TINY SURREALISM

TINY SURREALISM

SALVADOR DALÍ AND THE AESTHETICS OF THE SMALL

ROGER ROTHMAN

University of Nebraska Press / Lincoln and London

Publication of this volume was
assisted by the Virginia Faulkner
Fund, established in memory of
Virginia Faulkner, editor in chief
of the University of Nebraska Press.

Library of Congress
Cataloging-in-Publication Data
Rothman, Roger.
Tiny surrealism: Salvador
Dalí and the aesthetics of
the small / Roger Rothman.
pages cm
Includes bibliographical
references and index.
ISBN 978-0-8032-3649-3
(hardback: alk. paper)
ISBN 978-0-8032-8088-5
(paperback)
1. Dalí, Salvador, 1904–1989—
Criticism and interpretation.
2. Dalí, Salvador, 1904–1989—
Written works. 3. Modernism
(Art). 4. Proportion (Art) I. Title.
ND813.D3R68 2012
709.2—dc23 2012028076

Designed and set in Fanwood
by Nathan Putens.

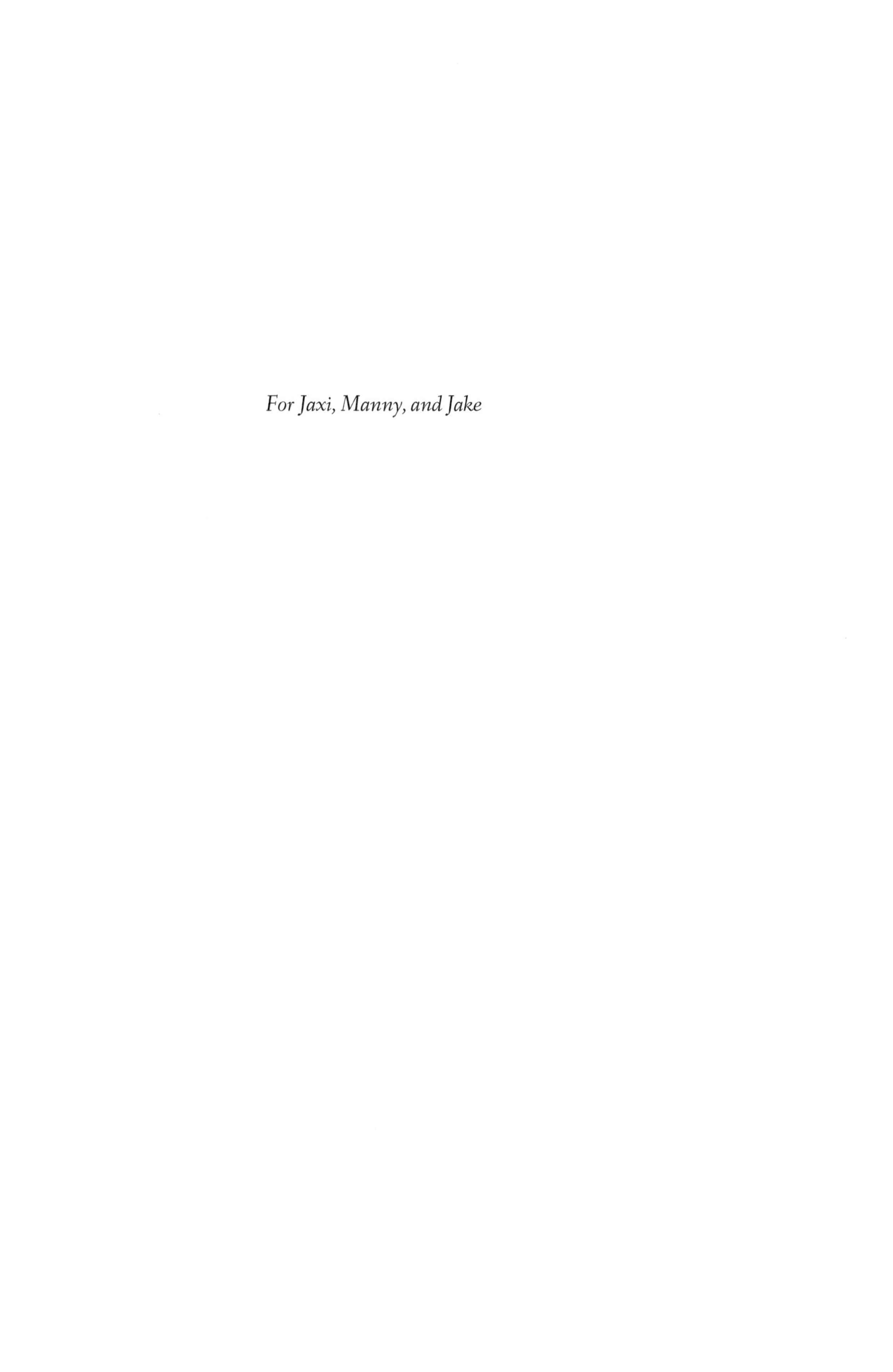

For Jaxi, Manny, and Jake

CONTENTS

ILLUSTRATIONS

ACKNOWLEDGMENTS

In researching and writing this book I was fortunate to have had the support of many individuals. The idea for this project began while I was writing my doctoral dissertation, and I would like to thank my advisors, Benjamin Buchloh and Rosalind Krauss, for their guidance and critical acumen. I would also like to thank Jonathan Crary, David Rosand, and David Freedberg for their support during my years at Columbia.

The book began in earnest while I was teaching at Agnes Scott College, and I would like to thank my colleagues Donna Sadler, Anne Beidler, Terry McGehee, and Nell Ruby for their encouragement and friendship. As the project developed Matthew Simms, John Westbrook, and Jordi Comas read numerous drafts and listened as I worked through my ideas. I am especially grateful to them for their input and friendship. I would also like to thank my colleagues in the Department of Art and Art History at Bucknell: Christiane

Andersson, Tulu Bayar, Janice Mann, Joe Meiser, and Roz Richards. During the early stages of my research support was provided by the Samuel H. Kress Foundation. Work over the summers was supported by research grants from Bucknell University. In the later stages crucial financial support was provided by the Office of the Dean of Arts and Sciences and the Office of the Provost as well as by the Bucknell University Association for the Arts. In this regard I am especially grateful to Renée Gosson, George Shields, and Mick Smyer.

For their comments on various drafts, I thank Ned Searles, Janine Mileaf, Elisabeth Guerrero, Benjamin Harvey, Samantha Kavky, and Diane Maas. I am also grateful to Neil Anderson, Peter Kresl, Steve Guattery, Jerry Mead, and Greg Clingham for their support and critical comments at various stages of the writing process. I would also like to thank the community of scholars I have met through The Space Between Society, in particular: Phyllis Lassner, Debra Rae Cohen, Kristin Bluemel, Genevieve Brassard, and Robin Rissler. I am grateful to Jenevieve DelosSantos for having invited me to speak at Rutgers University, where I tested significant aspects of the book's argument, and to Andrés Mario Zervigón, Tatiana Flores, and Olivia Gruber, for their comments after my presentation. I am also grateful to Michael Taylor and Elliott King for their gracious and generous assistance with acquiring reproductions for the book. Much of this book was written in the main room of the clubhouse of the Fire Island Summer Club, and I would like to thank Marty Handler and Marvin Mazur for their warm companionship over the course of those many summers together.

For their assistance with translations, I would like to thank Manuel Delgado, Frank Comas, and Pere-Albert Balcells Comas. Isabella O'Neil and Laura Riskedahl provided important library assistance, and Deane Clements was an invaluable copyeditor of the original manuscript.

At the University of Nebraska Press, I am grateful for the attention given to my manuscript by Ann Baker, Joy Margheim, and especially Kristen Elias Rowley. I would also like to thank the two anonymous readers for their many insightful comments and suggestions. Their responses to the original manuscript had a significant impact on the final version.

I am deeply grateful to my parents, Anne and Lewis Rothman, who encouraged me from beginning to end. I am also thankful to my in-laws, Barbara Gortikov and Stanley Israel, for the support and warmth that have made them second parents to me. Finally, I wish to thank my wife, Jaxi, and my two boys, Manny and Jake, for all that they have given me, especially the little things.

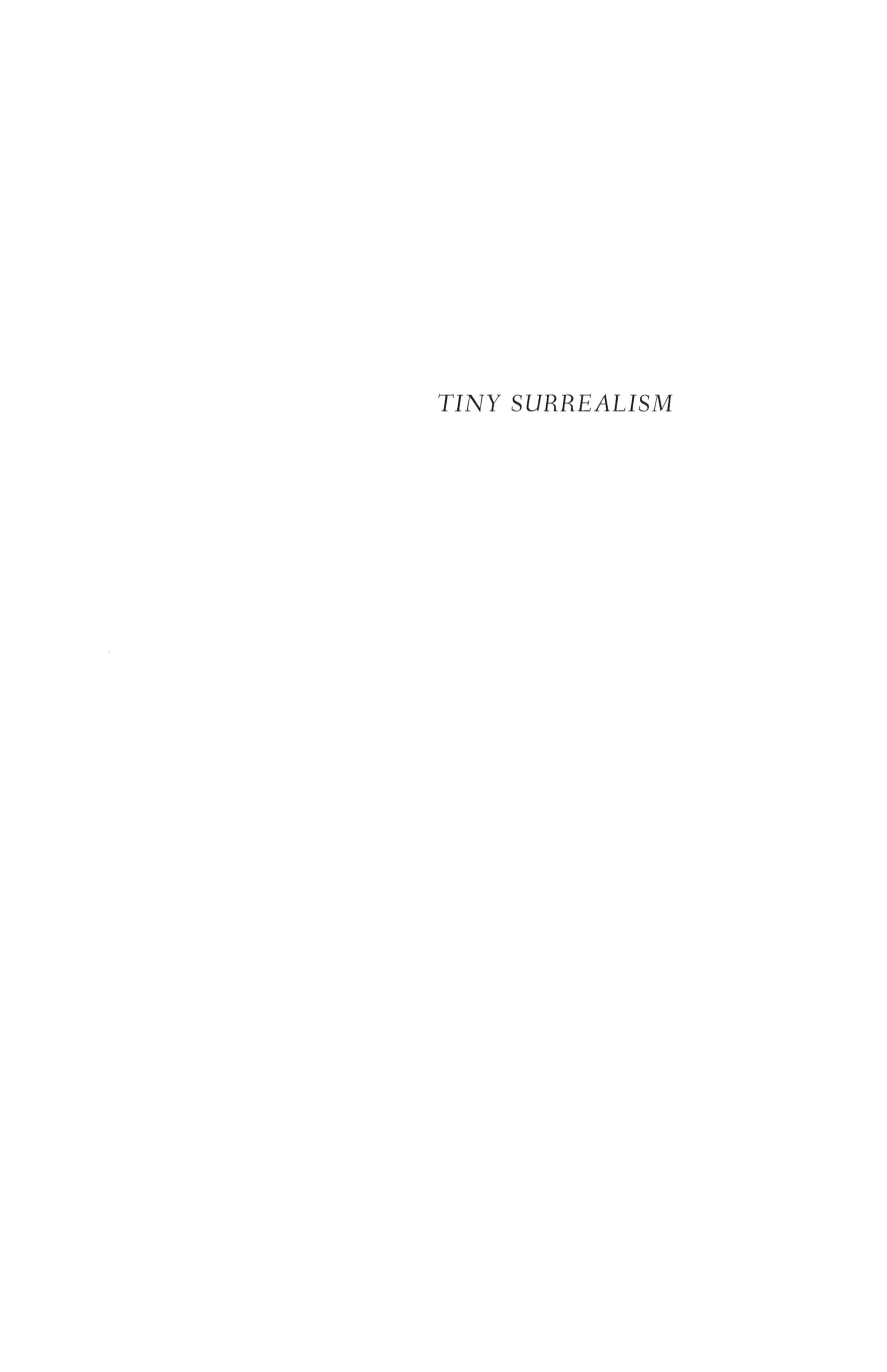

TINY SURREALISM

INTRODUCTION

DALÍ'S TININESS

Assuming that the subject on which the painter is laboring is grand, his next consideration is to keep away from minutiae.
NICOLAS POUSSIN, "Observations on Painting," ca. 1674

Ants. Pebbles. Bread crumbs. Hairs on the back of the neck. Sewing needles. Record needles. Blackheads. Subatomic particles. Strands of DNA. Salvador Dalí loved tiny things. He loved them in the twenties, when he was living in Barcelona and searching for an artistic direction that would be his own. He loved them in the thirties, when he was living in Paris among the surrealist painters and poets. And he loved them in the forties, fifties, sixties, seventies, and eighties, when he was living in New York as an artist of international fame. Indeed, if there was one constant in Dalí's career it was the love of the tiny. Throughout the many years of his career, Dalí embraced a wide range of sometimes contradictory orientations and perspectives: Federico García Lorca's poetics of the folk, Le Corbusier's modernism of the machine, André Breton's surrealism of the marvelous. These, however, were short-lived identifications (even the last one). His love of little things, on the other hand — of things that exist at the boundary of perception and on the edge of cognition — was a love Dalí never abandoned.

This book aims to account for the depth and complexity of Dalí's abiding fascination with things tiny. It begins in the midtwenties and ends in the late thirties, because these were the years in which Dalí's engagement with little things was most developed. These were also the years in which Dalí's aesthetic of the small was the most transformative. It was during these years that Dalí constructed a surrealism of the tiny to rival not only Breton's surrealism of the marvelous but also Georges Bataille's surrealism of the formless and Antonin Artaud's surrealism of suffering.

Dalí's identification with things small was to influence almost every aspect of the painter's art and writing. It shaped his conception of modernism, of the avant-garde, and above all, of Sigmund Freud and his significance. Of course, all of the surrealists were influenced by Freud; in this regard, Dalí was no different. What distinguished him from his contemporaries was that, in his mind, Freud was most properly understood as a theorist of the tiny. For at the core of Dalí's most significant and lasting contribution to surrealism's psychoanalytic discourse — the concept of "paranoia-criticism"— was a belief in the power of little things to dig deep within our mind and then to resurface anew to wreak havoc on reality.

Despite the myriad distortions and fabrications that Dalí inserted into his 1942 autobiography, *The Secret Life of Salvador Dalí* (indeed announced by the very title of chapter 4: "False Childhood Memories"), it is nevertheless clear that Dalí's fascination with little things can be traced back to the painter's childhood. Chapter 6, for example, begins with an account of the moment he discovered his newly emerging pubic hairs ("very slender and widely scattered") and continues with an account of his morbid and profound fear of little insects, grasshoppers in particular.[1] In the years that followed, little things began to form a distinct class of objects. Some were natural, some man-made. Some were tender, others aggressive. Different though they were among themselves, they shared a common set of properties not found in the world of the large. By the time he reached his twenties, Dalí came to believe that little things had strange powers that, under certain circumstances, enabled them to disrupt and undo beings a hundred times their size.

Of all his early writings on the subject of the small, the most evocative is a poem that Dalí first wrote in Spanish in the fall of 1927 and then published in Catalan in the August 31, 1928, issue of the journal *L'Amic de les Arts* (Friend of the arts).[2] Titled "Poema de les cosetes" (Poem of little things), this brief, ten-line verse articulated Dalí's universe of the tiny as a realm of infinite transformation in which soft flesh turns sharp and spiky, solids become gas, and "little charms prick":

> There's a tiny little thing in a spot up high.
> I'm happy, I'm happy, I'm happy, I'm happy.
> The sewing needles plunge into sweet and tender little bits of nickel.
> My girlfriend's hand is made of cork full of thumbtacks.
> One of my girlfriend's breasts is a calm sea urchin, the other a swarming wasp's nest.
> My girlfriend has a knee of smoke.
> The little charms, the little charms, the little charms, the little charms, the little charms, the little charms, the little charms, the little charms . . .
> THE LITTLE CHARMS PRICK.
> The partridge's eye is red.
> Little things, little things, little things, little things, little things, little things, little things, little things, little things, little things, little things, little things . . .
> THERE ARE LITTLE THINGS AS STILL AS A LOAF OF BREAD.[3]

For many readers "Poem of Little Things" stands as an early exploration of what would become the centerpiece of Dalí's surrealist practice: the juxtaposition of irrational images and events.[4] Indeed, it seems entirely of a piece with the form of surrealist production that Breton had dubbed "psychic automatism": "to express — verbally, by means of the written word, or in any other manner — the actual functioning of thought."[5] It was no surprise, therefore, that when Breton first saw Dalí's paintings in 1929, he was moved to declare, "With the coming of Dalí, it is perhaps the first time that the mental windows have been opened really wide."[6]

In the wake of Breton's enthusiasm for the psychoanalytic elements on display in Dalí's work, critics and scholars have come to understand the painter as among the most deeply Freudian of the surrealists. Most influential in this regard was the publication, in 1982, of Dawn Ades's *Dalí and Surrealism*. Ades's text, which was written when Dalí was still alive, has remained a cornerstone of Dalí scholarship. (Dalí died in 1989, and Ades revised and updated it in 1995.) In it, Ades not only initiated the psychoanalytic readings that would form the basis of so much later scholarship on Dalí but also, by devoting a chapter exclusively to the analysis of Dalí's concept of "paranoia-criticism," gave substance to the idea that this was indeed the painter's signal contribution to surrealist thought.[7] Hal Foster, Robert Lubar, and David Lomas are among the more recent scholars to have built on Ades's work by introducing the writings of Jacques Lacan and Bataille into the discussion of Dalí's engagement with psychoanalytic thought.[8] Especially significant was the publication, in 1996, of Haim Finkelstein's monograph on Dalí, as it offered the most fully realized analysis of Dalí's complex engagement with Freud's writing and the discourse around it.[9]

Alongside those who have explored the psychoanalytic aspects of Dalí's surrealist period, others have dug deeper into the painter's early years in Madrid and Barcelona. In 1999 Fèlix Fanés, former director of the archives at the Salvador Dalí Museum in Figueres, published a landmark study of Dalí's years as a young man. Fanés study provides the most detailed account to date of Dalí's complex reception of the competing forms of modernism that dominated Spanish culture in the teens and twenties.[10] Still others have attended to Dalí's rich dialogue with popular culture, not only in the fifties and later, where this connection is the most obvious, but throughout the painter's career.[11] Dalí's engagement with the cinema has provided yet another avenue for scholars, as has the role of modern science in shaping Dalí's post-surrealist work and thought.[12]

By approaching Dalí's work through the lens of the small, this book diverges from the prevailing scholarship. Nevertheless, it seeks to draw connections between Dalí's identification with little things and his engagements with psychoanalysis, modernism, popular culture, and, briefly, modern science.[13] As will be addressed in the chapters to follow, Dalí's relationship to psychoanalysis was mediated by an identification with small and apparently insignificant thoughts and gestures. In a similar vein, Dalí's participation in the discussions around modernism in Spain was framed in terms of the small-scale technological innovations of the period. With regard to Dalí's interest in mass culture, it will be seen that it typically involved actors and scenarios that were regarded as insignificant, of little consequence. And when it came to the sciences, Dalí was especially attracted to discoveries of the most microscopic elements of the organic and inorganic world.

In this regard the book addresses the complexities and contradictions inherent not in the surrealist subject but rather in the surrealist *object*. Surrealism has long been a crucial node in the study of subjectivity by virtue of its thoroughgoing critique of the rational subject. "We are still living under the reign of logic," Breton famously declared, and it was up to surrealism to put an end to its supremacy. His demand was therefore "the total liberation of the mind and all that resembles it."[14] Thus did the surrealists set out to redefine the subject's inner logic and defining boundaries. In this their influence was incontestably enormous, as generations of theorists were influenced directly and indirectly by the surrealist deconstruction of subjectivity. This would include Lacan's linguistically structured unconscious, Louis Althusser's subject of ideology, and

Judith Butler's performative subjectivity, to name only the most recognizable. As a result, it has become clear that the subject is irreparably divided against itself, pocked with holes, and overflowing in ways that were hardly recognized in the years before the surrealists.

But what of the object? To what extent can we say that we have uncovered its divisions, holes, and overflowings? Of late there has been a resurgence of interest in examining the complexities of the object in ways that have long shaped the study of the subject. I say resurgence because, as Bill Brown — one of the key figures in the rise of what some have called "object studies"— pointed out in 2004 in an essay titled "Thing Theory," an interest in understanding the complexity of things has never disappeared, although it has remained an enterprise on the margins in some periods.[15] In the wake of Brown's call for a return to the object, studies have emerged in fields as diverse as anthropology, epistemology, phenomenology, political theory, and psychoanalysis. In addition to a number of single-authored texts, edited publications like *Things that Talk* (2004), *The Secret Life of Things* (2007), and *The Object Reader* (2009) look to make sense of objects with the same level of complexity that has been applied to human subjects.[16]

Brown points to the 1920s as a crucial decade for contemporary theorists of the object to consider, for it was in this period, he claims, that "things emerge as the object of profound theoretical engagement in work of Georg Lukács, Martin Heidegger, and Walter Benjamin, and which is the decade after objects and things are newly engaged by (or as) the work of art for [Ezra] Pound, Marcel Duchamp, [William Carlos] Williams, Gertrude Stein."[17] (In a later essay Brown adds to this list Bronisław Malinowski, Marcel Mauss, and Jean Piaget, as well as Karl Abraham, Melanie Klein, Ernst Bloch, and André Breton).[18] The contemporary analyses that have drawn on these earlier theorists are sometimes radically destabilizing. For example, Bruno Latour has argued that "modernity artificially made an ontological distinction between inanimate objects and human subjects, whereas in fact the world is full of 'quasi-objects' and 'quasi-subjects.'"[19] Within the context of Latour's conception of modernity, Dalí's relevance emerges as particularly significant. Not only does Dalí's identification with things that are small and overlooked bear on Latour's concept of quasi-objects and quasi-subjects but so too does the concept of paranoia-criticism. For what distinguishes the paranoid subject from all others is the very fact that he sees himself as a quasi-object and the things he perceives as a collection of quasi-subjects. Indeed, the particularities of Dalí's identification with little things open new avenues of inquiry within the field of object studies.

Dalí's identification with little things also bears on the "fatal strategy" that Jean Baudrillard proposed as the solution to the crisis of the subject. Why is it, Baudrillard asks, that "we have always lived off the splendor of the subject and the poverty of the object"?[20] Although he makes no mention of Dalí in his text, his identification with the position of the object makes it seem as though he had been reading Dalí carefully. In fact, Baudrillard comes especially close to Dalí's own perspective on little things when he declares that "the pure object is sovereign, because it is what breaks up the sovereignty of the other and catches it in its own trap. The crystal takes revenge."[21] To use the language that Dalí favored, the crystal "pricks."

To consider Dalí's work within the context of object theory is not as eccentric as it might at first appear, since it was Benjamin who first proposed that surrealism was a movement fixed on the problem of the object.[22] Indeed, in a short essay titled "Dream Kitsch," Benjamin went so far as to insist, against the claims of the poets and painters themselves, that the surrealists were "less on the trail of the psyche than on the track of things."[23] For Benjamin, surrealism's significance rests less on its exploration of the inner world of the unconscious mind than on its consideration of the exterior world of objects — in particular, those objects that rational thought routinely overlooks. Benjamin's claim is especially resonant with Dalí's practice, for, as will be elaborated in the chapters to follow, Dalí was, like the object theorists of today, as interested in the secret life of things as his contemporaries were in the nocturnal world of the unconscious.

To make sense of Dalí's relation to little things requires that one also attend to the manner in which these little things were painted. Yet very few critics and historians have taken it upon themselves to make sense of Dalí's technique. Indeed, many dismiss his paintings as nothing more than illustrations, as diagrams of ideas. The ideas themselves may be of interest, but not the way in which they have been rendered. The effect has been that Dalí's mass appeal has far and away eclipsed scholarly opinion. Consider, for example, the recent textbook on twentieth-century art by Hal Foster, Rosalind Krauss, Yve-Alain Bois, and Benjamin H. D. Buchloh, *Art since 1900: Modernism, Antimodernism, Postmodernism* (2004). Individually as authors, and collectively as the editors of the journal *October*, Bois, Buchloh, Foster, and Krauss have done more to transform the discourse of modernist studies than any other group of art historians. It is therefore especially compelling to note that the account of Dalí's painting in *Art since 1900* is limited to a single phrase at the tail end of a sentence that begins by addressing the work of other surrealists: "On the other hand, a certain type of modernism wants to claim those parts of Surrealism's visual production that seem acceptably abstract — [Joan] Miró and the half of [Max] Ernst that confines itself to frottage — while disencumbering itself of everything that seems retrograde and antimodernist because too suavely realistic — other parts of Ernst, late (and repetitious) [Giorgio] de Chirico and René Magritte, and, after 1930, Salvador Dalí's photographically rendered dream pictures."[24]

At the core of the prevailing dismissiveness of Dalí's painting is the fact that the techniques employed in their production were entirely at odds with those of the dominant strain of modern painting. For modern painting distinguished itself by its commitment to dismantling the traditional conventions of pictorial representation. These conventions included the careful modeling of individual forms with light and shadow and the use of linear and atmospheric perspective to construct a realistically three-dimensional environment in which to situate these forms. They also included an established set of traditional materials and their manipulation: the mixture and application of various oils (linseed, stand, poppy, walnut), solvents, resins, and varnishes. Dalí employed all of these techniques and materials and, on occasion, went so far as to adopt the rarified practice of glazing and scumbling translucent layers of oil-saturated pigments over opaque layers of underpainting. This technique required an understanding of pigments and binders that the vast majority of artists of the time had no interest in acquiring. Perhaps most symbolic of Dalí's aberrance was his use (and exaggerated display) of a mahl stick: a thin rod, traditionally of bamboo, that was covered at its tip with a ball-shaped pad. For Dalí the mahl stick was both a tool of his trade and an emblem of his identification with the outmoded practices of premodern painting.

Despite the evident commitment with which Dalí applied himself to the task of emulating the techniques of the old masters, critics and historians have had remarkably little to say on the subject. Instead, the vast majority of attention has been paid to the iconographic elements within the paintings. Indeed, evidence of a critical prejudice against Dalí's technique is everywhere in the literature, even among those who would be counted as supporters. Among the earliest and most succinct belongs to Douglas Goldring, who, in the pages of the *London Studio* in 1935, referred to Dalí as "a virtuoso in paint" and compared his technique to the Pre-Raphaelites. Nevertheless, as far as he was concerned, "it is only when we leave on one side the quality of the actual painting and consider Dalí's subject matter and content — *what* he paints rather than *how* he paints — that he appears startling and revolutionary."[25]

Goldring's early assessment of Dalí as a virtuosic yet ultimately unoriginal technician whose work is of interest only on account of its imagery has been regularly repeated throughout the years. A few decades later, for example, Sarane Alexandrian, a late member of the surrealist movement, put the matter similarly: "[Dalí's] act of painting has no further function save that of using a perfected *trompe-l'œil* technique to make the images of this organized delirium unforgettable."[26] For Alexandrian, as for Goldring, Dalí's mastery of chiaroscuro, linear perspective, and other techniques of the old masters has but one function: to make the depicted elements more memorable. More recent reiterations of this point of view include Ades's suggestion that we understand Dalí's technique as "an expedient, a means more or less efficient to express a given idea or image." It also includes Finkelstein's claim that Dalí is more accurately described as an "illustrator" than a "painter," as well as Lomas's proposal that Dalí's masterful illusions be considered akin to a "lure" that hooks us and reels us in for a closer look.[27] In all of these instances Dalí's technique is judged to be secondary, if not entirely inconsequential; what really matters in these paintings is *what* they depict, not *how* they depict.

It should be noted that Dalí himself seemed to endorse those who would seek to set aside questions of his technique as a painter. In a well-known interview with Alain Bosquet in 1966, Dalí insisted that "painting is only one of the means of expression of my total genius, which exists when I write, when I live, when in some way or other I manifest my *magic*."[28] To take Dalí as a painter and not a universal creator whose genius manifests in multiple forms is, it would seem, to misunderstand him. Nevertheless, there exist other, less frequently cited, statements by Dalí that suggest that technique played a far more significant role. Some of the most compelling of these comments pertain to Dalí's fascination with the work of Jan Vermeer. Over the course of his long career Dalí associated his work with a wide range of predecessors (including Paul Cézanne, Le Corbusier, de Chirico, Arnold Böcklin, and later Raphael and Leonardo), but none of them came close to rivaling Vermeer. Throughout his life Dalí remained entirely unwavering in his belief that Vermeer was the greatest painter who ever lived and the artist whom he most dearly wished to emulate.

In fact, one of the central claims of this book is that Dalí's abiding commitment to what he referred to as Vermeer's "probity" and "photographic" method suggests that technique was not only the means by which Dalí depicted his subjects but also, at times, the very subject of his work. To suggest this is, in turn, to propose that the iconographic elements within the paintings are not always Dalí's main concern but are sometimes themselves the lure, the device through which the viewer is drawn near to the painting so as to attend to its technique. To consider Dalí's work from this perspective is, in effect, to turn Goldring's 1935 assessment upside down: *It is only when we leave on one side Dalí's subject matter and content and consider the quality of the actual painting*—how *he paints rather than* what *he paints — that he appears startling and revolutionary.* Seen in this way, it may turn out that the most disruptive of all of Dalí's little things is the very manner in which they were painted.

For many viewers of Dalí's work, the painting that most immediately calls to mind the artist's Vermeer-like attention to detail is *The Persistence of Memory* (fig. 1). Completed in 1931 and exhibited in Paris the same year, the painting was purchased for the modest sum of $250 by the American collector and dealer Julien Levy. The following year Levy exhibited *The Persistence of Memory* at his gallery in New York, and in 1934 Mrs. Stanley B. Resor, who had purchased it from Levy, gifted it to the Museum of Modern Art. Almost immediately thereafter *The Persistence of Memory* became one of the most recognizable works of modern art and a painting that would become metonymic of Dalí's art as a whole. It is remarkable, therefore, that this painting has consistently failed to attract the sort of extended analysis that one would expect of a work of such mass popularity and art historical importance. Unlike Édouard Manet's *Bar at the Folies Bergère*, for example, or Picasso's *Les demoiselles d'Avignon* — both of which have achieved popular acclaim as well as critical consideration — there is an enormous gap between the public's deep fascination with *The Persistence of Memory* and the attention that scholars have given it.[29] For many art historians Dalí represents modern art at its most kitsch. It is inauthentic and all to easily digested. It is, as suggested by its near-total absence within the pages of *Art since 1900*, an object to be addressed glancingly, if at all. Indeed, insofar as *The Persistence of Memory* stands for Dalí's production in total, it has come to play the role of a Kleinian bad object: a pollutant best left alone.

Then again, the notion of a work of art as pollutant is entirely consistent with Dalí's own ambitions, and thus each of the six main chapters of this book begins with a short description of one small aspect of *The Persistence of Memory*. Each description includes an interpretive perspective on the painting that, in turn, performs in miniature the central argument of the chapter it begins. Together these six views of *The Persistence of Memory* serve as a condensation of the book's overall argument, and similarly, each of the six chapters of the book can be understood as an extended consideration of this one painting. These six views serve another function as well. Some of Dalí's paintings include a wide range of little things, and some of these little things function in radically different ways. As such, the best way to get a grasp on them is to clutch them with different grips. Thus, although most of the works that appear in this book are addressed in only one chapter, a few are examined in two or more. As such, the six epigraphic descriptions that introduce each chapter recapitulate the book's overarching practice of examining Dalí's work from different angles.

Chapter 1 focuses on the emergence, in the mid-1920s, of Dalí's interest in and sensitivity to a variety of little things. The objects of Dalí's attention included those of the natural world (ants, flies, fish, birds, olives, seashells, grains of sand, breadcrumbs, ashes) and the urban environment (temperature gauges, phonograph needles, cigarette paper, adding machines and their small, numbered buttons, nickel-plated bathroom fixtures, small metal appliances). The chapter argues that the little things that most interested him were almost invariably modest, humble, ordinary, and inconsequential. In addition, the chapter traces the construction of a model of visual perception and pictorial practice that Dalí believed would best serve the interests of these humble and inconsequential objects, a model based on the work of Vermeer and the mechanical precision of the camera. The chapter also examines Dalí's consideration of these little things as existing under the oppressive order of the big and, with it, his subsequent commitment to what he called the "liberation" of the little things.

Chapter 2 follows Dalí's turn, in the late twenties, toward the prevailing concerns of the surrealists. Its particular focus is on the way in which Dalí's conception of little things informed his most significant contribution to surrealist discourse: the concept of paranoia-criticism. Central to this chapter is the examination of the way in which the concept of paranoia developed from, yet fundamentally transformed, Dalí's earlier identification with little things and their liberation. Considerable scholarship has been devoted to Dalí's complex engagement with Freud's writing, and this chapter aims to expand on this literature by fleshing out the ways in which Dalí's earlier preoccupations shaped his subsequent reception of Freud. It argues, for example, that Dalí saw the paranoiac's apparent delusions as in fact evidence of a visual hyperacuity akin to that of a camera lens. In other words, paranoia was for Dalí a form of cognition born of a heightened sensitivity to little things. And this is to say that, in contrast to much that has been written on Dalí, psychoanalysis was not the central animating concept of his work but rather was an elaboration on and transformation of a prior and more fundamental engagement with things tiny.

Chapter 3 examines the little things to which Dalí turned in the thirties. During this period the playful little things that had once interested him took on a more aggressive cast. They turned against their hosts as invasive little parasites. The invaders he fixed upon were often those within our own bodies: mucus, blackheads, and errant hairs on one's arm. At the same time Dalí began to transform his own work into little things. He shrunk his paintings to miniscule proportion and mimicked the miniaturist style of Ernest Meissonier.

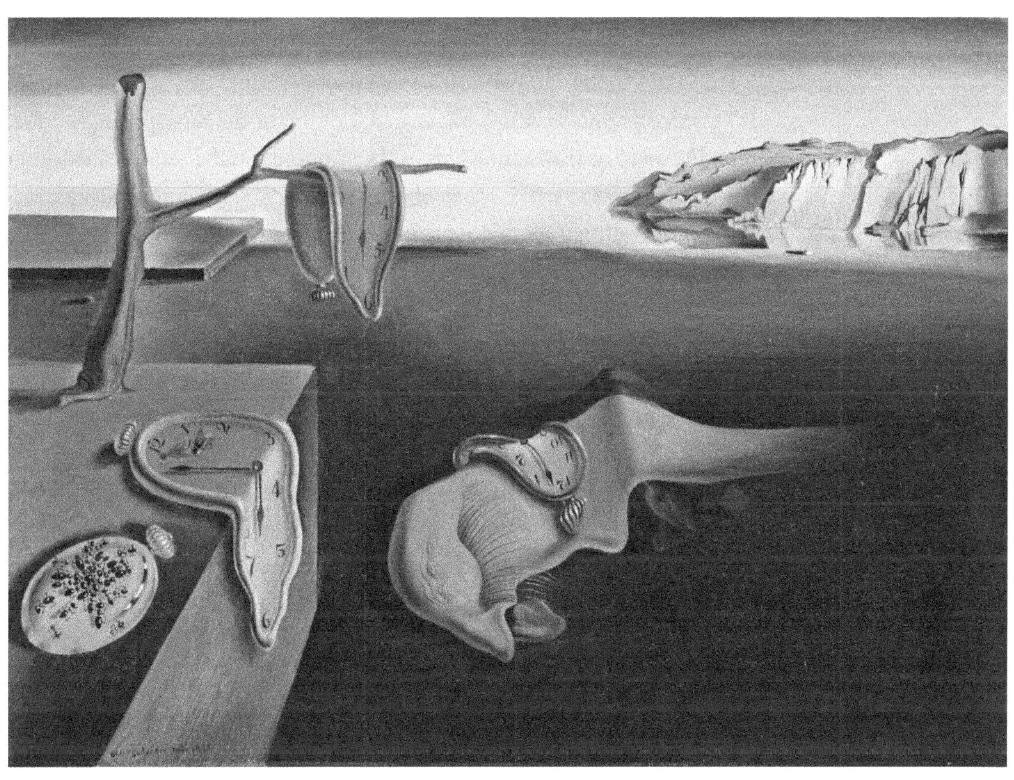

1. Salvador Dalí, *The Persistence of Memory*, 1931. Oil on canvas, 24.1 × 33.0 cm (9½ × 13 in.). Given anonymously. The Museum of Modern Art, New York NY. Dalí, Salvador (1904–89) © ARS, NY. Digital Image © The Museum of Modern Art/Licensed by SCALA/Art Resource, NY.

In so doing he identified yet another parasite to emulate, this time a parasite on the history of art.

Chapter 4 focuses on the relationship between the discourse of the small and that of the superficial. It begins with the observation that many of Dalí's favorite little things were organisms that grew from or lived on the surface of another, larger thing: ants crawled across the surface of a freshly painted canvas; hairs emerged from the back of a girl's neck; sea urchins pricked the skin on the bottom of a foot; blackheads erupted from the pores on a face. Whereas "The Rotting Donkey" has for many years served scholars as the urtext of Dalí's thought and practice, this chapter looks to its lesser-studied twin, "The Sanitary Goat," as a means of uncovering Dalí's consideration of the disruptive potential of superficiality and the disorientations of the simulacrum. More than any other chapter, this one seeks to make sense of Dalí's hyperfine illusionism as a practice engaged not in illustrating unconscious thoughts but, more significantly, in manifesting a universe of destructive simulacra.

Chapter 5 addresses the relation that Dalí established between the small and the submissive. The chapter begins with the observation that for Dalí, to make oneself into a little thing is to engage in an act of radical self-restraint. It continues by examining the ways in which self-control and self-denial influenced Dalí's practice as a painter. The chapter demonstrates that Dalí considered submission to a rule to be an act of subversion more potent than any declaration of freedom. The chapter also argues that Dalí's self-imposed restrictions act not only against a modernist affirmation of absolute liberation but also in opposition to norms of sexuality and gender and as such deserve to be understood as explicit gestures of anti-masculinism. In contrast to the mutilated female bodies of Hans Bellmer, for example, Dalí's perversions suggest a radically inverted dynamic of power.

Whereas chapter 5 concerns the interpersonal implications of littleness, Chapter 6 concerns its historical implications. History's victors are transcendent; history's vanquished are buried under rubble. When the vanquished reemerge, they do so as anachronisms — as uncanny reminders of a distant and decrepit past. This chapter examines in detail the emergence and development of Dalí's conception of anachronism, a term that first appeared in Dalí's writings in the midthirties. It considers the various ways in which Dalí exploited the anachronistic techniques of the old masters as tools aligned against the underlying pictorial values of the moment — that is, the values of the surrealist avant-garde in particular and European modernism at large. In this last transformation of the small Dalí set his little things against the very order that would seek to define their place within the history of modern painting.

The afterword addresses in brief the transformation of Dalí's interest in the small that took place after his official exclusion from the surrealist movement.

Rather than offer an outline of the various interests and practices of the forties, fifties, and beyond, the chapter focuses on the most distinctive feature of Dalí's post-surrealist work and thought: the turn to modern science. That Dalí found himself no less fascinated by cellular structures and subatomic particles than he had once been by pebbles and ants suggests that, in some form at least, the logic of the tiny remained a significant aspect of his thinking. To end where the book begins, the afterword returns one last time to consider *The Persistence of Memory*, now within the context of Dalí's new ideas about the types of little things that matter most.

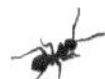

To a great extent, the image we today have of Dalí's work was cast in 1929 when the painter exhibited his first explicitly surrealist paintings at the Galerie Goemans in Paris. Accounts of Dalí's eccentric personality and the success of *Un chien andalou* had laid the foundation for a dramatic entrance into the Parisian scene. For the exhibition catalog Breton wrote an essay in which he praised the paintings for what he perceived to be their uncompromising exploration of the unconscious. But Breton's essay began on an equivocal note: "Dalí is like a man who wavers between talent and genius, or, as it used to be called, vice and virtue." Of Dalí's vices, one that particularly troubled Breton was his manner of painting; more precisely, what troubled him was the fascination that others seemed to have with Dalí's technique. "'It is splendid,' they say, 'for a man to paint such little things so well (and that it is even better when he *enlarges* them).'" In the face of this delight, Breton set out to defend what he considered to be Dalí's real contribution. What mattered to Breton, and what he worried might become lost in the hands of an artist so clearly invested in a particular style of painting (the "vice" mentioned above), was the way in which Dalí managed to illustrate so clearly the "interior showcase" of the mind as it is brought to life by "the power of voluntary hallucination."[30] For Breton, not only was the way Dalí painted unimportant, it was in fact an impediment to the work's profound significance.

Bataille, too, had been struck by the paintings that Dalí had shown in Paris. Having seen examples of them a few months before they were exhibited at Galerie Goemans, Bataille used them in an essay titled "The Language of Flowers" to exemplify and illustrate his philosophy of "base materialism." For Bataille, Dalí's paintings were especially useful in counterposing what he took to be the idealism implicit in Breton's embrace of the "voluntary hallucination" as the key to making manifest the beauty of the unconscious and revealing what Breton called "the marvelous." Indeed, it was precisely this orientation toward

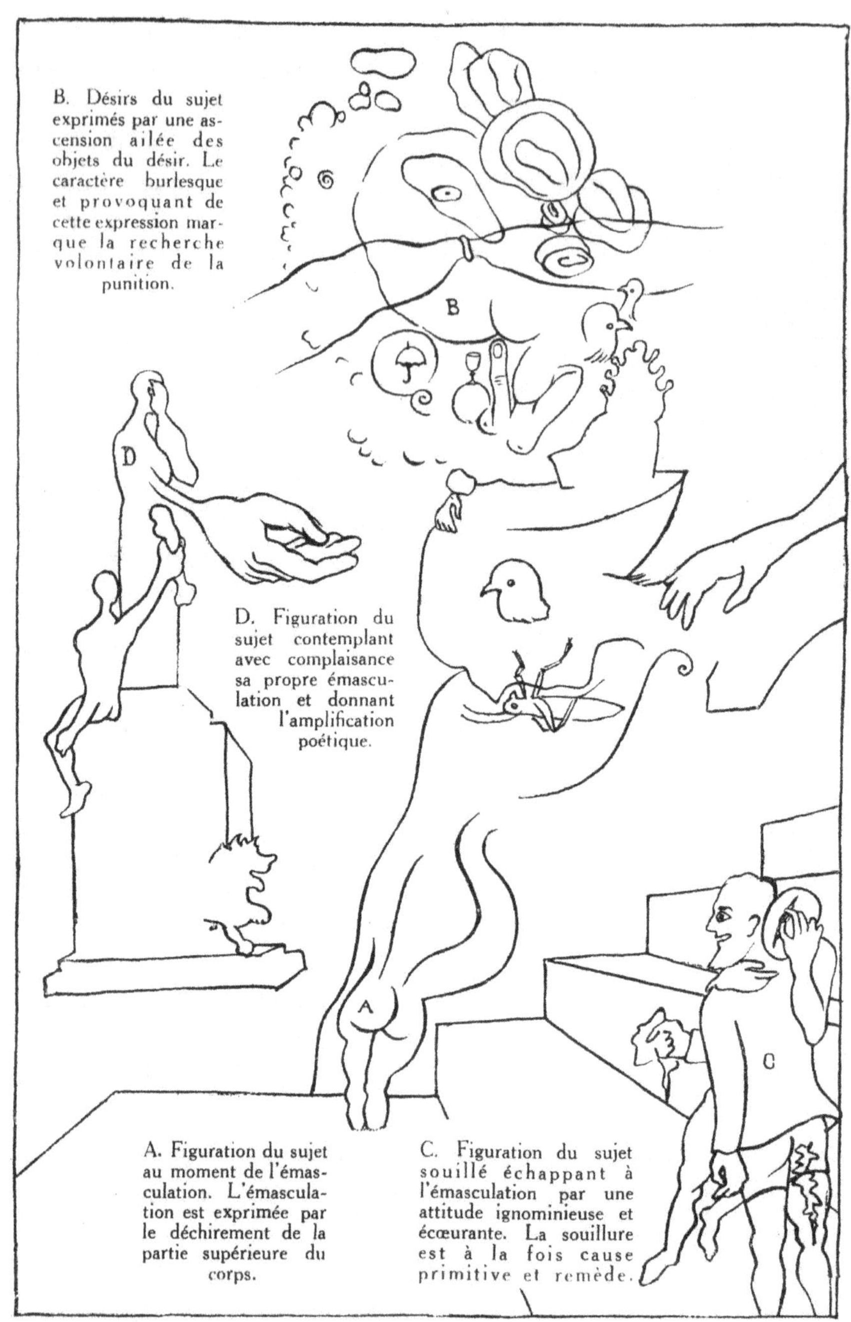

2. Georges Bataille, "Psychoanalytic Schema of the Contradictory Representations of the Subject in *The Lugubrious Game* of Salvador Dalí." *Documents* 7 (December 1929): 37.

the beautiful that Bataille found most suspicious. "If one says that flowers are beautiful," Bataille claimed, "it is because they seem to *conform to what must be*, in other words, they represent, as flowers, the human *ideal*." Bataille insisted that such idealism is but a ruse that conceals the ugly truth that most flowers are in fact "badly developed and are barely distinguishable from foliage; some are even unpleasant, if not hideous."[31] Dalí's work seemed to Bataille to recognize this ugly truth. In his eyes, Dalí's paintings depicted the world as it really is: hideous. They showed the unconscious to be, like the flower, unpleasant and badly formed. When one examines it up close, as Dalí did, the mind is revealed to be a grotesque lump of shame, fear, and self-reproach. To illustrate his point, Bataille included a diagram of Dalí's *The Lugubrious Game* (figs. 2, 19) in which the significant iconographic elements were tagged with short descriptive identifiers. Together these descriptive tags pictured *The Lugubrious Game* as a revelation of the mind's inner ugliness. For example, Bataille read the swirling mass of elements at the top of the painting not as Breton would have (as a record of the unconscious set free) but rather as symbols of profound shame and, with it, the ignominious desire for "punishment" and "emasculation."[32]

Although Breton and Bataille held fundamentally opposed interpretations of Dalí's work, the two implicitly agreed that what most deserved consideration was its imagery, not its technique. This was not true, however, of Louis Aragon. Like Breton and Bataille, Aragon saw Dalí's work soon after it was first shown in Paris, and like them, Aragon was stunned. In particular, Aragon was struck by a work that Dalí had exhibited in March 1930. The exhibition, also held at Galerie Goemans, included a diverse group of collage-based works. The show included Cubist *papiers collés* by Georges Braque, Picasso, and Juan Gris as well as Dadaist collages by Jean Arp, Ernst, Duchamp, Francis Picabia, and Man Ray. It also featured recent works by surrealists, including works by Miró, Magritte, Yves Tanguy, and Dalí. Inspired by the surrealist collages he had seen in reproduction while living in Barcelona, Dalí had begun experimenting with a variety of nonart materials in the late twenties. In some he glued on grains of sand and tiny seashells; in others he cut and pasted little bits of photographs and magazine illustrations. It was this latter form of collage that was exhibited at Goemans and was at odds with the other collages on view for having been crafted so meticulously that it was nearly impossible to distinguish the elements that were glued to the surface from those that were painted by Dalí's own hand.

Aragon wrote an essay to accompany the exhibition in which he proposed that collage-based practices should be divided into two fundamentally different categories. In "La peinture au défi" (In defiance of painting), Aragon distinguished between the aestheticism at work in the collages of the prewar period (prior to 1914) and those constructed in its wake.[33] The former group — which would include, for example, Picasso's deftly constructed collages of guitars and café tables — are oriented toward the aesthetic contemplation of line, shape, and color. The latter — which would include both dadaist and surrealist collages — were oriented toward the exploration of the hidden surreality of the world.[34] For Aragon, the former was of little real consequence, as the role of the collaged elements is merely to "enrich the palette." The latter, by contrast, uses collage to enrich the world. In fact, Aragon argued, it is precisely by negating the palette (that is, by negating traditional aesthetic experience) that this latter form of collage succeeds in enriching the world, since its deployment of real-world materials makes a mockery of traditional aesthetic experience (of line, shape, and color). Such collages are, wrote Aragon, not simply *other* than painting, they are "in absolute opposition to painting." Their oppositional stance marked them as a weapon not only against aesthetic experience itself but also against the bourgeois value system in which aesthetic experience is maintained. Such collages are, Aragon proposed, a "materialization of a moral symbol in violent opposition to the morals of [the present] world."[35] For Aragon, the collages that most effectively symbolized this violent opposition were those that used inexpensive materials and simple, even crude, methods of construction. These were the collages that were most "in defiance" of both painting and the bourgeois values that subtend it.

Aragon's conception of collage as an anti-aesthetic practice made Dalí's skillfully crafted works especially puzzling. What is one to make of Dalí's masterful ability to hide the distinction between the painted and the collaged, the man-made and the manufactured? How, Aragon wondered, is one to make sense of a collage that refuses to announce itself as such? For Aragon, these were the central questions posed by Dalí's work. In the end Aragon was moved to conclude that, although employing the same practice of cutting and pasting that was on display in the rest of the exhibition, Dalí's work was based on an entirely different set of principles:

> Salvador Dalí's use of collage probably best defies interpretation. He paints with a magnifying glass; he knows how to imitate chromolithography so that the effect is invariably successful: the scraps of pasted-on lithograph appear painted on, while the painted areas appear to be pasted on. By this is he trying to baffle the eye, and does he rejoice in the error he has caused? It's possible to think so, yet still find no explanation for this double game, which can be imputed neither to the painter's despair before the inimitable, nor to his indolence before the fully expressed. . . . What are we to make of Dalí's meticulousness [*minutie*]?[36]

That Aragon recognized the importance of meticulousness and the value of deception marks his analysis as altogether different from those of Breton and Bataille. For Breton, Dalí's miniaturism was something of a minor irritant; for Bataille, it was entirely irrelevant. But for Aragon, it was a cause for concern. Although he found himself unable to comprehend it, he was, nevertheless, fully cognizant of its significance.

In the years that followed the initial interpretations of Breton, Bataille, and Aragon, it was Breton's Freudianism and Bataille's base materialism that shaped the way Dalí's work came to be understood. Aragon's puzzled recognition that Dalí's technical precision and his deceptive manipulation of tiny scraps of glued paper were significant failed to generate the same level of curiosity. Nevertheless, it is still possible to return to Aragon's bewildered fascination with Dalí's technique and thereby develop an alternative pathway, one that runs away from Poussin's world of grand subjects toward the realm of minutiae, of little things that prick.

1

LITTLE THINGS

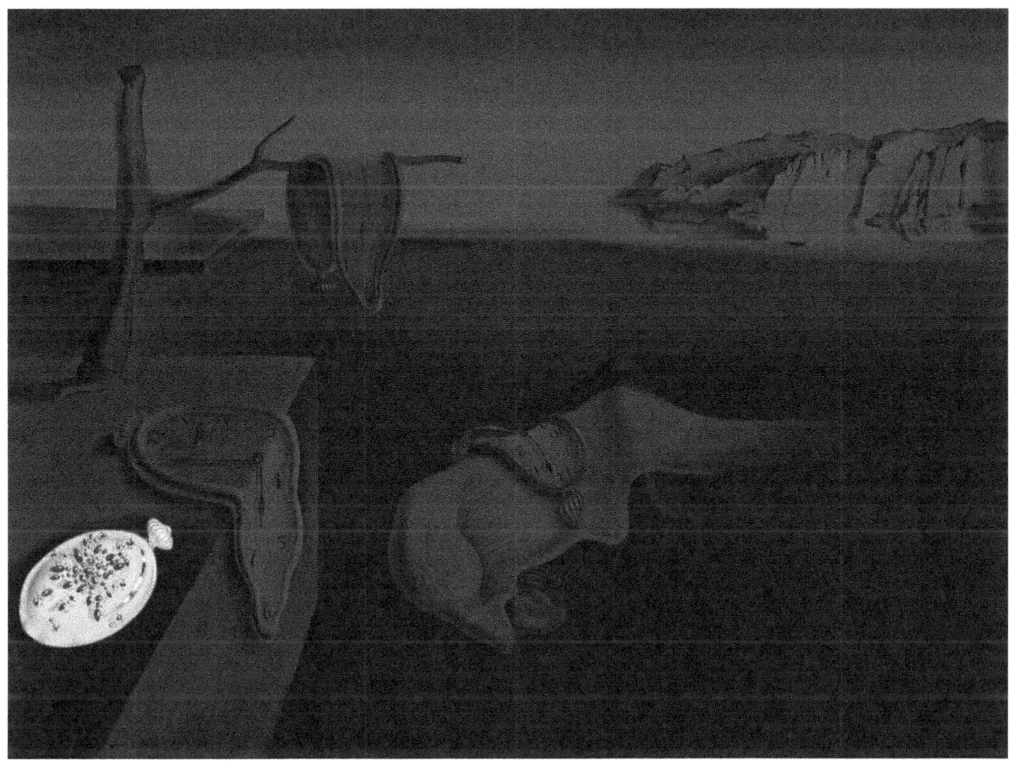

Atop the metal cover of the pocket watch crawl two dozen ants. From a short distance away each segment and limb is visible and the larger ants are easy to distinguish from the smaller ones. But from a greater distance the black ants resemble the markings one expects to find on the watch's face. They give the impression that the three hands of the clock and the fifteen digits that circle the dial had magically transformed themselves into a colony of ants. No longer following the prescribed rhythm of the clock's circular motion, the hands and digits have been liberated, free to determine their own rhythm, perhaps even to wander off the watch completely if that is their desire.

One irony of Dalí's lifelong fascination with the small is that the man was an egotist of enormous proportion. One need look no further than the famous opening lines of his autobiography, *The Secret Life of Salvador Dalí*: "At the age of six I wanted to be a cook. At seven I wanted to be Napoleon. And my ambition has been growing steadily ever since."[1] Salvador Dalí y Domenech was born on May 11, 1904, in Figueres, a Catalan town in northeastern Spain. He and his family spent summers in the fishing village of Cadaqués, and many of his early paintings include motifs derived from both locales.[2] In the summer of 1916 Dalí was exposed, through the collection of Ramón Pichot (an artist and friend of Picasso), to the paintings of the French impressionists. The works made an immediate impact; they were, he later recounted, "my first contact with an anti-academic and revolutionary esthetic theory."[3]

In 1922, at the age of eighteen, Dalí moved to Madrid to attend the Residencia de Estudiantes. There he befriended a number of young writers and artists, including Luis Buñuel and Federico García Lorca, six years Dalí's elder and already a poet with a significant reputation. In 1923 Dalí was suspended from the Residencia for recalcitrance, but it would prove a minor obstruction, since in 1925 he was offered his first one-man exhibition at the prestigious Galiere Dalmau in Barcelona. Dalmau's gallery was the first in Spain to exhibit the works of the cubists (in 1912), and throughout the teens and twenties it was a critical site for avant-garde artists in the city. Dalí's 1925 exhibition included works in two diametrically opposed styles: some, like *Venus and Sailor* (*Homage to Salvat-Papasseit*) (fig. 3), drew on the fractured shapes and disjointed spatiality of cubism and the rigid geometry of purism, while others, such as *Portrait of My Father* (fig. 4), relied on traditional techniques of modeling and perspective that characterized the works of the antimodernist naturalism of the *rappel à l'ordre* that arose in the years immediately following the conclusion of the First World War.[4] The tension between tradition and modernity was not lost on critics who reviewed the exhibition, but the show was in general a striking success — especially for an artist who was only twenty-one years old.

The following year Dalí was invited to show his works at a number of group exhibitions, and the year after that he had a second one-man show at Dalmau's gallery (December 1926–January 1927). Yet again, the paintings on view ranged widely, almost chaotically, in their stylistic diversity. Works such as *Still Life by Moonlight* (fig. 5) include references to Picasso's classicizing linearity; the contrasting colors and flat, simplified forms of synthetic cubism; and the puzzling juxtapositions characteristic of Giorgio de Chirico's metaphysical interiors.

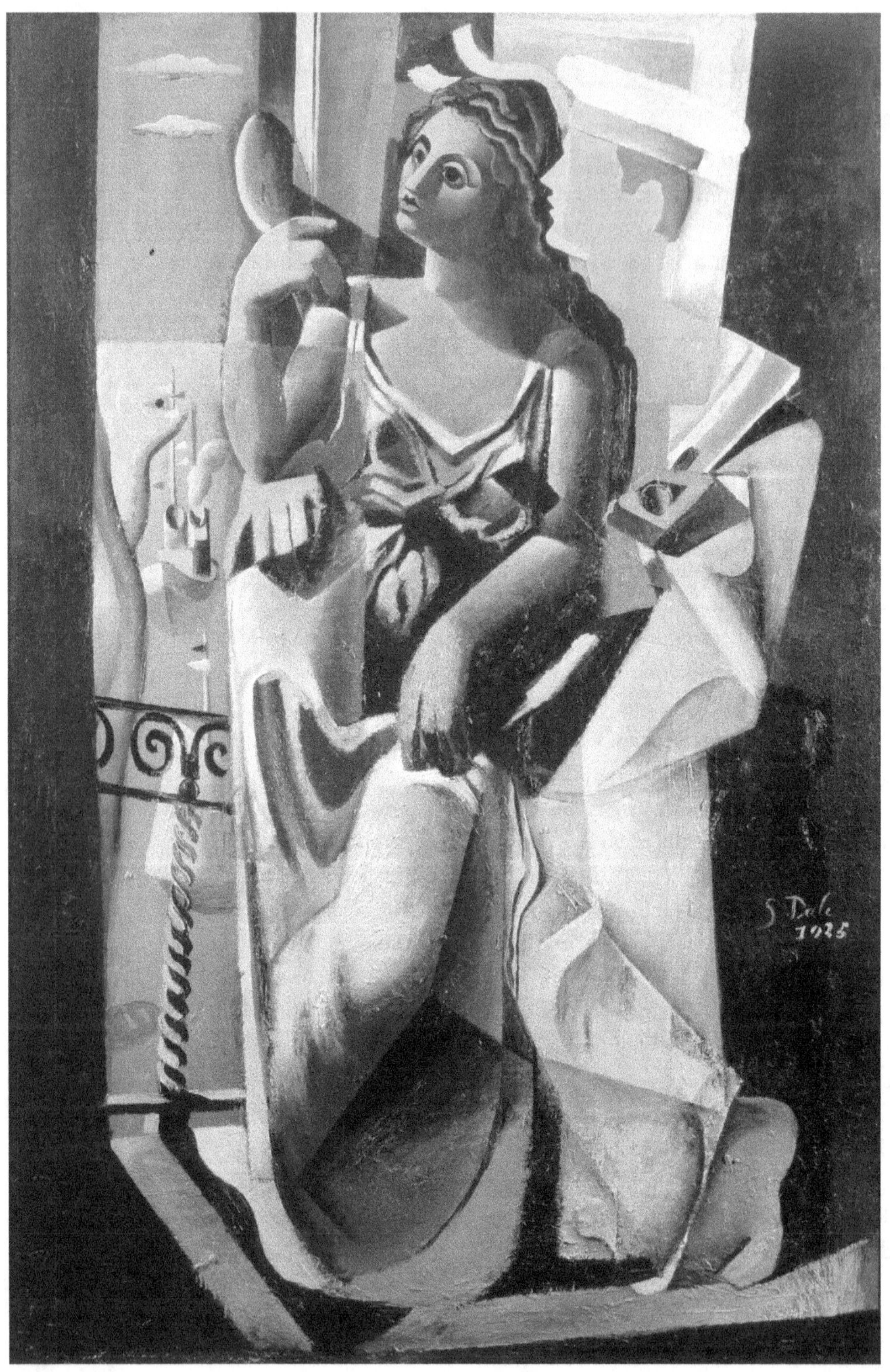
S. Dali
1925

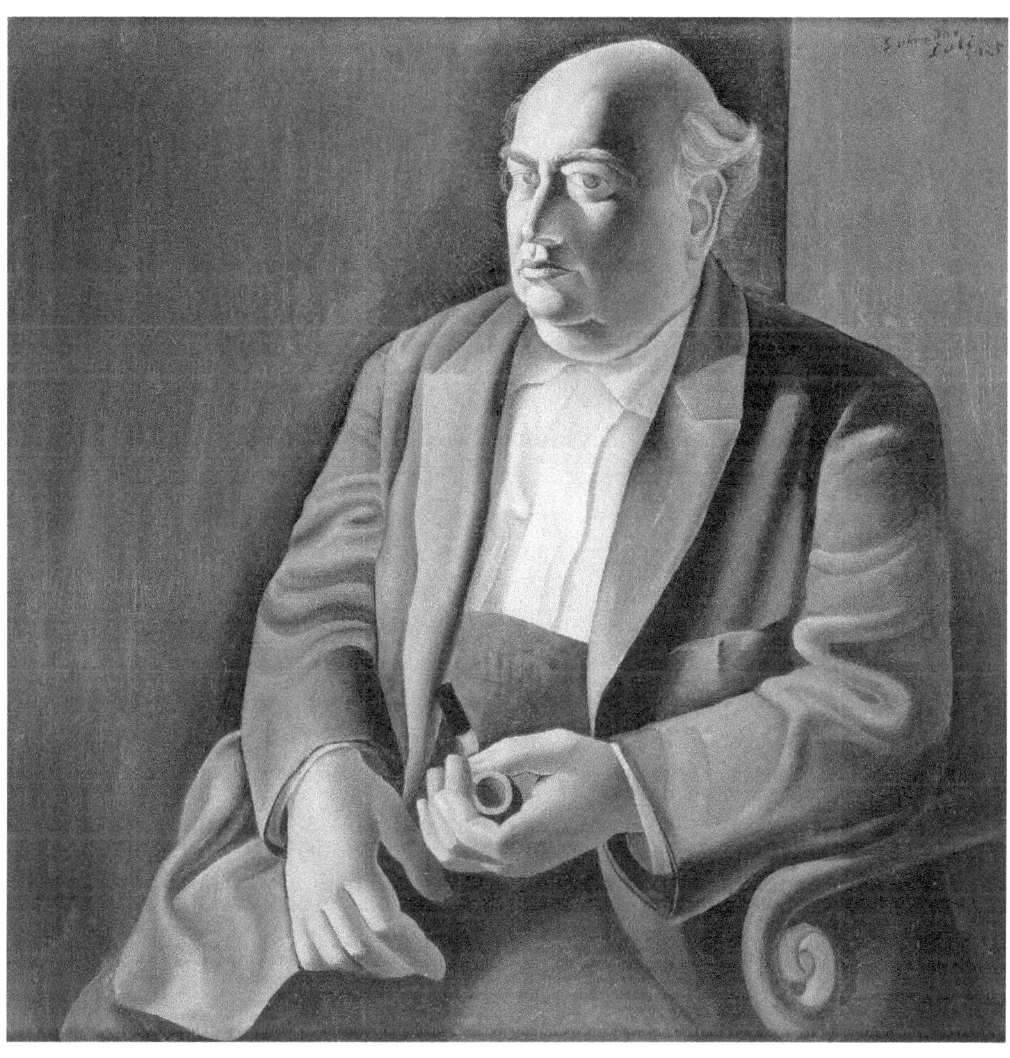

3. (*left*) Salvador Dalí, *Venus and Sailor* (*Homage to Salvat-Papasseit*), 1925. Oil on canvas, 215.0 × 147.5 cm (84.65 × 58.07 in.). Ikeda Museum, Shizuoka, Japan. Dalí, Salvador (1904–89) © ARS, NY. Photo credit: Bridgeman-Giraudon/Art Resource, NY.

4. (*above*) Salvador Dalí, *Portrait of My Father*, 1925. Oil on canvas, 104.5 × 104.5 cm (41.14 × 41.14 in.). © MNAC – Museu Nacional d'Art de Catalunya, Barcelona. Photographers: Calveras/Mérida/Sagristà. Dalí, Salvador (1904–89) © ARS, NY.

Others, such as *The Basket of Bread* (fig. 6) exhibited what some critics took to be the realism of the Dutch baroque. It was becoming clear to his contemporaries that Dalí was not going to commit himself to any one style. Some accused him of insincerity and craven manipulation of the market; others, more charitably, attributed his stylistic contradictions to the confused voracity of youth.[5]

The critical response to Dalí's paintings did little to arrest his stylistic experimentation. In works from 1927 and 1928 — for example, *Honey Is Sweeter than Blood* and *Instrument and Hand* (*Aparell i mà*, sometimes translated as *Apparatus and Hand*) (fig. 7) — Dalí introduced still more artistic references into his work, including elements drawn from the playfully abstracted figures of Joan Miró, the eerily vacant landscapes of Yves Tanguy, and the puzzling juxtapositions of Max Ernst's collages. In sum, from 1925 to 1928 Dalí's paintings managed to incorporate almost every artistic style in circulation at the time.

In addition to the two explanations for Dalí's stylistic promiscuity mentioned above (youthful experimentation and market exploitation), there is another possibility. This third explanation understands the diversity of styles as the sign of an underlying unity of conception that had not yet found its appropriate expressive form. As this chapter will argue, Dalí's divergent styles during the late twenties were the result of an effort to construct a visual language that would speak to the artist's emerging identification with little things. His writings, both public and private, express this identification clearly, and they suggest that the rapid and often contradictory movement from one style to another was the result of Dalí's struggle to express this identification in paint. A close look at the writings makes it clear that Dalí's attempt to find a pictorial language suited to the small led him not only through the range of avant-garde styles of the time but also and most transformatively to a conception of the camera lens as the mechanical object ideally suited to the observation of little things and to an understanding of Vermeer as the artist who gave the small the greatest respect and understanding. At that point Dalí's stylistic meandering came to an end. By combining the mechanical objectivity of the camera lens with the sensitivity of Vermeer, Dalí had found a visual language he was happy with, a visual language with which he could give form to little things and show how they "prick."

Dalí's closest friend throughout the mid- to late twenties was Lorca, and the two corresponded frequently. Although Lorca's letters have been lost, Dalí's remain, and they offer a fascinating window into the painter's identification with the small.[6] This is especially evident, for example, in a letter that Dalí wrote to Lorca in March 1926. The letter begins, as did most of his letters to Lorca, by informing his friend of the various projects that interested him at that moment. Gradually, however, the language begins to break down, and by the

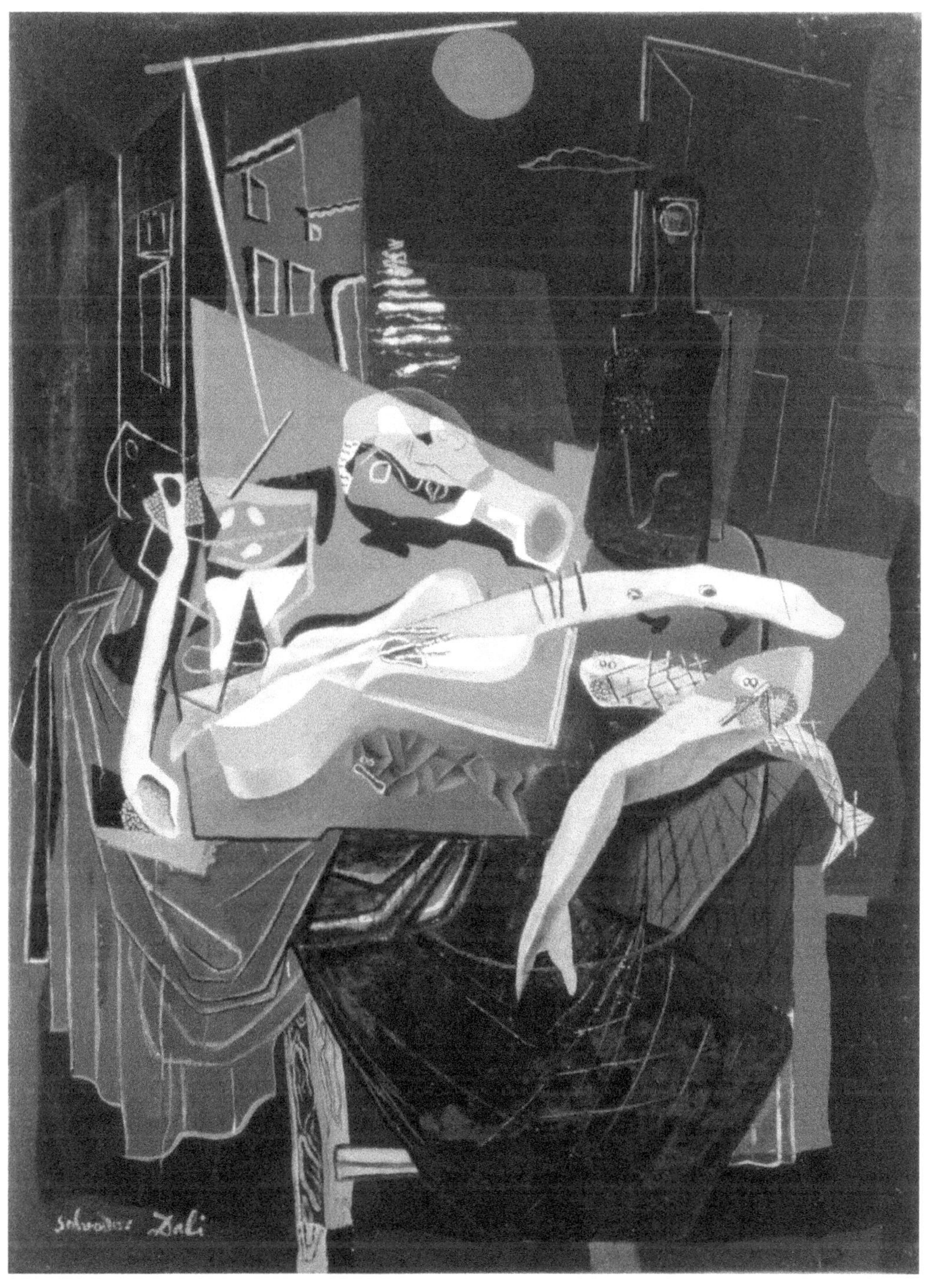

5. Salvador Dalí, *Still Life by Moonlight*, 1926. Oil on canvas, 199 × 150 cm (78.35 × 59.06 in.). Museo Nacional Centro de Arte Reina Sofía, Madrid. Dalí, Salvador (1904–89) © ARS, NY.

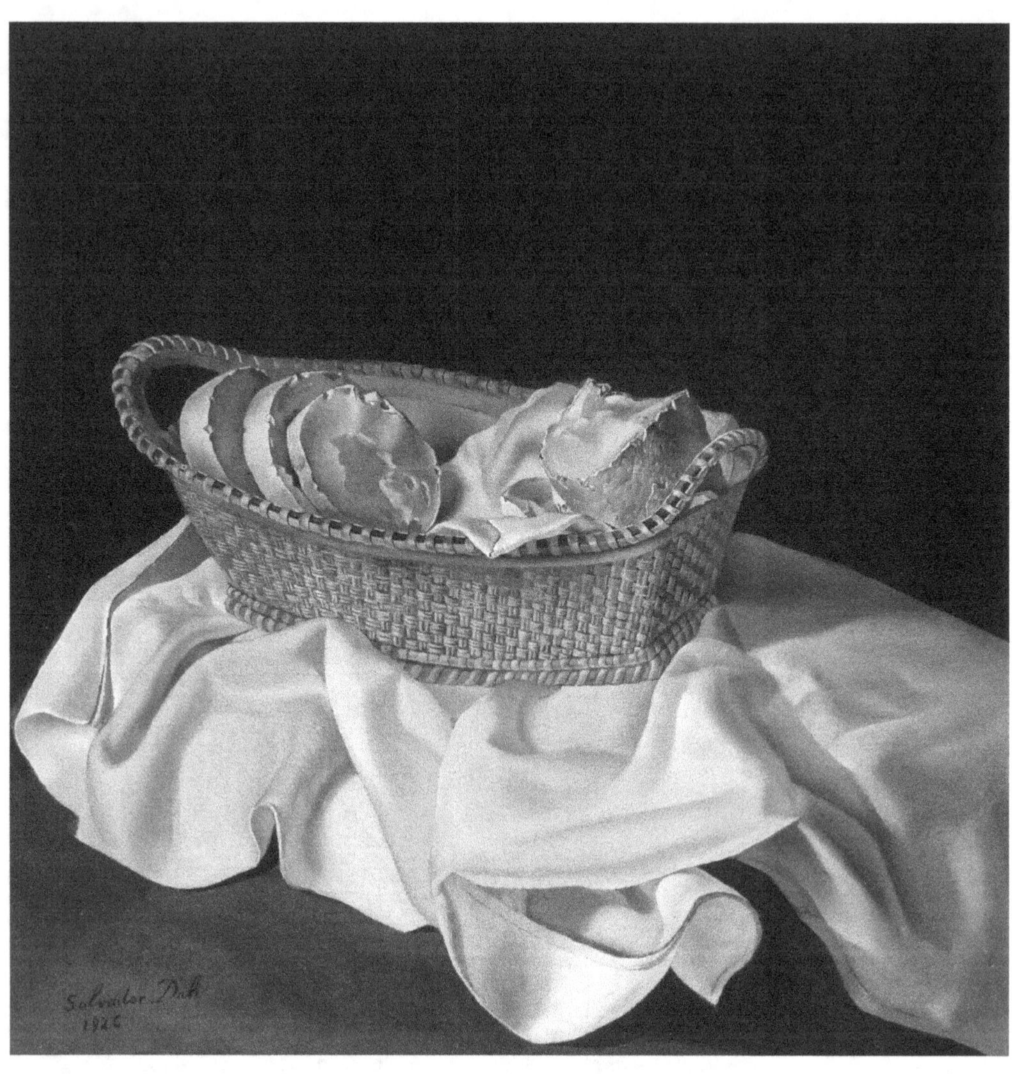

6. (*above*) Salvador Dalí, *The Basket of Bread*, 1926. Oil on panel, 31.5 × 31.5 cm (12½ × 12½ in.). © Salvador Dalí. Fundació Gala-Salvador Dalí (Artists Rights Society), 2011. Collection of the Salvador Dalí Museum, Inc., St. Petersburg FL, 2011.

7. (*right*) Salvador Dalí, *Aparell i mà* (*Instrument and Hand* or *Apparatus and Hand*), 1927. Oil on panel, 62.2 × 47.6 cm (24½ × 18¾ in.). © Salvador Dalí. Fundació Gala-Salvador Dalí (Artists Rights Society), 2011. Collection of the Salvador Dalí Museum, Inc., St. Petersburg FL, 2011.

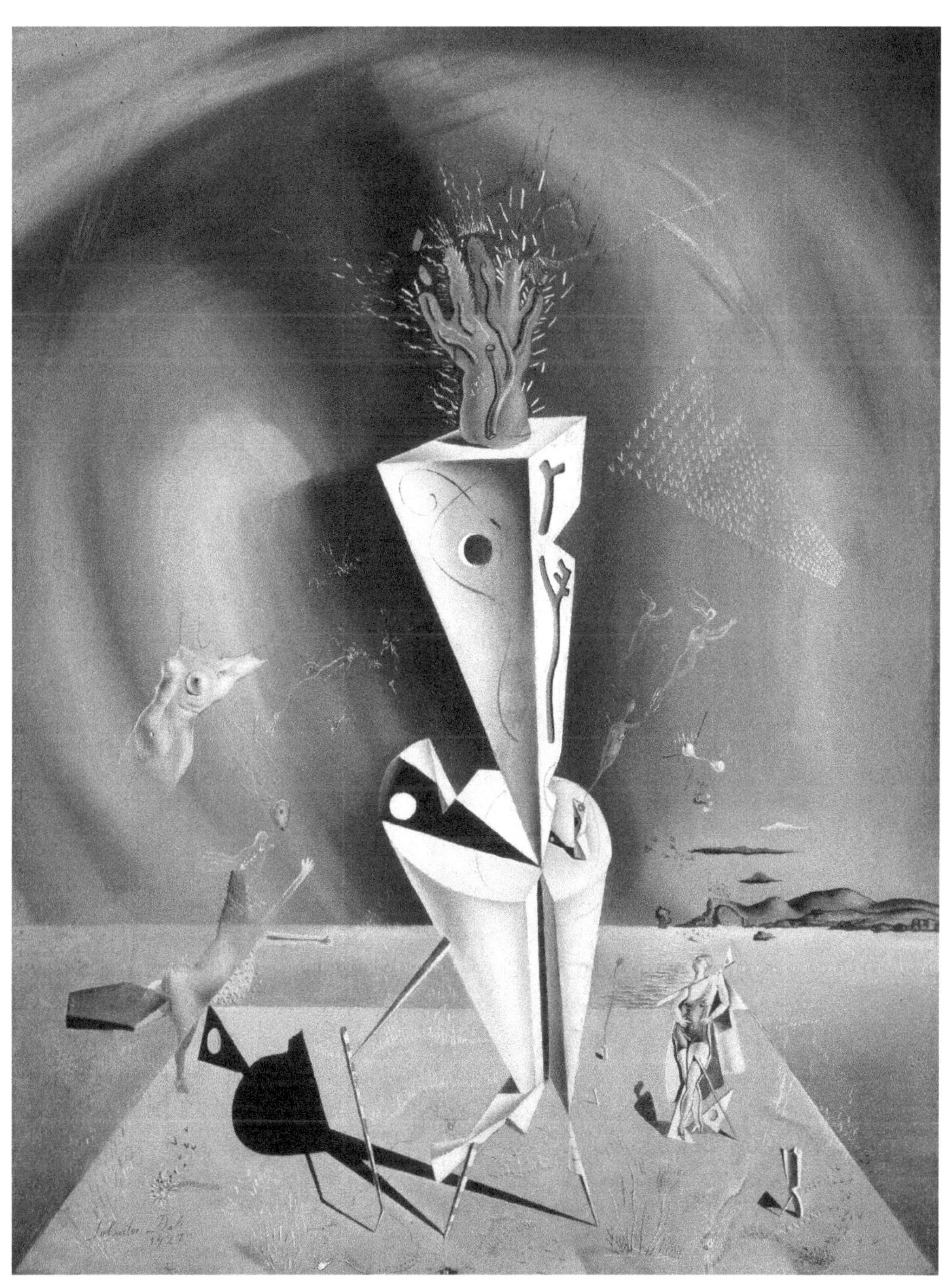

middle it reads as an incoherent string of utterances, interrupted occasionally by momentary bursts of apparent cogency.[7] For example, in one section of the letter a flurry of word fragments, "ri ri ri ri ri ri ri ri ri cccccccccc," is followed by "¡Sí señor! ¡No señor!" On the next page, Dalí's orthography erupts:

Look, an i with lots of dots on top

.
.
.
.
.

i *and another with even more dots*

.
.
.
.
.
.
.
.
.
.
.
.
.

i

The eruption continues on the following page, where an enormous O fills almost the entire sheet of paper. Beneath it appears a second, much smaller *o*, and at the very bottom of the page, in capital letters, "QUE COSAS" (which literally translates as "what things" but is more meaningfully translated as "imagine that!") (fig. 8). The next page is the letter's last. In it, Dalí offers Lorca a few remaining fragments of his thinking along with another lowercase *i* that, like the two that appeared earlier in the letter, appears to erupt in a welter of dots.

As far as little things (*cositas*) go, the dots atop the lowercase *i* may well qualify as among the littlest of all. When one is trained to write in cursive they are, like the cross on the lowercase *t*, an afterthought, an element to be affixed to the word after the completion of all the other letters in the word. When Dalí exclaims, "que cosas," he is making Lorca aware of these otherwise invisible dots as *things* worth examining in themselves.[8] Suggesting that his reader forget for a moment the *meaning* of the words within which the letter *i* might be included, Dalí invites him or her to delight in its own seemingly self-propelled escape from the page. As the dots multiply they describe an upward movement, away from the short vertical stem above which the first dot would have been expected to sit. One imagines Dalí ticking off the dots, his hand drifting up and away from the vertical line at the letter's base. The result is the picture of a letter in which one of its parts — its smallest — has been set free, released from its bondage to the pen stroke below it and the word within which it had once been held captive. No longer fixed in its place, it flies away of its own accord and multiplies as it wishes, first five times, then thirteen times, and finally, at the end of the letter, some thirty times, as it weaves its way in and out of the other words on the page.

The production of nonsense effected by Dalí's dots in flight recalls what Gilles Deleuze and Félix Guattari called the "deterritorialization" of language in Kafka's writing. For them, the term is useful as a means of identifying key moments in Kafka's writing as it devolves from sense to nonsense. In those moments, they write, "The sound or the word that traverses this new deterritorialization no longer belongs to a language of sense, even though it derives from it, nor is it an organized music or song, even though it might appear to be. . . . Everywhere, organized music is traversed by a line of escape — in order to liberate a living and expressive material that speaks for itself and has no need of being put into a form."[9] Their description of Kafka's nonsense as the eruption of elements that speak for themselves as they exist outside of linguistic form echoes Dalí's string of deterritorialized dots. Now that the dot on the top of the letter *i* has been released ("liberated," as Deleuze and Guattari put it) from the word, it follows its own, deterritorialized, "line of escape."

Once liberated, what becomes of these little things? What did Dalí imagine was the nature of this new "expressive material"? Here it is useful to consider the distinction between "object" and "thing" that Bill Brown has proposed. Drawing on a wide range of sources (including the philosophical reflections of Michel Serres, Maurice Merleau-Ponty, and Francis Ponge, as well as remarks by Rainer Maria Rilke, Leo Stein, and others), Brown has argued that objects and things ought to be distinguished by the way in which we, as subjects, relate to them. Brown proposes that we think of objects as items that we use to do work, create meaning, construct social relations. Things, on the other hand, are items (or properties of an item) that we cannot use, that fail to generate meaning, that dissolve social relations. Under particular circumstances an object can become a thing and vice versa. An object becomes a thing, Brown suggests, when it is *misused*: when work is interrupted, meaning suspended, social relations unraveled. "To the degree that the 'thing' registers the undignified mutability

6

Mira una i con muchos puntos en cima

i otra con mas puntos

i

como se llama?
ANTONIO Moreno

Antonio Moreno, decia el Moreno Villa mordiendose el vigote

Que COSAS!

¡que COSAS!

8. Salvador Dalí, pages from a letter to Lorca, March 1926. Fundación Federico García Lorca.

mira ahora te dibujaré una o 7

o

una o

QUE COSAS!

of objects, and thus the excess of the object (a capacity to be other than it is), the 'thing' names a mutual mediation (and a slide between objective and subjective predication) that appears as the vivacity of the object's difference from itself."[10] From the observation that the object contains within itself an "excess" that manifests as its "difference from itself," Brown constructs what he calls an "axiomatic distinction" between objects and things:

> The sort of objectification that takes place during those operations that produce use value, sign value, cultural capital will never produce a thing. Producing a thing — effecting thingness — depends, instead, on a fetishistic overvaluation or misappropriation, on an irregular if not unreasonable reobjectification of the object it dislodges from the circuits through which it is what it typically is. Thingness is precipitated as a kind of misuse value. By *misuse value* I mean to name the aspects of an object — sensuous, aesthetic, semiotic — that become legible, audible, palpable when the object is experienced in whatever time it takes (in whatever time it is) for an object to become another.[11]

As an example, Brown considers the use one might make of a knife when faced with a task for which a screwdriver would be the proper tool. The moment of its "misuse" is the moment when the knife's "thingness" is revealed:

> In the process of using a knife as a screwdriver, of dislocating it from one routinized objectification and deploying it otherwise, we have the chance (if just a chance) to sense its presence (its thinness . . . its sharpness and flatness . . . the peculiarity of its scalloped handle, slightly loose . . . its knifeness and what exceeds that knifeness) as though for the first time. For the first time, perhaps, we thus also sense the norms by which we customarily deploy both knife and screwdriver. . . . The life of things made manifest in the time of misuse is, should we look, a secret in plain sight — not a life behind or beneath the object but a life that is its fluctuating shape and substance and surface, a life that the subject must catalyze but cannot contain.[12]

Moments such as this, like moments when objects fail to do what they should, when they cause you to "cut your finger on a sheet of paper, . . . trip over some toy, . . . get bopped on the head by a falling nut" are moments that, although "outside the scene of phenomenological attention, . . . nonetheless teach you that you're 'caught up in things' and that the 'body is a thing among things.'"[13] Thus does Brown propose that we distinguish objects from things: objects have a transparency about them (a transparency of function and meaning), while things are opaque:

> As they circulate through our lives, we look *through* objects (to see what they disclose about history, society, nature, or culture — above all, what they disclose about *us*), but we only catch a glimpse of things. We look through objects because there are codes by which our interpretive attention makes them meaningful, because there is a discourse of objectivity that allows us to use them as facts. A *thing*, in contrast, can hardly function as a window. We begin to confront the thingness of objects when they stop working for us: when the drill breaks, when the car stalls, when the windows get filthy, when their flow within the circuits of production and distribution, consumption and exhibition, has been arrested, however momentarily.[14]

In the end, Brown conceives of objects and things as two sides of a single coin. The coin rarely flips, however, so we have become accustomed to thinking about only one side (the object side). Only rarely, and then but fleetingly, does the coin flip to reveal the thing side. Witnessing the flip requires that the subject engage in a particular type of attention that runs counter to the type of attention that objects require. To see objects we need to attend to uses, meanings, and connections; to see things we need to attend to misuses, failures of meaning, and ruptures.

Dalí's own attention to the "deterritorialized" dot as it flees the stem of the letter *i* and proliferates on its own accord has much in common with Brown's understanding of what is required to make visible the "thingness" of an object. In the process of transforming from a mark in the construction of a letter into a string of dots, the mark is transformed from an object into a thing. Like the knife that suddenly becomes a screwdriver or the sheet of paper that suddenly becomes a knife (when it cuts our finger) or the toy that suddenly loses its playfulness when we trip over it, the dot atop the letter *i* effects a sudden transformation from a linguistic object (transparent and meaningful) to an opaque and asignifying thing. Like Brown, Dalí initiates the transformation from meaningful object to meaningless thing by engaging in a "fetishistic overvaluation or misappropriation" of the object: the dot is looked at in the wrong way and with the wrong intentions. Also like Brown, Dalí believes that the pivotal moment in which the transformation takes place is the moment in which the object "stop[s] working for us." Finally, and yet again like Brown, Dalí draws great pleasure from witnessing these moments of transformation, moments in which, as Brown put it, we "catch a glimpse of things" before they flip back again to their obverse side and thus return to the world of objects.

Dalí's paintings of the period include no direct transcriptions of this scene of escaping dots, but they nevertheless include elements that suggest a similar dynamic of escape and dispersal, of the object that becomes a thing. The dots that flee their base-stroke have their analog in the tiny insects and birds that are scattered about the surface of paintings such as *Instrument and Hand* and *Little Ashes* (figs. 7, 10). In a letter to Lorca, Dalí described the delight he experienced at the thought of rendering the chaotic scene of a myriad of little things jostling against each other, detaching themselves — like the dot above the *i* — from the structures to which they were intended to remain affixed:

> Just now I'm painting a very beautiful smiling woman, *bristling* with *feathers of every color*, held up by a little marble dice that is *on fire*. The marble dice is supported, in turn, on a quiet, humble little plume of smoke. In the sky are donkeys with parrot heads, grass and sand from the beach, all about to explode, all clean, incredibly objective, and the scene is awash in an indescribable blue, the green, red and yellow of a parrot, an edible white, the metallic white of a stray breast (you know that there are also "stray breasts," just the opposite of the flying breast, for the stray one is at peace without knowing what to do and is so defenseless it moves me).
> — *Stray breasts* (how beautiful!) (*Pechos extraviados* [¡qué bonito!])[15]

Dalí rendered these "stray breasts" not only in *Instrument and Hand* and *Little Ashes* but also *Honey Is Sweeter than Blood* and other paintings of the period. In them the stray breasts soar in the sky like birds. They are — again, like the dots on the tip of the letter *i* — object fragments that have been released from the larger structure from which they had once functioned as a meaningful part.

Stray breasts were but one of a long list of little things that Dalí sought to deterritorialize. He was also, for example, drawn to the thought of the liberation of the hands of a clock. Bound to its circular rhythm, the hands of a clock are little things that are forced to follow another's command. But what, Dalí wonders as he attends to the clock with the eyes of one in search of its "thingness," would happen if the hands were to dislodge themselves from the clock's face? What would happen if they stopped functioning as useful *objects* and became instead a collection of meaningless, broken, and useless *things*? What movements would they choose to make once they were left to their own desires? Would they *stray* like the breasts? Would they drift upward and off the canvas like the dots on the page? Dalí described his fantasy of the liberated clock hands in an essay from 1928. "Minute hands are truer," he wrote, "when they cease being subject to their special function, the moment they are given to a rhythm other than that of following the circumference, acquiring the slightly mad choking caused by their articulation with bread crumbs."[16]

The thingness of the minute hand is, it would seem, bound to the thingness of the similarly liberated bread crumbs. In fact, of all of Dalí's little things, crumbs may be the most perfect emblem of a "thing" as Brown has described it. When attached to the loaf of bread, they are, in fact, not crumbs at all but parts of the loaf. They are useful: they can be eaten. In this capacity they are "objects." But once these small parts become dislodged from the rest of the loaf they take on different qualities. Once dislodged they lose their usefulness and thus become "things." From an object to be eaten they have been transformed into a thing to be swept away as waste. A crumb as such (what we call a crumb in distinction to what we would refer to as a small piece of a loaf) is an especially rare item, for it exists primarily in a state of thingness. Left to itself a crumb is useless and therefore visible to us in its thingness, but when amassed with thousands of other crumbs and modified through heat, moisture, and combination with other substances it becomes once again useful as a foodstuff. In so doing the thing is turned back into an object.

At this point it is useful to consider the question of scale. Note that to become a useless piece of bread (to become a crumb), the piece needs to be very small. A large crumb is not a crumb; it is still a piece of bread, albeit a smaller piece than the piece from which it was dislodged. It is only when the piece of bread is too small to be eaten that it is a crumb. One cannot deterritorialize large things. Only little things can effect this "flight" from use to nonuse, meaning to nonmeaning. Here is one place in which Dalí may offer something useful to theorists like Brown. Dalí's example of the crumb suggests that if we are interested in catching "a glimpse of things," we should fix our gaze on the small, on little things like crumbs and minute hands and dots on the letter *i*. These are items we typically consider only insofar as we recognize their function within a larger item. In themselves they are useless (the minute hand) or meaningless (the dot on the *i*) or inconsumable (the crumb). As such, under most circumstances these little things remain invisible to us. For Brown, as for Dalí, the goal is to find these things and bring them to light. And for Dalí, if not for Brown, it seems as though the best way to find them is to start paying more attention to things that are particularly small.

Dots, crumbs, and clock hands soon coalesced in Dalí's mind as constituting an alternative universe that was visible only under certain circumstances. In another letter to Lorca, Dalí reported that his investigation of the tiny had led him to conclude that the world is in reality a teeming swarm of little things without structure or sense. We only believe that it has meaning because we have pressed these little things into shapes and structures that are congenial to the subjective order of the mind. As such, true poetry — the poetry of the real as it exists outside the mind — must be a poetry in which the little things are set free to move about as they themselves see fit and not as the mind would like to imagine them. Thus did Dalí insist to Lorca that metaphor — the device by which the poet connects one thing to another and thereby creates order of the otherwise inchoate mass of little things — must be banished without remorse: "I'm convinced," he wrote to Lorca, "that in poetry our efforts only make sense when they lead us to evade the ideas our intelligence has forged artificially, and give things their exact, real sense." That this ought to be understood as a critique of poetic conventions — in particular of metaphoricity — is spelled out in the passage that follows:

> In reality, there is no relation at all between two dancers and a honeycomb, unless it be the relation that exists between Saturn and the little cockroach that sleeps in its chrysalis, or unless there is *no difference* between the dancing couple and the honeycomb. The minute hands of a clock (never mind my examples, I'm not exactly looking for poetic ones) begin to have real value at the moment they stop pointing out the hours and, losing their *circular* rhythm and the arbitrary role our intelligence has subjected them to (pointing out the hours), they *evade* the clock entirely and occupy the place that would correspond to the sex organs of little bread crumbs.[17]

Dalí's argument seems to be this: if we are to suppose that two things are in some way similar, we must then conclude that all things are in some way similar. Since this cannot be the case, all things must be dissimilar, no matter how similar they may appear to us. Similarity and difference belong to the mind of the individual, not the things themselves.

The only true and objective poetry is thus the poetry in which the mind's control has been suppressed to the point where the little things of the world are free to determine their actions and arrangements: "We must leave things *free of* the conventional ideas to which intelligence has subjugated them. At that moment those cute little things (estas cositas monas) will begin to act in accordance with their real, consubstantial manner of being."[18] Dalí concludes (with an analogy more directly applicable to the visual arts), "Let the things themselves decide where their shadows fall!"[19]

That Dalí understood his poetic practice in dialogical relation to the mainstream of modern poetry in Spain — indeed, as he put it, its "exact opposite"— is evidenced by his various references to the poetry of Juan Ramón Jimenez.[20] Ramón was among the most revered Spanish poets at the time, and his influence was central to the generation of writers who published regularly in journals such as *Verso y Prosa* and *Litoral* (both of which had published Lorca's work as well). Dalí's distain for the conventions practiced by these poets was unequivocal; he derided them as stuck in "the marasmus of putrefaction" and their work as "rotten sentimentality." Ramón, Dalí held, was the worst of the lot, the "commander in chief of poetic putrefaction."[21] Dalí considered him a "reactionary" who refused to admit any evidence of modernity into his poetic universe.[22] "I've reread *Platero y yo* [Ramón's most respected collection of prose poems]," Dalí wrote to Lorca, "it's *nauseating*, all that emotional ecstasy before things he doesn't see, that he doesn't see at all (que no ve en absoluto)."[23] Ramón's failure, according to Dalí, was the result of an adherence to the poetics of metaphoricity. For Dalí, to really see meant to recognize that the mind "subjugates" the little things of the world, holds them down and fixes them to our own needs and desires. Thus the only true poetry is poetry that sets them free.[24]

Ramón's *Platero y yo* tells the story of a wandering poet and his donkey, Platero, as they travel through the village of Moguer, the poet's hometown in southern Spain. Reading the text today one readily spots a host of passages that would surely have offended Dalí. At the beginning of the book, for example, Ramón describes Platero as "small, fluffy, soft; so soft on the outside that one would say he is all cotton, that he has no bones. That is, except for the jet mirrors of his eyes, which are as hard as beetles of black crystal."[25] The imagery here is exactly the sort to which Dalí objected: black as jet, hard as crystal. Both metaphors are comprehensible within the subjective framework of the human mind. For Dalí, proper seeing was anti-metaphorical; it required the suppression of the mind's power to make different little things appear similar. Eyes and jet are not the same; to see them as similar is to deny them their reality, their "thingness," and instead to expose them to the subjective order of the poet's mind. Had Ramón truly seen the donkey's eyes as they were and not as he subjectively imagined them, he would not have seen them as jet or crystal. He would not have seen them *as* anything; he would simply have seen them.

For Dalí, the only appropriate way to use metaphor was to use it so that the result would be an absurd image, an image that by virtue of its impossibility compels the reader to recognize the error of metaphoricity itself. Deployed by Dalí, metaphors result in nonsense, as, for example, in his description of his girlfriend's knee in "Poem of Little Things" as made of smoke or of his girlfriend's breasts as a sea urchin and a swarm of wasps (see introduction). Unlike Platero's jet-black and crystal-hard eyes, Dalí's metaphors are incoherent. By virtue of being mentally ungraspable, they are set free from the poet's mind and, as such, they underscore the distance that separates the real things from our mental image of them.

Dalí called this distance the sign of the poet's "objectivity." Poetic objectivity required a willingness to let the little things of the world wander freely, unmoored from the poet's mind. At the same time Dalí insisted that painters, too, must practice a similar form of objectivity. Defending the works he had exhibited at Barcelona's Autumn Salon of 1927, Dalí insisted that to understand his paintings one should forget the history of "*artistic* painting" and instead "merely look at them with pure eyes." "Is this an oddity? A living eye, the most insignificant and innocuous plant, a fly, are organisms infinitely more complicated, more mysterious, and more unusual, than any of my simple and primary organisms, that, on top of that, are described with the kind of clarity and precision which nature never offers us, [the latter] being always at the mercy of the least accident. To know how to look at an object, an animal, with your mind's eye, is to see it in its greatest objective reality."[26] With this, Dalí had begun to offer a public and explicit statement on painting in the service of the small.

Dalí's critique of metaphoricity was most explicitly declared in "The Liberation of the Fingers," which was published in March 1929. "Nothing is further removed from our true aspirations," wrote Dalí, "than the metaphoric image and the other methods of a defunct poetry, which are as unacceptable if not more so than the imagination itself." One should instead "wander around without method following unintentional paths, recording the simple facts that each day signify more violently within our consciousness the existence of an essential reason."[27] In other words, to see something "in its greatest objective reality" is to see without the artificial and misleading aid of metaphor, to see in such a way that even the most "insignificant and innocuous" little things are left to their own devices, unmolested by poetic subjectivity. It is, to return to Brown's distinction between objects and things, to refuse to see through them as one would see through objects and instead to recognize them in their opacity as things. The title of this particular essay makes Dalí's intentions especially clear: the poet's task is to "liberate" the fingers from the hand that holds them. Like the hands of the clock that detach themselves from the circular rhythm of the timepiece and the breasts that stray from their torso, the fingers of the hand are set free to move about as they wish, unbound by any supervening structure, sense, or application.

THE LITTLE PHOTOGRAPHIC INSTRUMENT

Most of the little things Dalí favored belong to the natural world. His paintings and poems included references to breadcrumbs and olives, ants and sea urchins, bird feathers and grains of sand. Of the few man-made elements that he favored, most tended to be ones that spoke of tradition more than modernity — the sewing needle and the pocket watch, for example. Of particular interest in this regard is the poem "Fish Pursued by a Grape," which, like "Poem of Little Things," was first written to Lorca in Spanish and later published in Catalan in *L'Amic de les Arts*.[28] The poem tells the story of a variety of things so small as to be described with a *double* diminutive — "tiny little." "That fish and that grape," the poem begins, "were nothing but tiny little things (cosetes petites), but these little things were rounder than others and were kept up quietly in their place." What follows is a veritable catalog of tiny little things and their curious properties: "there are small things that are shooting stars, that get altogether wet when their place is being changed. . . . There are small things that are flat; there are small things that stand on one leg. The others are merely a hair, the other had been salt."[29] As the poem continues the narrative grows more complex, but its underlying structure remains consistent throughout: precise descriptions of a host of small and seemingly inconsequential objects that exhibit bizarre properties and undergo curious transformations.

The poem's penultimate line — "the still olive is wearing a little skirt (una petita faldilla)"— leaves the reader with one last puzzling image, but the final line is curiously straightforward: "I have a nice photo of New York."[30] Because of its position at the very end of the poem, and because of its placement immediately following the reference to the "petita faldilla," the reader is inclined to understand the photograph as yet another *coseta petita*. Although only implicit, this final line performs yet another act of transfiguration: the great city of New York becomes, by virtue of its transformation into a photograph, a tiny keepsake. In the end New York City is, like the grape and the olive, simply another little thing.

That Dalí concluded this poem with a reference to New York alerts us to the rather surprising fact that, with rare exception, the world of urban modernity is almost entirely absent from Dalí's paintings of the late twenties. (The billboard advertisement in the background of *Young Girl in Figueres* (fig. 9), also known as *Woman at the Window in Figueres*, is a notable exception.) Nevertheless, in his letters and public statements, Dalí frequently lavished praise on the astonishing inventions of modern technology. In fact, the absence of the modern world was one of Dalí's principal complaints against Lorca's poetry: "Your songs are of a Granada with no trolleys and still without airplanes," Dalí lamented. "They are an old Granada with natural elements, far removed from today, purely popular and constant." The machine, he declared, "has changed *everything*."[31]

In this Dalí was drawing on his understanding of Le Corbusier's aesthetic of modern industry. "The machine," wrote Le Corbusier in *The Lesson of the Machine*, "is bringing about a reformation of the spirit across the world. . . . In place of the calcareous pebble or the imperfect orange, the machine brings shining before us disks, spheres, the cylinders of polished steel, polished more high *than we have ever seen before*: shaped with a theoretical precision and exactitude *which can never be seen in nature itself*. . . . A new desire; an aesthetic of purity, of precision, of expressive relationships setting in motion the mathematical mechanisms of our spirit: a spectacle and a cosmogony."[32]

Le Corbusier's ecstatic celebration of machinic perfection is echoed widely in Dalí's writings of the period and most explicitly endorsed in an essay from 1928 titled "Poetry of the Mass-Produced Utility." In it Dalí identifies Le Corbusier as the figure whose writings "make us see the simple and moving beauty of the miraculous mechanical and industrial world that, newly born, is perfect and pure as a flower." However, unlike Le Corbusier, for whom industrial beauty was best exemplified by airplanes, automobiles, ocean liners, factories, and turbines, Dalí was interested in the little objects of modern industry: "the metallic and brilliant thickness of phonographic needles"; the "little pieces of my cigarette paper"; "the mechanical and *matte* subtlety of the telephone"; "the tender joy of the little black and red numbers of the electric counting machine"; "the wash-basin with a pedal"; "the small metallic appliances in which endure the slowest nocturnal osmoses with all flesh, plants, the sea, the constellations"; and "the clarity of nickel taps in toilets made of porcelain."[33]

It is also worth noting here that Dalí's fascination with the material stuff of modern life was, like his interest in the little things of the natural world, oriented not only toward the physically small but also toward that which is metaphorically small — the banal, the marginal, the innocuous, and the trivial. Consider, for example, Dalí's interest in things like athletic jerseys and film comedies: "Modernity," he wrote in 1928, "does not mean canvases painted by Sonia Delaunay, nor does it mean Fritz Lang's *Metropolis*. It means hockey pullovers of anonymous English manufacturing. It means film comedies, also anonymously made, of the *loony* type."[34] Although briefly drawn to Chaplin and Keaton, Dalí singled out the actor Harry Langdon for special praise and did so by identifying him as tiny: "Harry Langdon is a little thing, that moves with greater thoughtlessness than little animals. . . . He moves the way the bean plant moves when it opens its leaves."[35]

More than the nickel taps on porcelain toilets and the matte finish of the telephone, and more than hockey pullovers and Langdon's thoughtless movements, the product of modernity that most fascinated Dalí was the camera. It was, for him, particularly special, for not only was it small itself but it had (as we saw at the culmination of "Fish Pursued by a Grape") the power to make other things small. Dalí understood the camera as a device capable of training us to see the world properly — with "maximum probity" (màxima probitat), as he sometimes put it.[36] In "Photography: Pure Creation of the Spirit," Dalí described this "petita màquina" as the greatest little thing in the world:

> Clear objectivity of the little photographic instrument (Clara objectivitat del petit aparell fotogràfic). Objective crystal. Glass of true poetry. The hand no longer intervenes. Subtle physiochemical harmonies. Plate sensitive to the most delicate precisions. The mechanism, perfect and exact, proves, by its economical structure, the joy of its poetic functioning. A light handling, an imperceptible tipping, a wise displacement in the spatial sense,

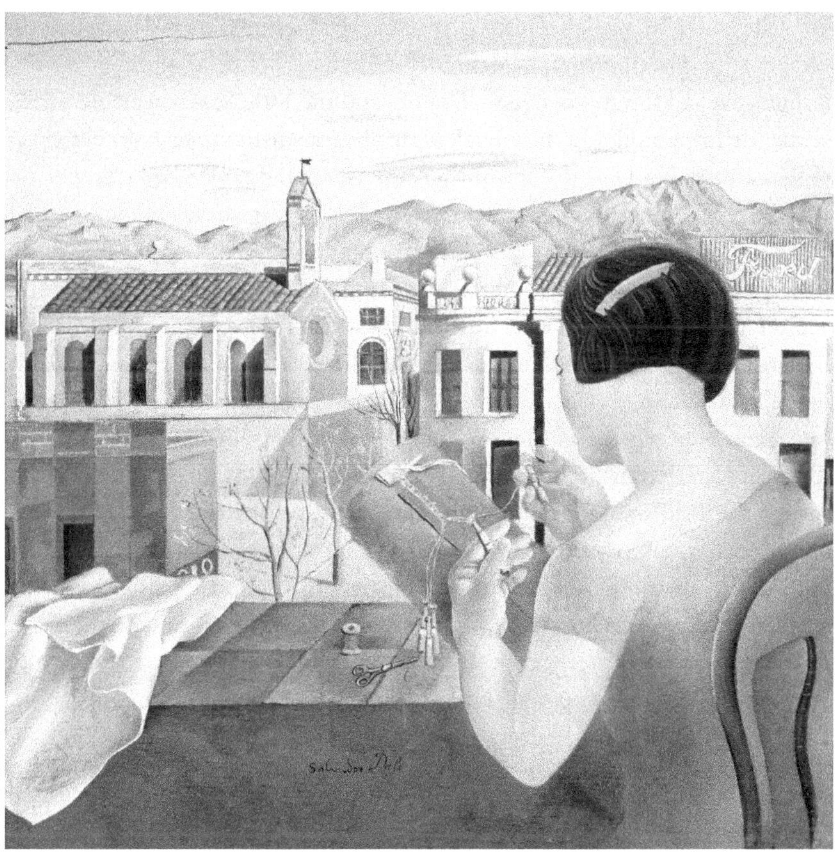

9. Salvador Dalí, *Young Girl in Figueres*, 1926. Oil on panel, 20.8 × 21.5 cm (8.19 × 8.46 in.). Coll. Juan Casanelles, Barcelona, Spain. Dalí, Salvador (1904–89) © ARS, NY. Photo credit: Erich Lessing/Art Resource, NY.

> so that — under the pressure of the tepid fingertips and the nickel-plated string — out of the pure crystalline objectivity of the glass there emerges a spiritual bird of thirty-six greys and forty new manners of inspiration. When the hand no longer intervenes, the mind begins to know the absence of turbid digital flowerings; inspiration is set loose from the technical process, which is strictly entrusted to the unconscious calculation of the machine. . . . No invention has ever been as pure as that created by the anesthetized look of the clearest eye, without eyelashes, of Zeiss; distilled and attentive, unaffected by the rosy efflorescence of conjunctivitis.[37]

This final line is intended as a swipe against the poetic excess of Ramón and his generation, for whom the ideal poetic image is that which sees the world through the transformative lens of metaphor. Dalí, in pursuing the "exact opposite" method, modeled his poetry after the absolute thoughtlessness of the camera lens. The photograph does not discriminate: before its anesthetized and lashless eye, all things are equal. The big and the little, the powerful and the weak, the important and the trivial: none of these distinctions hold in the eye of the camera. For Dalí, this was the great power of the camera's objectivity — it was the great enemy of order and reason and thus the great friend of the small.

Dalí's understanding of the camera's importance went beyond that of the photographic print itself; it applied just as much to the art of painting. For the camera was not simply another little thing; it was the little thing of little things, the little thing that teaches us to see the world with an objective eye — that is, without attempting to make sense of it, without attempting to order its elements into a coherent whole. The lens of the camera sees "things," not "objects," for it pays no heed to the mind's desire for order and significance; it seeks only to "caress the cold smoothness of white lavatories; pursue the drowsy lassitude of aquariums; analyze the most subtle articulations of electrical appliances with all the unreal precision of its own magic."[38] In contrast, painting is an art that has always been bound by its adherence to what Dalí called "the single experience and comprehension" (la sola experiència i comprensió), by which he meant the underlying organizing principle that the mind imposes on the little things it observes. The lesson of the camera is thus that the painter must inhibit the mind's impetus to make sense of the myriad little details that the eye captures on its retina and instead do as the camera does: record these little details without imposing on them any supervening structure or sense.

This lesson is especially evident in *Instrument and Hand* (fig. 7) and *Little Ashes* (*Cenicitas*) (fig. 10). Both paintings refuse to remain bounded by a "single experience" and instead depict objects as unorganized fragments, details without a whole. The title *Instrument and Hand* (*Aparell i mà*) seems designed to alert the viewer to the difference between the objective precision of the camera (*l'aparell fotogràfic*) and the subjective imprecision of the human hand while at the same time imagining a fusion of the two as a single unit. In the center of the painting, on a flat gray slab, stands a gigantic mechanical object with what appears to be a pulsating hand — red-hot and veined and bristling with pins and feathers. The (photographic) instrument and the (human) hand have merged to become a hybrid machine-organism that is also a hybrid subject-object, a being-thing that suggests the very complexities tracked by Bruno Latour in his various studies of the object-world of modern technology.[39] For Latour, the modern distinction between subject and object, between humans and artifacts, obscures the actual interpenetration of the two: "Men and things exchange properties and replace one another."[40] More precisely, "real objects are always parts of institutions, trembling in their mixed status as mediators,

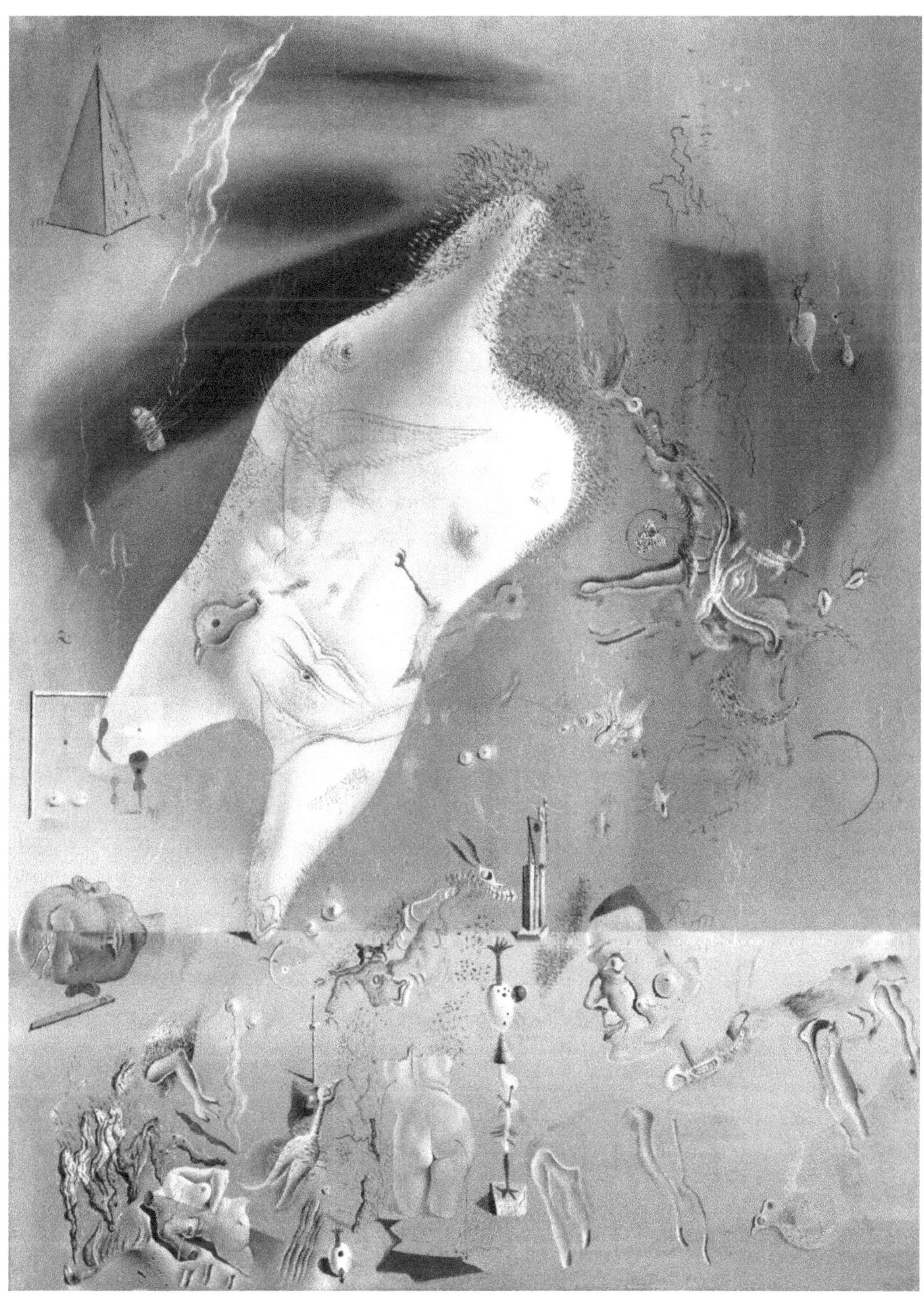

10. Salvador Dalí, *Little Ashes* (*Cenicitas*), 1928. Oil on panel, 64 × 48 cm (25¼ × 18⅞ in.). Museo Nacional Centro de Arte Reina Sofía, Madrid. Dalí, Salvador (1904–89) © ARS, NY.

mobilizing faraway lands and people, ready to become people or things, not knowing if they are composed of one or many, of a black box counting for one or of a labyrinth concealing multitudes."[41] Latour has applied this optic to a number of humble artifacts: the speed bump, the mechanical door closer, the weighted hotel key, and the camera. Regarding the last, Latour has proposed that humans and cameras effectively made each other: "The new amateurs and Eastman's camera co-produced each other."[42] The border between instrument and hand is, in reality, porous.

Around the hybrid hand-machine at the center of *Instrument and Hand* swirl a host of Dalí's favorite little things: flies, birds, and other swarming organisms; stray breasts; fish (both intact and stripped to the bone). All of these little things are painted crisply, precisely, and with little indication of the artist's hand. In doing so, Dalí seems to be attempting to articulate a pictorial practice that would produce the same disorientingly chaotic effect that he associated with the camera lens. It is not so much an attempt to mimic the appearance of a photograph as an attempt to mimic its epistemology, its manner of knowing the world.

Rather than direct the viewer's attention to the means by which the world's little things are recorded (the photographic *instrument* versus the painter's *hand*), the title of Dalí's other important painting of 1927–28, *Little Ashes* (*Cenicitas*) draws our attention to the little things themselves. Where, we wonder, are the *cenicitas*? Are they perhaps everything depicted here? The title certainly invites us to consider every object and organism as a type of little ash. As did *Instrument and Hand*, *Little Ashes* includes figures bristling with pins and feathers, flies and birds and other swarming animals. The stray breasts are here as well, as are the liberated fingers and other suspiciously genital organisms depicted with Miró-like abstraction. Scattered references to cubism appear in the guitars on the left, and viewers familiar with Tanguy's paintings will recognize echoes in the geometric figure in the upper left corner. The effect of all these object fragments and stylistic quotations is one of near-total chaos. Attempts to create order are thwarted, as it is almost impossible to determine a fixed hierarchy of importance among the objects or even a framework in which to organize them spatially or conceptually. The result is a painting in which we are asked to examine the depicted elements in the way that Dalí understands the epistemology of the camera. We are asked to see without thinking, to see without organizing the observed phenomena into mental categories. We are asked, that is, to do what Dalí believed Ramón was incapable of doing ("he doesn't see; he doesn't see at all"). Overwhelmed by the violence of the countless visual transpositions — a woman's torso merges with a man's profile; a donkey's neck becomes a feathered plume; a geometric cone supports an egg, which in turn sprouts a human hand, and so on — the viewer is incapable of establishing an order within which any metaphorical substitutions would be meaningful. As a result, we are left with only our vision and the pleasure of watching these little things jostling and scattering about the canvas.

Both *Instrument and Hand* and *Little Ashes* are thus photographic not because they *look* like photographs but rather because their depictions of the world are, like the camera lens, *attuned to the little*. Like the camera lens, they resist the inclination of the mind to make meaning of the things represented. This is what Dalí meant when he insisted on objectivity in painting. Objectivity is the suppression of the mind's organizational inclinations such that the eye can see things without making sense of them. Objectivity resists the imposition of order; it deterritorializes, transforms objects into things. The result is thus an irrational, incoherent, and in a strict sense, meaningless field of visual experience.

VERMEER, THE GREATEST PAINTER THERE EVER WAS

The letters Dalí wrote to Lorca throughout the mid- to late twenties make reference to a wide range of past and present artists, including Braque, Cézanne, George Grosz, Jules Pascin, and Henri Rousseau. But in the spring of 1926 Dalí drew Lorca's attention to an artist of an entirely different sort: "Believe me," he wrote, "the greatest painter that ever was is Vermeer of Delft."[43] Although he did not follow up with any specific defense of Vermeer's greatness, his letter proceeds with a suggestive reference to his own work in progress: "I am painting 'Girl in Figueras.' For the past five days, I've painted devotedly, patiently, the back of her newly shaved neck, and it's coming out very well, so well that it almost doesn't look (though it is) modern (or old)."[44] Although it isn't entirely clear from the letter, Dalí is likely referring to one of two paintings completed around this time: *Girl's Back* (fig. 11), which measures a little more than twelve by ten inches, or *Young Girl in Figueres* (fig. 9), which is even smaller.[45] The latter part of Dalí sentence, especially its strange interruption with parenthetical contradictions, will be examined in chapter 6, but here I would like to focus on Dalí's insistence on precision, patience, and attention to the small.

The diminutive size of Vermeer's paintings was (and still is) central to the awestruck response of viewers. *The Lacemaker* (fig. 12), for example, (a painting Dalí undoubtedly saw on his visit to Paris in April 1926) measures a mere nine and a half by eight inches. Although quite a bit smaller than *Girl's Back*, *The Lacemaker* is nearly identical in size to *Young Girl in Figueres*. Moreover, both paintings depict women working with needles on fabric (Dalí's seems to be decorating a pillow). As such, both paintings establish a mirror relationship between painter and subject in which the minute care and attention of the

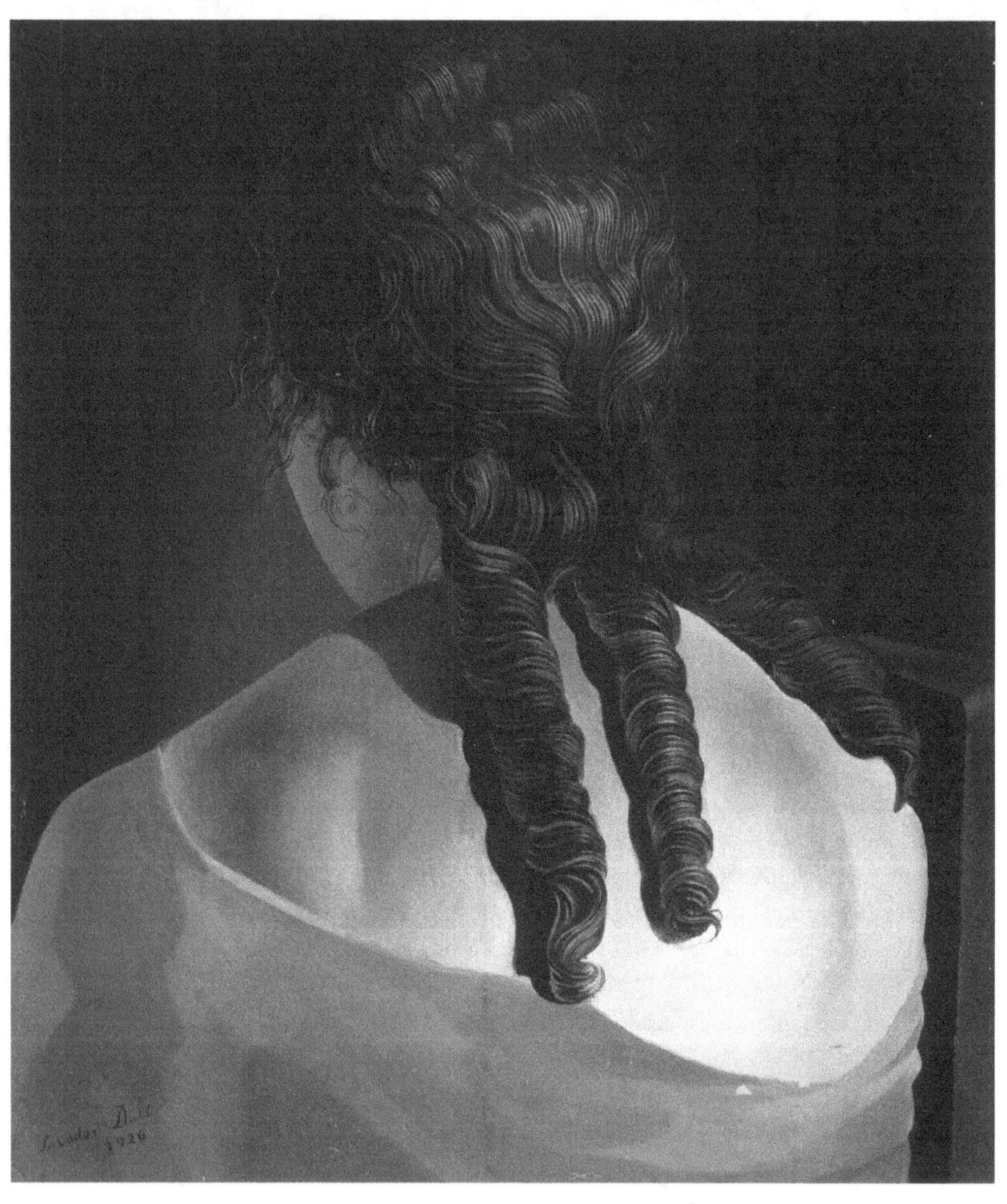

11. Salvador Dalí, *Girl's Back*, 1926. Oil on panel, 32 × 27 cm (12½ × 10¾ in.). © Salvador Dalí. Fundació Gala-Salvador Dalí (Artists Rights Society), 2011. Collection of the Salvador Dalí Museum, Inc., St. Petersburg FL, 2011.

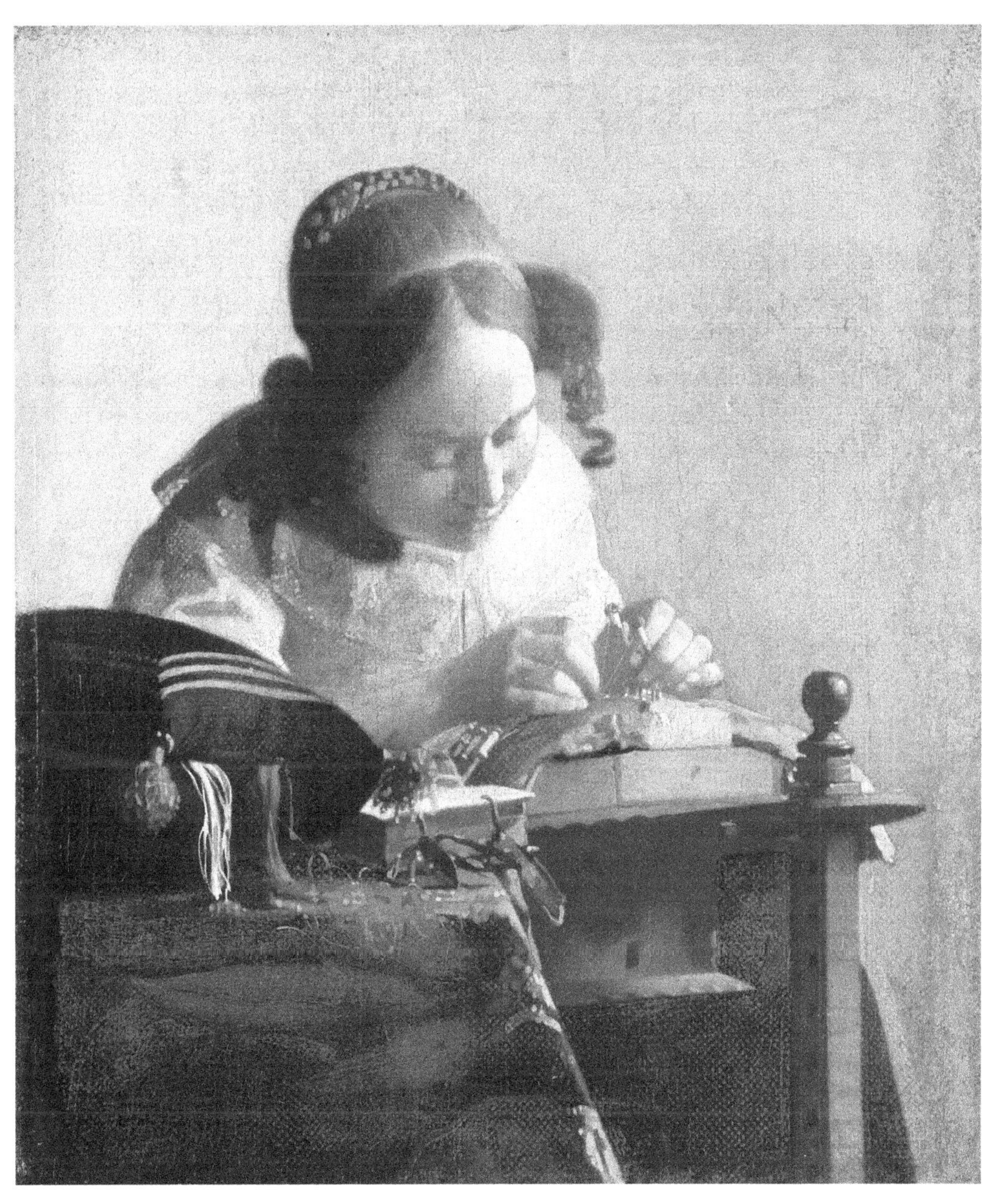

12. Jan Vermeer, *The Lacemaker*, 1669–70. Oil on canvas laid down on wood, 24 × 21 cm. Inv.: MI 1448. Photo: Gérard Blot. Louvre, Paris, France. Photo credit: Réunion des Musées Nationaux/Art Resource, NY.

subjects is echoed by the care and attention applied by the painters as they painted them.

At the same time, however, Dalí's two paintings are in significant respects wholly unlike Vermeer's. *Girl's Back* depicts a dramatically spare environment and glows with an intense luminosity more akin to the Spanish still lifes of Francisco de Zurbarán, Juan Sánchez Cotán, and Luis Meléndez.[46] *Young Girl in Figueres* employs a deliberately skewed perspective and a simplified treatment of surfaces less indebted to Vermeer than to Giorgio Morandi and Giorgio de Chirico.[47] Moreover, neither of these paintings manifests anything remotely resembling Vermeer's magical opalescence. Vermeer's influence — at least as it can be said to be present in these two small paintings — is in truth more conceptual than technical. It is not so much the particular style of Vermeer that Dalí has emulated but rather the *idea* of Vermeer — the idea, that is, of an artist who paints, as Dalí put it with regard to his own work in progress, with devotion and patience.

Then as now, art critics treated Vermeer as an astonishing exception, an outsider whose slow and deliberate practice (leaving behind only three dozen works) marked him as an aberration. Theophile Thoré, writing under the name William Bürger, set the tone for much of the subsequent reception of Vermeer with his 1866 essay in the *Gazette des Beaux-Arts*. Thoré's lengthy account of Vermeer's work included reference to all of the painter's known works (some of which have since been de-attributed). Above all, Thoré's text established Vermeer as an elusive mystery, a figure entirely apart from the history of art, and a painter about whom there existed almost no biographical details with which to unravel the mystery.[48] Writing of Vermeer as if addressing him directly, Thoré begins his account of the painter's life and work with, "You are one of those who attracts the Unknown, the Ignored. You are curious about both mystery and reality, shadow and light — the two sides of art and life."[49]

Thoré's text referred more than once to Vermeer's paintings as "petits tableaux," and subsequent commentators likewise emphasized their diminutive scale.[50] Gustave Vanzype, for example, wrote an influential book on Vermeer in 1908 in which he claimed that "often, when a museum owns a single Vermeer, this small painting becomes the jewel of its collection."[51] Roughly ten years later, Jean Louis Vaudoyer reiterated Vanzype's claim, indeed quoted it verbatim and credited Vanzype, while adding the idea that the small scale of Vermeer's paintings was linked to their status as "humble" (a term Dalí would later employ in his own reflections on Vermeer).[52] Vaudoyer, like those before him, emphasized the notion that Vermeer's technique — which he described as "faithful as a camera"— was unparalleled, "without relatives."[53] Above all, it was their "fidelity" to the "mundane" that distinguished these paintings from all others. What made these works astonishing, Vaudoyer insisted, was that Vermeer's faithfulness to these mundane and humble scenes somehow managed to transform them into tiny jewels of utmost preciousness: "We are dealing," he concluded, "with a magician."[54]

That Dalí, in his correspondences with Lorca, associated Vermeer's work with the same constellation of terms that Thoré, Vanzype, and Vaudoyer had used suggests that his conception of Vermeer was by no means unusual. Dalí, like the French critics before him, imagined Vermeer as an outsider whose work was distinguished not only by its affection for the mundane but also, and more importantly, by the way this affection was manifest in his technique. Although he knew most of Vermeer's paintings only through reproduction, his trip to Paris and Brussels in early 1926 gave him an opportunity to see a few of the originals in person and to examine them up close.[55] The visit impressed him, and even six months after his return he was unable to let go of the experience: "I dream of going to Brussels," he wrote to Lorca in the fall of 1926, "to *copy* the Dutch painters in the museum."[56] He underlined the word "copy" so as to emphasize that his desire was not to adapt their techniques to the practices of the present (in the manner of Picasso's neoclassicism, for example), but straightforwardly to emulate them.

The following July (1927) Dalí publicly announced his admiration for Vermeer in an essay titled "Saint Sebastian." As did his letters to Lorca, this text referred to Vermeer as a model of "humble patience" (la paciència humil), which he likened to the imperceptibly gradual process by which fruit ripens on the tree.[57] A few months later, in "Photography, Pure Creation of the Spirit" (September 1927), Dalí again affirmed his admiration for Vermeer. This time he supplemented his image of Vermeer's patience and humility with one of self-restraint: "With all the temptations of light . . . Van der Meer, a new Saint Anthony, preserved intact the object, with an inspiration altogether photographic, an outcome of his humble and impassioned sense of touch."[58] Like Vaudoyer before him, Dalí likened Vermeer to a human camera. But Dalí pressed this metaphor further by noting that to make oneself after the model of a mechanical instrument was more than simply a technical skill. It was evidence (for Dalí at least) of an extraordinary character, unmatched anytime in the past or present: "In the history of looking," Dalí declared of Vermeer, "his eyes are the case of the highest probity" (el cas de màxima probitat).[59]

Dalí made yet another public affirmation of his identification with Vermeer in an essay published in December 1927. Here, for the first time, he specifically addressed the issue of scale: "Be careful about the innocent concept of grandiosity. Michelangelo with *The Last Judgment* is not greater than Vermeer of Delft with his *Lacemaker* in the Louvre, however small its dimensions are. Taking into account its plastic dimensions, Van der Meer's *Lacemaker*, alongside the Sistine Chapel, can be rated as having grandiose dimensions." Informed by the dramatic scalar manipulations characteristic of photography and the cinema (wherein, as Dalí noted, "a lump of sugar on the screen can *become* larger than the interminable perspective of gigantic buildings"), as well as by the precise and nondiscriminating gaze of the camera lens, Dalí concluded that the little paintings of Vermeer are themselves little things.[60] Both are physically small and both enable us to attend to the world of the small. For Dalí, both photography and the art of Vermeer are tools of deterritorialization. They liberate the tiny from the order of the mind and set them free to wander without order or sense. In so doing, they transform objects into things.

Even as he turned, in 1928 and 1929, toward the art and writing of the surrealists, Dalí maintained his allegiance to Vermeer's art of humility and patience. In "The New Limits of Painting," which appeared in February 1929, Dalí again described Vermeer as representing "the highest, most humble and most dramatic probity."[61] Thus, despite having abandoned the subtle lyricism of Lorca for the provocative excesses of surrealism, Dalí continued to maintain the same position he had first articulated in 1926. In Vermeer, Dalí had found the model of the painter he wished to be: a painter *of* and *for* the small. The camera was for Dalí a useful reference point, but Vermeer's practice was something that could be emulated. Indeed, what most distinguished Dalí's surrealism from that of his contemporaries was the way in which it was informed, at its most fundamental level, by an identification with the tiny and the still, small paintings of Vermeer.

2

PARANOIA

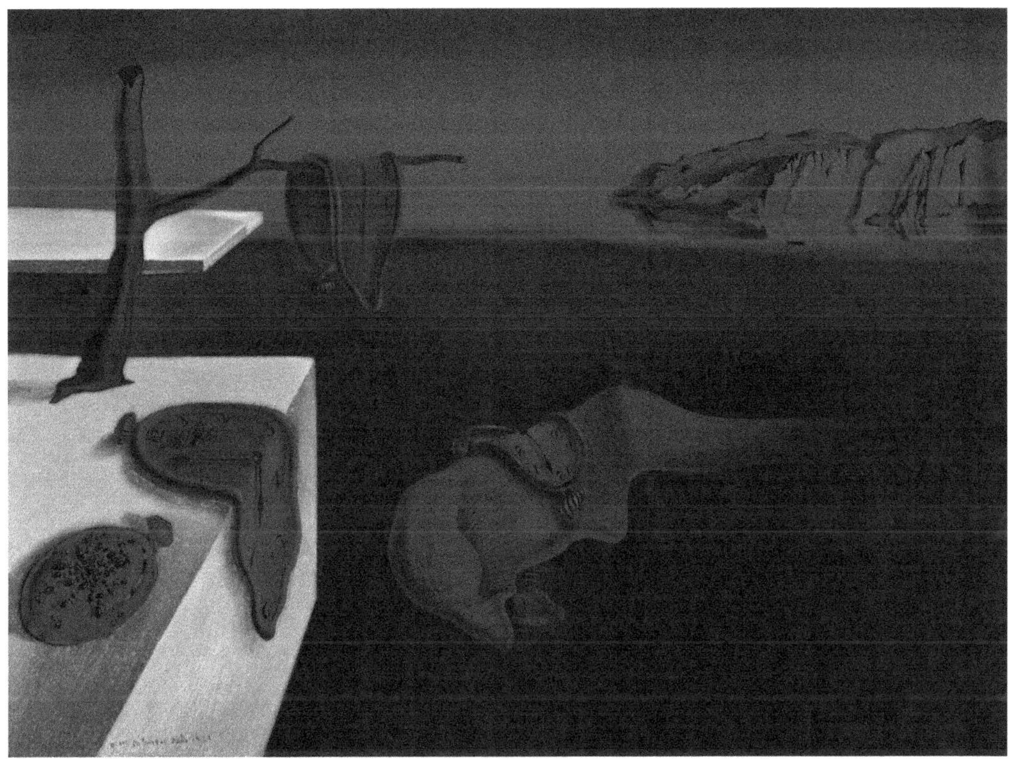

In the distance a rectangular pool abuts the shoreline. In the foreground a cubic block erupts from the picture's lower edge. Although less striking than the melting watches for which the painting is most famous, the pool in the distance and the block in the foreground are just as puzzling. Their geometric simplicity and rectilinear clarity mark them as alien elements. The cubic block in the foreground is especially curious, as it lacks the vertical and horizontal lines that identify the pool behind it as constructed of brick or stone. What is it made of? Is it sand that has somehow solidified? Or is it the materialization of a thought, the three-dimensional realization of the idea of a cube? If so, then perhaps the watches, ants, fly, and tree that sit on it are also products of the mind. Were this the case, then the painting as a whole would seem to be divided in two: one side a depiction of the little things that make up the natural world, the other side a representation of the little things that live inside the mind.

The previous chapter chronicled the origin and early development of Dalí's interest in little things. It argued that the ants, breadcrumbs, olives, sea urchins, phonographic needles, and household appliances that so fascinated Dalí constituted more than a collection of attractive objects: they were the protagonists in a narrative of liberation, a tale in which things small are set free from the supervening order to which they are typically beholden. For Dalí, "objectivity" was a deterritorializing practice in which the camera was the ideal modern instrument and Vermeer the exemplar in the realm of painting.

This chapter follows the shift that took place in Dalí's work in the late twenties. As he grew closer to the surrealists, Dalí's relationship with Lorca grew more distant. Yet rather than abandon his earlier identification with little things, Dalí adapted it to the surrealist discourse — or rather, he adapted surrealist discourse to his earlier identification. In doing so Dalí redefined the practices of surrealism as akin to the operations of a camera or a painting by Vermeer: Just as Dalí had conceived of the photograph and Vermeer's gaze as tools in the service of liberating the little things of the material world, he had come to see surrealism as a tool in the service of liberating the little things of the world of the mind. Most dramatically represented by what he called "paranoia-criticism"— a term he introduced in 1929 — Dalí's manipulation of Freudian psychoanalysis extended his earlier concept of "objectivity" such that it would now apply to the things that the mind sees when it turns inward. For Dalí, the paranoiac's mind is best understood as a camera of the psyche, an objective and nondiscriminating device that captures with equal precision thoughts both large and small, desires both significant and trivial. Thus disposed, surrealism became yet another tool in the service of the liberation of the small.

As we saw in the previous chapter, Dalí's oscillation between the traditional realism of *Portrait of My Father* (fig. 4) and *The Basket of Bread* (fig. 6) and the modernism of *Still Life by Moonlight* (fig. 5) and *Instrument and Hand* (fig. 7) was a sign of the painter's struggle to reconcile the "objectivity" of Vermeer with the pictorial conventions of the avant-garde. As his work grew increasingly oriented toward the practices and discourses emerging in Paris, he invited Miró and Miró's dealer in Paris, Pierre Loeb, to visit his studio in Figueres. The visit took place in September 1927, and afterward Dalí was hopeful that Loeb would take him on as one of his gallery artists. Unfortunately, like the Catalan critics before him, Loeb left his visit with concerns about the stylistic diversity of Dalí's work. "I find you are still veering too rapidly from one influence to another," Loeb wrote to Dalí after he returned to Paris, "and I am waiting for the opening up of your own personality. I am sure you will soon find a direction and with your gifts I feel certain that you will have a fine career as a painter."[1]

Whether influenced by Loeb's criticism or not, Dalí's work soon took another turn. He stopped trying to integrate Vermeer's realism with Picasso's cubism and stopped looking to Fernand Léger and Le Corbusier for inspiration. Burying himself in the pages of *La Révolution Surréaliste*, Dalí set himself on a rapid course of self-directed study of surrealist art and writing. Following the footsteps of Jean Arp, he cut and pasted colored paper in abstract arrangements (for example, *Four Fishermen's Wives in Cadaqués*, 1928) and affixed large pieces of cork to canvas and painted irregular, shadowlike black forms along the side (for example, *Female Nude*, 1928). In other instances, as with *The Rotting Donkey* (fig. 13) and *Bather* (fig. 14), he lifted elements from Miró, Tanguy, Ernst, and André Masson.[2] Although he had yet to commit himself to one particular style and was still, as Loeb put it, "veering from one influence to another," he was at least working within a more limited and aesthetically consistent set of practices.[3]

This is not to say that Dalí abandoned his earlier commitment to the small, the poetics of "objectivity," and the clear eye of the camera lens. The degree to which these commitments inflected Dalí's understanding of surrealism is evident, for example, in the artist's reception of Miró's paintings, the peculiarity of which is best gauged by comparing it with Breton's. In *Surrealism and Painting*, which appeared in February 1928, Breton praised Miró for having effectively translated the surrealist practice of automatic writing into the language of painting. He described Miró's method as "pure automatism" and proposed that the painter be recognized as perhaps "the most 'surrealist' of us all."[4]

When Dalí looked at Miró's paintings, he saw something altogether different. It was not the passages of automatism that struck him but rather the inclusion of so many little details. Works like *The Hunter* (*Catalan Landscape*) (fig. 15) are littered with them, and for Dalí, these tiny details were evidence of Miró's "objectivity." For Dalí, what mattered in Miró's paintings was not so much the contortions performed on the bodies of the little farm animals but rather the fact that so many of them were drawn with their little "hairs and pricks."[5] Breton may have seen Miró's work as evidence of a mind set free from conscious control, but Dalí saw it as the sign of a likeminded liberator of all things tiny.

THE PHOTOGRAPHIC DATA

Although Dalí had been drifting toward surrealism as early as 1926 and 1927, by the end of 1928 his conversion was all but complete. In December he wrote to his friend Pepín Bello to tell him that he was working to put together a surrealist magazine.[6] Although the magazine never materialized, Dalí edited the March

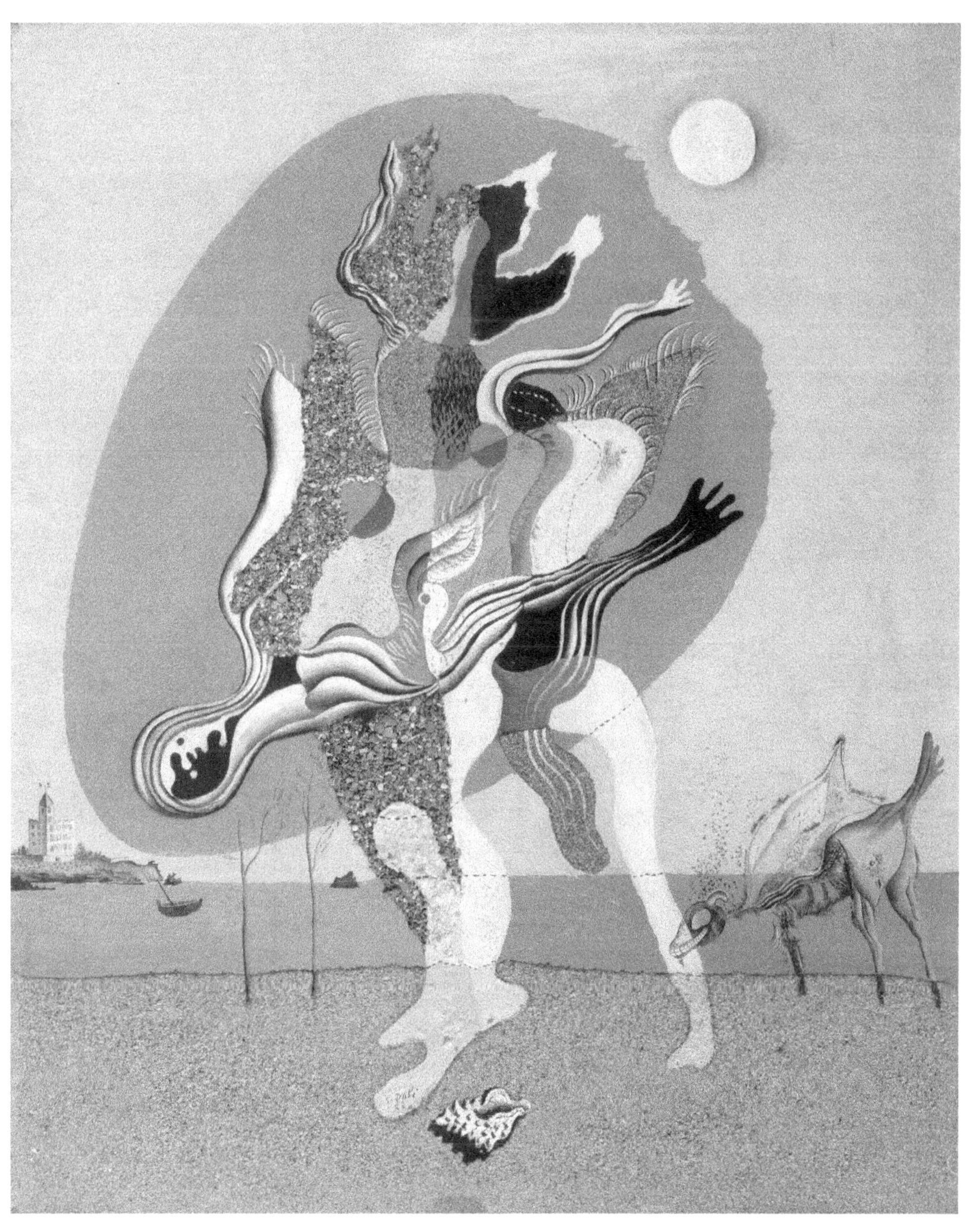

13. Salvador Dalí, *The Rotting Donkey*, 1928. Oil, sand, and gravel on wood, 61 × 50 cm (24.02 × 19.69 in.). Inv.: AM 1999-22. Photo: Jean-Claude Planchet. Musee National d'Art Moderne, Centre Georges Pompidou, Paris, France. Dalí, Salvador (1904–89) © ARS, NY. Photo credit: CNAC/MNAM/Dist. Réunion des Musées Nationaux/Art Resource, NY.

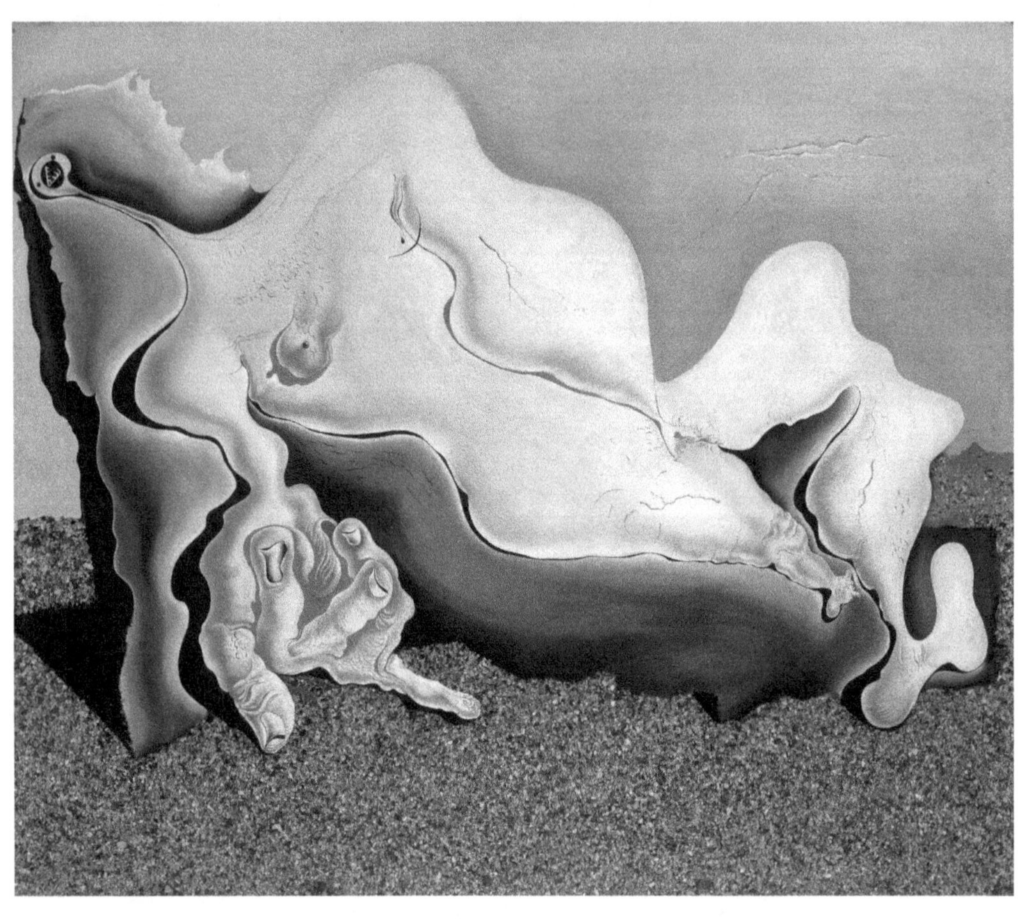

14. Salvador Dalí, *Bather* (*Beigneuse*), 1928. Oil on canvas, 63.5 × 75.0 cm (25 × 29½ in.). © Salvador Dalí. Fundació Gala-Salvador Dalí (Artists Rights Society), 2011. Collection of the Salvador Dalí Museum, Inc., St. Petersburg FL, 2011.

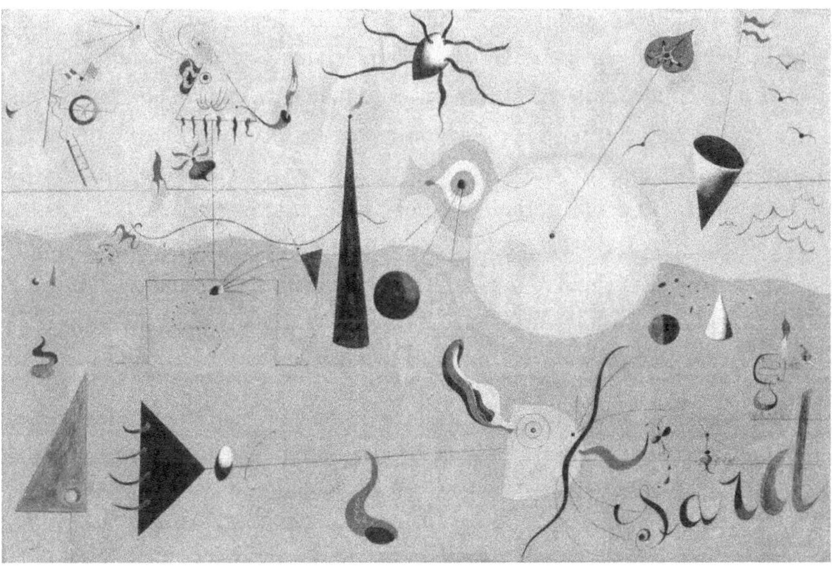

15. Joan Miró, *The Hunter* (*Catalan Landscape*), Montroig, July 1923–Winter 1924. Oil on canvas, 25½ × 39½ in. Purchase. (95.1936). The Museum of Modern Art, New York NY. Miró, Joan (1893–1983) © 2011 Artists Rights Society (ARS), New York/ADAGP, Paris. Digital Image © The Museum of Modern Art/Licensed by SCALA/Art Resource, NY.

1929 issue of *L'Amic de les Arts* and made it something of a special issue on surrealism. In the meantime Dalí continued to submit articles to other Catalan journals, and in February 1929 *La Gaseta de les Arts* published an essay of his titled "The Photographic Data."[7] As he had in his 1927 essay "Photography: Pure Creation of the Spirit," Dalí continued to praise the camera's cold objectivity, its resistance to "sentimental affectation." But this later text was not simply a reiteration of the earlier one. Although, like the earlier essay, it highlighted the camera's objectivity and its ubiquity in science and advertising, it also associated it explicitly with the practices of surrealism, Breton's in particular: "From strictly scientific works — natural histories, geographies, etc. — up to the recent ventures in the novel (André Breton's *Nadja*), the photographic data intervenes in them all as much as it does in advertising and in the pure poem."[8] But Dalí's goal was not to sing the praises of surrealist thought and practice, it was to demonstrate that, properly understood, surrealism was in fact a subspecies of the poetic and pictorial "objectivity" that Dalí had developed on his own. This is especially clear in the following passage, in which he claimed that the best evidence of surrealism's truth is the image seen through the lens of a camera:

> From the subtlety of aquariums to the most rapid and flitting gestures of wild beasts, photography offers us a thousand fragmentary images of a dramatized

totalization. The capital of a cathedral situated at the height of ten meters above ground in constant darkness is revealed to us by photography with the exaggerated meticulousness of detail with which we can become acquainted solely through the skillful photogenic process to which the photographer can subject things. Besides the great rigor to which the photographic data, for its part, subjects our mind, it is yet ESSENTIALLY THE MOST SECURE VEHICLE FOR POETRY and the most agile process for capturing the most delicate osmoses that are formed between reality and surreality. The mere fact of photographic transposition already implies a total invention: the capturing of an UNKNOWN REALITY (una REALITAT INÈDITA).[9]

This passage enunciates two crucial concepts. The first is Dalí's articulation of photography as effecting a radical disaggregation of reality: the notion that through the lens of the camera the eye registers "a thousand fragmentary images." The "totalization" that we take to be reality's underlying truth is demonstrated by photography to be an artifact of the mind. The "exaggerated meticulousness of detail" is the tool by which this fragmentation and disaggregation is effected, for it is this that undermines the mind's capacity to organize the details into a whole. The cathedral that Dalí describes, for example, is understood by the mind to be fixed to the earth, but when viewed at night through the camera lens, its upper register emerges as a separate element, severed from its base, like the wandering clock hands that Dalí had described in an essay the year before (see chapter 1).[10]

The second crucial concept is the notion that photography's capacity to disaggregate can be put to surrealist use. Because the camera produces images in which reality is disaggregated and because our minds demand that the world be recognized as unified, photographs offer us documents of "an unknown reality." Because the images produced by the lens of the camera have not been subjected to the organizing capacity of the human mind, they are primordial, brute facts. They are pictures of reality before it has been organized by cognition. Surreality for Dalí is thus a revelation born not in the mind but in the camera lens; it is the conclusion arrived at not through the consideration of the interior world of the psyche but through the examination of the exterior world as seen in a photograph. Thus did Dalí conclude that "nothing will prove Surrealism right as much as photography."[11]

The writings collected in the March 1929 issue of *L'Amic de les Arts* offer still more clues to the ways in which Dalí absorbed surrealism into his aesthetic of the small. The issue included manifesto-like texts along with poems and short pieces of prose. It also included an interview with Luis Buñuel. In the first text of the issue, titled "At the Moment," Dalí declared that surrealism is above all an epistemological project. Surrealism, he insisted, is rigorously "anti-imaginative." It should not be associated with romantic confabulation but rather with the cold, objective record of the "the psychic instrument" (l'aparell psíquic). As Dalí conceived it, the psychic instrument of the surrealist, like the photographic instrument of the camera (l'aparell fotogràfic) records only facts. Where the latter facts are material, the former are mental. And just like the camera, the irrationality of the surrealist mind "liberates" these mental facts so that they may be free to wander as they please, with no logic or sense.[12]

The texts that followed elaborated on this connection between the photographic documentation of little things and the surrealist processes of mental liberation. "Review of Antiartistic Tendencies," for example, included a subsection headed "Documentaries." In it Dalí elaborated on the claims he had made earlier in "The Photographic Data." He argued, first, that the visual documentation provided by photography and film should be understood as investigations operating in parallel to the textual practices of surrealism.[13] Above all, it is the "documentation of minutiae" (el documental minuciós) that serves as "proof of the constant osmosis between reality and surreality." Here again, the focus lies squarely on the small: "Let us hope that the first irrational attempts, free from any aesthetic sense, paralleling attempts that are strictly scientific, will present us with a documentary of the long life of the hairs of an ear, or a documentary of a stone, or that of the life of an air current in slow motion."[14]

Other texts in the issue returned to the distinction between the "sentimental" and "metaphorical" poetry of writers of Ramón's ilk and the "objective" and "real" poetry that Dalí sought. In a section headed "Wireless Imagination," he introduced a distinction between imagination and inspiration. "Imagination" (la imiginació), he contended, "always means intervention, action." It is like "a jet of water whose violence responds to our will." "Inspiration" (la inspiració), on the other hand, "is involuntary, a geyser that erupts unexpectedly."[15] Imagination, like metaphor, *intervenes* in the world of little things. Inspiration, like objectivity, allows the little things to erupt on their own. Similarly, in "The Liberation of the Fingers," Dalí declared that "nothing is further removed from our true aspirations than the metaphoric image and the other methods of a defunct poetry, which are as unacceptable if not more so than the imagination itself."[16] Both metaphor and imagination are condemnable for the control they exert over little things like a motionless stone, a slow-growing hair on an ear, and a microcurrent of warm air. Only objectivity and inspiration can set them free.

Also included in the issue was a prose piece that focuses on a man who, although not literally tiny, is described as so "insignificant" as to be no more remarkable than a crumb. The story lurches from one unrelated scenario to another, unified only by the recurrent invocation of tiny objects and organisms that suddenly change their properties. At one point, for example, the narrator notices some hair on his fingertip: "'How soft is all this!' I said, referring to these hairs (THAT CERTAINLY WERE ERECT LIKE NEEDLES). . . . Yes, truly, a hair that was erect like a needle." He then looks through a microscope and finds that the hairs are in fact "a row of fleas," each of which "is made up from an infinite number of small sea urchins." In one passage, the narrator notices a sponge on the ground. What interests him is not the sponge itself but the distance that separates it from a nearby shoe:

> This particular sponge was separated by 1 meter and 35 centimeters from the heel of a shoe worn by a person, standing upright in front of a beautiful rotting mouth (FULL OF SMALL INFECTED BLISTERS). But right away the person changed position and moved the leg backwards; the distance then between the sponge and the heel of this person's shoe became 1 meter and 40 centimeters; next, the person moved almost imperceptibly and the distance between the sponge and the heel of the above-mentioned person became 1 meter and 38 centimeters; by the end of a quarter hour, the distance between the sponge and the person's heel was again 1 meter and 35 centimeters; half a quarter of an hour later the distance was 2 kilometers . . .[17]

In passages such as this one it becomes difficult to disentangle material facts from mental facts. The result is a text in which surrealism's two "objective instruments," *l'aparell psíquic* and *l'aparell fotogràfic*, have become one and the same.

PARIS DOCUMENTS

Soon after the appearance of the March 1929 issue of *L'Amic de les Arts*, Dalí left for Paris to assist Buñuel in the shooting of *Un chien andalou*. He arrived in the second week of April, after having secured an agreement to provide a series of brief reports on life in Paris for the Barcelona newspaper *La Publicitat*. These reports, collectively titled "Documentary — Paris — 1929" appeared in six installments between April 26 and June 28. Together they provide evidence of the ways in which his time in Paris and his encounters with the surrealist poets and painters led him to extend and refine the thoughts he had first articulated in *L'Amic de les Arts*.

The first of the six installments was the most theoretical. Its role was to introduce Dalí's readers to the peculiar documentary method that would be used to produce the subsequent reports. It included a restatement of the claim Dalí had previously made in "The Photographic Data" (February 1929) that the properly constructed documentary — that is, the "objective" documentary — is similar to surrealist texts in that both serve as "proof of the delicate and constant osmoses established between surreality and reality."[18] Although the claim was merely asserted in the earlier text, here Dalí elaborated on the equivalence he was constructing between the documentation of minutiae (*el documental minuciós*) and surrealists' automatic writing (*l'écriture automatique*). The two are united, he argued, by their mutual antipathy toward the literary and the artistic. As such, they can do things that neither literature nor art can do: "The documentary notes in an antiliterary fashion things said to be in the objective world. In a parallel manner, the surrealist text transcribes, with the same rigor and in as much antiliterary sense as the documentary, the REAL and liberated functioning of thought, what actually goes through our mind."[19] In other words, for Dalí, the camera is a machine-made surrealist poet and the surrealist poet is an organic camera. By banishing all literary concerns the surrealist poet becomes a kind of instrument, a device that, like the camera, is capable of producing an objective record of the thoughts that live in our minds. Psychoanalysis, in this reading, is a tool at the service of the little — a device acutely attuned to the tiniest thoughts and feelings. As Dalí put it near the conclusion of his first dispatch: "Dream analysis has demonstrated beyond doubt that all that is considered to be insignificant is precisely what effects our mind in the MOST VIOLENT AND VIVID MANNER."[20]

While the first of the six dispatches was an explanation of the method of *el documental minuciós*, the ones that followed were a *performance* of the method. The objects and events that Dalí recorded in these subsequent dispatches were chosen for their triviality and disconnectedness. The second (April 28), for example, began with a typology of the mustaches sported by the guests of various Parisian hotels, followed by meteorological observations and, after that, a record of the objects held in the stocking of a woman Dalí saw at the bar of La Coupole ("a bunch of violets, three cigarettes, a 100 franc bill, the photograph of a boxer, and also, very close to the leg and under the stocking too, a diamond bracelet").[21] The second dispatch concluded with an account of the price paid at the recent sale of a painting by Miró and a list of the ingredients and flavors of a popular new cocktail called the Honolulu.

The third and fourth dispatches (May 7, 23) continued in the same vein, but the fifth (June 7) returned to theoretical concerns.[22] In it Dalí introduced his readers to what he considered to be the problem of "the riddle" (l'endevinalla). For Dalí, riddles were evidence of an outmoded poetic orientation toward metaphor and thus toward the subjective mind that attempts to impose meaning and order on what is objectively an inexplicable collection of objects and events.[23] The riddle, in other words, is an invitation to make order out of reality. As such, the documentary is the anti-riddle, the process by which reality is transcribed without the subjective imposition of order.[24] Unlike the riddle, the "pure documentary" (la pura documental) collects data that cannot be explained or made to signify anything beyond its own factual existence. As an example, he offered the following observation of objects on a table:

> "There are" eighteen buttons, the one closest to me has a hair (perhaps an eyelash or a tiger's hair) coming out of one of its holes. Three centimeters to the right of this button there is a cookie crumb. There are still five more crumbs situated in the manner indicated in the first illustration. Beyond the crumbs and continuing to the right there is a dark abyss two hand-spans in width. On the other side of the abyss "there is" a table hanging on a thin and long wisp of smoke. There are on this table the number 86, a cup, a teaspoon, four fingertips. When all this is noted, the crumbs change their place and form a new grouping. . . . The hair stays in the button, but, further away, two crumbs (the two on the extreme right) get off, flying fast. Suddenly the following things take place in a very rapid succession: seven hands follow one another, three gloves are introduced in three hands, two hands leap on top of a chair, one on top of a table three meters away.[25]

As practiced in passages like this one, "pure documentation" takes the reader to the endpoint of objectivity, the point at which everything is recorded and nothing makes sense.

The sixth and final dispatch concluded with yet another affirmation of the photographic document and the surrealist method: "From the documentary point of view, any postcard album 'whatsoever' of the streets and squares of Paris will have one day more value than all the literary descriptions that will be written by the best of writers. . . . What counts are only and exclusively the Surrealist documents and texts of today."[26] For readers who somehow managed to attend to all six of Dalí's microscopic accounts of the trivial and transient, this final report served as a reminder that what Dalí had attempted in the dispatches was to provide a purely objective account of sensory perceptions while simultaneously suppressing all urges to make them cohere. It was a reminder that his reports were meant to be read as the residue of a performance of minute documentation, of the attempt to provide an objective — and therefore irrational — record of each and every little thing that had passed before his eyes.

THE FIRST DAYS OF SPRING

By the time the final two reports appeared in print, Dalí had already left Paris for his family's home in Figueres. The timing of his departure was such that he was unable to attend the premier of *Un chien andalou* and thus missed the astounding reception it received. The film's success made Dalí an instant

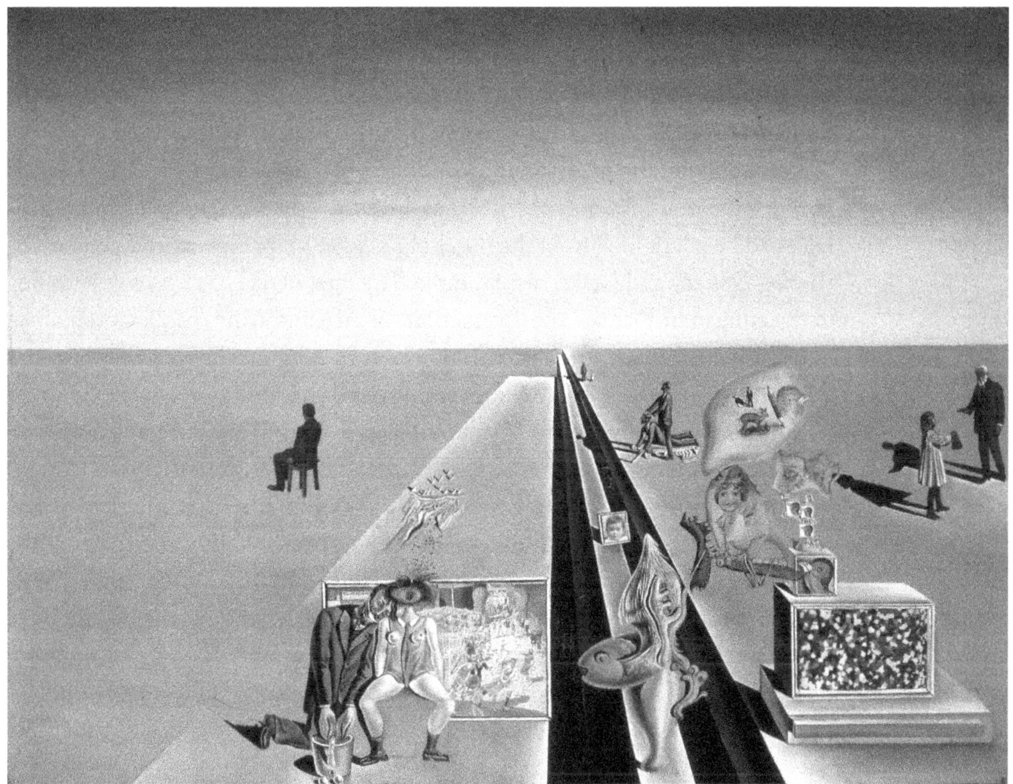

16. Salvador Dalí, *The First Days of Spring*, 1929. Oil on panel, 49.5 × 64.0 cm (19½ × 25¼ in.). Collection of the Salvador Dalí Museum, Inc., St. Petersburg FL, 2011.

celebrity in Paris, and he spent the summer months of 1929 preparing new works to be exhibited at Camille Goemans's gallery in the fall. Goemans, who had met Dalí while he was in Paris, offered him a contract that would cede to Goemans all his new work in exchange for a monthly stipend of one thousand francs.

Among the works that Goemans likely saw firsthand while Dalí was in Paris was *The First Days of Spring* (fig. 16).[27] Like *The Rotting Donkey* (fig. 13), *Bather* (fig. 14), and other paintings from 1928, *The First Days of Spring* employed elements of collage. But unlike these earlier works, in which Dalí chose to affix tiny things from the natural world (sand, pebbles, seashells, cork), it included instead elements that were manufactured by machine: images cut from newspaper clippings, picture postcards, chromolithographs, and in the center of the painting, a photograph of Dalí as a young child. On the far left Dalí cut from a newspaper illustration a drawing of a seated man with his back turned. Another black-and-white illustration — this time of a bearded man confronting a girl — appears on the far right. In the foreground are two multicolored images, each framed like the photographic self-portrait in the middle: on the left a scene of exuberant young couples and families enjoying themselves on the deck of a yacht; on the right an abstract composition of colored forms, vaguely pointillist in manner.

Undoubtedly the most significant stylistic shift evident in *The First Days of Spring* is the near-total absence of any of the forms, gestures, and other quirks that Dalí had been cribbing from the pages of *La Révolution Surréaliste*. Unlike *The Rotting Donkey* and *Bather*, for example, *The First Days of Spring* owes nothing to the cubism of Picasso, the abstractions of Arp and Miró, or the automatism of Masson and Ernst. Instead it draws most heavily on the Vermeer-inspired miniaturism of works like *The Basket of Bread* (fig. 6) and *Girl's Back* (fig. 11).

The elements depicted in *The First Days of Spring* are scattered across an almost featureless gray plane, bisected vertically by two steps that recede miles into the distant horizon and beneath an equally featureless blue sky (which, in the tradition of Dutch landscapes, occupies nearly half of the space of the picture). The elements that are painted and glued to the surface run from the most anodyne to the most dramatic, from the most self-evident to the most inexplicable. On the left is the aforementioned seated man; to its right are twelve tiny protrusions shaped like freestanding columns and steeply pitched pyramids, all of which cast dense black shadows on the ground. Beneath them lies a brightly colored abstraction, alternating streaks and zigzags of yellow, red, pink, and blue. Looking closer, one finds a diagonal row of five miniscule black circles nestled between two hair-thin lines of red. Below the colored abstraction a swarm of winged insects (likely flies) escape from what appears to be a rectal or vaginal opening. It is red and muscular and is framed perfectly by gently curled black hairs that suggest eyelashes. Gazing downward, the viewer recognizes this red-hot opening as a substitute for a head, for it sits atop a slender neck. The figure is dressed in a man's shirt, shoes, and socks and sports a long red tie. The tie runs from the neck to what appears to be a vagina, suggesting that the figure, although dressed in men's clothing, is in fact a woman. Her arms and legs are fully exposed, as are her breasts, which protrude impossibly through her shirt. Leaning against her is a fully clothed man whose mouth is gagged and whose hands are, in form and color, reminiscent of the strange, multicolored abstraction that hovers above him.

Moving across the painting, one is confronted with similarly puzzling objects, some of which are clearly benign: a child's colored pencil, a red fish, a pretty little drawing of lamb, and the head of a bird with a bright red eye (perhaps the partridge of Dalí's "Poem of Little Things"). Other details are decidedly ominous and grotesque: as well as the gagged man and the vagina-woman mentioned above, there is also a multicolored yet ghostly head that bites into the flesh of a mouthless male figure whose eyes have been grasped by an enormous grasshopper. A few others — like the aforementioned abstraction as well as the brown, spiky form to the left of the grasshopper and the multicolored object that seems to merge with the body of the red fish — are altogether impossible to identify.

In effect, *The First Days of Spring* is a translation into paint of the radically disaggregating effect of photography's "thousand fragmentary images." The "exaggerated meticulousness of detail" visible in the painting effects the same dispersal as the camera lens. As in a photograph, reality here is shown to be a fragmented collection of little things, each one liberated from whatever supervening order had once held it in place. Like the photographic document, *The First Days of Spring* seems designed as a device to record *una realitat inèdita*, reality as it is seen, not as it is ordered by consciousness. Indeed, the heterogeneous elements scattered about the surface are recorded with the same meticulousness that Dalí had used to describe the buttons, hairs, cookie crumbs, wisp of smoke, cup, teaspoon, fingertips, gloves, and chairs in the Paris dispatches. The painting is thus not a riddle but an attempt to record the world of things that have been "grant[ed] . . . their own liberty."[28]

Once back in Figueres Dalí continued to paint in this new manner. *Illuminated Pleasures* (fig. 17), *The Accommodations of Desire* (fig. 18), and *The Lugubrious Game* (fig. 19) all include collaged photographs and print illustrations, some of which are easily identified. Others — such as the severely cropped and reshaped photograph affixed to the sky-blue rectangle in the center of *Illuminated Pleasures* and the similarly shaped photographic fragment on the right-hand edge of *The Lugubrious Game* — seem designed to be unreadable (see chapter 6). As a result, these elements function as photographic abstractions: tiny manifestations of what Dalí had referred to in his dispatches as the mystery of the "pure documentary" and what he had described in "The Photographic Data" as "the most secure vehicle for poetry and the most agile process for capturing the most delicate osmoses that are formed between reality and surreality."[29] These fragments are particularly effective in performing the task of the "pure documentary" because, like photographs, they constitute real, verifiable facts. Indeed, their existence as photographs is precisely what substantiates their reality. And yet they are, on account of their having been so severely cropped and reshaped, almost entirely inscrutable.

THE MOST IMPERCEPTIBLE AND SUBTLE DETAILS

Following on the heels of his Paris dispatches and the paintings of 1929, Dalí began to develop a new lexicon. Indeed, he erupted with a flurry of new terms. Of particular significance were the concepts of "the gratuitous," "the double image,"

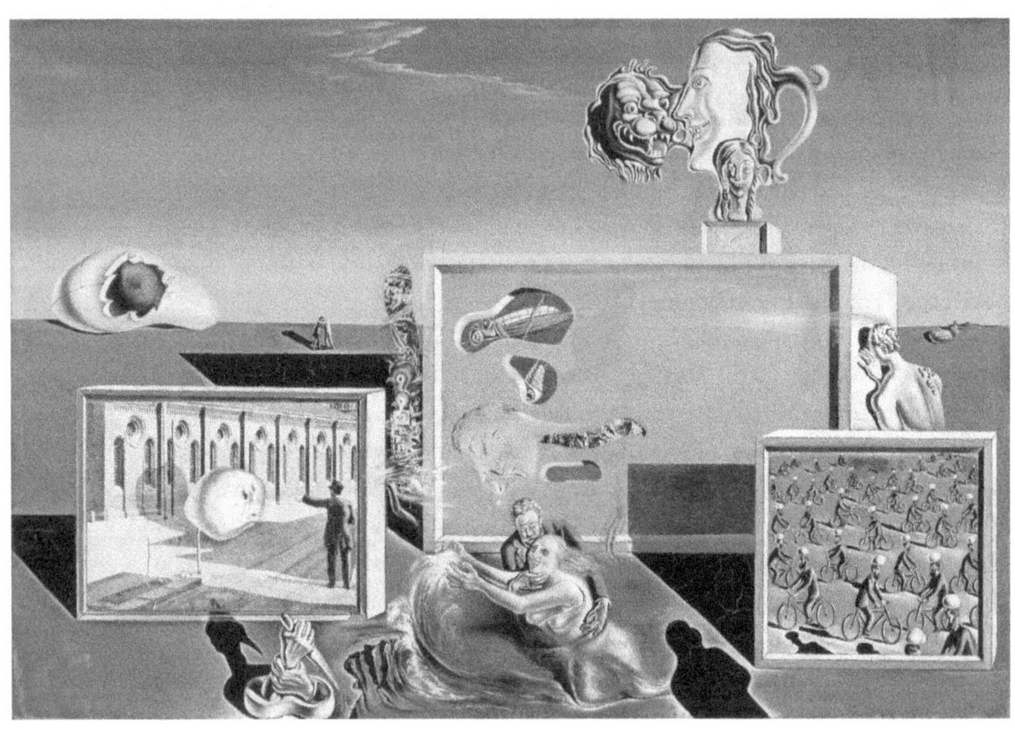

17. Salvador Dalí, *Illuminated Pleasures*, 1929. Oil and collage on composition board, 23.8 × 34.7 cm (9⅜ × 13¾ in.). The Sidney and Harriet Janis Collection. The Museum of Modern Art, New York NY. Dalí, Salvador (1904–89) © ARS, NY. Digital Image © The Museum of Modern Art/Licensed by SCALA/Art Resource, NY.

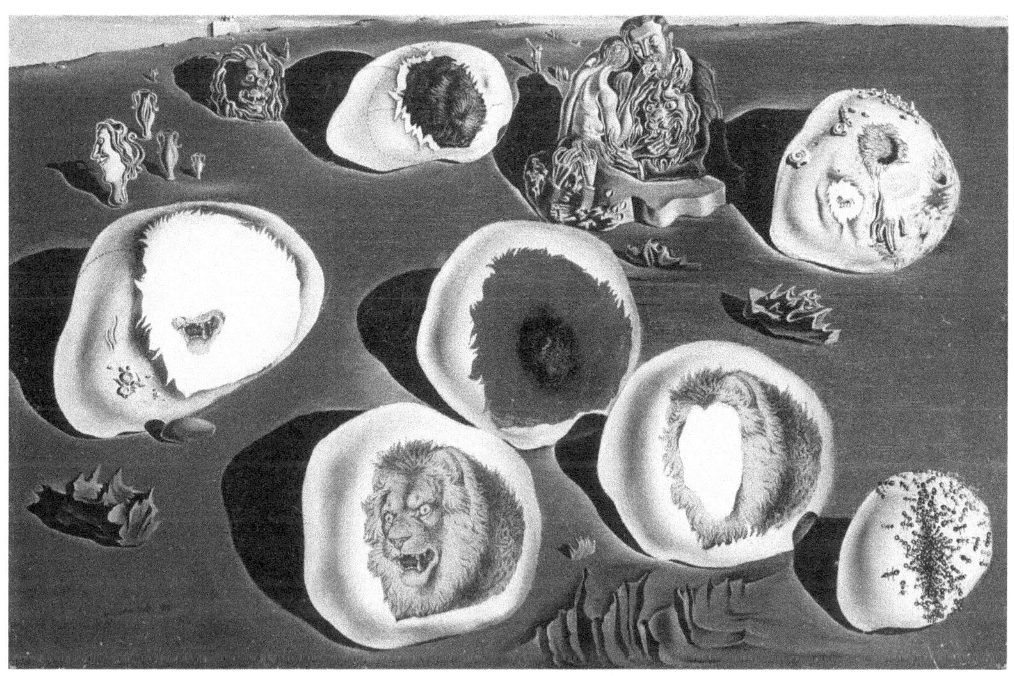

18. Salvador Dalí, *The Accommodations of Desire*, 1929. Oil and cut-and-pasted printed paper on cardboard, 22.2 × 34.9 cm (8¾ × 13¾ in.). Jacques and Natasha Gelman Collection, 1998 (1999.363.16). The Metropolitan Museum of Art, New York NY. Dalí, Salvador (1904–89) © ARS, NY. Image copyright © The Metropolitan Museum of Art/Art Resource, NY.

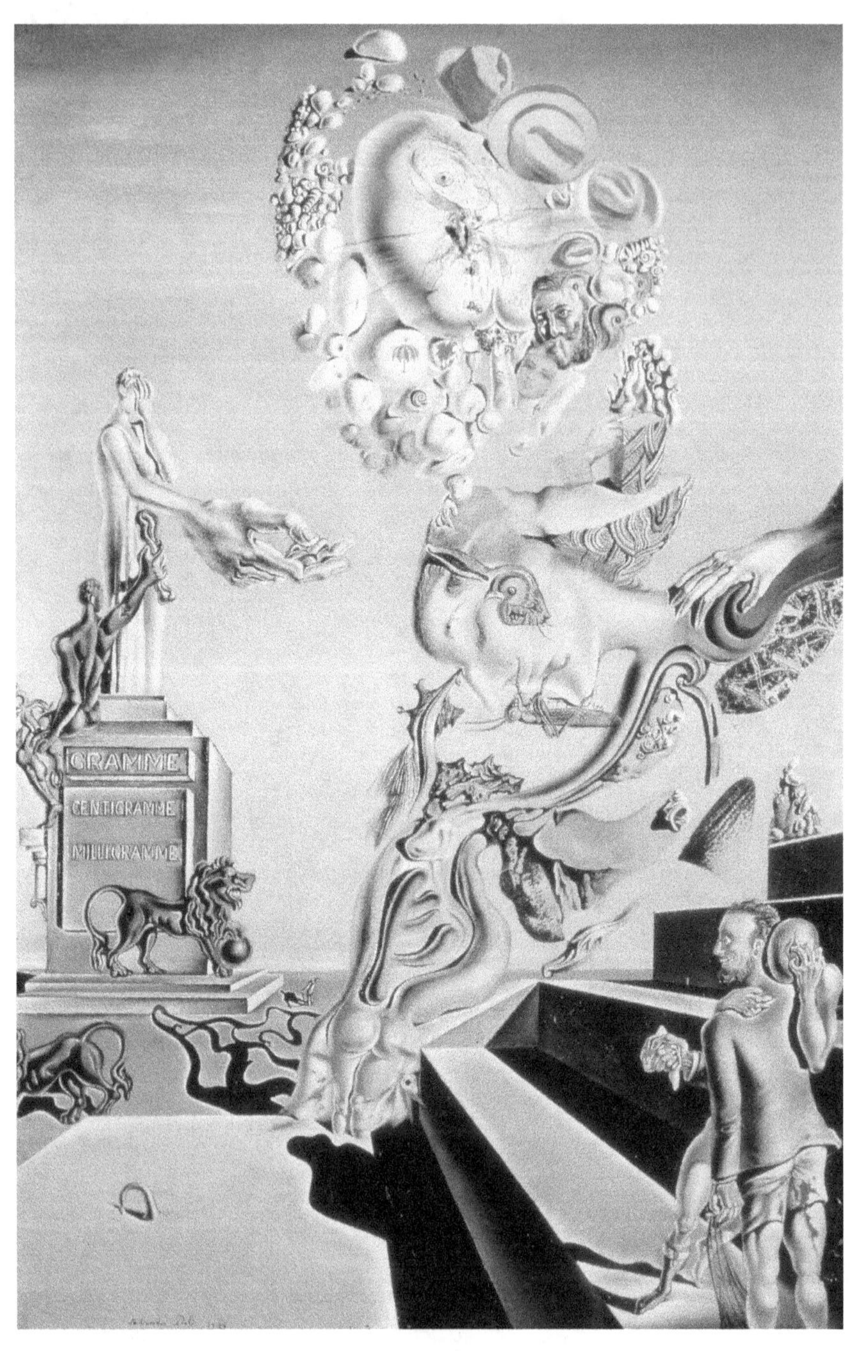

19. Salvador Dalí, *The Lugubrious Game*, 1929. Oil and collage on cardboard, 44.4 × 30.3 cm (17.48 × 11.93 in.). Private collection. Image provided by the Fundació Gala-Salvador Dalí. Salvador (1904–89) © ARS, NY.

and above all, "paranoia." Later chapters will examine at length the gratuitous and the double image, but here it is important to address Dalí's conception of paranoia, as it quickly became, like the poetry of objectivity and the liberation of little things, one of Dalí's central organizing principles.

Of all that Dalí wrote, it is his first statement on paranoia that is most remembered and recited: "I believe that the moment is drawing near when, by a thought process of a paranoiac and active character, it would be possible (simultaneously with automatism and other passive states) to systematize confusion and thereby contribute to a total discrediting of the world of reality."[30] Dalí used what he called "the paranoiac will" to produce a number of paintings from this period, most famously *The Invisible Man* (fig. 20) and *Invisible Sleeping Woman, Horse, Lion* (fig. 21). Like the famous image of the duck-rabbit, the objects perceived in these paintings oscillate between the different images, never settling on any one. As Dalí described it, "The double image (an example of which might be the image of a horse that is at the same time the image of a woman) may be extended, continuing the paranoiac process, with the existence of another obsessive idea being sufficient for the emergence of a third image (the image of a lion, for example) and thus in succession until the concurrence of a number of images which would be limited only by the extent of the mind's paranoiac capacity."[31]

More than any other phrase, "the paranoiac will to systematize confusion" has come to stand for Dalí's method as a whole. How Dalí arrived at it is still not entirely clear, but he was certainly influenced by the account of paranoia in Freud's work.[32] Freud refers to paranoia in *The Interpretation of Dreams* and more extensively in *Introductory Lectures on Psychoanalysis*, where he describes the illness ("dementia paranoides") as a manifestation of "an attempt to fend off excessively strong homosexual impulses."[33] In his most famous study of the illness, "Psychoanalytic Notes on an Autobiographical Account of a Case of Paranoia (Dementia Paranoides)," Freud elaborates on this etiology, arguing that Judge Daniel Paul Schreber's illness was "a means of warding off a homosexual wishful phantasy" and that his "delusions of persecution" were thus compensatory symptoms.[34]

While Freud's etiology was novel, his account of the primary symptoms was not. Since the Greeks, paranoia had served as a term applied broadly to any type of mental derangement; by the nineteenth century it often was described more specifically as a "persecution complex" of which the distinctive feature is an elaborate reasoning process that seems coherent and convincing to the subject but irrational and absurd to others.[35] In the early twentieth century it was defined by psychiatrists Paul Sérieux and Joseph Capgras as a particular type of *interpretive delirium*: "a false reasoning having its point of departure a real sensation, an exact fact, which, by virtue of associations of ideas linked to

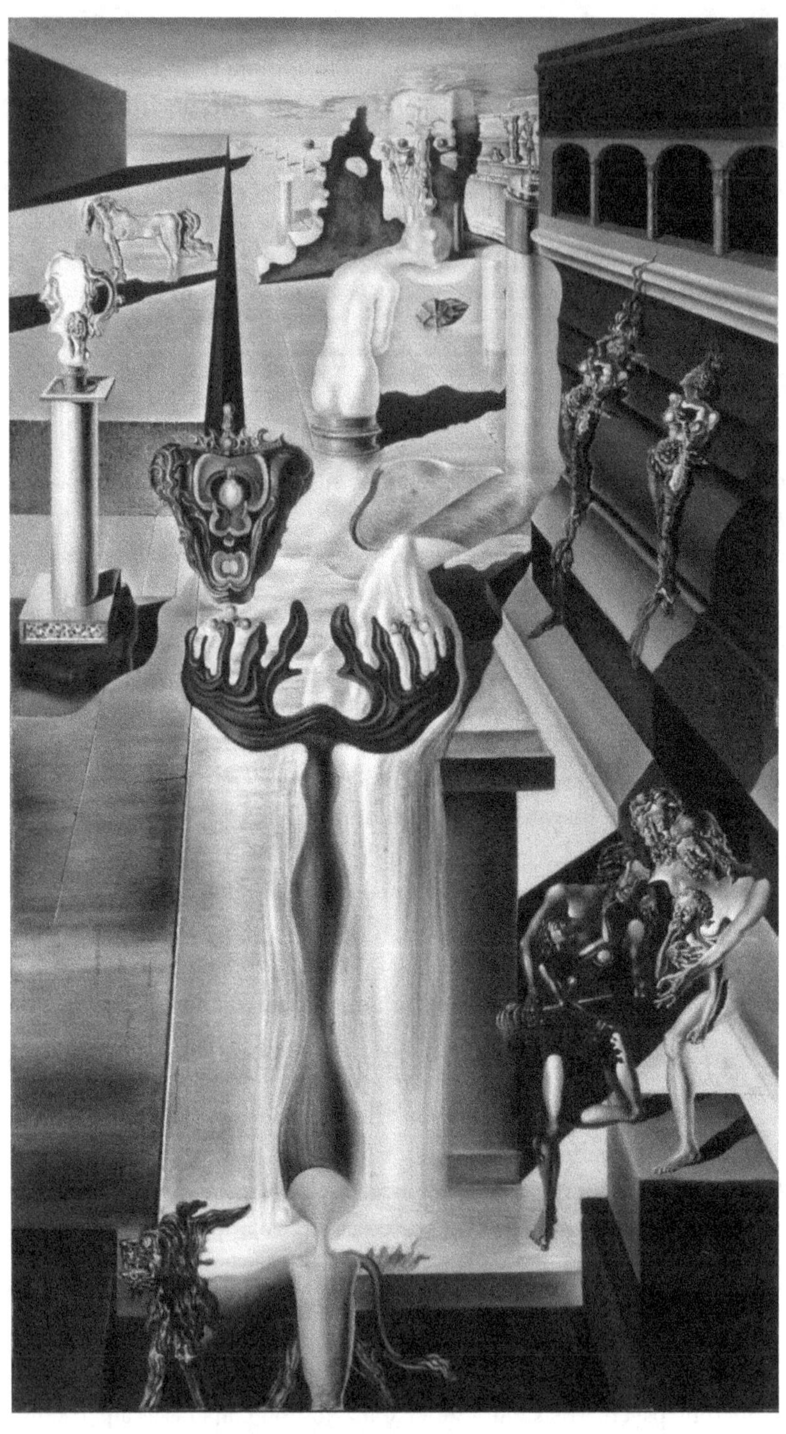

20. Salvador Dalí, *The Invisible Man*, 1929–32. Oil on canvas, 140 × 81 cm (55.12 × 31.89 in.). Museo Nacional Centro de Arte Reina Sofía, Madrid. Dalí, Salvador (1904–89) © ARS, NY.

tendencies, to affectivity, assumes, aided by erroneous deductions and inferences, a personal significance for the patient, compelled invincibly to relate everything to himself."[36]

In grasping Dalí's use of the term, however, the psychiatric literature can only take us so far.[37] The definition provided by Sérieux and Capgras, or for that matter by Freud, fails to coincide with much of Dalí's conception. First of all, Dalí insisted that the mental narratives and images produced by the paranoiac "nearly always defy psychological analysis."[38] That is, not even the most sophisticated psychoanalytic explanation would be able to make sense of the paranoiac's various "deductions and inferences."[39] This, of course, is entirely at odds with the psychoanalytic understanding of the illness; Freud's entire project was based on the premise that the analyst could interpret the symptoms like a riddle. Consider, for example, Freud's analysis of the claim made by Schreber that he possessed the superhuman power to look directly at the sun without burning his eyes:

> When Schreber boasts that he can (like the eagle of ancient mythology) look into the sun unscathed and undazzled, he has rediscovered the mythological method of expressing his filial relation to the sun, and has confirmed us once again in our view that the sun is a symbol of the father. It will be remembered that during his illness Schreber gave free expression to his family pride, and that we discovered in the fact of his childlessness a human motive for his having fallen ill with a feminine wishful phantasy. Thus the connection between his delusional privilege and the basis of his illness becomes evident.[40]

According to psychoanalysis, paranoia is without question a "false reasoning." The delusional images described by the paranoiac cannot undermine our faith in reality. Indeed, it is precisely the confidence that the analyst has in his or her conception of reality that enables him or her to recognize the paranoiac as such. When Schreber insisted, for example, that he was capable of communicating telephonically with distant and invisible others because he had been implanted with metal filaments, Freud never questioned reality as he himself understood it.[41] It was clear to him that Schreber's delusions were just that — false images of reality.[42]

Dalí's concept of the paranoiac image as "nearly always defy[ing] psychological analysis" is therefore fundamentally at odds with psychoanalysis.[43] On the other hand, it is entirely consistent with Dalí's pre-surrealist theory of objectivity and the documentation of minutiae.[44] For Dalí, paranoia was a process that deterritorializes mental things in the way that the camera deterritorializes material things. The distinguishing feature of the paranoiac's images is thus not their riddle-like nature but rather their astounding precision and subtlety,

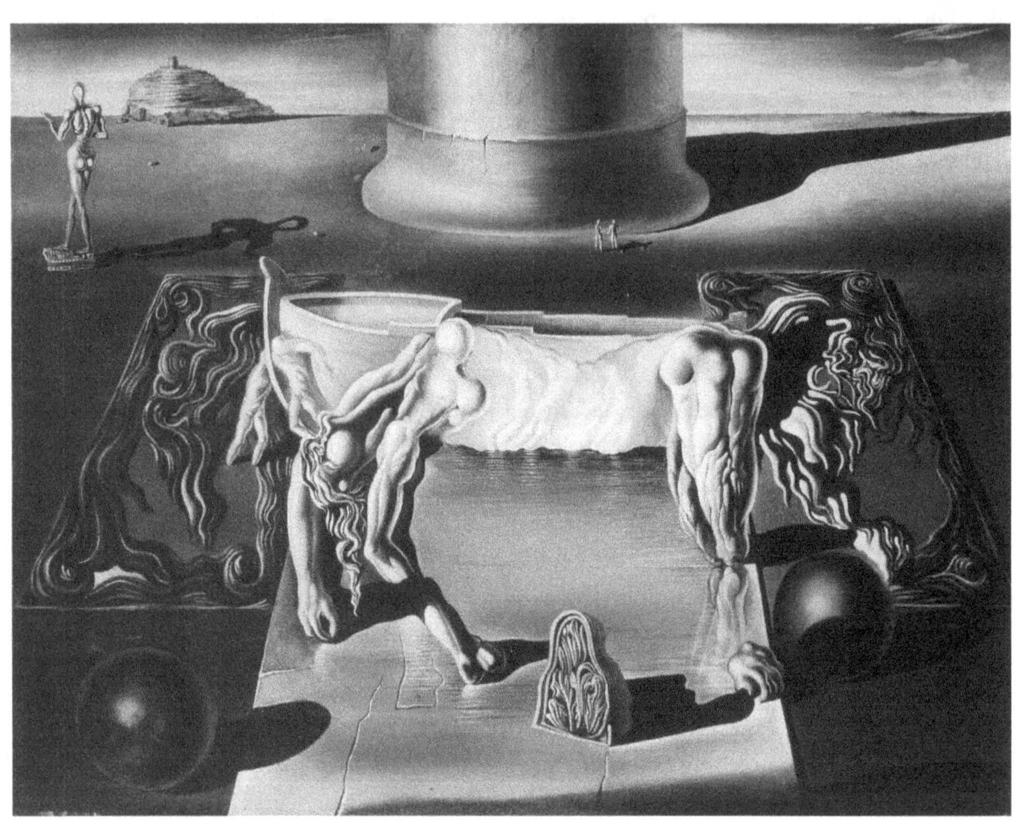

21. Salvador Dalí, *Invisible Sleeping Woman, Horse, Lion* (also called *Paranoiaque Woman, Horse*), 1930. Oil on canvas, 50.2 × 65.2 cm (19.76 × 25.67 in.). Inv. AM 1993-26. Photo: Philippe Migeat. Musee National d'Art Moderne, Centre Georges Pompidou, Paris, France. Dalí, Salvador (1904–89) © ARS, NY. Photo credit: CNAC/MNAM/Dist. Réunion des Musées Nationaux/Art Resource, NY.

their "most imperceptible and subtle details," their "associations and facts so refined as to escape normal people."[45] The images of the paranoiac are beyond analysis because their veracity "cannot be contradicted or rejected."[46] They are, for Dalí, no less objective than the "thousand fragmentary images . . . of exaggerated meticulousness" that the photograph records.[47]

The derangement of paranoia is thus the transformation of a normal individual into a camera, a recording device of such astonishing perceptiveness and objectivity that it manages to record the world without discriminating between the big and the small, the momentous and the trivial.[48] Like the camera, the paranoiac is radically disaggregating: his or her attention to the imperceptible details effects the same rending of reality that is effected by the camera lens.[49] Thus should the descriptions provided by the paranoiac force us all to abandon our insistence that the world has certain properties and not others. Following this to its logical conclusion, Dalí proposes that reality "exists merely as a function of each individual's paranoiac capacity."[50]

This final remark points to an aspect of the paranoiac process that goes beyond the disaggregating effect of the camera lens and is more directly related to the *re*-aggregating effect of the cinematic montage.[51] Although Dalí never analyzed the properties and implications of montage with the directness and complexity that he gave to the photograph, his reflections on his work on *Un chien andalou* offer some compelling clues to his thinking. In an essay published in *Mirador* in October 1929, Dalí defended his film in the very same way that he had defended the photograph. *Un chien andalou* was, he insisted, "a simple . . . recording of facts."[52] The narrative fragmenting that was so disturbing to viewers was, for Dalí, the means by which cinema could effect the disaggregation of little things. The experience of reality produced by the film's jarring visual juxtapositions was, like that of a photograph, "enigmatic, incoherent, irrational, absurd, *inexplicable*."[53] That we have habitually perceived the world as coherent, rational, and meaningful is, Dalí claimed, "a result of a process of accommodation quite similar to the one that makes thought look coherent, when its free functioning is incoherence itself."[54] In this way Dalí articulated a theory of film that was fully consistent with — even indistinguishable from — his prior account of the photographic image.[55]

What irritated Dalí about traditional narrative film was that it made it appear as though distinct and individual events in the world are somehow connected. "Alongside this made-to-order reality that fits the imbecility and the needed certainties, there are *facts*, simple *facts*, that are independent of conventions: there are hideous crimes; there are unspeakable and irrational acts of violence that periodically illuminate the desolate moral panorama with their comforting and exemplary splendor. There is the anteater, there is quite simply the bear

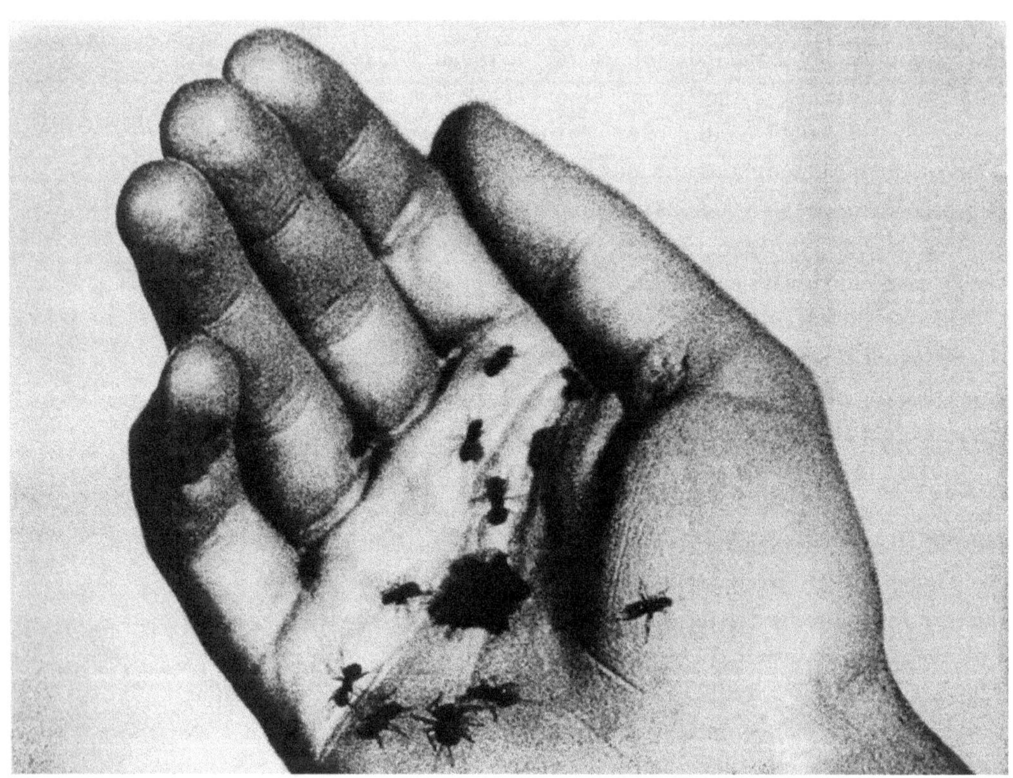

22. Salvador Dalí and Luis Buñuel, stills from *Un chien andalou*, 1929.

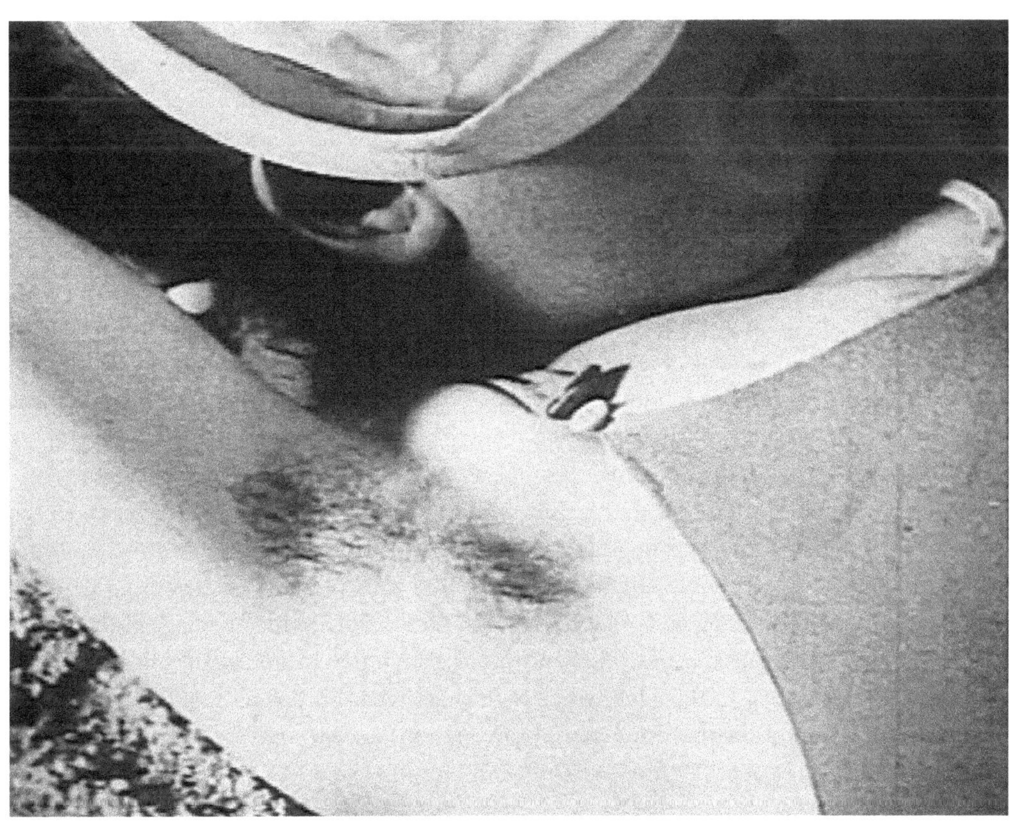

of the woods, there is, etc., etc."[56] Dalí's rejection of "made-to-order reality" is presented here in as a montage: a hideous crime is linked to a "desolate moral panorama," which is linked to an anteater, which is itself linked to a bear in the woods, and on and on indefinitely ("etc., etc."). Although photography may at times suggest such concatenations of unrelated elements, the cinematic montage enacts this disorienting reaggregration with unique command.

The disruptive potential of montage is exploited throughout *Un chien andalou*. It confounds interior and exterior, city and country, past and present. In one scene a man in an apartment is shot with a revolver and he falls to the floor. In the following scene we witness his fall continue, this time in a park. In another sequence a woman shuts the door of her city apartment only to find herself at the seashore. Alongside these scenes of spatial disruption the film also includes elements in which time is disturbed. Most striking is the sequence of shots that is suddenly interrupted by a title card that reads "Il y a seize ans" (Sixteen years before). The viewer expects a change of venue, but when the action resumes we find the very same scene that was interrupted. The title card had simply been inserted between two frames of the film. As a result, time is revealed as a "made-to-order reality" no less artificial than space.

Just as disruptive are the film's astonishing dissolves. One of the most remarkable is the series that begins with the close-up of an upturned hand. In the middle of the palm is a small black hole. In and around it a swarm of ants are crawling. Gradually the scene dissolves into an image of the armpit hair of a woman lying on the beach. This in turn dissolves into an image of the spines of a sea urchin and, following that, the strands of hair on top of a woman's head (fig. 22). In this Dalí was able to enact what his poems could only describe: impossible transformations from one substance to another.

PORTRAIT OF PAUL ÉLUARD

This chapter began with a consideration of the pictorial consistency that emerged in Dalí's work in 1929. Works such as *The First Days of Spring*, *The Accommodations of Desire*, and *The Lugubrious Game* transposed the disaggregating effect of the photographic image into the realm of painting. Other aspects of these works draw more directly from the cinema. For example, in *The First Days of Spring* the stack of bird heads mimics the vertical repetition of an unrolled film clip. More substantially, however, the paintings of this period emulate cinema's inherent paranoia by reaggregating the little things of the world into organisms of impossible shape and dimension.

Consider, for example, the portrait Dalí made of the poet Paul Éluard. Although stylistically similar to many of the other paintings he was making at

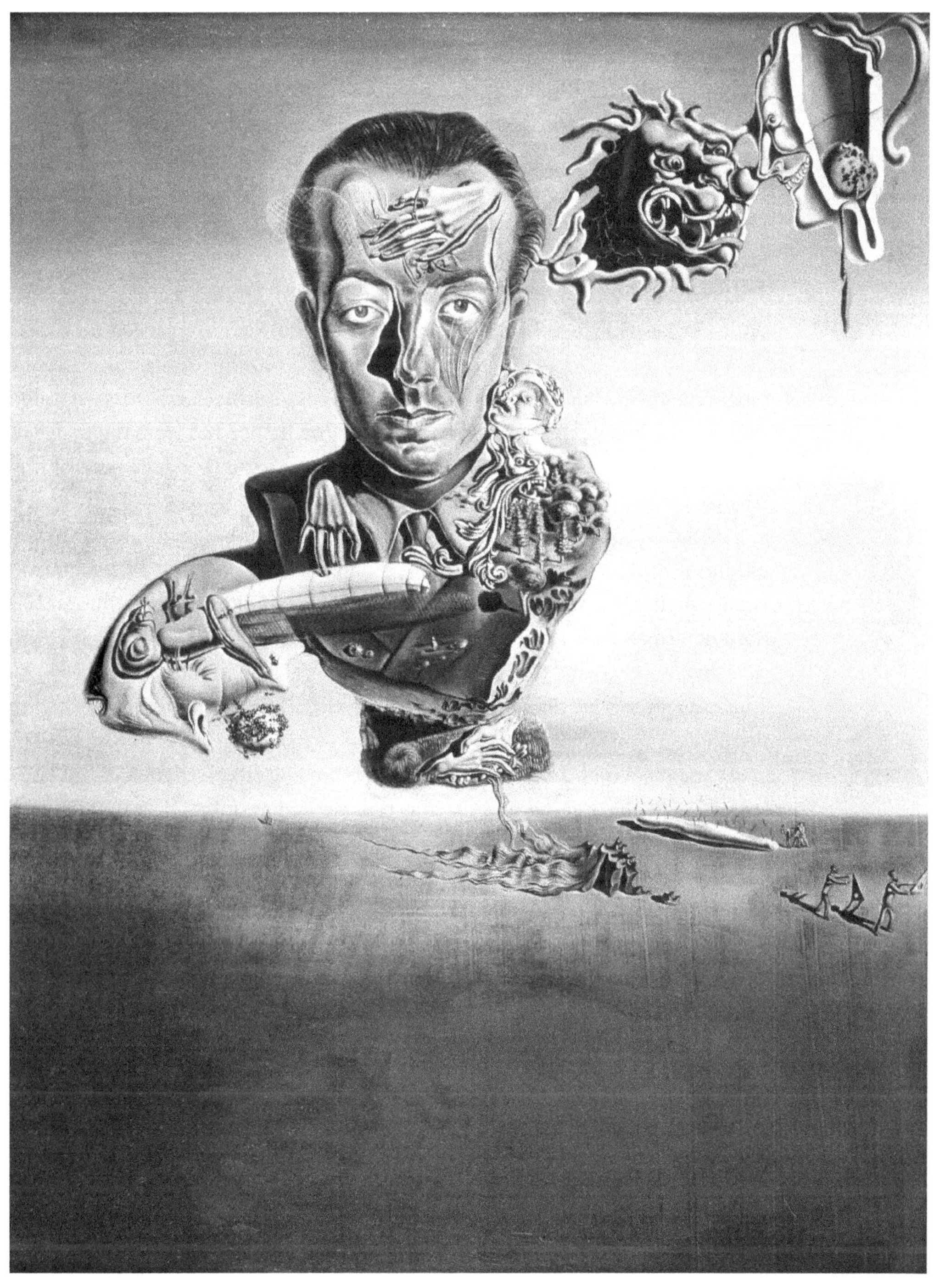

23. Salvador Dalí, *Portrait of Paul Éluard*, 1929. Oil on cardboard, 33 × 25 cm (12.99 × 9.84 in.). Private collection. Image provided by the Fundació Gala-Salvador Dalí. Dalí, Salvador (1904–89) © ARS, NY.

the time, *Portrait of Paul Éluard* (fig. 23) draws on a number of iconographic elements that first appeared in Dalí's works from 1927 and 1928. Most important is the depiction of Éluard as an enormous figure hovering above the horizon that recalls the gigantic fleshy torso in *Little Ashes* (fig. 10). Also similar to the torso in *Little Ashes* is the depiction of him as inundated by various objects and organisms. The hands that cling to different parts of Éluard's anatomy are likewise a feature of *Little Ashes*, as well as of *Instrument and Hand* (fig. 7) and *Honey Is Sweeter than Blood*.

Portrait of Éluard includes another curious element that seems drawn from these earlier paintings. On the right-hand side, between the jagged rocks and the pair of male figures marching rightward off the edge of the canvas, sits a long, smooth, and shiny object. What it represents is unclear, but its extended shape and white color suggest that it was originally derived from the image of an animal bone picked clean by insects (indicated, perhaps, by the mass of tiny pin-like shapes hovering above it). Despite its puzzlingly abstract nature and its position at the margin of the painting, this object (along with the swarm of pin-like forms) serves as a tiny distillation of the painting at large, for the portrait is nothing if not a depiction of Éluard as a man assaulted by little things. His unmoving expression reads as stoic resolve in the face of the dawning recognition that he is hostage to a swarm of little things, each of them rendered with "the exaggerated meticulousness of detail" that Dalí had earlier attributed to the photographic image.

Other aspects of the painting recall the startling effects of the cuts and dissolves in *Un chien andalou*. Éluard is represented as linked by a slender tube of flesh or a clump of hair to a lion's head, which is itself bound by its cheek to the nose on a head that has been fashioned into a jug. Beneath Éluard's chest, two hands clasp a strand of hair that seems to become a roiling wave along the horizon. Like the series of dissolves in which a mass of ants is transformed to become a woman's armpit and then a sea urchin, the strand of hair in *Portrait of Éluard* begins as a wave and then, as it stretches rightward, solidifies to become the jagged cliffs of Cadaqués.

As Dawn Ades has pointed out, the portrait is distinctive within the genre by virtue of its inversion of the expectation that such representations include attributes of the sitter.[57] In this instance the attributes depicted are not those of Éluard but of Dalí. The elements included were drawn, Dalí claimed, from his own childhood recollections and persistent anxieties (a fear of grasshoppers, the craggy rocks of Catalunya, etc.). Indeed, the notion that the sitter has been invaded by the artist is literalized in the figure depicted beneath the grasshopper, the yellow form that is fused with the red fish. Turned on its side it is recognizable as a portrait of Dalí himself, distorted as if reflected in a carnival mirror.

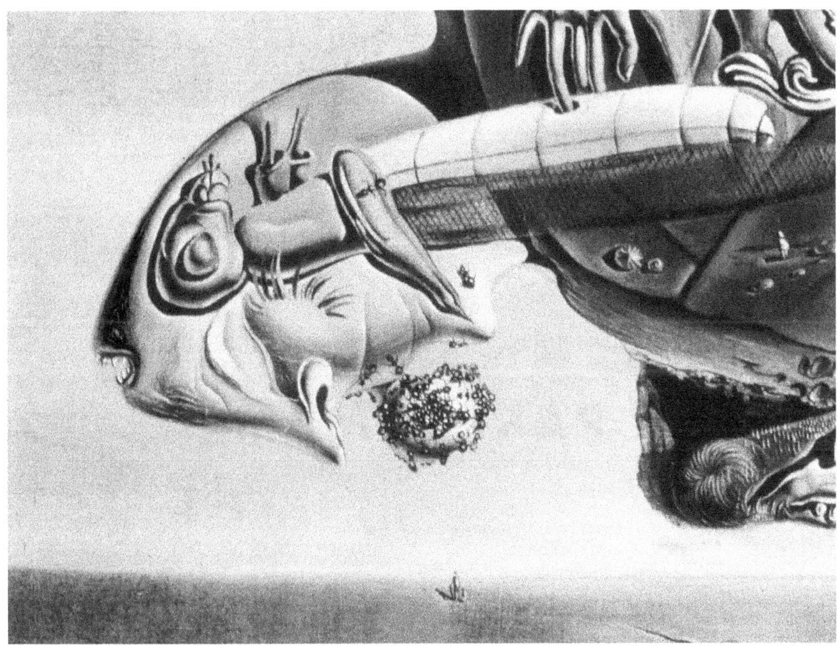

24. Salvador Dalí, detail of *Portrait of Paul Éluard*, 1929. Oil on cardboard, 33 × 25 cm (12.99 × 9.84 in.). Private collection. Image provided by the Fundació Gala-Salvador Dalí. Dalí, Salvador (1904–89) © ARS, NY.

He is painted in profile, with arched brow and closed eyes. Blood trickles from his nostril and ants swarm about his mouth (fig. 24). Like the grasshopper and the lion and the cliffs, Dalí is represented here as one thing among many. In cinematic and paranoiac fashion, he has been reaggregated to become but a tiny part of the heap that is his sitter, an insect clinging to Éluard's body like the ants that cling to his own face. Dalí's little things, himself included, no longer wander freely; instead they fuse themselves together to become a single, gigantic little thing. So united, they overwhelm their host with the force of a mass of parasites.

3

PARASITISM

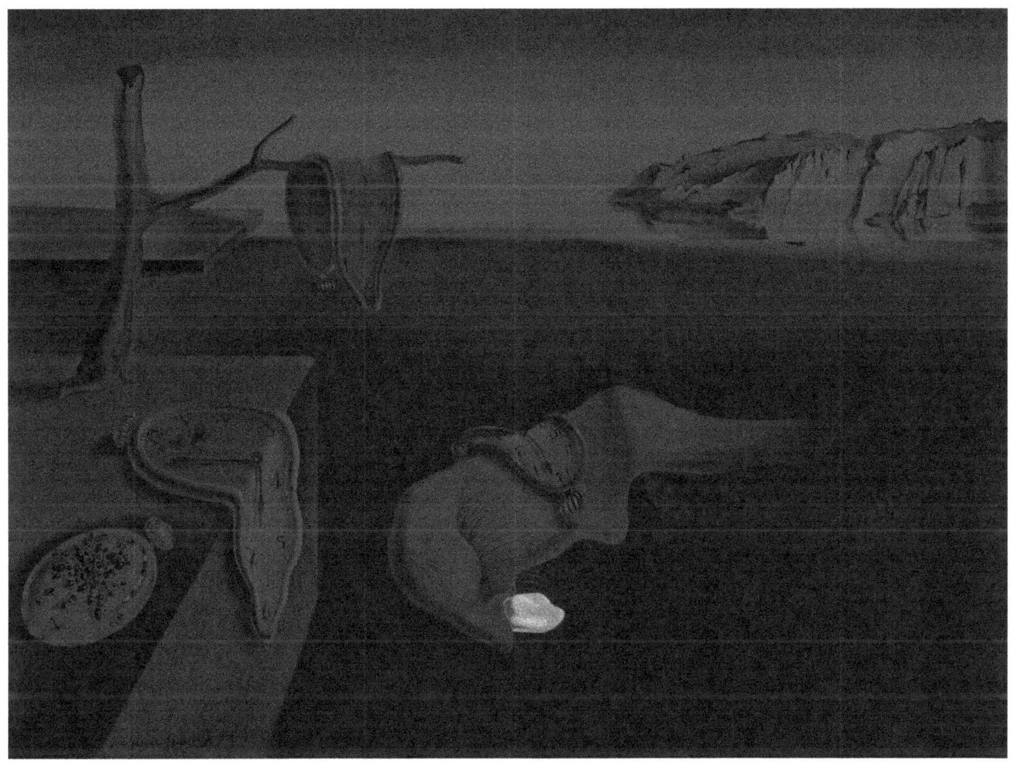

Near the tip of the central figure's nose is a strangely globular substance. It might be blood, but it's not red. Perhaps it's mucus or a tongue. On the other hand, it's possible that it's not a part of the figure at all but rather something that it's resting on, a pillow, perhaps, or a stone. Or it might be an imagined object, a materialized dream image of some kind. Or perhaps it's something that has arrived from an altogether different universe, something neither real nor imagined. Maybe it's an ideal object of some unknown origin, a Platonic form that's invaded from another realm and affixed itself to the figure like a parasite in search of a host.

IT ENTERS THE BODY AND INFESTS IT

Chapters 1 and 2 chronicled the emergence of Dalí's identification with little things between the years 1925 and 1929. At first it was a question of how to find them and record them. This required Vermeer-like patience and camera-like objectivity. Then it was a question of how to set them free, of what it took to "liberate" them from the structures and meanings that would otherwise contain them. Soon after they were put to use as tools of surrealist disruption, evidence of the fundamental irrationality of the world, and the seeds of paranoiac cognition. As Dalí's work developed over the course of the nineteen thirties, the concept of the small metastasized more radically. Little things came to be seen as indications of a realm of superficiality and, at the same time, as disruptively submissive creatures. And they were also, for Dalí, the shadows of ghostly anachronisms that haunt the present. The connections between the small and the superficial, the submissive, and the anachronistic will be addressed in chapters 4, 5, and 6, respectively. This chapter concerns the relationship between the small and the parasitical, and it follows Dalí as he identifies and catalogs his favorite little parasites, from ants, blackheads, and boogers to the tiny paintings of Ernest Meissonier.[1]

Parasitism, argues Michel Serres, is a tactic of the weak and small.[2] Its weakness makes parasitism necessary; its smallness makes parasitism possible. The parasite eludes detection by virtue of its stealth and guile, by redirecting the superior force of another toward its own benefit. For Serres, parasitism does not merely destroy; it creates, even as the parasite itself is abject and repellent and almost always expelled eventually. The creativity of the parasite stems from the fact that it is constantly compelled to invent "something new": "Since he does not eat like everyone else, he builds a new logic. He crosses the exchange, makes it into a diagonal. . . . People laugh, the parasite is expelled, he is made fun of, he is beaten, he cheats us; but he invents anew."[3]

In addition to its unique manner of inventiveness, the parasite is distinguished by the way it makes use of its relative position "on the side, next to, shifted." The parasite, by virtue of its marginal position, is thus the being that knows positionality best and is therefore best able to play positionality against the otherwise superior force of the host. As Serres puts it, "The producer plays the contents, the parasite, the position. The one who plays the position will always beat the one who plays the contents. The latter is simple and naïve; the former is complex and mediatized."[4]

This aspect of Serres's argument is particularly useful not only because it reinforces the relational aspect of parasitism but also because it highlights the parasite's dual nature as small yet disruptive. As such, the parasite's success is dependent above all on its adaptability: "It enters the body and infests it. Its factious power is measured by its capability to adapt itself to one or several hosts. This capability fluctuates, and its virulence varies along with its production of toxic substances. They lie dormant, rise up, lose wind, are lost for a long time."[5]

At the same time, by virtue of its ubiquity, parasitism shapes the sphere of the social at its most basic level. As Lawrence Schehr notes in his introduction to Serres's text, "For Serres, the parasite is the primordial, one-way, and irreversible relation that is the base of human institutions and disciplines: society, economy, and work; human sciences and hard sciences; religion and history. All of these have the parasitic relation as their basic and fundamental component."[6]

Dalí's small, marginal, and disruptive little things share much in common with Serres's parasites. At the same time, it is important to recognize the existence of a crucial point at which the analogy breaks down. Unlike Dalí, Serres does not identify with the parasite. He does not advocate for the parasite or delight in the parasite's disruptive acts. Serres's interest lies almost entirely in the question of what the parasite can do *for the host*. For Serres, it is important that we recognize the contributions of the parasite: "He makes others laugh; he takes, gives, takes again, directs speech, communicates a small, warm shudder to the others that assures us that we are together. Without him, the feast is only a cold meal. His role is to animate the event."[7] Dalí approaches the relationship between host and parasite from the other side; his identification lies with the experience of the little creatures who disrupt the host rather than the host's feeling of disruption. Dalí, unlike Serres, chooses to see the world through the eyes of the parasite. The inventiveness that matters to him is thus that which aids the parasite, not the host.

THE EXTREME OF LITTLENESS

Dalí was embraced by the surrealists almost immediately upon his arrival in Paris. His exhibition at Goemans's gallery was accompanied by the reproduction of two of his paintings in the final issue of *La Révolution Surréaliste* (*Accommodations of Desire* and *Illuminated Pleasures*), and his paintings and writings were regular and prominent features in the surrealists' subsequent journal, *Le Surréalisme au Service de la Révolution* (SASDLR). In almost no time at all Dalí had moved from the margins of the movement to its center.[8]

Perhaps out of a desire to accommodate himself to the established discourse of his new environment, Dalí set aside some of his earlier interests. For one, Le Corbusier's modernism in *L'Esprit Nouveau* was understood to be antithetical to the surrealist project. Thus it is probably not a coincidence that Dalí stopped singing the praises of modern industry and its nickel-plated bathroom fixtures,

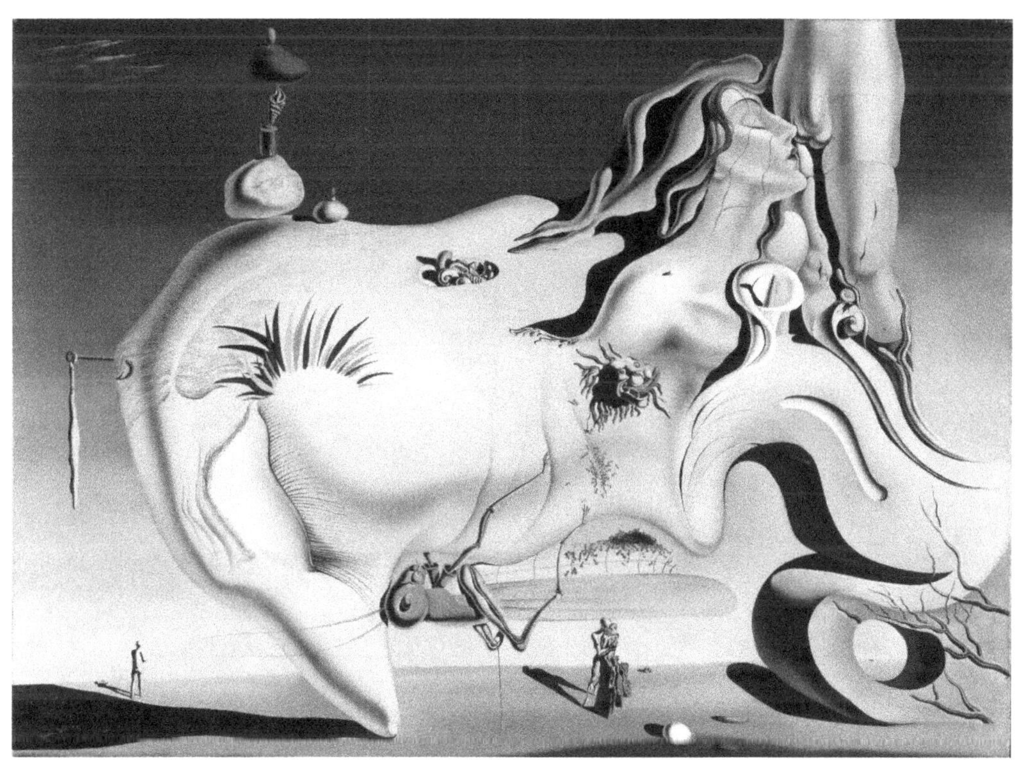

25. Salvador Dalí, *The Great Masturbator*, 1929. Oil on canvas, 110 × 150 cm (43.31 × 59.06 in.). Museo Nacional Centro de Arte Reina Sofía, Madrid. Dalí, Salvador (1904–89) © ARS, NY.

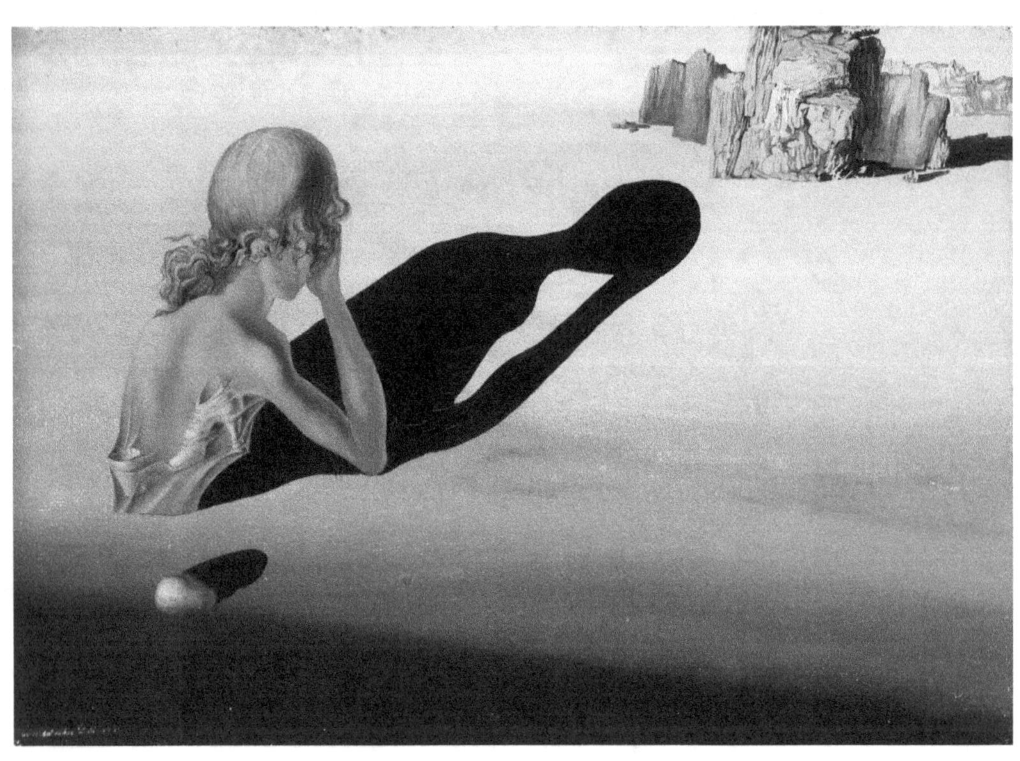

26. Salvador Dalí, *Remorse, or Sphinx Embedded in the Sand*, 1931. Oil on canvas, 19.05 × 26.67 cm (7½ × 10½ in.). Kresge Art Museum, Michigan State University, gift of John Wolfram, 61.8). Dalí, Salvador (1904–89) © ARS, NY.

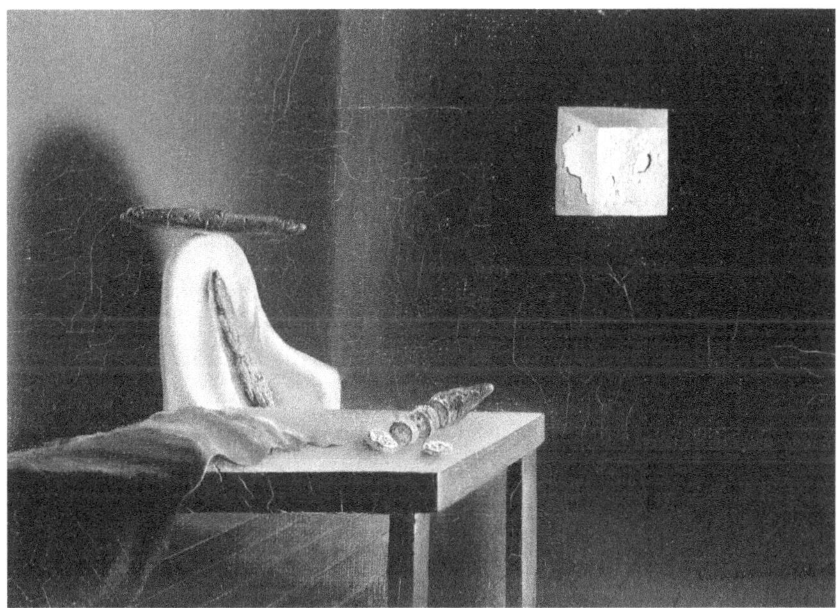

27. Salvador Dalí, *The Invisible Man*, 1932. Oil on canvas, 16.5 × 23.8 cm (6½ × 9⅜ in.). © Salvador Dalí. Fundació Gala-Salvador Dalí (Artists Rights Society), 2011. Collection of the Salvador Dalí Museum, Inc., St. Petersburg FL, 2011.

shiny metal appliances, and tiny phonographic needles. At the same time, he also introduced a host of new things, many of which were far more morbid and violent than the stray breasts and liberated fingers of his pre-surrealist period.

Of particular significance in this regard was the figure that Dalí called the "Great Masturbator." In the eponymously titled 1930 poem, the Great Masturbator is described as having an immense nose, closed eyes, horrible wrinkles in his forehead, and a swollen neck, "seething with ants." A hardened membrane covers his mouth, on top of which clings an enormous, motionless grasshopper.[9] Like the poem, the painting *The Great Masturbator* (fig. 25) depicts the beast with a huge nose, a closed eye, and a wrinkled brow. Also as in the poem, he is depicted as under assault by a mass of ants and an enormous grasshopper. In the painting the pitiful nature of the ironically enormous creature is underscored by the inclusion of a host of other invading objects: stones and shells, a fishhook, a lion's head, a lily blossom, a woman's face (also in profile), and the lower half of a man in white undergarments. Unable to see or speak, the beast is incapable of resisting the barrage of tiny violations. Here, as in *Portrait of Éluard* (fig. 23), *Phantasmagoria*, and *Illuminated Pleasures* (fig. 17), the Great Masturbator is represented as an impotent and beleaguered host ravaged by the tiniest of parasites.

With the exception of *The Great Masturbator*, all of these paintings are quite small. In fact, most of the paintings that Dalí made in 1929, including *Illuminated Pleasures*, *Portrait of Éluard*, *Accommodations of Desire*, and *Man of Sickly Complexion Listening to the Sound of the Sea (The Two Balconies)*, are smaller than ten by fourteen inches. So too are a number of paintings that Dalí completed in 1930 and 1931: for example, *Premature Ossification of a Railway Station* (12½ × 10⅝ in.), *The Persistence of Memory* (9½ × 13 in.), and *Remorse, or Sphinx Embedded in the Sand* (7½ × 10½ in.) (fig. 26). In 1932 and 1933 he painted a number of even smaller works, such as *The Invisible Man* (fig. 27) and *The Phantom Cart* (fig. 28). In all, between 1929 and 1936 Dalí painted more than fifty works whose longest side was less than twelve inches long.

More than thirty of these paintings were completed between 1932 and 1934, and in each of these three years Dalí painted one work no larger than three and a half inches on one side. *Portrait of Gala* (fig. 29), from 1932–33, is the smallest. *Portrait of Gala with Two Lamb Chops Balanced on Her Shoulder* (fig. 30), from ca. 1934, is slightly larger, as is *Dreams on a Beach*, from ca. 1934 (3½ × 2¾ inches). The diminutive size of these three paintings is all the more remarkable on account of the meticulousness with which they have been painted. Their effect owes only a tertiary debt to their subject matter — indeed, *Portrait of Gala* is iconographically unremarkable. Based on a photograph of Dalí's wife, Gala, standing in front of an olive tree, the painting mesmerizes its viewer on account of its technique and scale, not its imagery. Of course, *Portrait of Gala with Two Lamb Chops Balanced on Her Shoulder* offers the viewer a more puzzling image to consider. Nevertheless, relative to many of Dalí's other works of the period, the scene depicted here is rather ordinary. What charges it with intensity is less the subject matter than the style: the sense that reality has been compressed into a nearly microscopic space, as if the world were in the process of shrinking to a point.

While these three paintings are exceptionally small, many of Dalí's other paintings, although larger, include vast expanses of empty space. The enormity of the vacant space often serves to make the objects within them seem all the more diminutive. This is the case, for example, in works such as *Remorse, or Sphinx Embedded in the Sand* (fig. 26), in which the female figure is placed along the far left-hand side of the painting and opposed to an expansive and uninterrupted desert landscape, as well as in *Fried Egg on the Plate without the Plate*, 1932, in which a single egg hangs from a thin string in an otherwise empty field. In *Paranoiac-Astral Image* (fig. 48), perhaps the most troublingly vacant of all of Dalí's paintings, each of the principal figures is surrounded by a space so indefinite as to appear immeasurable. Unlike others that use their imagery to unsettle, these paintings provoke unease with their scale and method of manufacture.

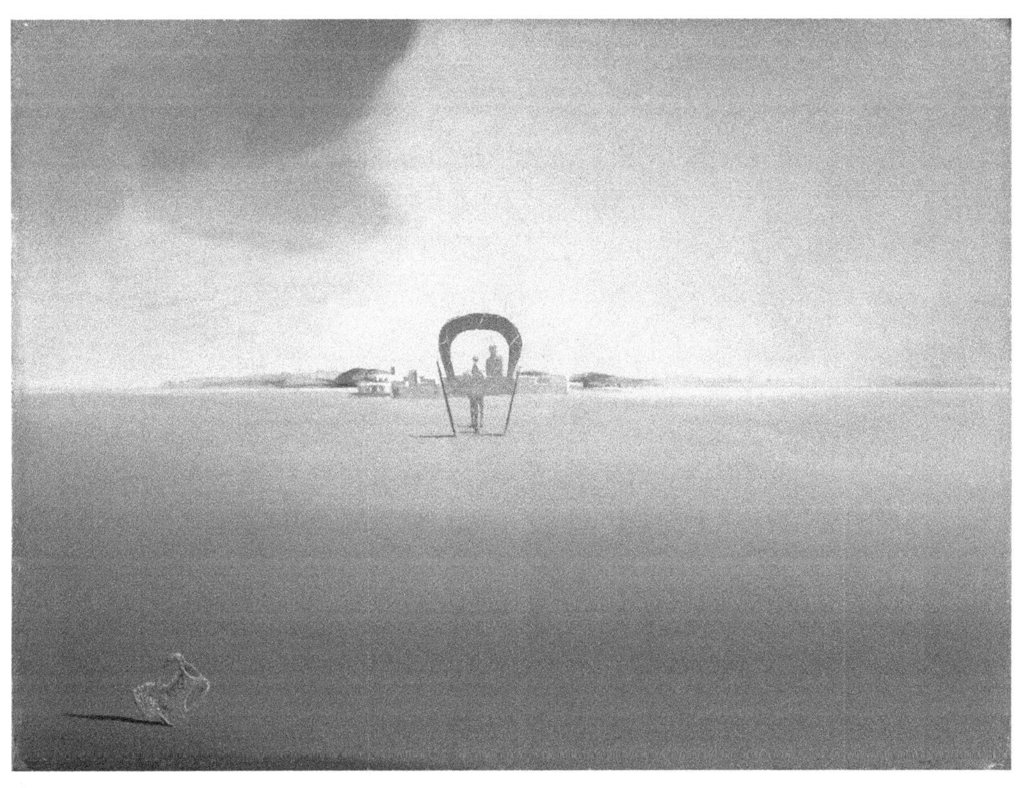

28. Salvador Dalí, *The Phantom Cart*, 1933. Oil on wood, 15.9 × 21.9 cm (6¼ × 8⅝ in.). Gift of Thomas F. Howard. 1953.51.1. Yale University Art Gallery, New Haven, Connecticut. Dalí, Salvador (1904–89) © ARS, NY. Photo Credit: Yale University Art Gallery/Art Resource, NY.

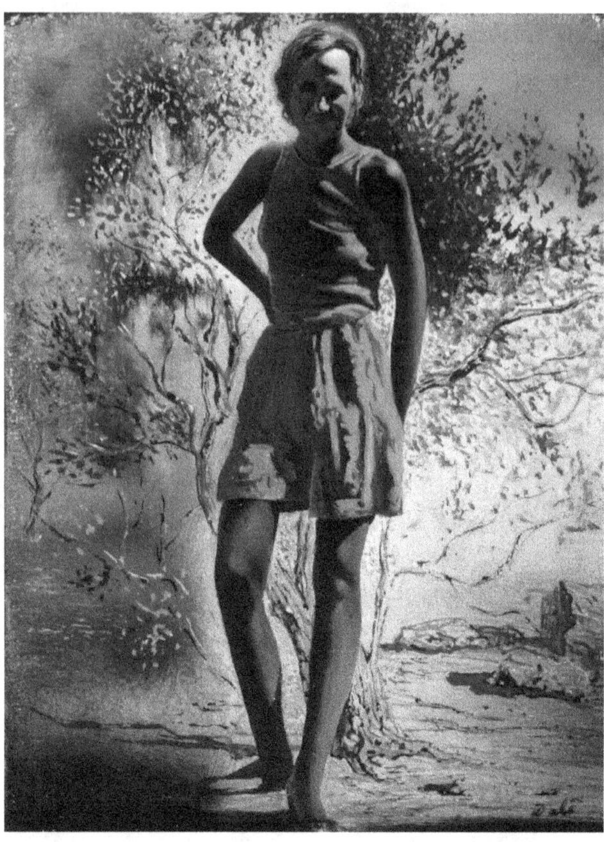

29. Salvador Dalí, *Portrait of Gala*, 1932–33. Oil on panel, 8.5 × 6.5 cm (3 7/16 × 2 5/8 in.).

Collection of the Salvador Dalí Museum, Inc., St. Petersburg FL, 2011.

There is a term for this particular experience of disorientation in the face of the extremely small: the "miniature sublime." Edmund Burke coined the term as one instance of the sublime experience in general, which he defined as that which "excite[s] the ideas of pain, and danger, that is to say, whatever is in any sort terrible, or is conversant about terrible objects, or operates in a manner analogous to terror."[10] Burke attributed the sublime to five sources or occasions: *terror*, *obscurity*, *power*, and above all, *vastness* (and its ultimate expression, *infinity*). These five aspects of the sublime are widely intuited, but Burke insisted that there was also another occasion on which the feeling of sublimity may arise, an occasion he described as "the last extreme of littleness":

> As the great extreme of dimension is sublime, so the last extreme of littleness is in some measure sublime likewise; when we attend to the infinite divisibility of matter, when we pursue animal life into these excessively small,

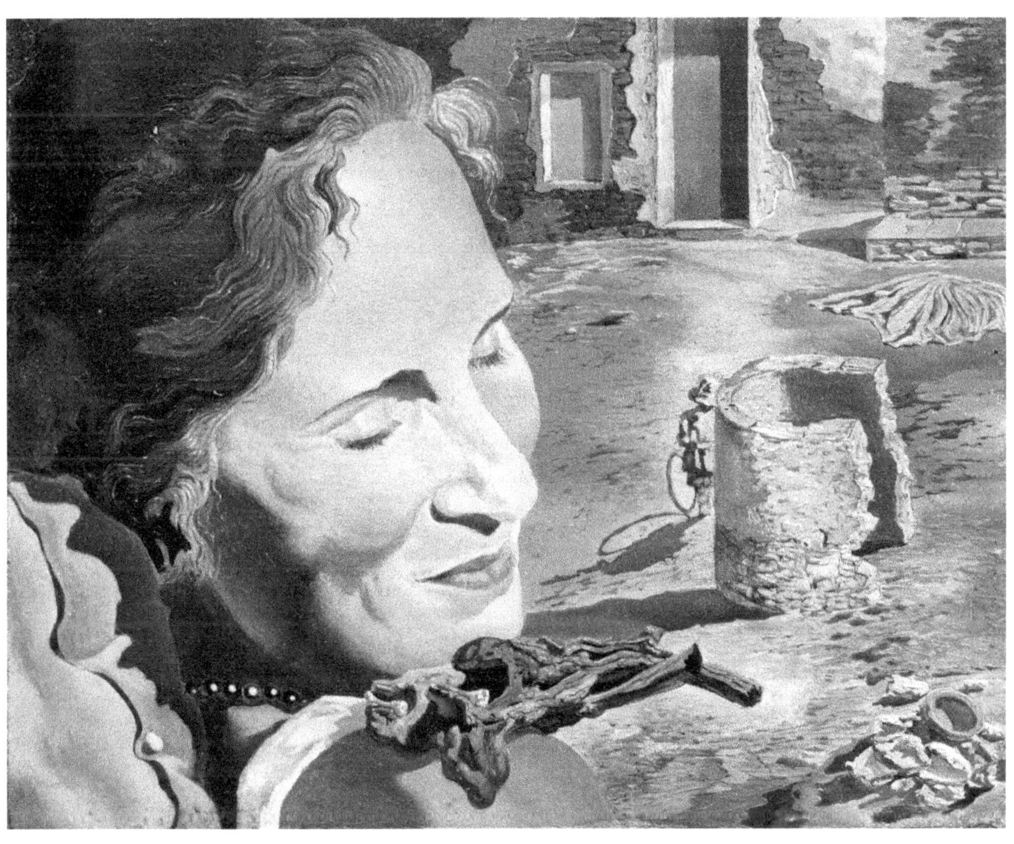

30. Salvador Dalí, *Portrait of Gala with Two Lamb Chops Balanced on Her Shoulder*, ca. 1934. Oil on wood panel, 6.8 × 8.8 cm (2.68 × 3.46 in.). Fundació Gala-Salvador Dalí, Figueres. Dalí, Salvador (1904–89) © ARS, NY.

and yet organized beings, that escape the nicest inquisition of the sense, when we push our discoveries yet downward, and consider those creatures so many degrees smaller, and the still diminishing scale of existence, in tracing which the imagination is lost as well as the sense, we become amazed and confounded at the wonders of minuteness; nor can we distinguish in its effect this extreme of littleness from the vast itself.[11]

It is a measure of the complexity of Dalí's developing concept of little things that a painting such as *Portrait of Gala* should follow soon after a painting like *The Great Masturbator*. The former, shown on a tiny block of painted olive wood, is understood to exhibit enormous power, while the latter, a monstrous giant, is revealed to be a bloated weakling. In both instances, big and small change places; the powerful shrinks and the little grows big.[12]

DRY AND MOTIONLESS MOCOS

Of all the parasites that Dalí introduced into his work after 1929, there is one that has almost entirely eluded critical attention. I am referring to the smooth and whitish object that appears in almost all of Dalí's paintings of this period. In *The Enigma of Desire, or My Mother, My Mother, My Mother* (fig. 31), for example, it appears in isolation at the bottom right of the painting and almost obscured by the lengthening shadow of a building that stands in some indefinite space beyond the picture plane. In *The Lugubrious Game* (fig. 19) the whitish, nearly round little thing has multiplied and now floats in what appears to be a circular rhythm in the blue sky at the top of the painting. It appears as well in the shadowed foreground in both *The Great Masturbator* (fig. 25) and *Premature Ossification of a Railway Station*. In *The Font* (fig. 32) Dalí has placed it very near the geometric center of the painting, as if all of the identifiable elements in this painting were circulating around it like planets around a sun. In *Remorse, or Sphinx Embedded in the Sand* (fig. 26) it is placed in the lower left-hand corner, initiating a diagonal line that extends through the shadow of the female figure to the sharp and ragged rocks in the distance. That Dalí was fascinated by this strange little thing is underscored by the fact that in a few instances it is clearly the painting's main subject. For example, in *Shades of Night Descending*, *Symbiosis of a Head of Seashells*, *The Sense of Speed* (fig. 33), and *Geological Destiny* (fig. 34) Dalí makes this small and mysterious element the principal object of consideration.

As far as I can tell, Dalí never definitively identified this strange little object. Nevertheless, on more than one occasion he did refer to a substance that bears a striking similarity to it. In a poem published in *La Gaceta Literaria* in April

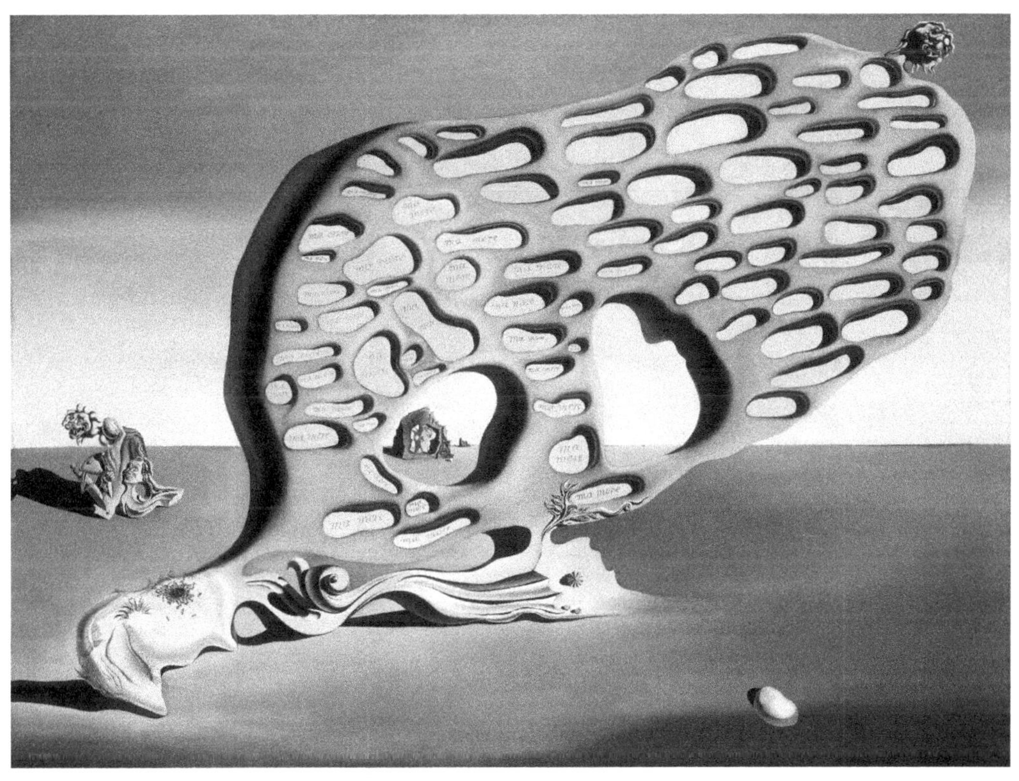

31. Salvador Dalí, *The Enigma of Desire, or My Mother, My Mother, My Mother*. 1929, Oil on canvas, 110.5 × 150.5 cm (43.50 × 59.25 in.). Inv. 14734. Pinakothek der Moderne, Bayerische Staatsgemaeldesammlungen, Munich, Germany. Dalí, Salvador (1904–89) © ARS, NY. Photo credit: bpk, Berlin/Bayerische Staatsgemaeldesammlungen/Art Resource, NY.

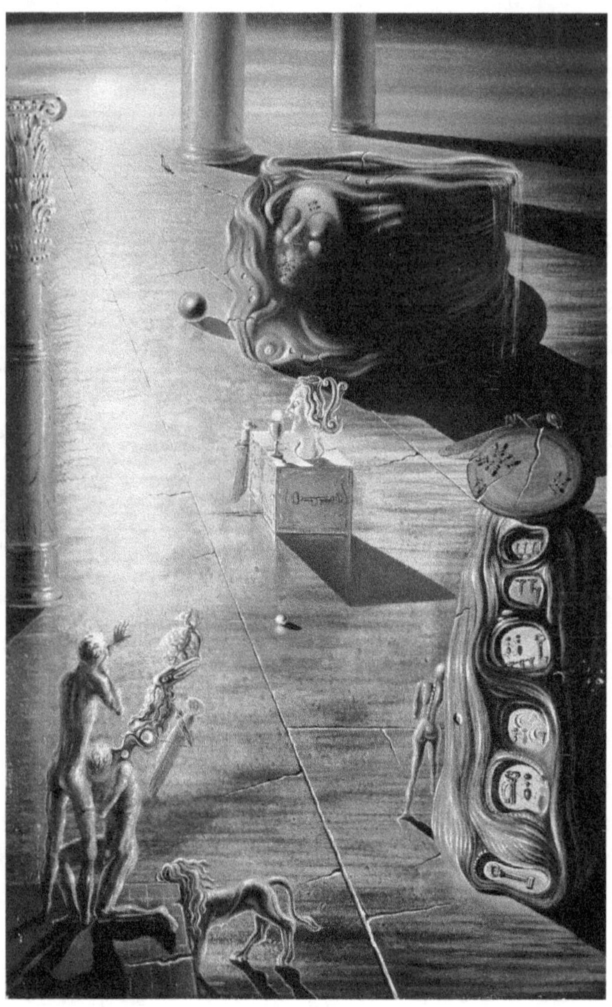

32. Salvador Dalí, *The Font*, 1930. Oil on panel, 66 × 41 cm (26 × 16¼ in.) © Salvador Dalí. Fundació Gala-Salvador Dalí (Artists Rights Society), 2011. Collection of the Salvador Dalí Museum, Inc., St. Petersburg FL, 2011.

1929, Dalí offered the reader a seemingly unending collection of dizzying metamorphoses.[13] The poem begins with a description of the head of a stag, dried out and resting on some moss. From the head spills a host of other organisms in a manner that suggests the literary equivalent of the ants and lion heads that burst from the surface of the white little things depicted in *Accommodations of Desire*. The narrator follows the tumbling of these organisms as they spill from the stag's head. The spillage eventually leads to a river where, in a cabin, lives what is described in the poem as "a booger" (un moco en una cabaña).[14]

The poem describes the booger's cabin as unadorned save for a photograph of a squirrel. Its one piece of furniture is a "freshly peeled almond that hangs on a string affixed to the ceiling." Nothing more is said about this solitary *moco*, and the poem then again redirects the reader's attention toward other objects and organisms.

One year later, however, in the poem "The Great Masturbator," Dalí returned to the theme of the tiny *moco*. In one passage the reader is confronted with a collection of classical vases "adorned with tiny hermaphrodite faces with golden curls and mustaches." Nearby one finds "tiny multicolored parasols" and "dry and motionless boogers" (les morves sèches et immobile).[15] Like the reference to *un moco* in the earlier poem, this poem's reference to *les morves* is momentary and glancing, and the poem quickly moves on to other things. Nevertheless, the image of snot that is dry and motionless — adjectives Dalí more often used to describe the crust of a loaf of bread — is graphic enough that one is led to wonder if this is also perhaps the clue that identifies those mysterious little things that populate so many of Dalí's paintings. Might the small, whitish, nearly round blobs be *les morves sèches et immobile*?

Dalí's attraction to mucus can be seen as of a piece with the surrealist fascination with excrement. Bataille, for example, was drawn to a wide variety of human waste: urine, feces, and saliva as well as, of course, all of the fluids associated with sexuality.[16] Artaud, too, took the concept of excrement as central to his understanding of poetic expression.[17] Mucus is different in that, unlike feces and urine, it suggests a more juvenile sort of repugnance. Boogers are a staple of children's jokes because of their relative harmlessness, and Dalí's image of a little *moco* living in a cabin by a river captures some of the jejune playfulness typically engendered by this particular form of human effluvia.[18]

That mucus is small and inconsequential makes it an obvious object of attraction for Dalí. But there is another aspect of it that surely interested him as well: its malleability. It can be sticky and stringy, gelatinous and rubbery, or dry, flaky, and hard.[19] Most suggestive in this regard is Dalí's poem "With the Sun," which was published in *La Gaceta Literaria* in March 1929. Unlike the two poems mentioned above, in which the references to mucus were brief and fleeting, "With the Sun," places the figure of the tiny *moco* at the center of the story and serves as the generative core of its logic of endless metamorphosis:

With the sun, there is a booger standing up at the edge of a curbstone.
And another booger, standing up on my fingertip, ready to fly away,
And another booger, upright 20 meters away, on a stone that looks like a
monument to parrots,
And another booger, calm on a moth 40 meters away, that is a happy song.

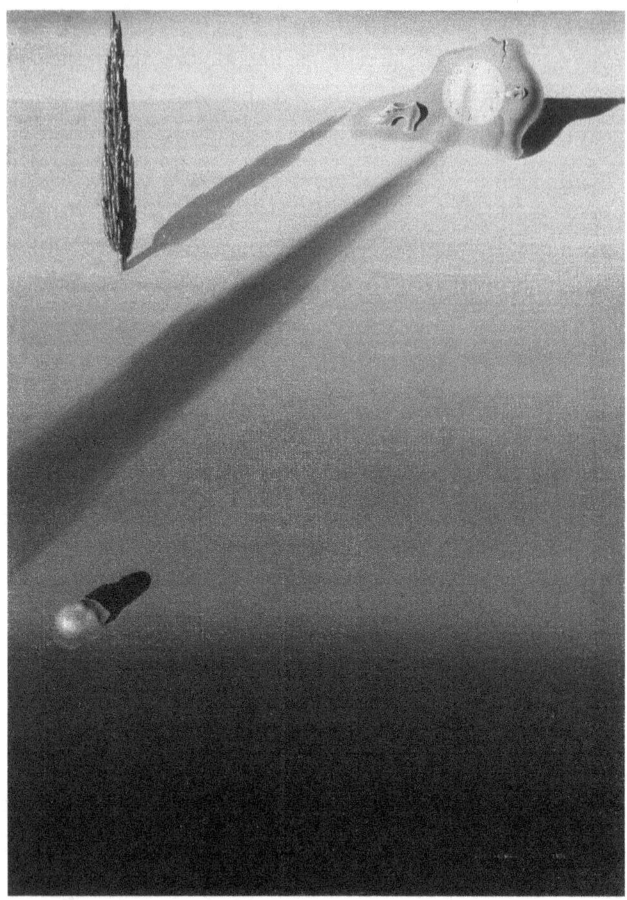

33. Salvador Dalí, *The Sense of Speed*, 1931. Oil on canvas, 33 × 24 cm (12.99 × 9.45 in.). Fundació Gala-Salvador Dalí, Figueres. Dalí, Salvador (1904–89) © ARS, NY.

And another dry booger that is a curve,
And another flying booger that is a tailor costume,
And another cramped booger that is the history of a walnut.[20]

Although there is insufficient evidence to definitively identify this shape-shifting *moco* with the smooth and whitish little things in *Shades of Night Descending*, *The Sense of Speed*, and *Geological Destiny*, it bears enough similarities to make this association worth considering. In both the paintings and the poems a formless little thing is monumentalized and invested with a mesmerizing power. Its ability to draw our gaze toward an endless series of tiny morphological transformations is the source of its disruptive potential. This is the essence of the parasitical *cosita* as Dalí conceived it. Its insertion into the scene provokes the crumbling of scalar distinctions and the unraveling of identity.[21]

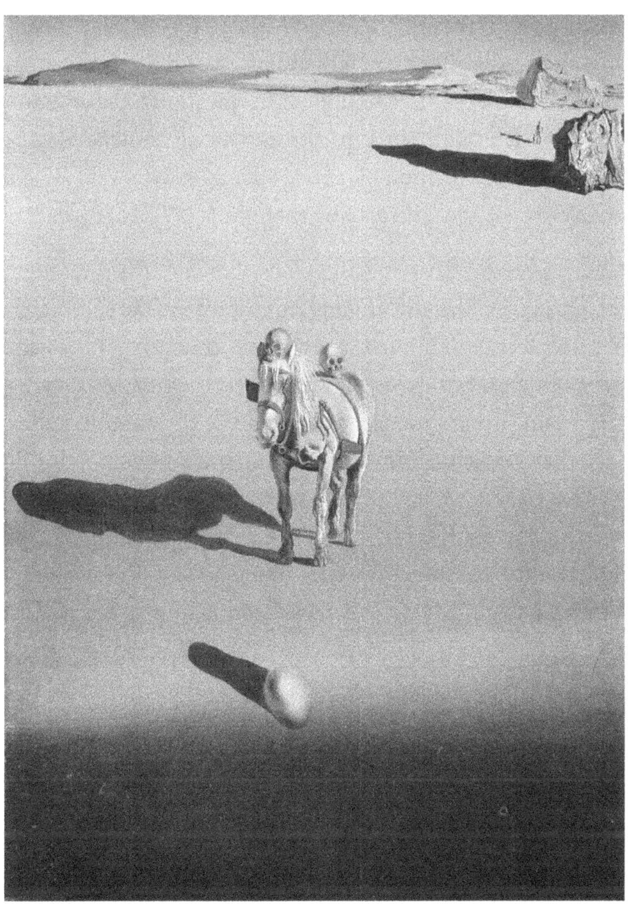

34. Salvador Dalí, *Geological Destiny*, 1933. Oil on wood panel, 21 × 16 cm (8.27 × 6.30 in.). Private collection. Image provided by the Fundació Gala-Salvador Dalí. Dalí, Salvador (1904–89) © ARS, NY.

THE AERODYNAMIC COMEDO

In 1934 Dalí introduced yet another bodily excretion into his collection of little things: the blackhead. If mucus represented the indefinite state between liquid and solid, the blackhead represented the region between organic "beings" and inert "objects." In "Aerodynamic Apparitions of 'Beings-Objects'" Dalí introduced his analysis with the following assertion:

> All of my readers, I am sure, will have had the satisfaction of feeling that stubborn tenacity, that hypnotizing obstinacy, that anxiety-ridden perseverance that scoffs at the giddiness preceding the pleasure owed to the intimate act of causing to spurt out of the pores of the nose, by means of a dextrous and painful squeezing applied about them, a slippery, new, and

aerodynamic comedo, more commonly known by the name of "blackhead" [point noir]. . . . Do not stupidly shrug your shoulders, you among my readers who would hold the extraction of the comedones in question to be a matter of little import; know you that this seemingly ultraprosaic cleaning is nothing less than ultraconcrete personalization of what is the most vital and lyrical in contemporary moral, scientific, and artistic thought.[22]

Like the *moco* that lives by the river and the *moco* that stands up ready to fly, the pasty substrate that is the blackhead yields an infinite variety of beings and objects. "It would be enough," Dalí insisted, "that a general compression be applied by both hands to have hundreds of tiny objects (night tables, skulls, bottles, lampshades, etc.) come up in slow ascension (like the Paramount orchestra), spiking the surface that just a few minutes ago was still supersmooth."[23]

By virtue of the hidden existence of blackheads beneath the surface of the skin, Dalí's description of the "giddiness" of the search for them and their eventual transformation into "hundreds of tiny objects" offers an analogy to the workings of the paranoiac as we have witnessed it in chapter 2.[24] In Dalí's understanding of the disorder, the paranoiac is not deluded but gifted with powers of discernment more precise than those of ordinary individuals ("associations and facts so refined as to escape normal people"). The paranoiac sees what lies beneath the surface, what is invisible to others. Once revealed, however, the paranoiac's observations are irrefutable ("conclusions that often cannot be contradicted or rejected").[25] Blackheads, for Dalí, functioned similarly. Ordinarily invisible, their exposure requires precision and attention to detail. And like the paranoiac's "associations and facts," their exposure is disruptive. The smooth skin of one's face — like the logical order of reality as perceived by normal individuals — is disfigured by the blackhead's eruption. Indeed, the blackhead is a perfect emblem for the world as it is pursued and revealed by the paranoiac.

Dalí's most literal representation of emerging comedones appeared in small portrait of Gala that he painted around 1933. Just under eight by nine inches, the painting depicts Gala in profile with a lobster resting on her head (fig. 35). She gazes intently to her left, apparently oblivious to her condition. She is also oblivious, so it seems, to the presence of a tiny, two-seat airplane attached to the tip of her nose. Like the night tables, skulls, bottles, and lampshades that Dalí described as emerging slowly from the pores on one's face, the small (and by definition *aerodynamic*) airplane that emerges from Gala's nose is none other than a mysterious and giddy comedo.

Although Dalí doesn't explicitly refer to blackheads in his writing until the "Aerodynamic Apparitions of 'Beings-Objects'" (nor does he return to the

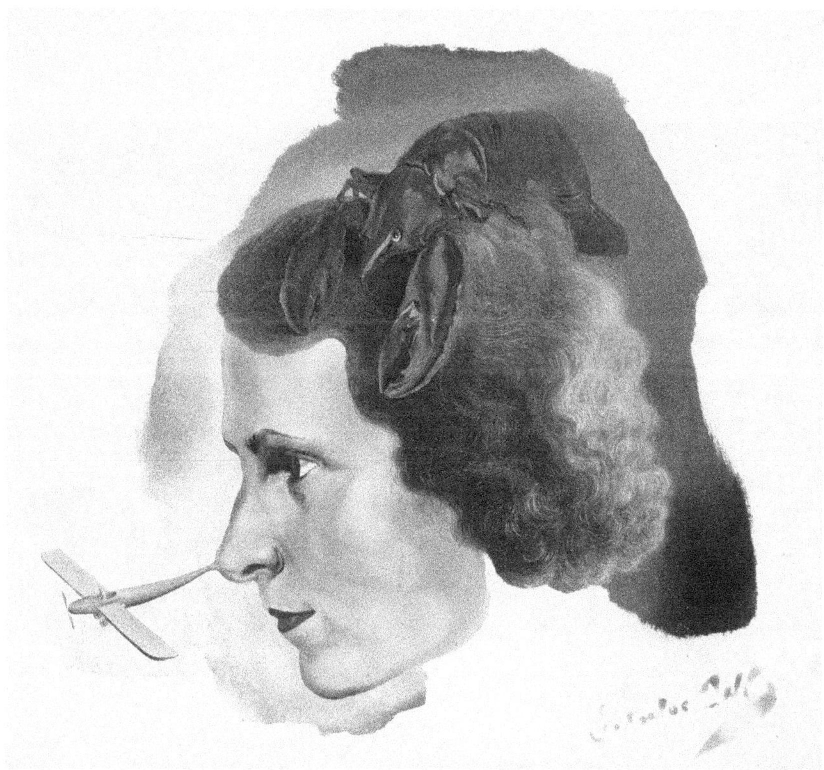

35. Salvador Dalí, *Portrait of Gala with Lobster*, ca. 1933. Oil on plywood panel, 20.0 × 22.5 cm (7.87 × 8.86 in.). Private collection. Image provided by the Fundació Gala-Salvador Dalí. Dalí, Salvador (1904–89) © ARS, NY.

subject at any length thereafter), many of his paintings are littered with objects that one would be justified in associating with the "strange bodies" that emerge from the pores on one's face. The woman and the white lily that emerge from the face of the figure in *The Great Masturbator* (fig. 25) as well as the enormous globular substance that bursts from the same face in *The Enigma of Desire* (fig. 31) share all of the properties of the aerodynamic comedo as Dalí would later articulate it. Likewise the lion and woman-vessel that erupt from Éluard's head in *Portrait of Éluard*. In *William Tell* (fig. 36) a pianist at his piano erupts from Tell's shoulder. And in *Birth of Liquid Desires* (fig. 37), also based on Dalí's version of the myth of William Tell, an entire Böcklinian landscape emerges, much like the airplane in Gala's portrait, from the loaf of French bread on Tell's head.

Similar eruptions are depicted as well in *Atavism at Twilight* (fig. 38), one of Dalí's many transformations of Jean-François Millet's famous mid-nineteenth-century painting *L'Angélus*. In Millet's work a wheelbarrow and pitchfork are

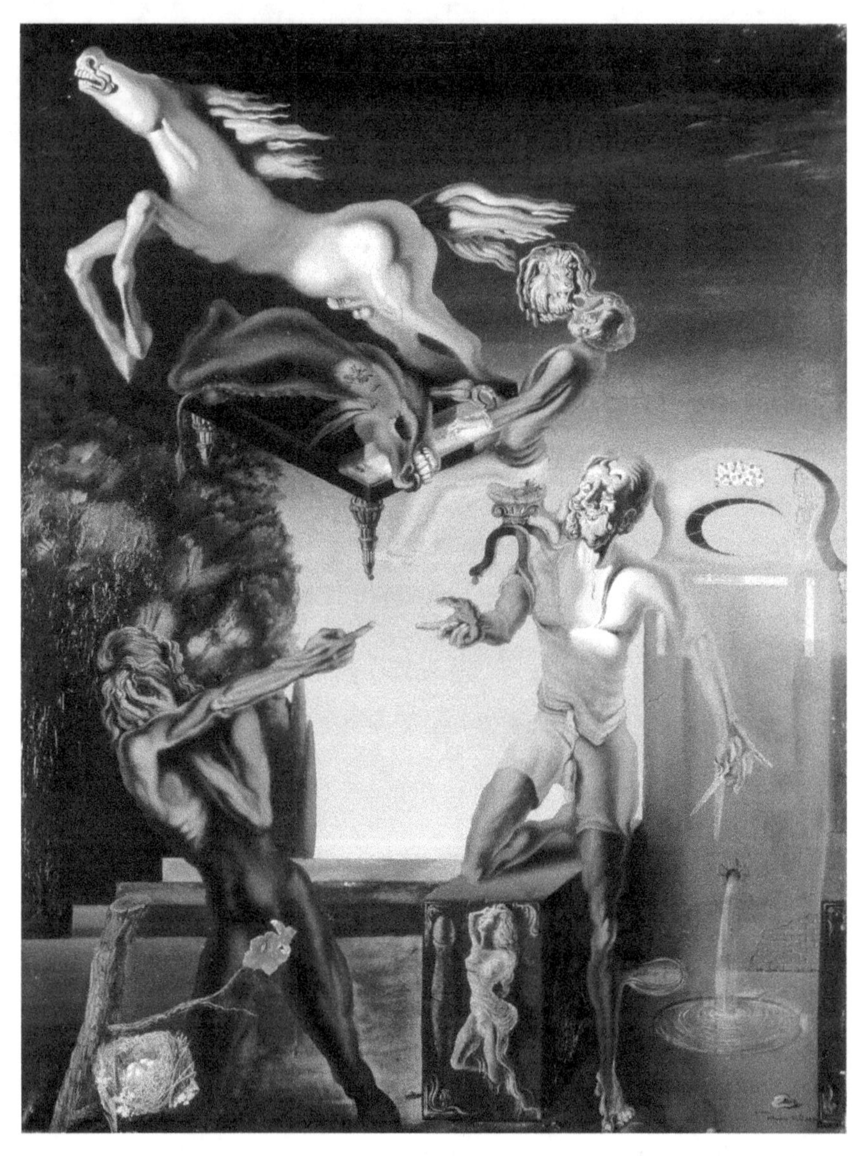

36. Salvador Dalí, *William Tell*, 1930. Collage of diverse materials, textile, paint, 113 × 87 cm (44.49 × 34.25 in.). AM 2002-287. Photo: Jean-Claude Planchet. Musee National d'Art Moderne, Centre Georges Pompidou, Paris, France. Dalí, Salvador (1904–89) © ARS, NY. Photo credit: CNAC/MNAM/Dist. Réunion des Musées Nationaux/Art Resource, NY.

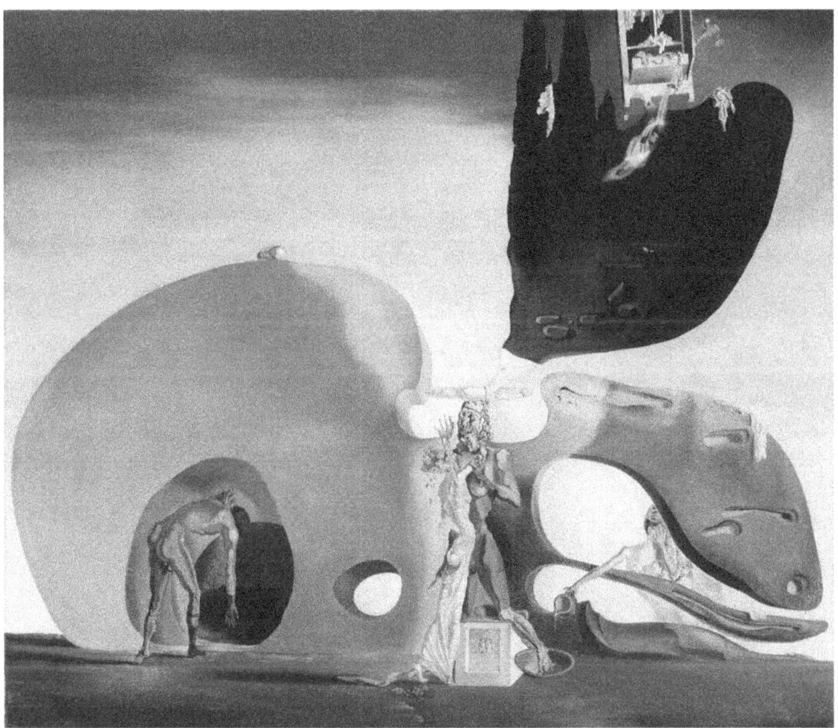

37. Salvador Dalí, *Birth of Liquid Desires* (*La naissance des désirs liquides*), 1931–32. Oil and collage on canvas, 96.1 × 112.3 cm (37⅞ × 44¼ in.). The Solomon R. Guggenheim Foundation, Peggy Guggenheim Collection, Venice, 1976. 76.2553.100. Dalí, Salvador (1904–89) © ARS, NY.

set beside a farmer and his wife as the two bow their heads in silent prayer. In *Atavism at Twilight* Dalí has included the key elements of Millet's painting but has moved them around: the loaded barrow grows from the man's head, and the pitchfork erupts from the woman's arm. In *Architectonic Angelus of Millet* (fig. 39) Millet's central figures have been transformed into ambiguous objects of enormous proportion — interpretable on the one hand as blocks of weathered rock and on the other as a pair of grotesquely outsized *mocos*. That Dalí may have associated these figures with the "comical and mysterious game" of squeezing blackheads is suggested by the long, thin protrusion that extends from the abstract figure on the right: a perfectly aerodynamic comedo.

Dalí described his many variations on Millet's painting as concrete manifestations of the world as revealed through paranoia-criticism.[26] *Atavism at Twilight* and *Architectonic Angelus of Millet* are not so much manipulations of Millet's painting as they are revelations of a hidden disorder rumbling beneath the surface of its gentle and gauzy hymn to rural life. In much the same way that the fingers' "dextrous and painful squeezing" unearths hidden forms beneath

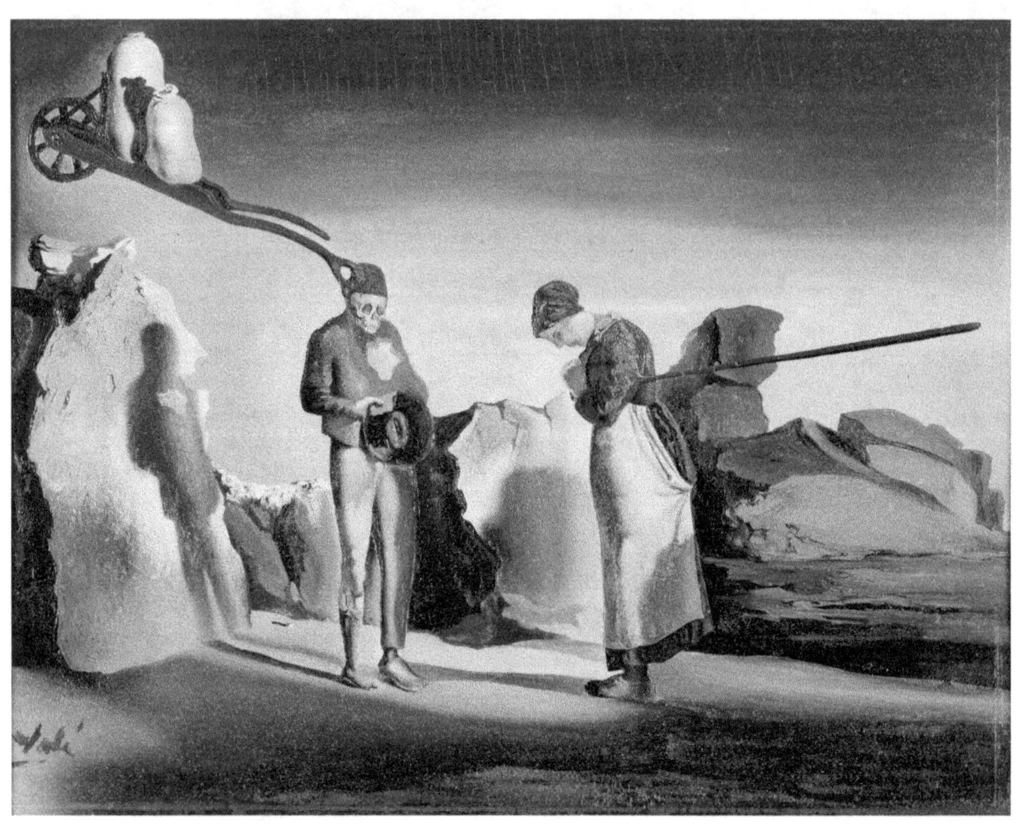

38. Salvador Dalí, *Atavism at Twilight* (*Obsessive Phenomenon*) (*Les atavismes du crépuscule* [*Phénomène obsessif*]), ca. 1933. Oil on panel. 13.8 × 17.9 cm (5.43 × 7.05 in.). Kunstmuseum Bern, Legat Georges F. Keller 1981, Inv. Nr. G 82.006. Dalí, Salvador (1904–89) © ARS, NY.

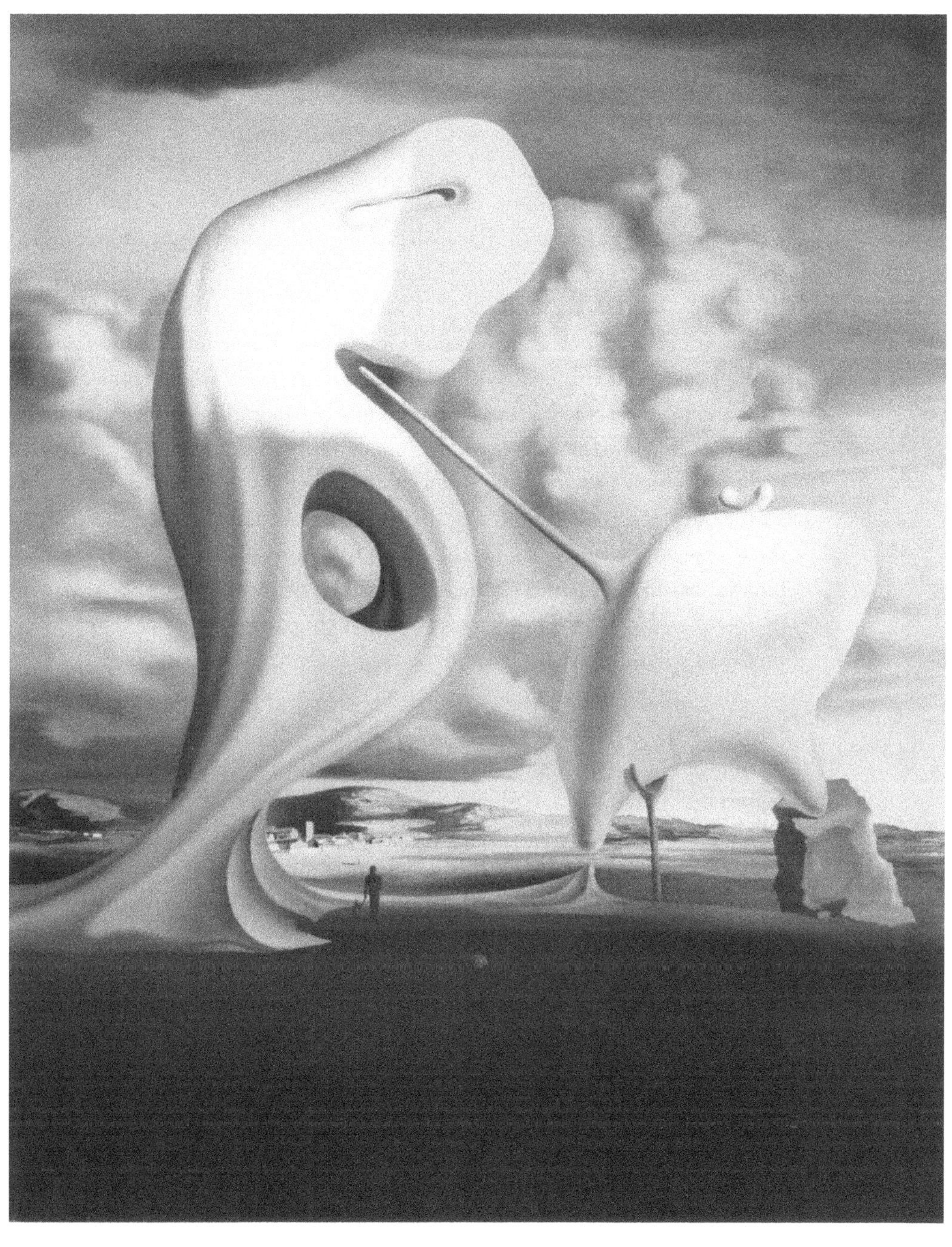

39. Salvador Dalí, *Architectonic Angelus of Millet*, 1933. Oil on canvas, 73 × 60 cm (28.74 × 23.62 in.). Museo Nacional Centro de Arte Reina Sofía, Madrid. Dalí, Salvador (1904–89) © ARS, NY.

the surface of the skin, Dalí conceived of paranoia-criticism as an instrument capable of squeezing Millet's painting so as to unearth a collection of mysterious and repulsive little things.

LA BOBINE SANS FIL

Throughout the nineteen thirties Dalí continued to propose new little things to consider and new terms to describe their effect. For example, in "Non-Euclidian Psychology of a Photograph," 1935, Dalí offered yet another term to describe the *point noir* at which an object or an image is unraveled by the interruption an unexpected little thing. He called it "la bobine sans fil" (the threadless spool) after an object he spied in the far corner of a photograph that he claimed had been puzzling him for some time. The photograph captures three figures, a man and two women, at the entrance of a city building (fig. 40). One woman stands on the curb and the other on the first step. Behind them, largely obscured by the shadowed entryway, stands the man. Only his face is visible, which makes him appear to be floating bodilessly above the two women. This, along with their stiff and awkward poses and the stoic expressions on the women's faces, produces a noticeably strange and menacing effect.

Similar to the admonition he had given to those "who would hold the extraction of the comedones in question to be a matter of little import," Dalí begins his analysis of the photograph by insisting that the menacing gaze of the three figures is not, in fact, its most disturbing element: "Do not believe, dear reader, that I draw your attention to this striking photograph because of its obvious pathetic and disconcerting quality, which arises quite naturally from the climate of criminality surrounding the three psychological beings." Instead, he asks us to pay attention to a tiny detail in the lower left-hand corner of photo. There, barely visible beneath the shadow cast by the curb, sits a small cylindrical object shaped like a tiny dumbbell (fig. 41). "Divert your eyes . . . away from the hypnotizing center of this photograph," Dalí implores, "and direct them with prudent caution toward its lower left corner": "For there, just above the sidewalk, you might observe with amazement — completely naked, completely pale, completely peeled, immensely unconscious, clean, solitary, tiny, cosmic, non-Euclidean — a threadless spool [une bobine sans fil]. Fasten your eyes on this threadless spool, so that its insignificance will not make you doubt its small but real presence, its hard and pure objectivity; fasten your eyes on this threadless spool, for it is about it that Salvador Dalí is going to talk to you."[27]

For the reader familiar with Dalí's pre-surrealist aesthetic of objectivity, the reference in this passage to the spool's "hard and pure objectivity" recalls the painter's previous studies of photography ("Photography: Pure Creation

t absolues des objets présentés par
cette intuition pure, qui aurait pu
e immensément solitaire et exacte,
rse une crise de plus en plus aiguë, et
ıt les sciences particulières, c'est que
l en pis.
re, cette
ès avoir
ıte d'un
ontinua
i lui of
promis-
culières,
ent au
t par la
plorable
ge mise
ison de
ntres et
la fille
pure »,
nt dans
les tem-
ıce, les-
de vé-
que les
maisons
ntuition
dont la
ppeal »
viendra,
qui do-
et en
et qui
dominer
i en fin
traduire
grandio-
lien, et
uo impossible et malheureux de
le la physique de Newton, duo
ut cas généralement illustré par

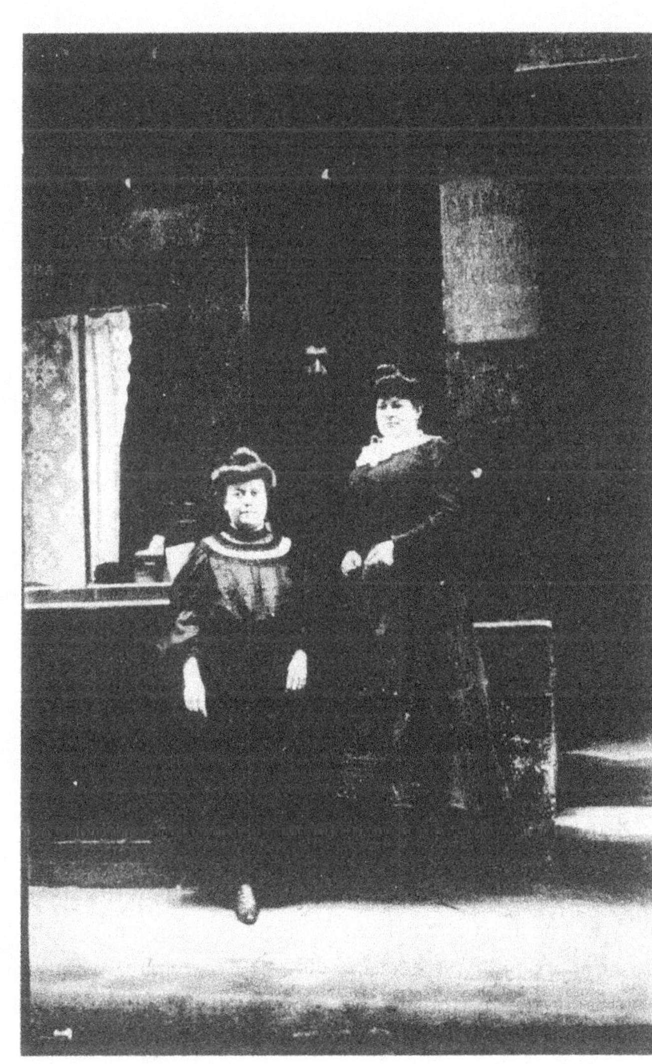

La « bobine sans fil », thème obses
pour Kant n'aurait été qu'un objet e
c'est-à-dire ayant une place précise e
l'espace, cesse d'être compréhensible d
où, comn
localisatic
totalemen
déjà bien
pitoyable
métaphys
théorie d
de Kant.
été répu
tiques. M
m'appara
une espèc
de l'aut
pure » p
sivement
sciences
elle récla
pirique q
lui payer
trop lour
miers av
portent e
a fini pa
pure, nu
bine que
de consi
le répète,
coin de l
n'est pa
du derni
la fille le
plus que
même de
fil qui e

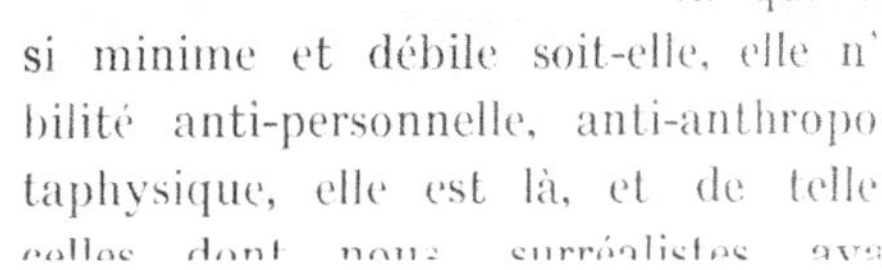

si minime et débile soit-elle, elle n'
bilité anti-personnelle, anti-anthropo
taphysique, elle est là, et de telle

40. Photograph from *Minotaure* (Paris), June 7, 1935.

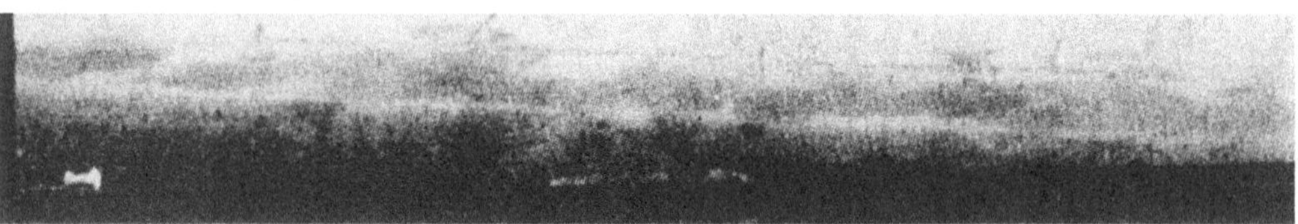

41. Detail of photograph from *Minotaure* (Paris), June 7, 1935.

of the Spirit," 1927; "The Photographic Data," 1929) and his concept of the "documentation of minutiae" (see chapter 2). What is new in this text is that, for the first time, Dalí has chosen to analyze a particular photograph rather than reflect on photography in general. "Non-Euclidean Psychology of a Photograph" effectively sets out to perform what Dalí's two previous texts on photography merely described. It attempts to locate within the objective lens of the camera evidence of a mysterious world incompatible with the one we think we know through reason. It also recalls Dalí's paranoia-criticism of *L'Angélus*: Just as viewers of *Atavism at Twilight* and *Architectonic Angelus of Millet* are asked to reconsider the apparent insignificance of the hat in the hand of Millet's pious farmer, Dalí's analysis of this strange photograph asks readers to fix their gaze on the tiny spool in the corner of the photograph.

Whether Dalí has accurately identified the tiny object in the corner of the photograph is, to my mind, an open question. I find it too small and ill-defined to identify with any certainty. Furthermore, Dalí's evident pleasure in working with the pun "bobine sans fil"/"bobine sans fille" (daughterless spool) and the Freudian possibilities it offers makes the identification suspiciously fortuitous.[28] That said, the identification itself matters less than the insistence that we draw our eyes away from what are clearly the most compelling figures in the picture and toward an object of no consequence at all. In this Dalí was identifying the photograph's own blackhead, the site at which the picture's apparent comprehensibility will be burst apart. The three figures in the center of the photograph may grant the image a "pathetic and disconcerting quality," but this is nothing compared to the profoundly disruptive effect of the threadless spool:

> This threadless spool indeed cries out loudly for an interpretation, for this most exhibitionistic object, because of its "imperceptible existence," and through its character and its invisible nature, which lend themselves to the sudden irruption peculiar to "paranoiac apparitions" (it is by this mechanism that its presence has assailed and struck me), this object, I say, appeals, once it is visible, once it is discovered, for a logical solution that would allow a reduction, even a partial one, of the flagrant and incomprehensible delirious

> phenomenon it embodies. . . . The least we could say of this silhouette of a ghastly and precise scrap of refuse that is the spool under consideration . . . is that we are talking about a "crazy thing" [chose folle].[29]

In other words, the threadless spool is, for Dalí, the photograph's *point noir*, and his analysis of it is the act of squeezing it.[30]

Dalí ended the essay by invoking Kant's notion of "pure intuition" and proclaiming that the spool is evidence of the truth of both non-Euclidean geometry and Einsteinian relativity. The argument is hyperbolic and scientifically ridiculous, of course, and it was meant to be. Dalí's concern lies not with the photograph's representation of physical space but rather with its representation of "psychological space." What the text sets out to impress on us is that the three menacing figures are in fact comprehensible to us — comprehensible *as menacing*. That we can easily comprehend them as such is, for Dalí, analogous to the easy comprehension of Euclidean space. The spool, on the other hand, is much more powerfully disorienting because it is, like Einsteinian space-time, incapable of being comprehended within the rational system to which we have grown accustomed:

> This spool, I repeat, smooth and new, abandoned at the corner of the street of psychology, is not only the symbol of the last thread of pure intuition, Kant's legitimate daughter. . . . Stupid and insignificant [minime et débile] though it may be, . . . it is there, and of such insignificance as the ones whose solicitations we Surrealists have, first and foremost, learned to listen to, solicitations revealed to us by dreams as characterizing our age, our life, with the utmost violence.[31]

Stupid and *insignificant*: we have seen these adjectives before. They are the attributes of the little things that had for years fascinated Dalí. From sea urchins and ants to boogers and blackheads, the little things that Dalí pursued were almost invariably stupid and insignificant. Indeed, the stupidity and insignificance of these tiny parasites served as the very source of their disruptive potential.

Moreover, by associating his account of the threadless spool with the "solicitations revealed to us by dreams," Dalí has offered an alternative perspective on the reception of psychoanalysis. Insofar as psychoanalysis is understood to be coordinated around concepts such as the primal scene and the oedipal drama, Dalí's analysis of the "crazy thing" at the edge of the photograph suggests that such coordinating concepts are merely the "hypnotizing center" of Freudian thought. The more profound elements are the ones in the margins, the stupid and inconsequential little things in the corners of psychological experience. Like the observations of the paranoiac, they cannot be made to conform to reality as we have come to comprehend it; rather, they force us to consider the possibility that the world is entirely irrational and inescapably mysterious — far more mysterious, in other words, than the mysterious gaze of the three menacing figures at the center of the photograph.

THE BROKEN AMPHORA AND THE ANTI-GEODESIC HAIR

Given the complexity of Dalí's account of the "threadless spool," it is surprising that no such object appears in any of his paintings of the period.[32] In contrast, Dalí's textual references to the Great Masturbator coincided with painted representations of the figure, as did his writings on the "stray breast," the "liberated finger," the "motionless loaf of bread," the "aerodynamic comedo," and almost every other little thing about which he had written. Nevertheless, Dalí's account of the disorienting effect of the tiny, inconspicuous spool in the corner of an otherwise dramatic photograph can be applied to any number of his paintings in which one spies in the margins an apparently ordinary and anodyne object that, on further consideration, threatens to unravel the painting as a whole.

Consider, for example, *Mediumnistic-Paranoiac Image* (fig. 42). On a nearly desolate beach at the end of the day, a bicyclist approaches in the distance, while a woman in the middle distance sits with her back turned to the setting sun and two men in the foreground stare directly at the viewer as if they had been momentarily interrupted from their labors. The careful arrangement of the elements creates an effective illusion of three-dimensionality, and the meticulous application of paint, which hides all traces of the brush, gives the impression that we are looking at a photograph, a snapshot of a moment in time. The eeriness of the scene recalls the "hypnotizing" aspect of the three menacing figures in the photograph Dalí analyzed.

What, then, is the viewer to make of the broken amphora at the base of the painting? Although easily overlooked at first glance, on closer consideration its presence is puzzling. An object of ancient history, it seems an intruder in this otherwise contemporary scene.[33] Underscoring its out-of-placeness is its color and facture. Unlike the icy tones of the rest of the painting, the amphora is warmly and elaborately multicolored, with flecks of purple, pink, red, yellow, orange, and green. The crepuscular lighting — consistent throughout the painting — somehow fails to darken it. In addition, the brushstrokes are textured and have a literal depth, suggesting that the amphora is somehow more substantive than the human figures around it. A closer look reveals it to be canted at an odd, if not altogether impossible, angle. The more one examines this little amphora in the foreground, the more it begins to appear like a parasite whose intrusion serves to unravel the carefully constructed unity of the rest of the scene. It is,

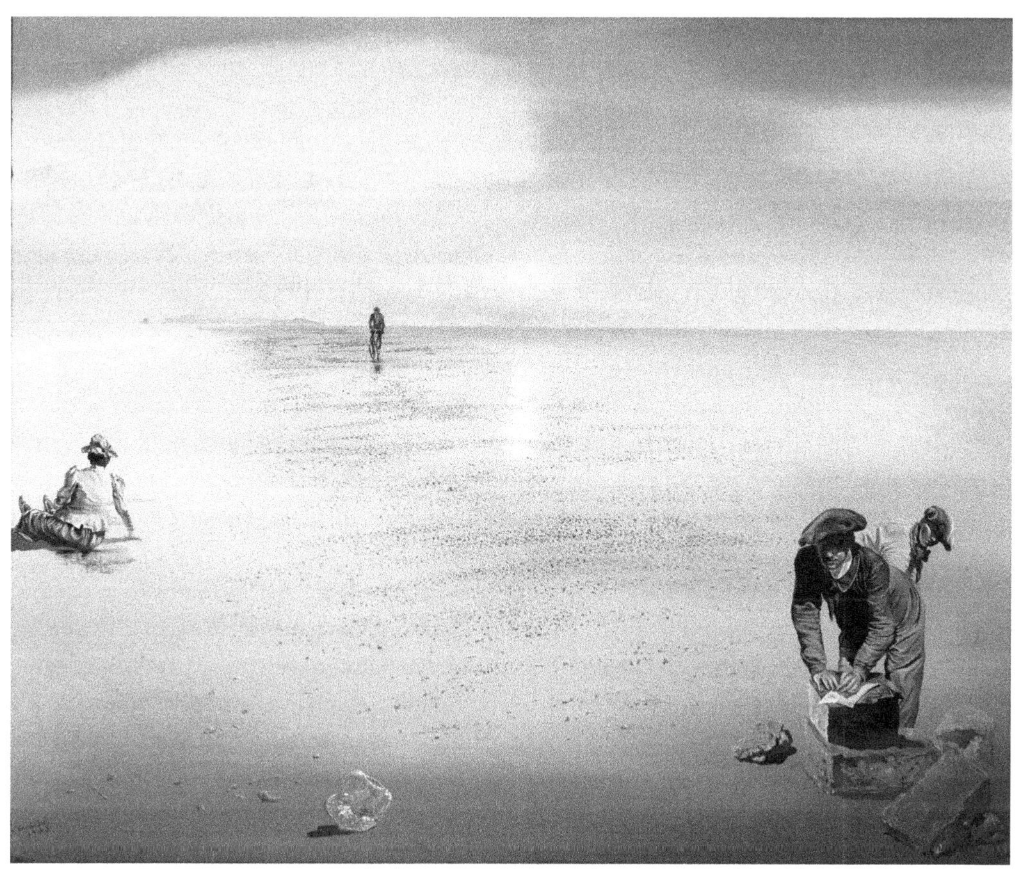

42. Salvador Dalí, *Mediumnistic-Paranoiac Image*, ca. 1934. Oil on panel, 19.0 × 22.8 cm (7.48 × 8.98 in.). Fundació Gala-Salvador Dalí, Figueres. Dalí, Salvador (1904–89) © ARS, NY.

like the threadless spool, the little thing in the corner through which the picture's order comes undone.

Dalí included amphorae in a number of other works from the midthirties. One appears, for example, in *The Fine, Average, Invisible Harp* (fig. 43), in which it functions as the fixed and banal center in an otherwise hallucinatory scene. In *The Phantom Cart* (fig. 28) the amphora occupies the position it does in *Mediumistic-Paranoiac Image*, in the corner and overshadowed by the dramatic double image in the center of the painting (a depiction of a couple riding in a horse-drawn carriage is at the same time the silhouette of a pair of buildings in the city toward which the couple is headed). Like *The Invisible Man* and *Invisible Sleeping Woman, Horse, Lion* (figs. 20, 21), which Dalí had painted earlier, and *The Endless Enigma* and *Apparition of Face and Fruit Dish on a Beach* (fig. 44), which he would paint later, *The Phantom Cart* demonstrates Dalí's facility with the invention of a seemingly limitless number of variations on the theme of the figure-ground gestalt switch. In itself, the double image is a clever curiosity, but the broken amphora in the near corner is a visual puzzle of a different order. In its variegated color it seems not so much part of the space in which it is painted as affixed to the surface like a collage. And its impossibly angled pitch (which also appears in *Mediumnistic-Paranoiac Image*) makes it all the more alien and disruptive.

A broken amphora also appears in *Paranoiac-Astral Image* (fig. 48) and *White Calm* (fig. 49).[34] Like *The Phantom Cart* and *Mediumistic-Paranoiac Image*, both works are quite small and are painted with an unparalleled degree of photographic illusionism.[35] They exhibit no shape-shifting, no transgressive acts of violence or sexuality, no paranoiac double images. Instead, they follow in the footsteps of works like *The Basket of Bread* (fig. 6) from 1926 and the portrait of Gala standing in front of an olive tree (*Portrait of Gala*, fig. 29). Like them, *Paranoiac-Astral Image* and *White Calm* lack the obviously fantastic and dreamlike distortions and mutations that Dalí typically relied on to attract viewers' attention. As such, the disruption caused by the presence of the amphora is smaller and subtler than the disturbances caused by Dalí's more graphic and violent imagery.

In 1936 Dalí proposed that one think of these small and subtle disturbances as akin to a hair on one's arm or leg that fails to follow the direction of the other hairs as they lay neatly atop the skin. He called these occasionally unruly hairs "anti-geodesic," in reference to the geometric lines that define the surface of a two-dimensional form that is curved in three-dimensional space (see chapter 4). In "First Morphological Law Concerning the Hairs in Soft Structures," Dalí described the "anti-geodesic" hair like this: "Had the hair adapted exactly, like a thread, to the soft surfaces, one could still have hoped to have straightened

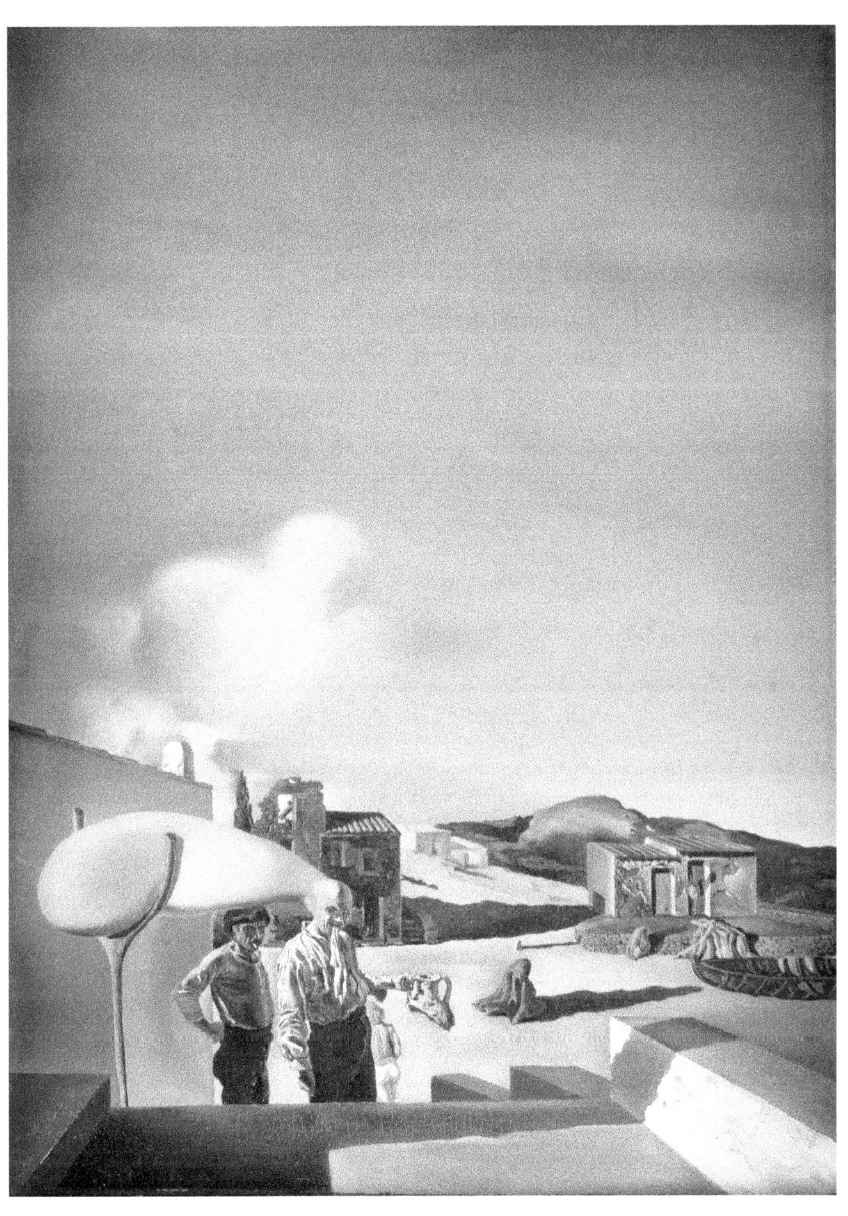

43. Salvador Dalí, *The Fine, Average, Invisible Harp*, 1932. Oil on canvas, 21 × 16 cm (8.27 × 6.30 in.). Private collection. Image provided by the Fundació Gala-Salvador Dalí, Figueres. Dalí, Salvador (1904–89) © ARS, NY.

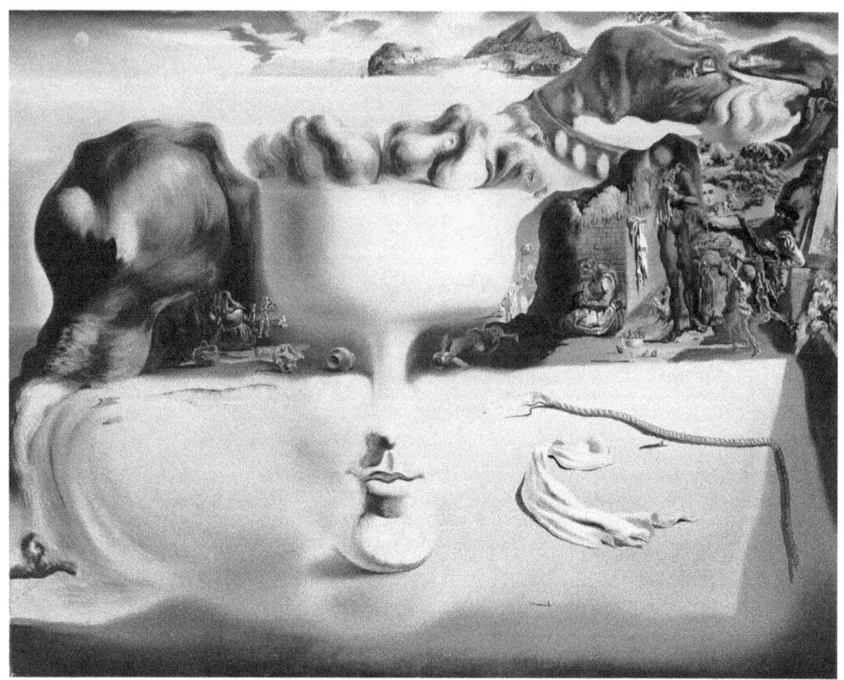

44. Salvador Dalí, *Apparition of Face and Fruit Dish on a Beach*, 1938. Oil on canvas, 114.30 × 143.83 cm (45 × 56⅝ in.). The Ella Gallup Sumner and Mary Catlin Sumner Collection Fund. 1939.269. Wadsworth Atheneum Museum of Art, Hartford, Connecticut. Dalí, Salvador (1904–89) © ARS, NY. Photo credit: Wadsworth Atheneum Museum of Art/Art Resource, NY.

things out. But the hair, in spite of its thinness, and even when soaked, continues always to maintain its shape. It is partially adaptable, but this is worse still, for it rises up in a horrible curve precisely in the most irreparable and criminal spot."[36] In its refusal to follow to the curve of the flesh, the anti-geodesic hair — like the blackhead, the threadless spool, and the broken amphora — functions once again as an intractable little thing that undoes the order of the world around it.

THE LITTLE, EDIBLE, AND FINE PAINTER, MEISSONIER

Throughout this period Vermeer remained Dalí's model of objectivity and meticulousness, a painter of little things whose exacting and uncompromising vision was the vehicle through which one glimpses the irrational. Hence did Dalí declare, in 1937, that Vermeer was "Surrealism Integral."[37] On the one hand, the statement was made to demonstrate his independence from the surrealist movement at a time when its members had grown increasingly unsympathetic to his ever-expanding sense of self-importance and commercial ambition (Breton famously dubbed him "Avida Dollars"). On the other, it was an expression of

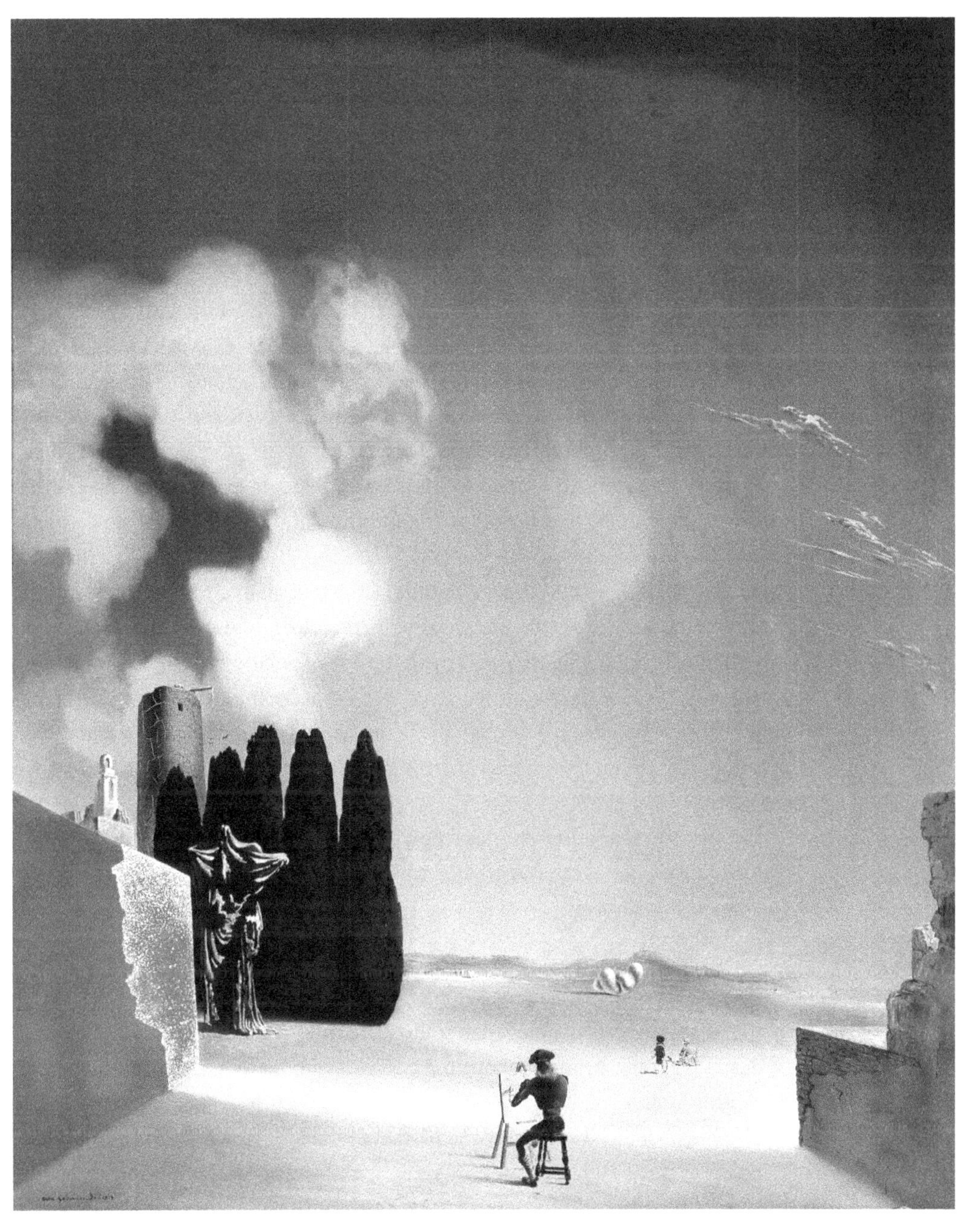

45. Salvador Dalí, *Enigmatic Elements in a Landscape*, 1934. Oil on panel, 72.8 × 59.5 cm (28.74 × 23.62 in.). Fundació Gala-Salvador Dalí, Figueres. Dalí, Salvador (1904–89) © ARS, NY.

his continued commitment to Vermeer's objectivity and identification with the small. Indeed, on more than one occasion Dalí paid homage to his imaginary mentor by inserting him, in ghostly form, directly into his paintings (*The Ghost of Vermeer van Delft, Enigmatic Elements in a Landscape* [fig. 45]).

Vermeer was not, however, a little thing like a blackhead or a booger. He may have been unjustly marginalized by historians who favored other artists whom Dalí considered less worthy, but he was by no means an object of derision or embarrassment. But there was a painter that Dalí admired whose relation to art history is more akin to a *moco* or a comedo: Ernest Meissonier. As the epitome of art at its most academic and antimodern, Meissonier's work could well be considered a kind of blackhead on the face of late-nineteenth-century art, an unsightly eruption on an otherwise grand history of avant-garde painting to which Dalí and his contemporaries were heir.

Dalí declared his allegiance to Meissonier in an open letter to Breton that served as the catalog text for his 1933 exhibition at the Galerie Pierre Colle (in which he showed, among other works, *The Fine, Average, Invisible Harp* and *Fried Eggs on the Plate without the Plate*). The text gives ample evidence of the growing tension between surrealism as Breton articulated it and Dalí's own surrealism of the tiny. Dalí began the letter by associating his newest paintings with a collection of disorienting phenomena that included photography, paranoia, art nouveau design (see chapter 6), the feeling of déjà vu, and trompe-l'œil painting. All of these phenomena, he said, are disruptive to our settled sense of the world.

But there was another phenomenon to be considered, one that Dalí thought Breton should be taking more seriously: the "little, edible, and fine aspect" of Meissonier's paintings.

> Meissonier, who, all of a sudden, has just recovered in my life, in my thoughts, in my preferences, the most obvious and parched relevance; a relevance that is solely comparable, I can tell you, to that of the very subtle, small, and desirable thirst brought about for a few days now by the representation of a certain table — half made of poached eggs, half of stone. . . . My solitude becomes huge and incurable the moment when, having arrived voluptuously parched at the cellar, I suddenly think with beating heart of Napoleon at the head of his army, in the Russian campaign, the horses with all their regulation straps in this snow of light and fine thirst that covers the landscape the "way" Meissonier painted it in a well-known and immortal picture.[38]

Dalí was, of course, fully aware that to champion the paintings of Meissonier was to mock surrealism: their meticulous realism was at odds with surrealism's conception of the mind and their heroizing of Napoleon an affront to surrealism's politics. Nevertheless, it is important to recognize that Meissonier was a tiny affront, a minor irritant. Had Dalí wished to champion the work of a major artist who could be said to stand as emblematic of reactionary politics and the robust manner of the European tradition, he might have chosen Hyacinthe Rigaud's *Portrait of Louis XIV* or David's *Portrait of Napoleon on Horseback*. That Dalí chose to endorse Meissonier's paintings was thus an expression, yet again, of his identification with all things "minime et débile" (stupid and insignificant). Indeed, for any number of Dalí's contemporaries, Meissonier's status within the art historical canon might well have been likened to a bread crumb or an insect on a picnic blanket: something to be brushed aside and quickly forgotten.[39]

Dalí's admiration for the "fine and edible" canvases of Meissonier is thus a logical endpoint to his decade-long search for "little things that prick." Like the sea urchins and sewing needles described in "Poem of Little Things" (see introduction) and the stray breasts and liberated fingers depicted in *Instrument and Hand* and *Little Ashes* (see chapter 1), Meissonier's miniaturist works were irritating little things, parasites on the body of art's great history. To propose that Meissonier be appreciated as "immortal" is to propose an absurdity, and the evident pleasure that Dalí derived from doing so recalls the giddiness he expressed to Lorca when he imagined the wild flight of dots escaping the letter *i*.

4

SUPERFICIALITY

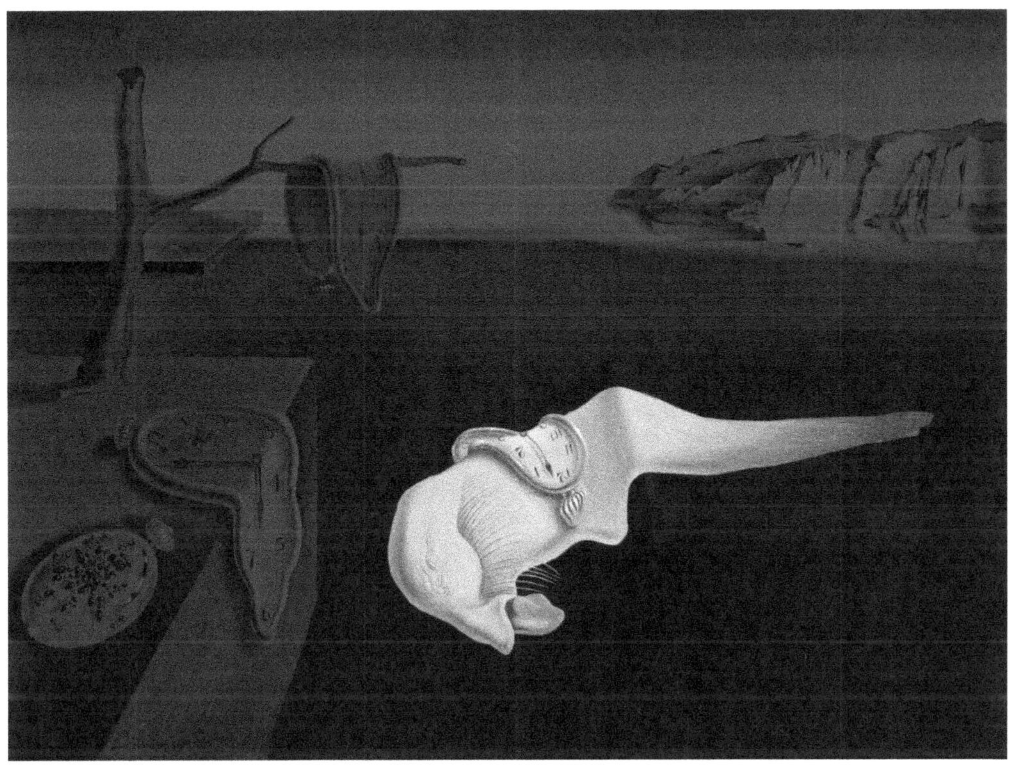

The self-portrait in the center of the painting depicts the artist in profile, with his left eye firmly shut and his lashes curling gently, his brow furrowed, and his hair closely cropped and slicked back against his scalp. His nose is impossibly large and he seems to have no mouth at all, but what is most disconcerting about this portrait is the fact that the head seems to have been drained of its internal organs, as if the bones, muscle, fat, and brain tissue had been sucked out of it by a vacuum cleaner. The result is that it looks less like a human head than a deflated balloon. It seems that what we are faced with is a portrait of the artist as an exterior without an interior, a being of surface alone, an envelope with nothing inside it.

SMOOTH SURFACES, ROUGH SURFACES, POLISHED SURFACES, STIPPLED SURFACES

This chapter asks two questions. First, to what extent did Dalí's engagement with the small serve as the foundation for a similarly complex engagement with the superficial and the simulacral? Second, in what ways was this engagement oriented in response to injunctions, modernist and surrealist alike, to reveal an inner world, one that was thought to be more "real" (more authentic and determinative) than the world of surfaces, the world of "mere" appearance? This chapter argues that Dalí's tiny surrealism was also a *superficial* surrealism. Like his surrealism of the small, Dalí's surrealism of the surface was developed in response to a range of aesthetic discourses in which depth and origin were privileged over surface and copy.

My argument begins with the simple observation that the little things that Dalí favored were often those that lived on or just beneath the surface of larger things: ants that crawled across a canvas and sea urchins that pricked the bottom of a foot (chapter 1), mucus that dripped from the nose and blackheads and hairs that emerged from beneath the skin (chapter 3). Likewise Dalí admired the camera for its fixed attention to the surface of things and paranoia-criticism for its refusal to embrace the demand that one's thought emanate from a rational core (chapter 2). As will be seen in this chapter, Dalí's celebration of surfaces (both industrial and natural) deserves to be understood as a particularly subversive celebration, as it ran counter to various modernist and avant-garde injunctions to "forget appearances," as Georges Braque once declared.[1] The injunction required, as Maurice Raynal put it, that one treat the techniques of the old masters as "arbitrary and rather childish" efforts to establish an art of "mere imitation."[2] By insisting to the contrary that the world of mere appearance was indeed the world that mattered, Dalí set out to offer an alternative ontology — one in which the surface was more significant than the interior and the copy more important than the original.

Like his interest in little things, Dalí's fascination with the world of surfaces emerged in the midtwenties. In a letter from June 1927, flush with enthusiasm for the technological marvels of modernity, Dalí declared to Lorca, "No epoch has ever known the perfection of ours. Until Machines were invented, there had never been anything perfect, and man had never seen anything as *beautiful* or *poetic* as a *nickel-plated* engine. . . . We are surrounded by perfect, novel beauty, which brings about new states of poetry."[3]

That Dalí delighted in the objects of modern industry was by no means exceptional. There was, however, something distinctive about the particularity of Dalí's delight, and this distinctiveness was underscored elsewhere in Dalí's letter. "I'm superficial," he declared, "and the outside of things is what delights me."[4] What Dalí hoped to make clear to Lorca was that the real beauty of the nickel-plated engine was not to be found in the engine's inner workings but in its outer appearance, its surface and shine. More than the engine itself, it was the nickel plating that Dalí found marvelous. (Indeed, in Dalí's letter it was the word *niquelado*, not *motor*, that was underlined for emphasis.) What mattered was not what the engine was able to *do* but what it *looked like*.

Published in 1928, Dalí's "Poetry of the Mass-Produced Utility" singled out objects like the telephone and the "little phonograph" not only because of their small scale but also, and no less significantly, because of their surface qualities, their texture and sheen.[5] Describing the photographic advertisements that fill magazines and newspapers and cover building walls and hoardings as "magnificent invitations to the sense and the voyage of discovery," Dalí focused in particular on the mesmerizing surface qualities of women's shoes as presented there: "Shoes occupying the entire page, perfect products, the eurythmic play of curves; alterations of diverse qualities, smooth surfaces, rough surfaces, polished surfaces, stippled surfaces; reflections that are clear, morbid, and intellectual, indicators of real mass, pure structural metaphors of the physiology of the foot. Marvelous photographs of shoes, as poetic as the most moving works of Picasso."[6]

Whereas Le Corbusier and others were interested in the methods of industrial manufacture and the functionalism of modern design, Dalí was unabashedly superficial. Rather than focus on construction or function, Dalí insisted that we fix our gaze on the myriad surfaces — smooth, rough, polished, stippled — of the objects captured in the lens of the camera.[7]

Dalí's comparison of advertising photographs with Picasso's work reminds us that at this moment Picasso was at the forefront of his mind. Paintings like *Still Life by Moonlight* (fig. 5), *Bather* (fig. 14), and *The Rotting Donkey* (fig. 13) clearly derive from Picasso's post-cubist pictorial vocabulary. Nevertheless, although compositionally indebted to Picasso, Dalí's work attends to surface effects with unique enthusiasm. In *Bather* and *The Rotting Donkey*, for example, the rough texture of the grains of sand and tiny pebbles affixed to the surface contrast sharply with the nearly glass-like finish of the painted areas. As Ades was the first to point out, Dalí was experimenting at this time with a variety of resins and often avoided using oil in his pigments.[8] The result was an enamel-like finish, with a surface of near-glass hardness and shine that, more so than Picasso's works, focused the viewer's attention as much on texture as on composition. In effect, Dalí was attempting to mimic the "poetry" of surfaces effected by the advertiser's use of photography.

In this Dalí was running counter to what Alain Badiou has described as the modernist "passion of the real" that figures such as Henri Bergson argued was the main source of art's significance: "Between nature and ourselves, nay, between ourselves and our own consciousness, a veil is interposed: a veil that is dense and opaque for the common herd — thin, almost transparent, for the artist and poet. . . . So art, whether it be painting or sculpture, poetry or music, has no other object than to brush aside the utilitarian symbols, the conventional and socially accepted generalities, in short, everything that veils reality from us, in order to bring us face to face with reality itself."[9]

Bergson's conception of the artist as one who boldly abandons convention so as to "bring us face to face with reality itself" is reflected in almost every subsequent defense of modern art. It played a crucial role, for example, in the development of cubist theory. As Jacques Rivière put it, "The true purpose of painting is to represent objects as they really are; that is to say, differently from the way we see them." Cubism, he argued, makes good on this by presenting to the viewer the "sensible *essence* [of objects], their presence; this is why the image it forms does not resemble their *appearance*."[10] Likewise, Robert Delaunay declared in 1912, "The first paintings were simply lines that traced the shadow of a figure made by the sun. But how far removed we are, with our contemporary means, from these simulacra — we who possess light."[11] Indeed, remarks like this are further evidence of what Geoffrey Hartman has called the modernist "quest for a pure representation," in which "the body itself becomes, in its contact with the physical world, the source and often the end of cognition."[12]

With regard to surrealism in particular, Breton considered the achievement of what Hartman referred to as "unmediated vision" to be the movement's animating ambition. Surrealism, Breton argued, peeled away the veneer of controlled, rational behavior to reveal the hidden world of aggression and desire. In this sense the prefix "sur-" in surrealism is misleading, for the movement was understood by its participants as a project dedicated to plumbing the depths of the real, digging beneath its superficial outer layer. "Surrealism," Breton declared in 1930, "aims quite simply at the total recovery of our psychic force by a means which is nothing other than the dizzying descent into ourselves, the systematic illumination of hidden places and the progressive darkening of other places, the perpetual excursion into the midst of forbidden territory."[13] As Maurice Nadeau put it in his retrospective account, surrealism's main ambition was to reveal "the hidden order that surrounds us."[14]

The extreme to which surrealism would go in pursuit of this endeavor to reveal the "hidden order" of the world and thereby "bring us face to face with reality itself" is detailed by Gilles Deleuze in his account of the writings of Antonin Artaud. Artaud's ambition, Deleuze argues, was to create a language of the body, a pure expression of desire and distress unmediated by ratiocination, a language of "depths without surfaces." "The consequence of this," writes Deleuze, "is that the entire body is no longer anything but depth — it carries along and snaps up everything into this gaping depth which represents a fundamental involution. . . . In this collapse of the surface, the entire world loses its meaning." Artaud's ambition was thus not only to remove the veil of outer appearance but, more radically, to create a language in which there would be no outer appearance at all — a language in which, as Deleuze puts it, "there is not, there is no longer, any surface."[15]

According to Deleuze, Artaud's language of pure depth is one of two opposing critiques of meaning production. The other — represented by Lewis Carroll — produces a form of nonsense in which it is depth that is banished, that is, a language of pure surface. While "Artaud is alone in having been an absolute depth in literature, . . . Carroll remains the master and the surveyor of surfaces."[16] Deleuze's distinction between Artaud's nonsense of depth and Carroll's nonsense of surface is especially useful in clarifying the degree to which Dalí's exuberant embrace of superficiality was at odds with one of surrealism's fundamental aspirations. Like Carroll, Dalí perceived the irrationality of the world as a manifestation of surface, not depths. Whereas for Artaud the most emblematic expression of unconscious desire was the scream that emanated from the depths of one's body, for Dalí it was the "eurythmic play of curves" and other purely superficial effects.

IT IS ALWAYS THE FALSE ONES THAT LOOK THE MOST REAL

"It's the same. But it's better in the picture, because in it you can count the waves."[17] According to Dalí, this is what Enriquet, a local fisherman in Cadaqués, once said while looking at one of his paintings. At the time Dalí had recently completed a number of seascapes in which the viewer can indeed count the waves (*Rocks of es Llaner* [fig. 46], 1926; *Penya-Segats* [*Woman on the Rocks*], 1926). The idea that a representation might be superior to the thing itself is one that fascinated Dalí at the time, and he tried to instill the same fascination in Lorca. "I've been painting all afternoon," he wrote to his friend, "7 cold, hard waves like the ones in the sea . . . , tomorrow I'll paint 7 more. I feel good because I've painted them *well* and every day the sea looks more and more like my painting."[18] Still a few years from embracing surrealism, Dalí was already fascinated by the idea of confounding our stable sense of reality. To what extent, he wondered, could representations supersede the object itself? It was a question that he continued to ask in the years that followed, and one that he understood to be closely connected to the issue of superficiality and the objectivity of the camera lens.

It was also, Dalí understood, a question that pertained to the distinction between the authentic and the fake, the original and the replica. That Dalí

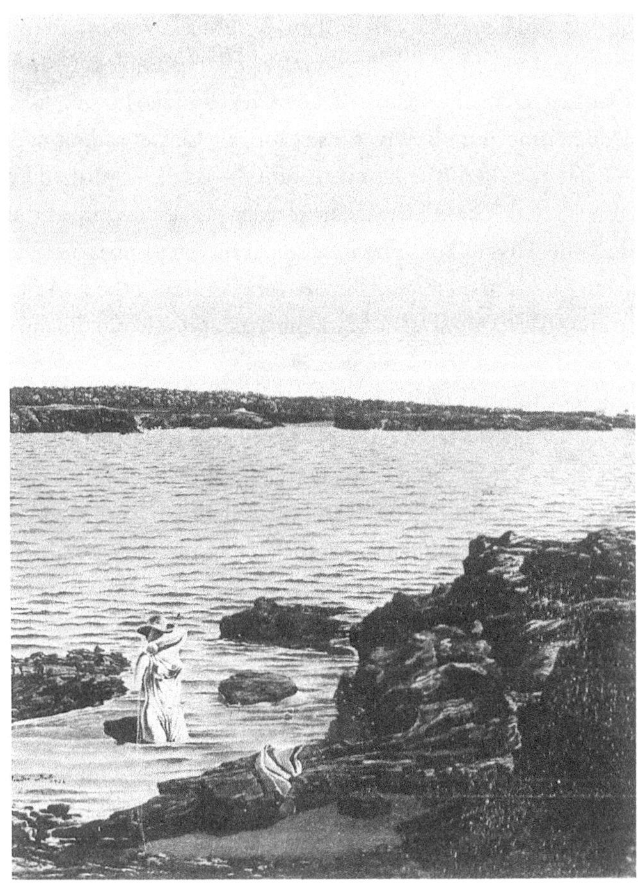

46. Salvador Dalí, *Rocks of es Llaner*, 1926. Oil on cardboard, 61 × 46 cm (24.02 × 18.11 in.). Fundació Gala-Salvador Dalí, Figueres. Dalí, Salvador (1904–89) © ARS, NY.

was attuned to this distinction and was drawn to the idea of confounding it is made clear in a passing remark he offered in an essay published in April 1928. Included among a collection of objects and observations that gave evidence of surrealism's significance (a list that included the "liberated" minute hands of a clock and a nude by Miró) was a reference to "wax museum figures on view at side-shows." That such things are devoid of real life and that they derive their compelling power from their deceptiveness does not, insisted Dalí, make them any less real.[19]

Like the distinction between appearance and reality, the distinction between the real and the fake was central to modernist discourse. Few taboos were more trenchant than the one that pertained to the inauthentic, and the dubious pleasure of the popular wax figure was among the most emblematic. Adolf von Hildebrand, for example, condemned wax figures alongside panoramas and the sculptures of Antonio Canova for their flagrant refusal to maintain the proper distance between reality and representation.[20] Similar examples abound, including Gustave Flaubert's diatribe against "fake materials, fake luxury, fake pride."[21] Nearer to Dalí in time and place was José Ortega y Gasset's identification of modern art — what he called "the new sensibility"— as distinguished by its resistance to what he called "sham," the clearest example of which was the mass spectacle of Madame Tussaud's: "The new sensibility, it seems to me, is dominated by a distaste for human elements in art very similar to the feelings cultured people have always experienced at Madame Tussaud's, while the mob has always been delighted by that gruesome wax hoax."[22]

Given his affirmation of the superficial and the visually deceptive, it is not surprising to find that Dalí was drawn not only to "wax museum figures on view at side-shows" but to a host of fake things. In a text from December 1928, for example, Dalí described a table made of "a heap of dry shellfish" on which "a bunch of carnations . . . served as a fake table cloth."[23] The poem "The Great Masturbator" (1930) included an even longer of list of fakes: first "fake brick," "fake gold," and "fake bronze medallions" and then "a seemingly fake grasshopper made up of an infinite number of tiny yet perfectly clear photographs of sharks."[24] In 1937 the subject of fakes came up again when Dalí proposed in a letter to Breton that the new surrealist gallery ought to be clad in "fake marble."[25]

In addition to fake things of the external world, Dalí was also fascinated by fake things of the mind — what he called "false memories." This is especially evident in the pages of his autobiography, *The Secret Life of Salvador Dalí*. In chapter 4, subtitled "False Childhood Memories," Dalí devoted a section to a period in his childhood (around age seven) when he began fabricating what he called "false memories": "The difference between false memories and true ones," he wrote, "is the same as for jewels: it is always the false ones that look the most real, the most brilliant."[26] Although begun in the late thirties and published in the early forties, this statement and others like it reveal a continuity of thought that began in the twenties when Dalí marveled at the idea that Enriquet found his painting of the ocean superior to the ocean itself.

In fact, Dalí first expressed an interest in the idea of false memories in 1929. In "The Liberation of the Fingers" he recounted a disturbing experience he had as young child when he caught a fish near his house in Cadaqués. Held in his hand, the fish's head seemed to suddenly transform itself into a grasshopper. From that time on, Dalí claimed, he lived with a dread of grasshoppers. The account is in itself strange enough, but it becomes only more so when the reader learns that the incident had been completely erased from Dalí's mind and had returned to him only after his father had recounted the story to him some years later. In the intervening years, however, this dread — based on an event that had at that time been unknown to him — had driven him to invent what he described as a variety of "entirely false stories" to explain his phobia — stories that he had for some time thought of as true.[27] The lesson that Dalí claimed to have drawn from this confluence of the actual and the imaginary was that the latter was no less real than the former. Pictures are sometimes better than the real thing, tall tales as influential as true memories, fake diamonds as brilliant as real ones. Dalí was constructing for himself a world in which the distinction between the real and the imaginary, the original and copy no longer held. In such an environment the Bergsonian ambition that animated Breton, Artaud, and others was for Dalí entirely gratuitous.

Ironically, the most controversial of all of Dalí's fake things was one in which the controversy stemmed from the misperception that it was real. In the summer of 1929, as he was preparing for his show at Goemans's gallery in Paris, Dalí was visited by Éluard and Gala as well as by Luis Buñuel, René Magritte, and Camille Goemans. Upon being presented with *The Lugubrious Game* (fig. 19), a number of them said they were disturbed by the depiction of the man in the lower right-hand corner whose white pants were stained with feces. As he recounted in *The Secret Life*, "The drawers bespattered with excrement were painted with such minute and realistic complacency that the whole little surrealist group was anguished by the question: Is he coprophagic or not?" The appearance of this figure in the corner was not the only evidence that lead them to ask this question; apparently Dalí had spent a good part of their time together regaling his guests with a host of excremental fantasies. "Imagine to yourselves," he said one day to his visitors, "that you see in your own mind a certain very respectable person. All right. Now go on and imagine a little sculptured owl perched on his head — a rather stylized owl, except for his face which must be quite realistic." After feeling convinced that everyone had managed to plant this image in their mind, he asked them to "imagine on the owl's head a piece of my excrement! . . . Of my own excrement!" According to *The Secret Life*, Gala was compelled to take him aside and confront him: "It's a very important work," Dalí recalled her saying,

> And it is precisely for this reason that Paul and I and all your friends would like to know what certain elements, to which you seem to attach a special importance, refer to. If those "things" refer to your life we can have nothing in common, because that sort of thing appears loathsome to me, and hostile to my kind of life. But this concerns only your own life, and has nothing to do with mine. On the other hand, if you intend to use your pictures as a means of proselytism and propaganda — even in the service of what you may consider an inspired idea — we believe you run the risk of weakening your work considerably, and reducing it to a mere psychopathological document.[28]

"I swear," Dalí replied in his defense, "I am not 'coprophagic.' I consciously loathe that type of aberration as much as you can possibly loathe it. But I consider scatology as a terrorizing element, just as I do blood, or my phobia for grasshoppers."[29]

His response seemed to satisfy her, but by the time the painting was shown at Goemans's gallery later that year, word of Dalí's excremental antics had traveled to Paris and the figure in the lower right-hand corner of *The Lugubrious Game* had buried itself deeply into Breton's mind. In *The Secret Life* Dalí recalled an encounter with Breton in which he expressed, as had Gala the summer before, distress over the scatological element in *The Lugubrious Game*. "The involuntary aspect of this element, so characteristic in psychopathological iconography, should have sufficed to enlighten him [Breton]," Dalí recounted. "But I was obliged to justify myself by saying that it was merely a simulacrum. No further questions were asked. But had I been pressed I should certainly have had to answer that it was the simulacrum of the excrement itself."[30]

Neither Gala's concern nor Breton's displeasure was enough to stop Dalí from returning to the subject of scatology. A similarly stained pair of pants appears on the figure of the piano player in the upper register of *William Tell* (fig. 36) and more egregiously still in the explicitly coprophagic characters depicted in the frontispiece to *La femme visible* (fig. 54). Buried within the thicket of densely crosshatched lines, a pair of bearded men open their mouths to receive the excrement expelled from two naked behinds.[31]

Some scholars have interpreted his assurance to Breton that his depiction was "merely a simulacrum" (as well as his subsequent refusal to permit Bataille to include a reproduction of *The Lugubrious Game* in "The Language of Flowers") as an indication that Dalí was buckling before surrealism's most powerful figure.[32] However, there is more compelling evidence to support the claim that when Dalí assuaged Breton by insisting that the excrement-stained man in *The Lugubrious Game* was "merely a simulacrum" he was in fact telling him the truth.

As we have seen, Dalí had developed a fascination with things like fake gold and false memories, so there is little reason to question his interest in simulated excrement. Indeed, "The Great Masturbator" includes not only references to fake gold, fake bronze, and fake brick but also to fake shit:

> Farther away
> past the second face of the Great Masturbator
> rose
> two large sculptures of William Tell
> one made
> of real chocolate
> the other of fake shit [fausse merde][33]

Given Dalí's longstanding interest in wax figures and the idea that a painted picture could be in some way superior to the view itself, Dalí's statement to Breton cannot be so easily dismissed as craven misrepresentation. His response to the poet was clever indeed, not because it was dishonest but because it managed to appease him while surreptitiously suggesting something altogether more subversive: that the depiction of fake shit might in fact be more disruptive than the depiction of the real thing.

NEW AND MENACING SIMULACRA

The 1942 publication of *The Secret Life* was not the first time that Dalí used the word *simulacrum*. In fact, the term appears in each of the four texts published collectively in 1930 under the title *La femme visible* ("Le grand masturbateur," "L'amour," L'âne pourri," and "La chèvre sanitaire"). (The word *simulacre* appears occasionally in the first two texts and frequently in the latter two.) Although *La femme visible* is typically mined for its analysis of the double image (as it appears in works such as *The Invisible Man* and *Invisible Sleeping Woman, Horse, Lion* [figs. 20, 21]) and for its theory of paranoia criticism,[34] it is just as valuable for its insights into Dalí's conception of the simulacrum. That the title of the book is the *visible* woman is the first indication that what was at stake for Dalí was the means by which a thing becomes a representation.

The *visible* woman — as distinct from the *actual* woman — is the simulacrum at the center of Dalí's concern in these four texts. In its everyday usage — more common in French than English — a simulacrum is simply a representation, an image in two or three dimensions of an object or event in the real world. Dalí sometimes used the word *simulacrum* in this way, but most often he inflected it with a sense of being a *false* representation of some sort.[35] For Dalí, the simulacrum mattered not because it represented an object or event but rather because it somehow undermined the very object or event it represented. Such simulacra were, as Dalí put it, "corrosive."[36] What they corrode is the divide between reality and representation, the original and the copy. Like the seascapes admired by Enriquet the fisherman, corrosive simulacra mesmerize us to the point where we find ourselves drawn more to the painted picture than to reality. As Dalí put it in "The Rotting Donkey," the simulacra that interested him were those that "systematize confusion and thereby contribute to a total discrediting of the world of reality."[37]

Lomas has argued that "Dalí's penchant for simulation and the simulacral" was a solution to a "defining problematic for Surrealism."[38] This is certainly true, although it is important to underscore that for Dalí this was not only a response to an issue within surrealism, it was also a logical extension of his own pre-surrealist theories of superficiality.[39] The closest analog to Dalí's understanding of the simulacrum is the one proposed by Deleuze in his analysis of Plato's distinction between "good" and "bad" copies (*eikon* and *phantasma*). The *eikon* is a "good copy" because it truly resembles its model; the *phantasma* (which Deleuze renames the *simulacrum*) is a "bad copy" because it only appears to resemble its model. According to this definition, the simulacrum is endowed with a unique power unavailable to the faithful *eikon*, what Deleuze calls the power of "the false." Like Dalí's "corrosive" simulacrum, the *phantasma* "engulfs all foundation, it assures a universal breakdown."[40]

Considered in this light, "The Rotting Donkey," which is typically read for its clues to Dalí's understanding of paranoia, is in fact more accurately understood as an attempt to provide a catalog of the different types of "corrosive" simulacra (the *phantasma*'s power of "the false"). Although he did not explicitly enumerate them as such, the "bad copies" that interested Dalí can be divided into five distinct types: the paranoiac image, the double image, the repulsive simulacrum, the solidified desire, and the gratuitous point.

The first order of corrosive simulacra — the paranoiac image — systematizes confusion in the manner discussed in chapter 2: the images produced by the mind of the paranoiac are simultaneously irrational and indisputable. Were they merely one or the other, they would fail to corrode our sense of reality. Their "precision" and "objectivity" make them impossible to reject, and at the same time, their irrationality makes them impossible to accept. As Dalí put it, "All physicians are of one mind in recognizing the swiftness and inconceivable subtlety commonly found in paranoiacs, who, taking advantage of associations and facts so refined as to escape normal people, reach conclusions that often cannot be contradicted or rejected and that in any case nearly always defy psychological analysis."[41] Dalí's paintings of this period give ample evidence of the "swiftness and inconceivable subtlety" of the paranoiac — one finds them, for example, in the objects and events that litter the landscape in *The First Days of Spring* (fig. 16) as well as those that erupt from the torso of the central figure in *The Lugubrious Game* (fig. 19).

The second order of corrosive simulacra — the double image — is a special instance of the first. Under certain circumstances, Dalí claimed, the mind of the paranoiac is capable of producing an image that is not only subtle, precise, and completely irrational but is also simultaneously a depiction of two entirely different objects. "It is by a distinctly paranoiac process," he claimed, "that it has been possible to obtain a double image; in other words, a representation of an object that is also, without the slightest pictorial or anatomical modification, the representation of another entirely different object."[42] The example Dalí gave is that of his recently completed painting, *Invisible Sleeping Woman, Horse, Lion* (fig. 21), in which a representation of a woman with her head thrown back is at the same time a representation of both a horse and a lion. Pictures such as this one were made to serve as proof that reality is not given to us but is instead produced by our mind in its capacity to invent and reinvent reality at will. As he put it in "The Moral Position of Surrealism": "I would be curious to find out what it is that the image under consideration really represents, what is the truth; and, right away, doubts are raised in our minds regarding the question of whether the images of reality itself are not merely products of our own paranoiac capacity."[43]

Dalí's third type — what I am calling the repulsive simulacrum — is an image that disturbs us not because it is irrational but rather because it is overwhelmingly terrifying. The examples Dalí included — "blood, excrement, and putrefaction" — appear in a number of paintings of this period — not only in the figure with the soiled pants in *The Lugubrious Game* but also in the depiction of the tiny stream of blood that sometimes drips from the nose of Dalí's alter ego, the Great Masturbator, as well as in myriad depictions of rotting carcasses (*The Rotting Donkey* [fig. 13]; *William Tell* [fig. 36]).[44] Whereas Dalí provided an extended analysis of the first two types, the repulsive simulacra were left largely unexplained. Nevertheless, it is possible to understand them, as Lomas has, as instances of Kristevan abjection.[45] Things such as blood, excrement, and putrefaction exist, Julia Kristeva proposed, in the gap between subject and object: they contain aspects of life and death, the animate and the inanimate, the nutritive and the morbid.[46] As such, they threaten the basic distinction between self and other on which our identity in the world depends. In "The Rotting Donkey" Dalí presented the repulsiveness of blood, excrement, and putrefaction as further evidence of the divide between appearance and reality: "Nor do we know if the three great simulacra, excrement, blood, and putrefaction, do not expressly conceal the coveted 'treasure land.' Connoisseurs of images, we have long ago learned to recognize the image of desire hidden behind the simulacra of terror, and even the awakening of 'Golden Ages' in the ignominious scatological simulacra."[47]

The fourth type — the solidified desire — is a three-dimensional object that has been extruded (like a blackhead) from the mind. Dalí's main example of desire made real was art nouveau design: "This imposing mass of frenzied and cold buildings spread over all of Europe, despised and neglected by anthologies and scholarly surveys." They are despised and neglected, he claimed, because they refuse to recognize the modernist imperative toward functionality. Rather than follow the demands of usefulness, the organic mimicry of Hector Guimard's famous Métro stations and other cast-iron works introduce an elaborate organicism of simulated flora that Dalí understood as "a dream world so pure and so disturbing . . . a true realization of solidified desires."[48]

Three years after the publication of "The Rotting Donkey," Dalí elaborated on his conception of Guimard's designs as betraying "a hatred of reality and the need to find refuge in an ideal world."[49] In "Concerning the Terrifying and Edible Beauty of Art Nouveau Architecture" Dalí juxtaposed photographic details of Guimard's buildings with captions that seemed to suggest that the inanimate objects had sprung to life only to demand that they be released from their newfound existence. ("Eat me!" demands one. "Me too," pleads another [fig 47].)[50] As suggested by Dalí's claim that such objects hate reality and wish "to find refuge in an ideal world," the corrosiveness of art nouveau derives from the sense that this is an architecture that refuses to accept itself as such, an architecture that in some way would prefer that it were a picture or a dream. That the designs are unable to exist as representation and are instead consigned to persist as real is the source of their unremitting distress.

The gratuitous point — the fifth and final type of corrosive simulacra — is the most complex and difficult to summarize. In effect, it is the inverse of the fourth in that it begins as a material object only to end up as a mental image. If art nouveau architecture is desire made real, then the gratuitous point is reality made into desire. More precisely, the gratuitous point is the moment when the former becomes the latter, when the real thing becomes the mind's desire.

"The Rotting Donkey," mentions this concept only in passing (as the manifestation of the simulacrum's "lack of congruity with reality"), but Dalí develops it at great length in "The Sanitary Goat."[51] (The title offers a clue to the essay's structure and significance as it echoes inversely "The Rotten Donkey," with which it was paired in *La femme visible*: rotten/sanitary, donkey/goat.) Unfortunately, this essay is even more difficult to summarize than "The Rotting Donkey," and it contains few graphic phrases that can be extracted for isolated consideration. While it is certainly true that all of Dalí's texts are complex, digressive, and difficult to summarize, "The Sanitary Goat" is among the most impenetrable. The only way to make sense of this text is to examine a number of long and rambling passages (a few of which appear below). Nevertheless, it provides crucial evidence of Dalí's theory of the simulacrum. It also, and perhaps more importantly, makes it possible to comprehend a number of paintings (such as *Paranoiac-Astral Image* and *White Calm* [figs. 48, 49]) that would otherwise seem to be at odds with Dalí's more well-known works.

Because "The Sanitary Goat" is a dense and convoluted text, it is useful to begin by establishing a sense of its general structure and rhetorical technique. Dalí's intention seems to have been to reveal his central concept slowly and haltingly so as to manifest in the reader's mind the very confusion that is the subject of the essay. Here, for example, is the opening passage:

> At the moment when doubting the evidence of our senses has just assumed the systematic form of a rigorous process, of which we should expect nothing

fonctionnaliste dans les architectures connues du passé, dans le Modern' Style ne sert subitement plus à rien du tout, ou, ce qui ne saurait lui concilier l'intellectualisme pragmatiste ne sert plus qu'au « fonctionnement des désirs », d'ailleurs les plus troubles, disqualifiés et inavouables. De grandioses colonnes et des colonnes moyennes, inclinées, incapables de se soutenir par elles-mêmes, telles le cou fatigué des lourdes têtes hydrocéphales, émergent pour la première fois dans le monde des ondulations dures de *l'eau sculptée* avec le souci photographique de l'instantanéité, jusqu'alors inconnu. Elles montent par vagues des reliefs polychromes, dont l'ornementation immatérielle fige les transitions convulsives des faibles matérialisations des métamorphoses les plus fugitives de la fumée, ainsi que les végétaux aquatiques et la chevelure de ces femmes nouvelles, plus « appétissantes » encore que la petite soif causée par la température imaginative de la vie des extases florales où elles s'anéantissent. Ces colonnes de chair fièvreuse, légèrement fièvreuse (37,5 dixièmes) ne sont destinées à soutenir rien d'autre que la fameuse libellule à l'abdomen mou et lourd comme le bloc de plomb massif où elle a été sculptée de façon subtile et éthérée, bloc de plomb de nature (par son ridicule excès de pesanteur qui introduit pourtant l'idée nécessaire de gravité) à accentuer, aggraver et compliquer perversement le sentiment sublime d'infinie et glaciale stérilité, à rendre plus compréhensible et plus lamentable le dynamisme irrationnel de la colonne, laquelle, par suite de toutes ces circonstances de fine ambivalence, ne peut manquer de nous apparaître comme la véritable « colonne masochiste » destinée uniquement à « se laisser dévorer par le désir », comme la véritable première *colonne molle* construite et découpée dans cette réelle viande désirée vers laquelle Napoléon,

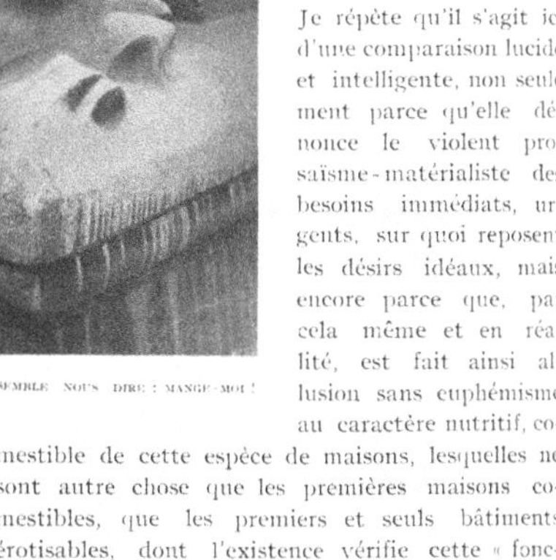

La base molle de cette colonne  semble nous dire : mange-moi !

comme nous savons, se dirige toujours à la tête de tous les réels et véritables impérialismes, qui, comme nous avons coutume de le répéter, ne sont autre chose que les immenses « cannibalismes de l'histoire » souvent figurés par cette côtelette concrète, grillée et savoureuse que le merveilleux matérialisme dialectique a placé, comme l'authentique Guillaume Tell, sur la tête même de la politique.

C'est donc, à mon sens, précisément (je n'insisterai jamais assez sur ce point de vue) l'architecture tout idéale du Modern' Style qui incarnerait la plus tangible et délirante aspiration d'hyper-matérialisme. On trouvera une illustration de ce paradoxe apparent dans une comparaison courante, employée il est vrai en mauvaise part, mais pourtant si lucide, qui consiste à assimiler une maison modern'style à un gâteau, à une tarte exhibitionniste et ornementale de « confiseur ». Je répète qu'il s'agit ici d'une comparaison lucide et intelligente, non seulement parce qu'elle dénonce le violent prosaïsme-matérialiste des besoins immédiats, urgents, sur quoi reposent les désirs idéaux, mais encore parce que, par cela même et en réalité, est fait ainsi allusion sans euphémisme au caractère nutritif, comestible de cette espèce de maisons, lesquelles ne sont autre chose que les premières maisons comestibles, que les premiers et seuls bâtiments érotisables, dont l'existence vérifie cette « fonction » urgente et si nécessaire pour l'imagination amoureuse : pouvoir le plus réellement manger l'objet du désir.

★

Le Modern' Style, architecture phénoménale.
Caractéristiques générales du phénomène.

72

47. An illustration from Salvador Dalí, "Concerning the Terrifying and Edible Beauty of Art Nouveau Architecture," *Minotaure* (Paris), December 12, 1933.

other than the collapse and unconditional surrender of reality, it is interesting to observe the backwardness of poetic thought, which could be considered without exaggeration, from the psychoanalytic point of view, as being anterior to the affective conflict, this thought having as its basis and as its sole criterion the most simple psychological reactions of sensations. The impressionism lingering in poetic thought has shown itself in a partial manner and as if skin-deep in the whole anti-intellectual trend, and in particular in the Ionian side of Bergson's ideas.[52]

Dalí's argument thus begins with the assumption that the naïve trust that once characterized our attitude toward the evidence of our senses no longer abides. In fact, doubting our senses has become a "rigorous process." In this we can recognize the same sensibility that subtended the Bergsonian imperative to lift the veil of deception so as to "bring us face to face with reality itself": at a moment in which we can no longer trust our senses to provide us with a true picture of "reality itself," we must proceed with caution, ever suspicious that our senses may deceive us.

Dalí's response to this condition, however, was entirely opposed to Bergson's. Where Bergson insisted that the veil be removed so that reality may be apprehended directly, Dalí asked that we instead focus our attention on the surface effects of the veil that hides reality. Although it is not yet stated explicitly in this opening paragraph, the reader begins to intuit Dalí's inversion of the Bergsonian imperative when confronted by the paragraph's denigration of "lingering" impressionism and "the backwardness of poetic thought." Insofar as poetry insists on pulling aside the veil of appearance, it betrays a foolish refusal to accept the fundamental uncertainty of our senses. For Dalí, the only proper response is to accept "the collapse and unconditional surrender of reality" and instead attend exclusively to the one thing we can know objectively: the veil itself.[53]

Following this initial assault on the modernist imperative to unveil the true world beyond the superficial particularities of appearance, Dalí proposed an alternative theory of representation, a theory that would take into account the unbridgeable divide between what we see "objectively" and what we "subjectively" imagine to exist behind appearances.[54] In particular, what interested Dalí was the moment when an individual suddenly realizes that the imagined connection between an observed phenomenon and an underlying truth of the matter does not hold. At this moment a tear is introduced into our experience of the world, a tear that did not exist at first and that, upon emerging, can never be repaired.

The name that Dalí gave to this moment was "the gratuitous point." As was the case with his introductory paragraph, the passage in which Dalí defined this concept does not lend itself to excerpting (and in fact requires, I believe, that the reader peruse it slowly and repeatedly in order to make sense of it):

> This gratuitous point . . . might take shape in the gesture, generally taken to be erratic, of a person who, without knowing how to play the piano, imitates (perfectly) on a marble table the confident fingering of a true pianist, convinced of the absolute similarity of his imitation. I have said that this geometric point would be, quite unlike a vague aspiration toward generalities, something strictly concrete, and I am going to finish proving this by adding that this point, in the case under consideration, would materialize precisely at the moment when the fake pianist would lose for a moment his absolute faith in his imitation, but would continue with it nonetheless with no less enthusiasm. I propose naming [this] geometric point . . . *The Sanitary Goat* . . . [because] to this very moment I have not found any conscious or unconscious relationship between this name and that which it serves to designate.[55]

Before unraveling this knotty passage, it is worth noting one of the more obvious aspects about it: in terms of the imagery evoked, there is nothing especially strange or extraordinary. Unlike the immediate puzzlement of the double image or the disturbing rants of the paranoiac and the repulsiveness of scatology and putrescence, the scene described here is altogether ordinary: someone is pretending to play the piano. What Dalí wants us to recognize is that at a certain moment the apparently banal act of pretending may suddenly become otherworldly. To label this moment "The Sanitary Goat" (a phrase inapplicable to any real-world phenomenon) is to underscore the gratuitousness at the heart of the phenomenon — the moment, that is, when the copy fails to resemble the thing it originally set out to copy. In other words, the phrase is itself a gratuitous point, a name without any relation to the thing it names.

Although the text includes no explicit connection between the concept of the "gratuitous point" and the paintings on which Dalí was working at the time, it nonetheless suggests a way of approaching them. It suggests, that is, that we think about them as "gratuitous points": representations that have at some point detached themselves from the world of reality to which they had once been connected (at least *thought* themselves connected: remember that this is a "fake" pianist whose gestures don't resemble those of someone who truly knows how to play the piano). Thus, although the prevailing accounts of Dalí's surrealist paintings argue that they should be understood as abandoning visible, outer reality for the invisible, inner reality of the unconscious, this is not what Dalí's text asserts. If we are to understand Dalí's paintings according to the example given here, then they are not to be understood as faithful representations of a dream world or an unconscious fantasy. In fact, they are to be understood as altogether false representations, that is, as *phantasma*, or "bad copies." Put another way, if Artaud is best understood as having attempted to create "depths without surfaces," as Deleuze put it, then perhaps Dalí's work should be understood as attempting to create surfaces without depths.

Consider, for example, *Paranoiac-Astral Image* (fig. 48) and *White Calm* (fig. 49). Both are small paintings and finely crafted, with hardly a single visible brushstroke. At first blush they look like photographs. Like *Mediumnistic-Paranoiac Image* (fig. 42, discussed in chapter 3), both *Paranoiac-Astral Image* and *White Calm* depict a collection of figures and figural groups dispersed across a wide and empty seashore. Like *Mediumnistic-Paranoiac Image*, both include in the foreground a curiously pitched and oddly colorful broken amphora. In all three cases the imagery is rather serene, almost bland. They include none of the elements for which Dalí is famous: no blood, feces, or putrefaction; no explicit violence; no distended figures; no monstrous beings; no double images. One might even wonder if they really are works by Dalí.

Upon closer inspection, however, certain small irregularities emerge. For instance, what is one to make of the windblown fabric that seems to be attached to the man on the left side of *Paranoiac-Astral Image*? Is such a thing possible? And what about the ghostly female form in the center, the woman in an oddly outmoded costume who seems not to walk on the sand but to glide above it? A similar conundrum emerges in *White Calm* when one seeks to make sense of the rigid frontality of the figures, all of whom address the viewer like objects arranged on a table.[56] The painting's disquieting artificiality is underscored by the rhythmical deployment of the figures: a man with a straw hat and pitchfork resting atop his shoulder; a young woman with her arms extended upward, her elbows bent, and her hands clasped behind her head; another woman in the distance, also with bent elbows, but this time with arms turned downward, hands on her hips. (Upon noticing that the women's arms mimic the amphora's two handles, the two human figures begin to appear all the more unnatural.) What looked at first to be a photograph suddenly seems too well arranged, too perfectly aligned.

The feeling one has when looking at these paintings is thus analogous to the feeling described by Dalí in "The Sanitary Goat." It is the feeling one has at the moment one realizes that the pianist is "fake." It is also the feeling of the pianist himself at the moment when he no longer cares that his fingering is wrong ("the moment when the fake pianist would lose for a moment his absolute faith in his imitation, but would continue with it nonetheless with no less enthusiasm"). This is the moment in which the pianist feels the pleasure of the *phantasma*. Whereas most of Dalí's works of the thirties set out to manifest the "corrosiveness" of the repulsive image and the double image, paintings such

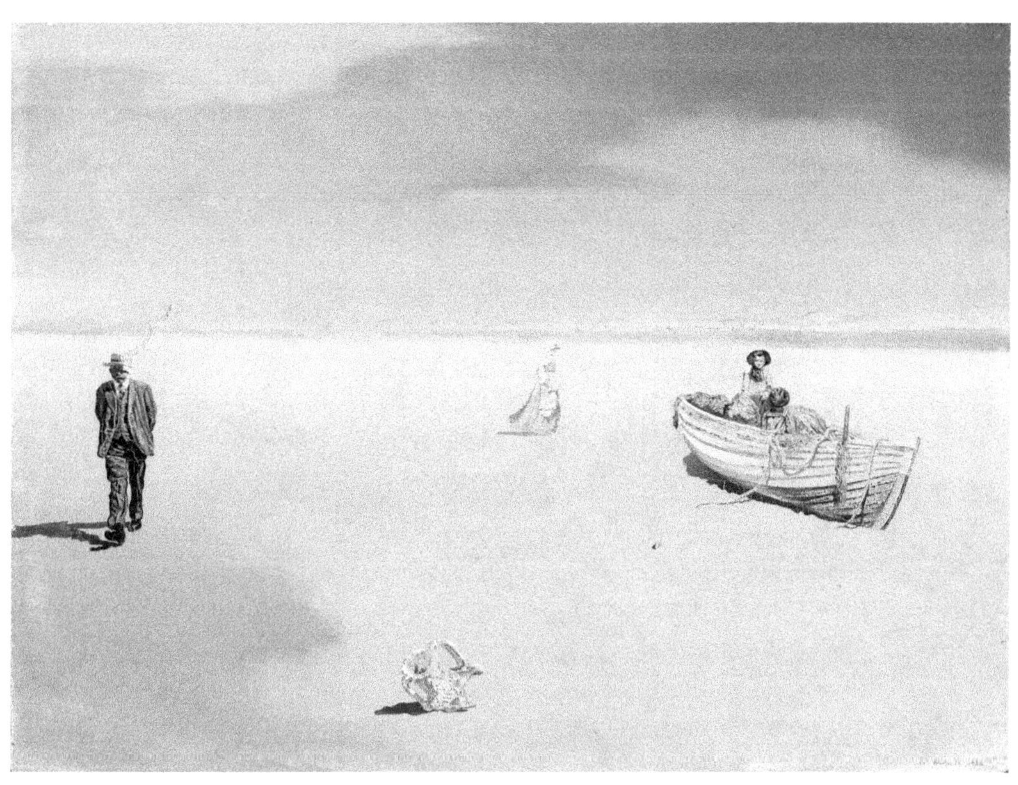

48. Salvador Dalí, *Paranoiac-Astral Image*, 1934. Oil on panel, 15.8 × 22.1 cm (6¼ × 8¾ in.). The Ella Gallup Sumner and Mary Catlin Sumner Collection Fund, 1935 (1935.10). Wadsworth Atheneum Museum of Art, Hartford CT. Dalí, Salvador (1904–89) © ARS, NY. Photo credit: Wadsworth Atheneum Museum of Art/Art Resource, NY.

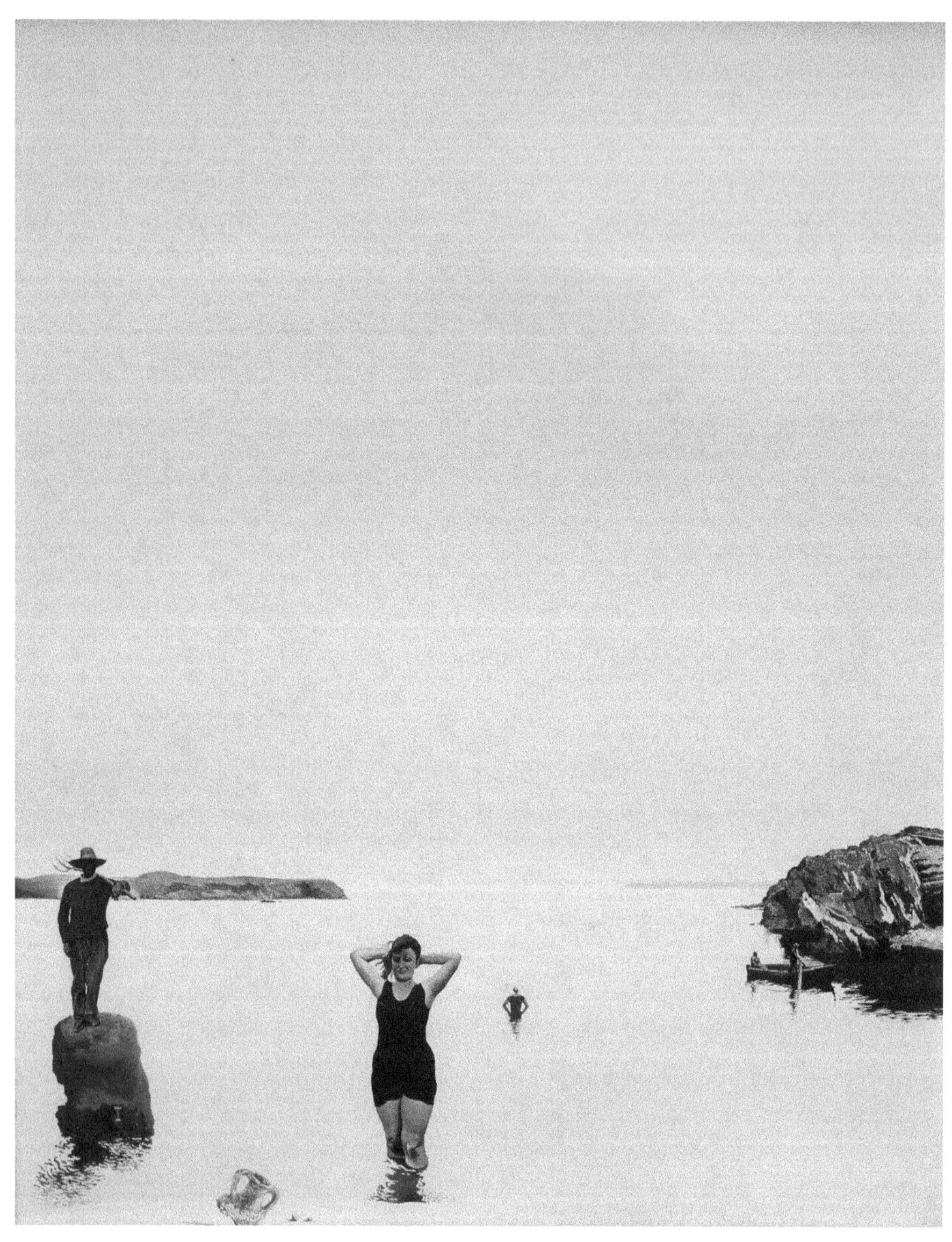

49. Salvador Dalí, *White Calm*, 1936. Oil on wood panel, 41 × 33 cm (16.14 × 12.99 in.). Private collection. Image provided by the Fundació Gala-Salvador Dalí. Dalí, Salvador (1904–89) © ARS, NY.

as these attempted the more difficult task of provoking the subtle disruption of the gratuitous. In such works the disruption is provoked not by a grotesque distortion or monstrous creation but rather by the momentary sensation of an almost imperceptible yet unbridgeable gap between reality and representation. In effect, the concept of the gratuitous point — the copy that "pricks" precisely because it is so perfect (both objective and precise) — is the limit point of Dalí's aesthetic of superficiality, the end result of his exuberant declaration to Lorca that he is "superficial" and that "it is the outside of things" that delights him.

THE ENVELOPE

Dalí, we have seen, had a habit of applying different names to the same underlying concept. Previous chapters have shown how the term "objectivity" was later referred to as "the documentation of minutiae," while terms such as "the aerodynamic blackhead," "the threadless spool," and "the antigeodesic hair" were used to denominate different instances of the same phenomenon. This is also the case with Dalí's concept of "the simulacrum." Although occasionally used in the years that followed (we saw Dalí use it in *The Secret Life* to describe *The Lugubrious Game*), it most often appeared under a different name. For example, in "The New Colors of Spectral Sex-Appeal" (1934) Dalí returned to the concept of the simulacra but this time referred to it as "the envelope." Like the five types of corrosive simulacra outlined in "The Rotting Donkey," the envelope "systematizes confusion" by hiding within it an entirely unknown world. In particular, the envelope corrodes our confidence in the existence of *volume*: "The envelope hides, protects, transfigures, stirs up, tempts, gives a misleading notion of volume. — It causes ambivalence with regard to volume and makes the volume become suspect — It promotes the birth of delirious theories regarding volume. — It provokes the giddiness of an ideal knowledge of volume, of an inconsistent knowledge of volume. — The envelope dematerializes the contents, the volume, debilitates the objectivity of volume, turns the volume virtual and agonizing."[57]

With this, Dalí offered his most explicitly formalist account of his practice. Paintings such as *Paranoiac-Astral Image* and *White Calm* — paintings that are difficult to reconcile with Dalí's more obviously surrealist works — are best understood as instances of the envelope's power to "hide, protect, transfigure, stir up, tempt, and give a misleading notion of volume." The "corrosiveness" of these paintings relies not on the particularities of the imagery but rather on the way in which that imagery is presented.

Two years after presenting the idea of "the envelope," Dalí introduced a more explicitly geometrical theory of superficiality. "The Spectral Surrealism of the

Pre-Raphaelite Eternal Feminine" (1936) offered a mockingly aggressive riposte to the legacy of Cézanne as manifested in the works of geometric abstraction. Against Cézanne — whom he described as a "Platonic bricklayer who is satisfied with a program consisting of the straight line [and] circle"— Dalí offered what he called "Pre-Raphaelite morphology."[58] Like the maligned academicism of Meissonier's work and the "despised and neglected" buildings of art nouveau, the paintings of the Pre-Raphaelites were anathema to the avant-garde and thus served Dalí as exemplary parasites. Their work "was summed up in the lukewarm and weak gravity of the 'depressive catenaries' of underwear adapting themselves to the most terrifying of strained and strict costumes, with the geodesic curves of sculptural bodies, of turgescent, disturbing, and imperialist flesh."[59] With this description of underwear Dalí offered a restatement of his concept of the envelope that "hides, protects, transfigures, stirs up, tempts, gives a misleading notion of volume." But by introducing what he called the "depressive catenary" Dalí oriented the concept in a new direction. With this he proposed a term with which to establish a theory of geometry that would stand in direct opposition to the theories of Léger, Piet Mondrian, and other abstractionists who were exhibiting together in Paris under the banners of "Cercle et carré" and "Abstraction-création."

Dalí was undoubtedly pleased by the idea that a catenary — in French, a "chaînette" (literally, "little chain") — is something of a geometric little thing. He was likely influenced as well by the fact that Antoni Gaudí used the catenary to construct his fluid forms. In addition, the catenary was a shape to which he could associate, in conjunction with the geodesic (see chapter 3), his evolving aesthetic of the soft and the hard. As a catenary is a shape produced by holding the two ends of a rope and tracing the sagging curve in the middle, it is, in a sense, the abstract representation of limpness, flaccidity as it is represented mathematically. By contrast, the geodesic is the geometrical shape of the erect, as it is the line formed by holding a rope taut against the surface of a three-dimensional curve. Of course, the catenary is also, as Dalí himself noted, a form readily associated with the old masters, as it is a shape that describes the folds that form at the base of a heavy curtain.[60] In other words, the catenary is the geometry of pictorial illusionism and thus the morphological antithesis of Cézanne's "sphere, cone and cylinder." Another way to put this is that whereas cones, spheres, and cylinders are the abstract forms of the interior, catenaries and geodesics are the abstract forms of the exterior. As such, they belong to the morphology of appearances, the geometry of the simulacrum.

As had been the case with so many of the neologisms that Dalí invented, the catenary vanished from his writing almost immediately after it emerged. The envelope, however, made a brief appearance in the midsixties when it was

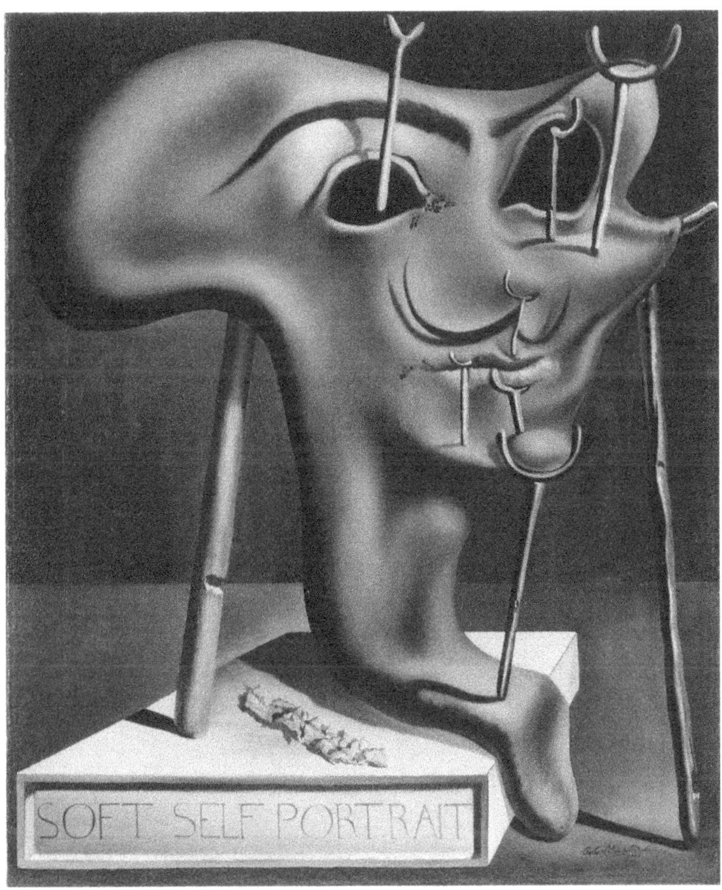

50. Salvador Dalí, *Soft Self-Portrait with Grilled Bacon*, 1941. Oil on canvas, 61 × 51 cm (24.02 × 20.08 in.). Town Hall of Figueres, on permanent deposit at the Fundació Gala-Salvador Dalí, Figueres. Dalí, Salvador (1904–89) © ARS, NY.

used it to describe a self-portrait Dalí had made in 1941, *Soft Self-Portrait with Grilled Bacon* (fig. 50). He described the painting as an "anti-psychological" self-portrait: "Instead of painting the soul — the inside — I wanted to paint solely the outside: the envelope, 'the glove of myself.'"[61] At the time, Dalí was working to distance himself from the psychoanalysis of his surrealist period, so one might question the interpretation of this painting as altogether "anti-psychological." However, it cannot be said that there was no precedent within Dalí's earlier writing to support such a radical interpretation. By returning to the concept of the envelope Dalí reminds us of the crucial role that superficiality played throughout his surrealist period and underscores the degree to which he had departed from psychoanalytic orthodoxy even during the period in which he was most profoundly influenced by it.

5

SUBMISSION

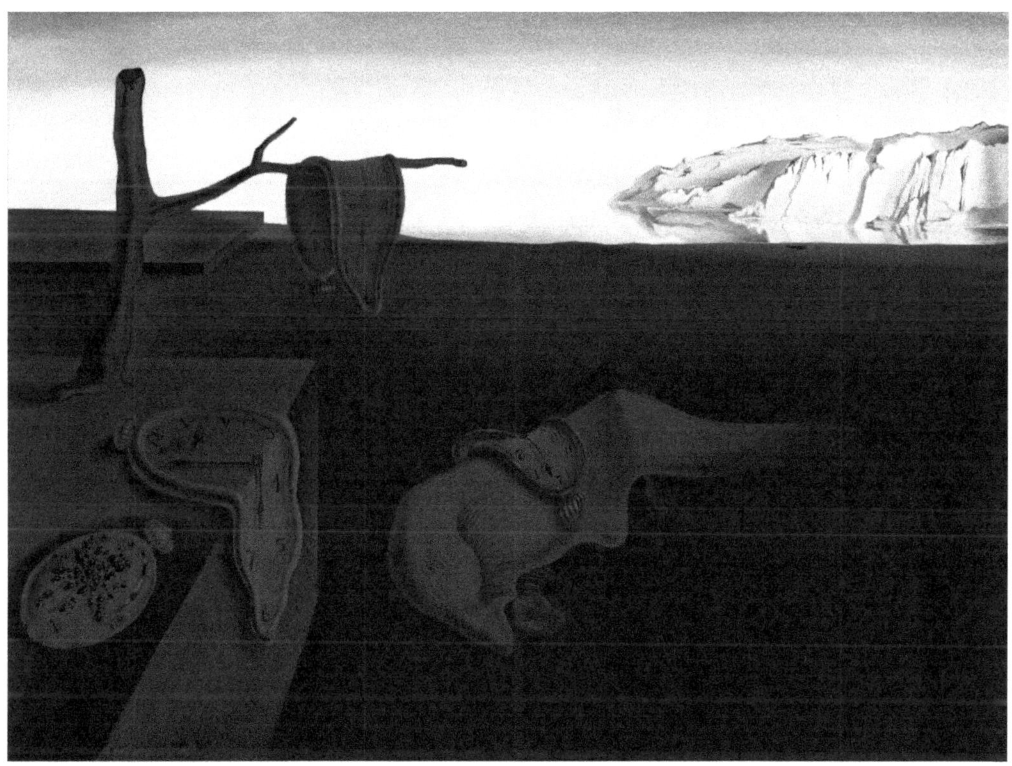

In the years preceding its completion, the artist typically depicted beaches as spaces of femininity. In these paintings women swim, relax, and enjoy the warmth of the sun on their exposed flesh. But here, on a beach in which the ocean is depicted as a thin sliver at the end of a vast sand-scape, Dalí has painted not a woman, but himself. Are we being asked to consider this a portrait of the artist as a woman? If so, it must be recognized that this feminized self is depicted quite differently than the women that appear in his other beach scenes. In this painting the figure appears lifeless, not relaxed, and the spotless landscape reads as desolate rather than pristine. This is a scene of pain, not pleasure, and as such suggests that sexual masquerade is not a liberating release from the self but a masochistic act of self-suppression.

Previous chapters have argued that Dalí's identification with little things shaped not only the ways in which he incorporated psychoanalysis into his work (chapter 2) but also the ways in which it informed his strategies of liberation (chapter 1), parasitism (chapter 3), and superficiality (chapter 4). This chapter and the next concern the ways in which Dalí redirected his tiny surrealism inward and outward. Directed inward, Dalí asked: What happens when one makes oneself a little thing? How does a little self respond to another? Directed outward, he asked: What happens to little things over time? How do history's little events endure in the present? This chapter pursues the inward turn of Dalí's little things and examines the development of a logic of "self-restraint," which for Dalí meant the suppression of the desire to expand, to penetrate, and to take control. The little self is the self that shrinks, remains on the surface, and relinquishes control to the other. In so doing it subverts the structures of power and penetration that subtend both modernism and patriarchy.

Dalí's engagement with the ethics and aesthetics of subversive self-restraint is evident, for example, in the painter's account of Vermeer as an artist of saintly humility and self-control. In Dalí's eyes Vermeer's paintings required the sort of intense concentration that, at its limit, exposed an ethical dimension. Vermeer's clear and calm depictions were indices of a modesty and self-restraint that recalled no one so much as the Father of All Monks, Saint Anthony. In Dalí's mind Vermeer's work not only prefigured the ontology of the photograph — its condition as a mechanical and thus "objective" documentation of the world — it also prefigured the ethics of the camera — its status as a small and humble recording instrument: "Vermeer of Delft was still another thing. In the history of looking, his eyes are the case of the highest probity. With all the temptations of light, however. Van Der Meer, a new Saint Anthony, preserved intact the object, with an inspiration altogether photographic, an outcome of his humble and impassioned sense of touch."[1]

Here Dalí has established Vermeer as the model anti-impressionist. Whereas the impressionists dissolved the object in a myriad of prismatic rays of light, Vermeer preserved and protected it from dissolution. Through saintly self-restraint, Vermeer purged himself of all intervening subjectivity so that the objects he saw could be recorded with photographic fidelity. Ultimately, it was less important that Vermeer's paintings *looked* photographic than that they were photographic in their "inspiration." If they looked like photographs it was only because they were the product of a photographic ethos — an ethos predicated on the humble preservation of the objects within the grasp of one's hand.[2]

The admiration that Dalí felt for Vermeer's humility and probity was reflected in his developing sense of himself as insistently, if not provocatively, self-restrained. For example, in a 1927 letter to Lorca Dalí rebuked his friend for having gotten drunk one evening. "You drank yourself sick?" Dalí asked, incredulously. "I'm living a life of the utmost virtue — I don't drink at all — *absolute* chastity. Vice is totally *artistic*."[3] For Dalí, self-restraint posed an alternative to what he perceived to be the excessive emotionalism of his Catalan contemporaries, whom he derided as "cry-baby transcendental artists, removed from all clarity, cultivators of all germs, ignorant of the precision of the graduated double decimeter."[4] At the time Dalí was struggling to distinguish himself from the artists of the Catalan avant-garde. Insofar as they considered themselves liberated from all morals and conventions, Dalí set out to identify himself as one who stood with virtue and thus with the ethics of self-restraint.

For Dalí, at the extreme end of this ethic lay the figure of Saint Sebastian. Sebastian was said to have been ordered by Diocletian to be bound to a stake and shot with arrows until he perished. Miraculously he endured the pain and survived. In 1927 Dalí published an essay titled "Saint Sebastian," and scholars have proposed that his interest in the figure stemmed from the fact that Sebastian's established association with homosexuality enabled the saint to serve as a covert symbol of Dalí's relationship with Lorca.[5] This may be true, but the figure of Saint Sebastian also served to indicate an ethic and aesthetic of patience that Dalí identified with Vermeer. For Dalí, there was a relationship between "the patience in the exquisite death throes of Saint Sebastian" and "the humble patience in the maturing process of the paintings of Vermeer of Delft."[6] In this Saint Sebastian became a model not only of ethical behavior but of artistic practice as well. In him one glimpses the virtues that distinguish Vermeer's work from all others': humility, patience, and self-restraint.

Perhaps the most telling statement Dalí ever made on the subject of self-restraint was from a short piece he wrote for *L'Amic de les Arts* in 1927 titled "The Common Sense of a Brother of the Order of Sant Joan Baptista de la Salle":

> As a small child, I learned a painting rule which I will never forget. It was in the painting class of the French Brothers. We painted aquarelles made of simple geometric elements first traced with a ruling pen. Our teacher told us: Painting this well, and, in general, painting well, consists of *not going beyond the line*. . . . Not going beyond the line! Here you have a conduct rule that may lead to a whole integrity and a whole ethic of painting. There always existed two kinds of painters: those who went beyond the line, and those who, patiently, and with respectfulness, knew how to just reach their limit.

> The first, because of their impatience, were qualified as being impassioned and inspired. The second, because of their humble patience, were qualified as being cold and solely good craftsman. If it is true, nevertheless, that going beyond the line is a form of impetuosity signifying always the beginning of intoxication, confusion and weakness, it is true as well that there exists a type of passion which consists precisely of the patience of *not going beyond the line*; and that this passion for balance is a strong passion and an enemy of all intoxication.[7]

What is especially significant about Dalí's insistence on the patience of "not going beyond the line" is that it underscores, in inverted form, the modernist imperative to dismantle convention. In response to the modernist identification of passion with liberation and frenzied release, Dalí proposed to identify passion with patience. For Dalí, it is precisely the arbitrariness of these regulations — their inherent senselessness and lack of supervening justification — that warrants one's submission to them. "Not going beyond the line" is a rule to be followed for no reason beyond that of its existence as a rule.

In this regard it is worth noting in that even Dalí's most experimental works from 1928 were exceedingly controlled. The sand and shells in paintings such as *The Rotting Donkey* and *Bather* (figs. 13, 14) have been affixed with the sort of meticulous care that is entirely uncharacteristic of the treatment of such materials by the artists from whom Dalí had appropriated his technique. The lines that are delicate and pliable in Miró's work are, in Dalí's, hard and brittle; the sand that is rough and scumbled in Masson's is, in Dalí's, precious and fussy. That he transformed the explicitly "intoxicating" methods of automatism and turned them on their head is yet another sign of the perverse chastity that guided his hand.

ABSOLUTE REVOLT, TOTAL INSUBMISSION

Dalí was certainly aware that his celebration of patience, rules, and submission would be understood by his contemporaries as a provocation aimed at the avant-garde imperatives of originality, autonomy, and independence. These imperative were well established by the 1920s and can be traced at least as far back as Baudelaire. For Baudelaire, there were three distinct types of artists: realists, imaginists, and conventionalists. The first and second types were of interest to Baudelaire as they engaged in what he considered to be living questions about art and life in modernity. Artists of the third type, however, were hardly worth considering at all: "These men conform to a purely conventional set of rules — rules entirely arbitrary, not derived from the human soul, but simply imposed by the routine of a celebrated studio. In this very numerous but very boring class we include the false amateurs of the antique, the false amateurs of style — in short, all those men who by their impotence have elevated the 'poncif' to the honors of the grand style."[8]

By the early part of the twentieth century members of the avant-garde would go further than Baudelaire to discredit the work of this "very boring class" of rule-bound and reactionary artists. Cubists Albert Gleizes and Jean Metzinger, for example, associated academic conventions with artistic enslavement.[9] In a similar vein, Miró once referred to pictorial conventions as "poison."[10] With regard to surrealism in particular, one of its most distinctive features was its explicit and aggressive assault on convention in all its manifestations. In the first surrealist manifesto, for example, Breton declared that the only word that interested him was "freedom"; in the second he defined the movement as "absolute revolt [and] total insubmission."[11] Bataille, for his part, founded much of his thought on what he considered the primal opposition between "servitude and revolt."[12] For him, this opposition is at the heart of eroticism, which he defined in the 1940s as "a domain marked off by the *violation of rules*. It is always a matter of going beyond the limits allowed . . . so it is a matter of passing from the licit to the forbidden." Together, Bataillean *sovereignty* ("life beyond utility") and Bretonian *insubmission* were the twin poles around which surrealism oriented itself.[13]

In many instances the modernist imperative of liberty included a corollary: the imperative to possess. Robert Delaunay, for example, described himself as one "who possess light."[14] Likewise did Kasimir Malevich justify his new techniques as tools of control and possession: "I have overcome the lining of the colored sky, torn it down and into the bag thus formed, put color, tying it up with a knot. Swim in the white free abyss, infinity is before you."[15] Consider, too, the following statement from Paul Klee:

> [The artist] surveys with penetrating eye the finished forms which nature places before him. The deeper he looks, the more readily he can extend his view from the present to the past, the more deeply he is impressed by the one essential image of creation itself, as Genesis, rather than by the image of nature, the finished product. . . . This being so, the artist must be forgiven if he regards the present state of outward appearances in his own particular world as accidentally fixed in time and space. And as altogether inadequate compared with his penetrating vision and intense depth of feelings.[16]

Like Delaunay and Malevich, Klee figured modernism as possessive and penetrative. The modern painter pierces beneath the surface of the visible world (the world as it is "accidentally fixed in time and space") so as to lay claim to the "image of creation itself." The arrogation of godlike powers is wholly unmistakable in this passage, yet its presentation as metaphor serves almost to disguise its underlying violence.[17]

For the surrealists in particular, the dialectical conception of freedom and possession was inspired above all by the writings of the Marquis de Sade. In a 1942 lecture at Yale Breton himself traced the surrealist fascination with Sade back to Apollinaire, who, in his 1909 introduction to a selection of Sade's writings, referred to the marquis as "cet esprit le plus libre qui ait encore existé."[18] Similarly, Bataille argued that the primitive urge to create art is itself an expression of a natural, sadistic urge: "Art, since it is incontestably art, proceeds in this way by successive destructions. Thus insofar as it liberates instincts, these are sadistic."[19] As Maurice Nadeau recalled in 1944, "The Surrealists wove a legend around [Sade]; for them he represented the highest and most stirring example. His lucid materialism, his search for the absolute in all forms of pleasure, notably in the sexual realm, his opposition to the traditional values and to those representing them, his gifts as a visionary, form the perfect figure of man as they conceived him."[20] For Nadeau, the surrealist dialectic of freedom and violence was captured best by the sadism at work in Aragon's famous declaration (from *Les aventures de Télémaque*, 1923), "Laws, moralities, esthetics have been created to make you respect fragile things. What is fragile should be broken."[21]

The most succinct, albeit retrospective, formulation of the surrealist conception of Sade was penned by Maurice Blanchot in 1949. In an essay titled "Sade's Reason," Blanchot asserts that "between the normal man who locks the sadistic man in an impasse and the sadistic man who turns this impasse into an escape hatch, the latter is the one who is nearer to the truth, who understands the logic of his situation, and who has a deeper intelligence, to the point of being able to help the normal man understand himself, by helping him modify the foundations of all perceptions."[22] For Blanchot, the perception of Sadean violence as a perversion of normal desire is but a mask to protect one's fragile sensibilities. Beneath this mask lies the ineradicable desire to possess and control the Other.

The surrealists' fascination with Sadean violence is nowhere so nakedly present than in the photographs of Hans Bellmer (fig. 51). Although there exists some debate as to the ultimate implications of Bellmer's perverse constructions, there is no question that they are, as Abigail Solomon-Godeau put it, "staged in a way that emphasizes spectatorial mastery and domination."[23] Hal Foster has suggested that Bellmer's sadistic imagery may actually serve as a critique of violence. Bellmer's dolls, Foster suggests, "may go beyond (or is it inside?) sadistic mastery to the point where the masculine subject confronts his greatest fear: his own fragmentation, disintegration, and dissolution. . . . Is this why Bellmer

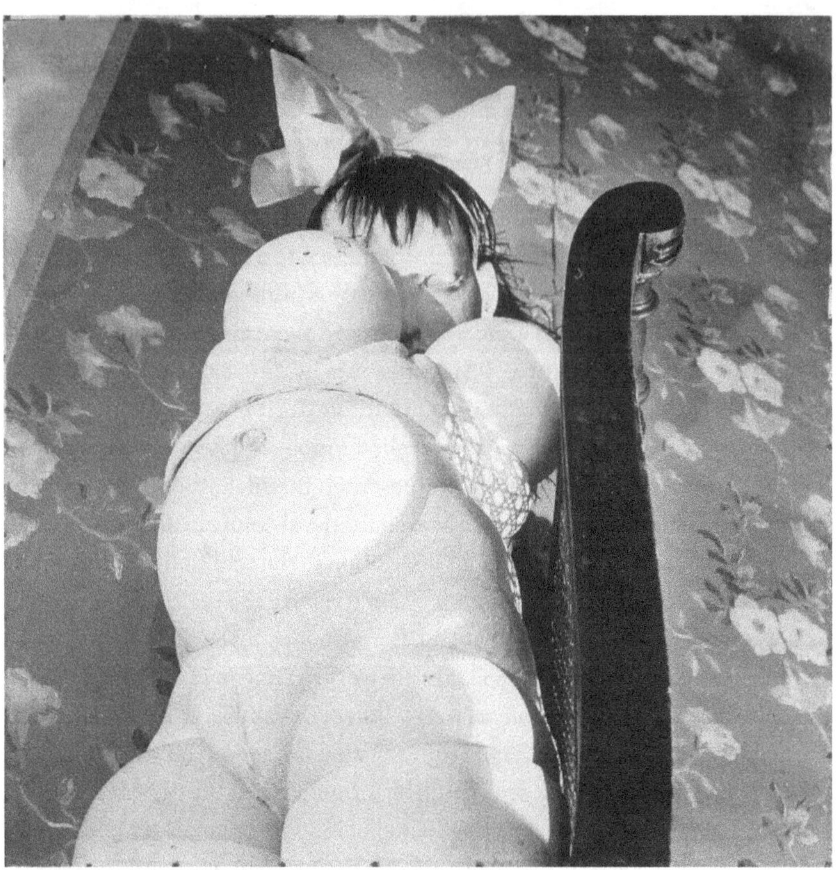

51. Hans Bellmer, *The Joy of the Doll* (*Le jeux de la poupee*), 1938–49. AM1996-206(15). Photo: Philippe Migeat. Musee National d'Art Moderne, Centre Georges Pompidou, Paris, France. Bellmer, Hans (1902–75) © 2011 Artists Rights Society (ARS), New York/ADAGP, Paris. Photo credit: CNAC/MNAM/Dist. Réunion des Musées Nationaux/Art Resource, NY.

appears not only to desire the (dis)articulated female body but also to identify with it, not only to master it sadistically but also to become it masochistically?"[24]

More recently, Sue Taylor and Therese Lichtenstein have expanded on Foster's attempt to reframe Bellmer's photographs as acts of social and political critique.[25] Nevertheless, I agree with Solomon-Godeau's claim that it is not so easy to recuperate Bellmer's work for these purposes:

> Neither the claim that Bellmer's doll photographs are a "critical" representation of gender nor Lichtenstein's parallel contention that "in front of these photographs, both male and female spectators can identify with the masochistic doll or the sadistic spectator, or oscillate between both positions" clinches the argument. A picture that is desublimatory (for example, a

"beaver shot" from *Hustler*) is not necessarily critical. Similarly, the fluidity of identification Lichtenstein attributes to the doll photographs is a mechanism at work in all encounters of a spectator with an image, and is thus not necessarily a function of any given picture itself, much less the intention of the person who made it.[26]

In this respect Solomon-Godeau is pursuing a line that Foster himself suggested: "The poupées produce misogynistic effects that may overwhelm any liberatory intentions. They also exacerbate sexist fantasies about the feminine . . . even as they exploit them critically."[27] Taylor has put it similarly: "Despite their roots in an emasculating masochism and the (mitigating) factor of the artist's feminine identification, we are still left with the misogynistic effects of the sadistic scenarios of female abuse Bellmer devises. . . . There is little to suggest that Bellmer did not in fact subscribe to the very stereotypes of femininity he is sometimes purported to expose in his extravagantly clichéd images." Taylor's more general assessment of avant-garde practices also deserves consideration: "The fantasized assaults on the female body that characterize so much of the iconography of twentieth-century artistic avant-gardes, as much as we may want to read them as an overturning of the repressive conventions of an entrenched aesthetic category (the idealized classical nude), must also be interrogated for their complicity with a dominant (male) ideology."[28] Indeed, as Amy Lyford has demonstrated, surrealist invocations of Sade often served to mask underlying anxieties of masculinity that had emerged in the years after World War I.[29]

And there is yet another question posed by surrealist depictions of sadistic violence, a question that neither semiotics nor psychoanalysis can answer without the help of sociological study: To what extent, if any, have these works instigated, encouraged, or aggravated acts of real-world sadism? For it is one thing to depict and promote images of simulated violence and quite another to perform and perpetuate acts of real violence.[30] Nevertheless, as Jonathan Eburne has shown, Sade's discourse on violence played an undeniably central role in surrealist investigations of psychic and social liberation.[31] In this regard it participated — alongside the writings of Malevich, Klee, and others — in a widespread discourse on the aesthetics and politics of possession and penetration.

MORE MASTERED THAN MASTERING

In light of the surrealists' insistence on the "total liberation of the mind and all that resembles it" and with it the fascination with extremes of Sadean violence, what are we to make of Dalí's own particular brand of sexual perversion?[32] More precisely, in what ways does Dalí's work make use of the language of

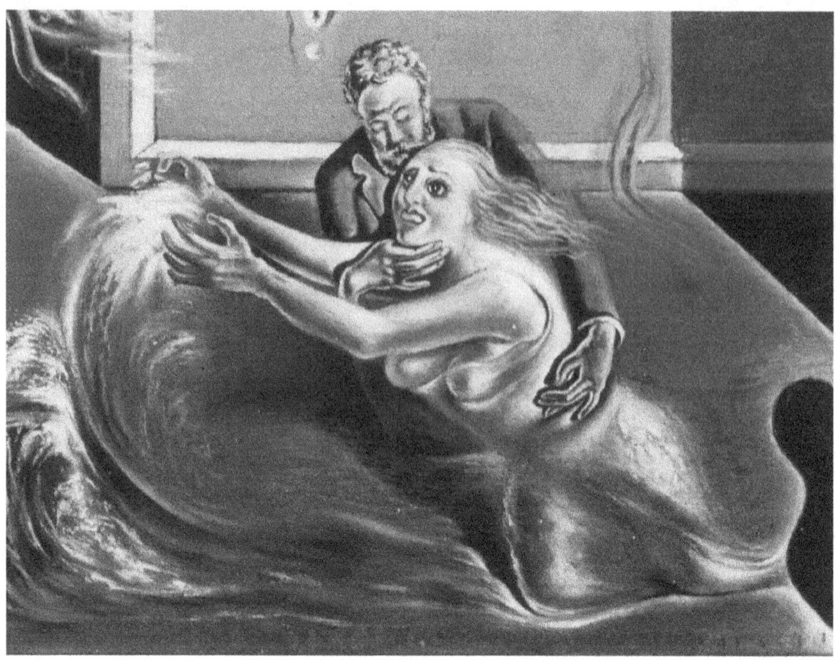

52. Salvador Dalí, detail of *Illuminated Pleasures*, 1929. Oil and collage on composition board, 23.8 × 34.7 cm (9⅜ × 13¾ in.). The Sidney and Harriet Janis Collection. The Museum of Modern Art, New York NY. Dalí, Salvador (1904–89) © ARS, NY. Digital Image © The Museum of Modern Art/Licensed by SCALA/Art Resource, NY.

self-restraint as a means of subverting the conventions of aggressive masculinity evident in the discourses of Breton, Blanchot, and Bellmer?

Like Breton and Bataille, Dalí recognized Sade as a crucial precursor to surrealism and considered Sade's writings to be no less important to the movement than those of the Comte de Lautréamont, Leon Trotsky, Freud, and Heraclitus.[33] "We cherish Sade," Dalí wrote, and he "possess[es] the purity of a diamond."[34] Given Dalí's fascination with perversion, this is hardly surprising and is obviously central to the sexual dynamics as presented in *Un chien andalou* — most notably in the famous opening sequence in which a man uses a razor blade to slice open a woman's eye (fig. 55).

Depictions of sexual violence toward women are also present in a number of Dalí's paintings of this period. For example, in *Little Ashes* (fig. 10), a grotesquely veined woman — whose legs, right arm, and head have been severed — squirts a thin stream of milk from her breast. More aggressive still is the inclusion, in *Illuminated Pleasures*, of a man shooting a pistol at an enormous floating egg-like object and another man strangling a woman (figs. 17, 52).

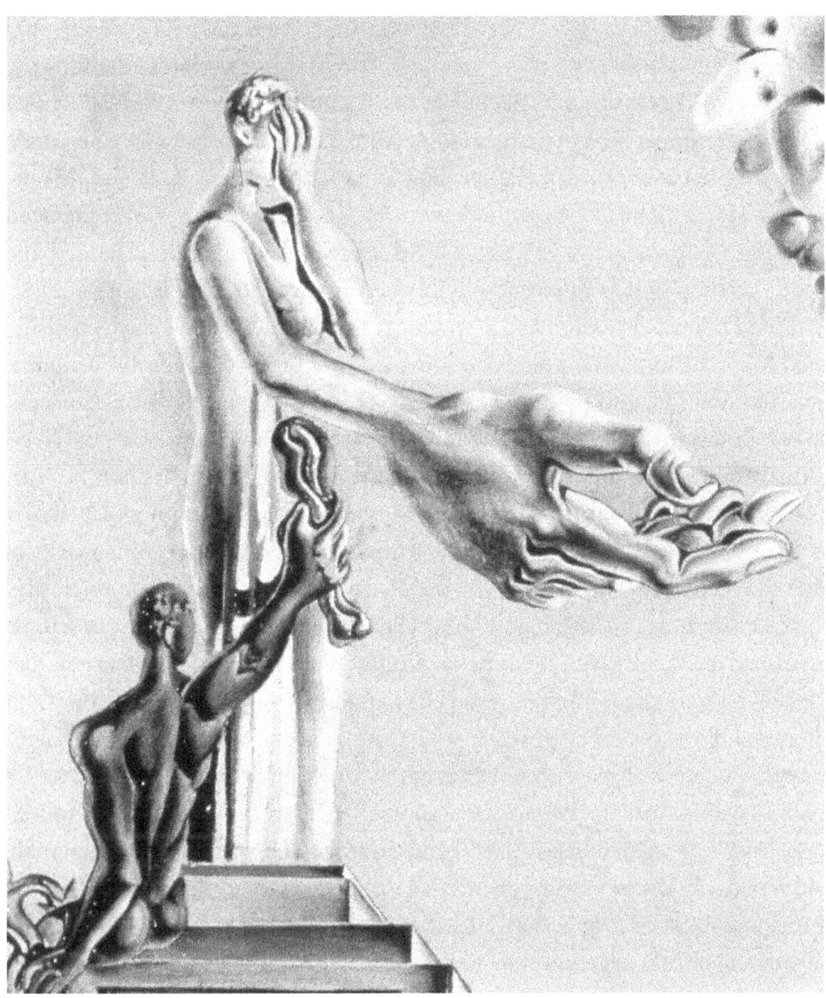

53. Salvador Dalí, detail of *The Lugubrious Game*, 1929. 44.4 × 30.3 cm (17.48 × 11.93 in.). Private collection. Image provided by the Fundació Gala-Salvador Dalí. Dalí, Salvador (1904–89) © ARS, NY.

It is worth noting, however, that the period in which Dalí regularly depicted such acts of sadism was remarkably brief and coincided, unsurprisingly, with his first few years inside the surrealist orbit. Scenes like those in *Illuminated Pleasures* appear in other paintings from the late twenties and early thirties, but after that they disappear almost entirely. For Dalí, sadism seems to have been an alien, uncomfortable perversion, one to which he consented unwillingly so as to curry favor with Breton and others whose support he so desperately desired when he first arrived in Paris.

Indeed, the inclination toward self-denial and rule following resembles the perversion of masochism far more than it does that of sadism, and there is at least as much evidence that Dalí was drawn to the writings of Leopold von Sacher-Masoch as he was to those of the Marquis de Sade. Perhaps the most explicit application of Sacher-Masoch's writing appears in Dalí's essay "Picasso's Slippers." In 1935 Christian Zervos asked Dalí to contribute an article on Picasso to *Cahiers d'Art*. Rather than write his own piece, Dalí simply took Sacher-Masoch's book *La pantoufle de Sapho* (Sappho's slipper) and replaced the name "Sappho" with "Picasso." With a few additional modifications, the essay was then sent to Zervos and published as a work of Dalí's own hand.[35]

That Dalí was attracted to the writings of Sacher-Masoch is worth pausing over. Masochism, as a complex of erotic pleasures derived from acts of submission, humiliation, and pain, was typically elided in surrealist discourse, mentioned almost invariably as the second half of so-called sadomasochism. Given surrealism's commitment to insubordination and sovereignty, it is hardly a surprise to find that the writings of Sacher-Masoch were read simply as corollaries to those of Sade. Bataille, for example, equated the humiliation of masochism with the consequence of timidity in the face of truth and referred to the pitiful creatures in such a situation as "the servile."[36] For Bataille, masochism is to be explained as one of two phenomena: as either "an excess of sadism, wherein the subject's cruelty is finally turned back against the subject himself" or as "an alteration of the sexual disposition, with the man displaying feminine behavior toward a woman of masculine behavior."[37] With this, Bataille pointed to the real force of masochism even as he dismissed it. That force lies in its potential to disrupt "the sexual disposition" by upending the distinction between male and female. In the process of dismissing masochism for its failure to offer anything new to the transgressions of sexuality articulated by Sade (beyond that of pushing sexual aggression to the point at which it is enacted on the self), Bataille fails to register the implications of his own suggestion that masochism confounds the otherwise rigid distinction between masculinity and femininity. In this regard it is telling that when Bataille analyzed *The Lugubrious Game* (figs. 2, 19, 53) he failed to notice (or neglected to mention) that the figure in the upper left corner of the painting — the figure that he interpreted as symbolic of "the genesis of emasculation and the contradictory reactions it carries with it"— is ambiguously gendered: not only are the lower limbs covered by what looks like the folds of woman's dress but the rounded bulge in the chest clearly indicates the presence of breasts.[38]

Dalí's interest in the masochistic subject is even more explicit in *La femme visible*. Along with the four texts, the book also includes a number of illustrations, of which the frontispiece is particularly compelling in this context (fig. 54). It is a densely drawn illustration of sexual perversity — featuring most notably one figure (arguably an avatar of the painter himself) engaged with apparent

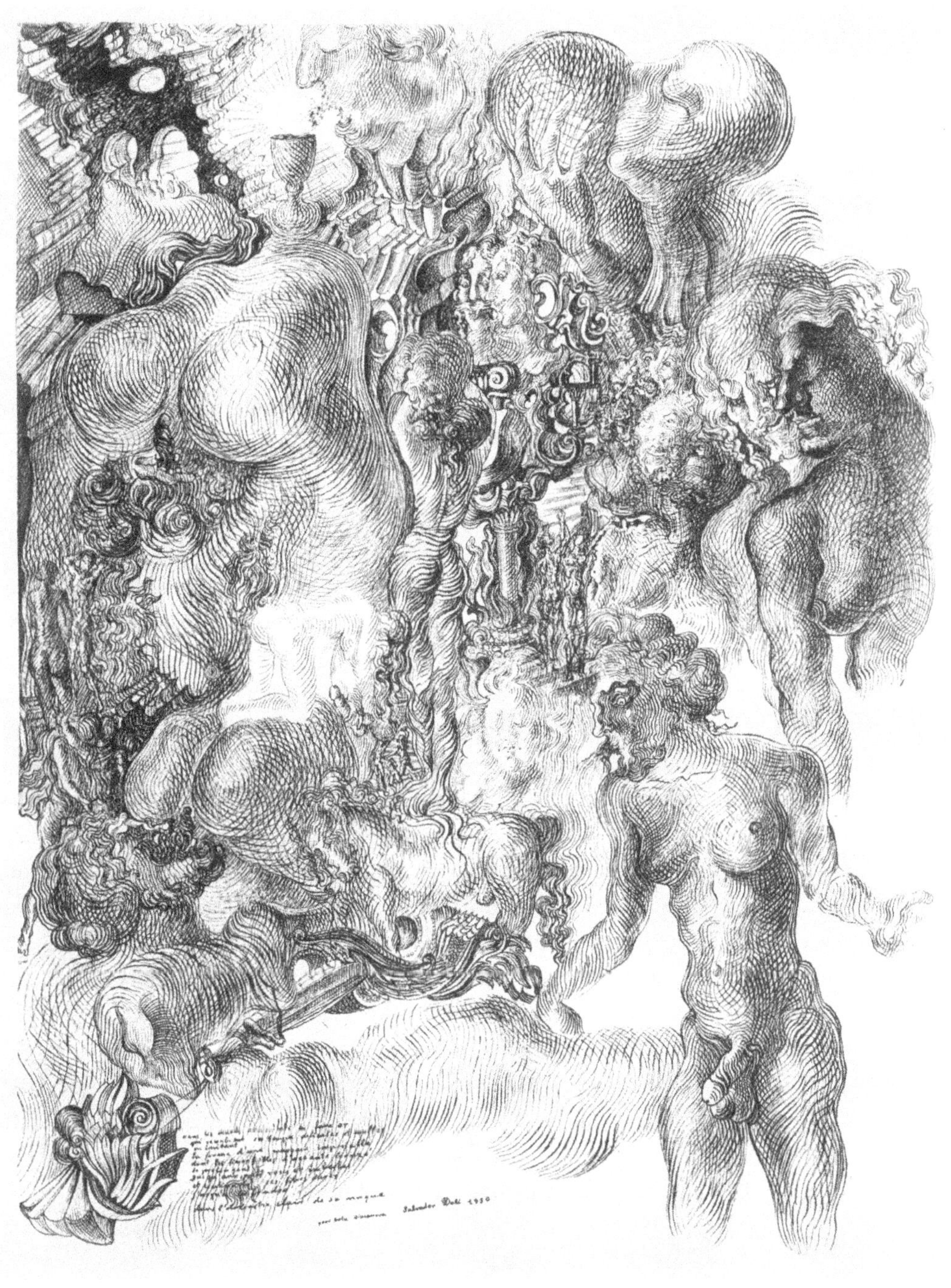

54. Salvador Dalí, frontispiece to *La femme visible*, 1930. The Museum of Modern Art, New York NY. Dalí, Salvador (1904–89) © ARS, NY. Digital Image © The Museum of Modern Art/Licensed by SCALA/ Art Resource, NY.

delight in the act of coprophagia. The effect of the illustration is particularly shocking because the thicket of tightly packet lines makes it especially difficult for the reader to make sense of it. Only after holding the page up close and focusing on it for some time is it possible to discern the figures and their actions. It is worth noting that despite its explicit pornographic quality — unequivocal evidence of a surrealist commitment to breaking taboos — the frontispiece depicts no violence toward women. Rather, it is the male figures who are passive and submissive, if not entirely limp. Against Bataille's sadistic sovereign, Dalí has here proposed the masochistic lover. "One loves completely," wrote Dalí in 1930, "when one is ready to eat the beloved woman's shit."[39] Indeed, a catalog of Dalí's exposed male figures reveals that the bulk of them, when not shown to be flaccid (*William Tell* [fig. 36], for example) are typically ashamed of their erections (*The Lugubrious Game*, for example); it is as if Dalí conceives of traditional masculinity (understood as active and penetrating) as a source of anxiety and fear. In any event, it is almost invariably undermined in one way or another.

This is especially evident in Dalí's self-representation as the Great Masturbator. Sometimes, as in *The Persistence of Memory* (fig. 1), he appears to be decaying or melting away; other times, as in *The Lugubrious Game*, he is assaulted by tiny insects eating into his flesh. In neither case is Dalí's alter ego figured as a sexual aggressor. He is limp, nearly lifeless, and thus incapable of protecting himself from outside forces — regardless of how small or weak those outside forces may seem to be. (Later in life, when Dalí looked back on the soft watches in *The Persistence of Memory*, he described them as masochistic: "Soft watches, biologically speaking, are the giant Dalínian DNA molecules which constitute the factors of eternity. They are masochistic, because they are so eternal. Like filets of sole, they are destined to be swallowed by the sharks of mechanical time."[40]) In effect, these paintings articulate masochistic self-negation as the endpoint of self-restraint, just as Bataille had articulated sadistic violence as the endpoint of sovereignty.

To better comprehend the radical implications of Dalí's identification with the masochistic subject, it is useful to return to the place of masochism in psychoanalysis. For Freud, sadism, although reprehensible, was nevertheless fully comprehensible as an exaggeration of normal desire: "Men are not gentle creatures who want to be loved," he wrote in *Civilization and Its Discontents*, "and who at the most can defend themselves if they are attacked; they are, on the contrary, creatures among whose instinctual endowments is to be reckoned a powerful share of aggressiveness."[41] Masochism — which Freud associated with the desire to be "treated . . . like a naughty child"— was thus a far more puzzling perversion.[42] Whereas sadism involves an exaggeration of normal masculinity, masochism involves its inversion, its transformation into femininity. As Freud put it, "If one has an opportunity of studying cases in which the masochistic phantasies have been especially richly elaborated, one quickly discovers that they place the subject in a characteristically feminine situation; they signify, that is, being castrated, or copulated with, or giving birth to a baby."[43]

The masochist, in other words, destabilizes gender norms in a radical way. For Kaja Silverman, it is thus masochism, not sadism, that is potentially the most subversive of the sexual perversions — subversive not only of heteronormativity but also, and more radically, of gender. With masochism, claims Silverman, the male subject calls into question his identification with the masculine position and in so doing "believes himself to be a woman at the deepest level of his desire and his identity." For Silverman, this is precisely where the sexual perversion of masochism takes on its most subversive aspect: "The male masochist as he is presented by Freud . . . not only prefers the masquerade of womanliness to the parade of virility, but he articulates both his conscious and his unconscious desires from a feminine position. And although he seems to subordinate himself to the law of the father, that is only because he knows how to transform punishment into pleasure, and severity into bliss. This male masochist deploys the diversionary tactics of demonstration, suspense, and impersonation against the phallic 'truth' or 'right,' substituting perversion for the *père-version* of exemplary male subjectivity."[44]

Silverman's analysis draws on Deleuze's account of the logic of violence and submission as it exists in the writings of Sade and Sacher-Masoch. In *Masochism: Coldness and Cruelty*, Deleuze argues that both sadism and masochism involve distinct modes of political and moral subversion. Sadism undermines the codes of law and morality by attacking their principles, while masochism undermines them by demonstrating the absurdity of their consequences. The distinction, Deleuze argues, is akin to the difference between the subversive logics of irony and humor:

> Sade's answer is that in all its forms — natural, moral, and political — the law represents the rule of secondary nature which is always geared to the demands of conservation; it is a usurpation of true sovereignty. . . . Here, the transcendence of the law implies the discovery of a primary nature which is in every way opposed to the demands and the rule of secondary nature. It follows that the idea of absolute evil embodied in primary nature cannot be equated either with tyranny — for tyranny still presupposes laws — or with a combination of whims and arbitrariness; its higher, impersonal model is rather to be found in the anarchic institutions of perpetual motion and permanent revolution.[45]

By contrast, with masochism the law is subverted not by overturning the law's principles but by assiduously following the law's consequences:

> What we call humor — in contradistinction to the upward movement of irony toward a transcendent higher principle — is a downward movement from the law to its consequences. . . . The law is no longer subverted by the upward movement of irony to a principle that overrides it, but by the downward movement of humor which seeks to reduce the law to its furthest consequences. A close examination of masochistic fantasies or rites reveals that while they bring into play the very strictest application of the law, the result in every case is the opposite of what might be expected (thus whipping, far from punishing or preventing an erection, provokes and ensures it). It is a demonstration of the law's absurdity. . . . The masochist is insolent in his obsequiousness, rebellious in his submission; in short, he is a humorist, a logician of consequences, just as the ironic sadist is a logician of principles.[46]

Thus, in Deleuzian terms, Silverman's account of the masochist's transformation of "punishment into pleasure, and severity into bliss" deploys a subversive humor to reveal the absurd consequences of the law of gender.

The real perversion of masochism is therefore not its violation of sexual taboos but rather its violation of gender: the masochistic identification with the feminine subject-position.[47] Silverman's analysis is especially significant in this context because of the pattern that emerges in Dalí's representations of himself and his avatars. In the depictions of himself as a flaccid and passive subject under assault by insects and timepieces or as the feces-eating male figure in the frontispiece to *La femme visible*, the pattern that emerges is one in which Dalí has identified with the masochistic subject.[48] In contrast to other surrealists, Dalí established the masochistic subject as the central figure in his dramas. The viewer was thereby put in the position of identifying with the submissive figure, which was, for the surrealists and beyond, the position of femininity.[49]

Paradoxically, Dalí's most renowned invocation of sadistic violence may well be seen as a radical act of masochistic identification. I am referring of course to the infamous prologue to *Un chien andalou*. In it a man (played by Buñuel himself) stands on a balcony in the moonlight and sharpens a straight razor in preparation for a shave; he pauses for a moment, looks out at a the night sky, and watches a thin cloud glide in front of a bright, full moon. Suddenly a woman appears and, moments later, the man reaches over her head and, mimicking the cloud's movement in front of the moon, pulls his blade across her left eye, slicing it in half (fig. 55).[50] So began what many consider the most revolutionary seventeen minutes in the history of avant-garde cinema.[51] As a number of scholars have pointed out, part of the fascination with the opening sequence

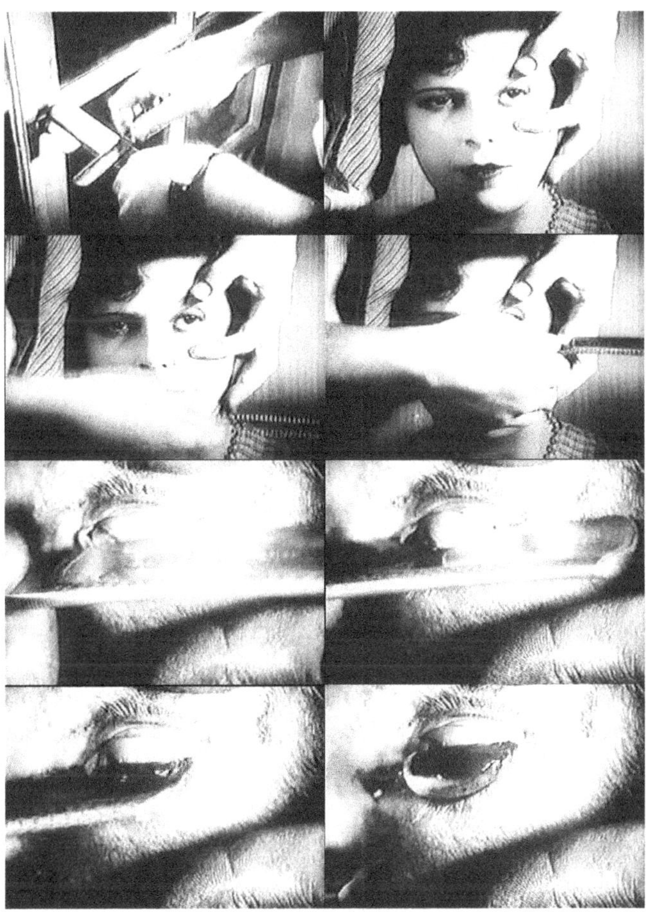

55. Salvador Dalí and Luis Buñuel, stills from *Un chien andalou*, 1929.

lies with the sadistic pleasure this scene unleashes in the psyche of the viewer.[52] In fact, Buñuel's character is typically referred to as the "sadistic barber."[53]

Nevertheless, what makes the scene most compelling — and what distinguishes it from other surrealist depictions of violence toward women — is the immediacy and force of the viewer's identification with the *victim*, who in this case is unequivocally and emphatically female.[54] The scene is voyeuristic, as indeed all cinema is. What distinguishes this particular instance of voyeurism is that it reverses the conventional structure of the spectatorial gaze — the structural inequality in which, as Laura Mulvey famously articulated, the viewer's active gaze is metaphorically invasive and aggressive.[55] In *Un chien andalou*, however, the viewer's gaze is positioned not as aggressive but as sympathetic, as one who identifies with the victim on the screen. And while such identification is clearly at odds with ordinary spectatorship, Silverman's reflections on what could be called "masochistic voyeurism" help to explain this anomaly. Silverman notes that, while "voyeurism has been heavily coded within western culture as a male activity, and associated with aggression and sadism," instances of female voyeurism (as recorded by Freud, for example) reveal a voyeur who is "more mastered than mastering." In such instances the voyeur's position relative to the observed scene of sexual domination is "less the site of a controlling gaze than a vantage point from which to identify with the [victim]."[56] The visceral shock and pained recoil provoked by the eye-slicing scene suggests that, on one level, the cinematic viewer is positioned as a masochistic voyeur whose gaze is identificatory rather than controlling.

THE ELEGANT LADIES OF MADRID

If this scene from *Un chien andalou* is thus torn between what Breton might have labeled the "sinister pleasure" of the sadistic voyeur on the one hand and the feminine, sympathetic position of the masochistic voyeur on the other, the vast majority of Dalí's representations of women are far less ambivalent. They are almost always identificatory. And this — Dalí's identification with the position of the female subject and its implicit self-demasculinization — it seems to me, is Dalí's most subversive perversion. Consider, again, *The Great Masturbator* (figs. 25, 56). At the top of the painting the head of a woman with long blond hair bursts forth from Dalí's neck like a blister or blackhead. That she is meant to be read as Dalí's feminine self is indicated by the way in which her features echo Dalí's: she has the same aquiline nose and thin, arched eyebrow. The fact that she, like Dalí, is shown with eyes closed only reinforces the sense that she is in some sense the painter's doppelgänger — not just attached to him, but of him.

Dalí's identification with the female subject long preceded his official introduction to the surrealists in 1929. Among his favorite subjects was his sister, Ana María, who would sit for hours for him, passing the time sewing as her brother meticulously crafted her likeness.[57] Between 1923 and 1926 Dalí painted more than a dozen portraits of his sister, many of which depict her quietly engaged in her needlework.[58] Dalí described his interest in capturing such moments in a 1926 letter to Lorca:

> I'm writing to you with great calm and serenity. Let me explain. We've already had some bad weather in this blessed September, it's raining, it's windy, a boat is anchored in the harbor, and all this makes one more aware of being inside, with the rustle of gentle, quiet labor. . . . My sister is sewing bed sheets or tablecloths at the window by my side and in the kitchen they're making buns and talking about putting out grapes to dry. All afternoon I have been

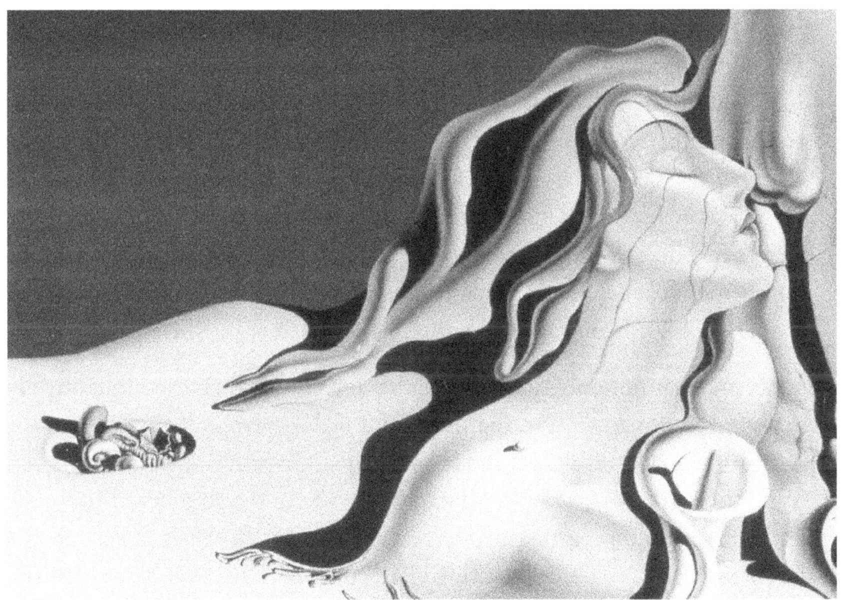

56. Salvador Dalí, detail of *The Great Masturbator*, 1929. Oil on canvas, 110 × 150 cm (43.31 × 59.06 in.). Museo Nacional Centro de Arte Reina Sofía, Madrid. Dalí, Salvador (1904–89) © ARS, NY.

painting — seven hard cold waves like the ones in the sea. Tomorrow I'll paint seven more. I feel calm because I have painted them *well* and every day the sea looks more like the one I am painting.[59]

It is noteworthy that many of the paintings of this period depict Dalí's sister from behind. Typical is *Girl's Back* (fig. 11), 1926, in which we understand from the way in which Ana María's head is bent downward that she is likely engaged in needlework.[60] The craft of painting, these works suggest, is in practice a feminine craft — small, careful, and bound to a tradition of rigidly prescribed techniques.[61]

Indeed, as chapter 4 pointed out, Dalí's work was decidedly anti-penetrative, and thus he refused to participate in the modernist imperative to pierce beneath the surface of things. In this regard Dalí's work echoes that of the Northern Renaissance painters as Svetlana Alpers has analyzed them. Where Italian artists understood the world as composed primarily of "human figures engaged in significant actions," northern artists "offer[ed] their pictures as description of the world seen. . . . [In northern art] it is the world, not the maker or viewer, which has priority."[62] Moreover, as Alpers has pointed out, the distinction between a depiction of the world as it is ordered in the mind and a record of the world as it exists in its state of natural disorder is one that has long maintained a set of gendered implications:

> It is part of our Western culture to find this kind of patient contemplation, this giving in and adapting to the world rather than seizing it and making it one's own, to be weak, not strong; feminine, not masculine. To want to possess meaning is masculine, to experience presence is feminine. This sexual designation is, however, not biologically determined but rather a matter of culture. And in the makings of art — these marvelous, gentle loving, strangely detached works by Vermeer, for example — we find a demonstration that the engagement of such modes of being is open to either sex. It is not the gender of makers, but the different modes of making that is at issue.[63]

Alpers's analysis not only underscores the degree to which the imperative to penetrate and possess is one that is central to Western culture but also the profundity of Dalí's intuitions about Vermeer's subversiveness.

With the arrival of Gala Éluard into Dalí's life in the summer of 1929, the painter's identification turned away from his sister. In *The Secret Life* Dalí told a story about Gala's first visit (with Éluard) to his house. Dalí wrote that she confided to him that she found him "an unbearably obnoxious creature because of my pomaded hair and my elegance." Dalí recalled that at the time he often wore shirts "with low necks and very full sleeves, which I had designed myself and which gave me a completely feminine appearance." He also described himself as preferring to shave his armpits so as to achieve "the ideal bluish effect . . . [of] the elegant ladies of Madrid" and as frequently donning a "fake pearl necklace" and his sister's earrings (fig. 57).[64]

In dozens of portraits Gala (whom Dalí married in 1934) is portrayed as both subject and object, self and other. One of the most astounding, by virtue of its scale at least, is *Portrait of Gala with Two Lamb Chops Balanced on Her Shoulder* (fig. 30), a jewel-like painting that measures a mere 2⅝ by 3½ inches. A work of virtuosic precision, this tiny painting includes not only a portrait of Gala and the two lamb chops of the title but also a detailed landscape that includes the image of a boy (Dalí as a child) and the ruins of a well that stood for years outside the painter's home in Port Lligat (fig. 58).[65] Here Gala seems more than just Dalí's love; she seems, in some sense, to be Dalí himself. Depicted as she is with her eyes closed, she seems to be recalling with an inner vision the landscape behind her. That this landscape belongs to Dalí's past suggests that she is not just depicted by Dalí but is — like the blond-haired woman in *The Great Masturbator* — part of Dalí. The smell of the lamb chops, like the scent of Proust's madeleine, evokes a flood of memories; here, however, the memories are not Gala's, but Dalí's.

In another portrait of the period, Dalí's identification with Gala is literally inscribed on the surface of the painting. *Angelus of Gala* (fig. 59) depicts what appears to be two Galas, one of whom has her back turned away from the

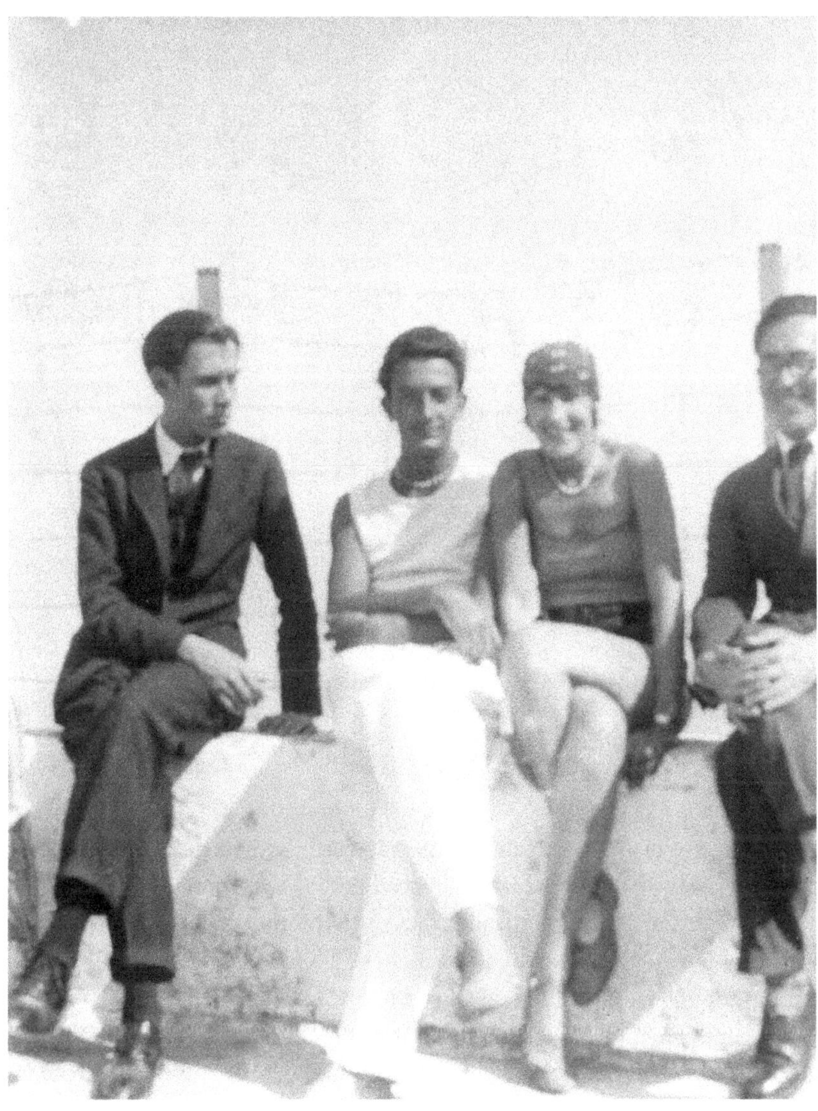

57. Photograph of Dalí and Gala, with Manuel Altogauirre (*left*) and Emilio Prados, Málaga, 1930.

viewer — in the position, that is, of the painter himself as he looks upon his model. In the lower right-hand corner of the painting lies the artist's signature — not "Salvador Dalí" but rather "Gala Dalí." (Dalí often titled his works with his wife's name, so as to indicate her role in their authorship.) Much of the peculiarity and tension in *Angelus of Gala* is derived from the strange suppression of Gala's femininity. The figure whose back is turned looks thick and vaguely masculine, as if to indicate that it is also a representation of Dalí. Dalí is Gala and Gala is Dalí. I argued above that Dalí's 1926 work *Girl's Back* suggests

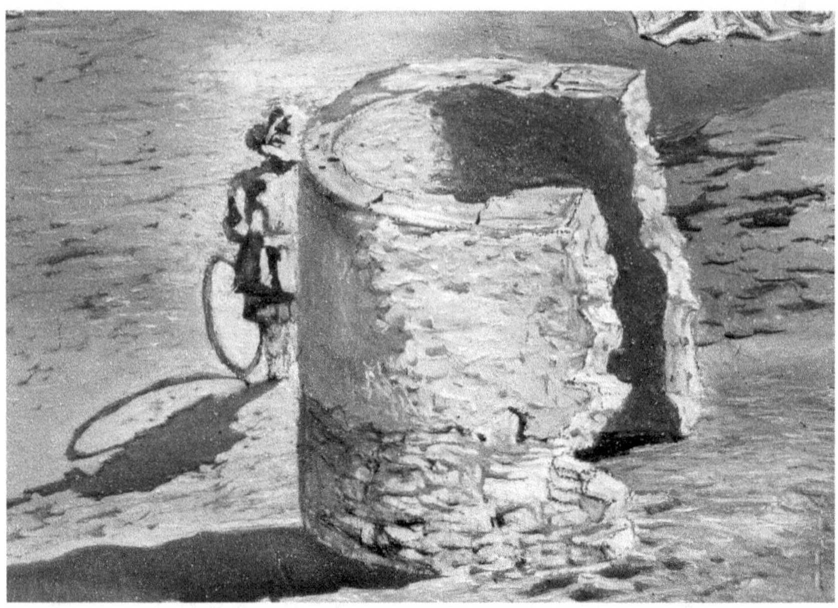

58. Salvador Dalí, detail of *Portrait of Gala with Two Lamb Chops Balanced on Her Shoulder*, ca. 1934. Oil on wood panel, 6.8 × 8.8 cm (2.68 × 3.46 in.). Fundació Gala-Salvador Dalí, Figueres. Dalí, Salvador (1904–89) © ARS, NY.

an identification between Dalí's painting and his subject's needlework. In the case of *Angelus of Gala* such an identification seems to me incontrovertible, as it is emphatically underscored by the mesmerizing precision with which Dalí depicted Gala's elaborately brocaded jacket. In this tiny section of the painting (measuring no more than six by three inches), Dalí has labored so finely that it seems as though every individual thread has been accounted for.

The gendered ambivalence of this portrait recalls the similarly ambivalent figure in *The Lugubrious Game* who hides his face in shame even as he reaches out with a grotesquely oversized hand. It is a work that strikes me as a perfect exemplification of Silverman's claim that, in the case of the masochist, the male subject's display of humiliation and shame is ultimately at the service of a deeper reorientation of subjectivity. The masochist, Silverman writes, "acts out in an insistent and exaggerated way the basic conditions of cultural subjectivity, conditions that are normally disavowed; he loudly proclaims that his meaning comes to him from the Other, prostrates himself before the gaze even as he solicits it, exhibits his castration for all to see, and revels in the sacrificial basis of the social contract. The male masochist magnifies the losses and divisions upon which cultural identity is based, refusing to be sutured or recompensed. In short, he radiates a negativity inimical to the social order."[66]

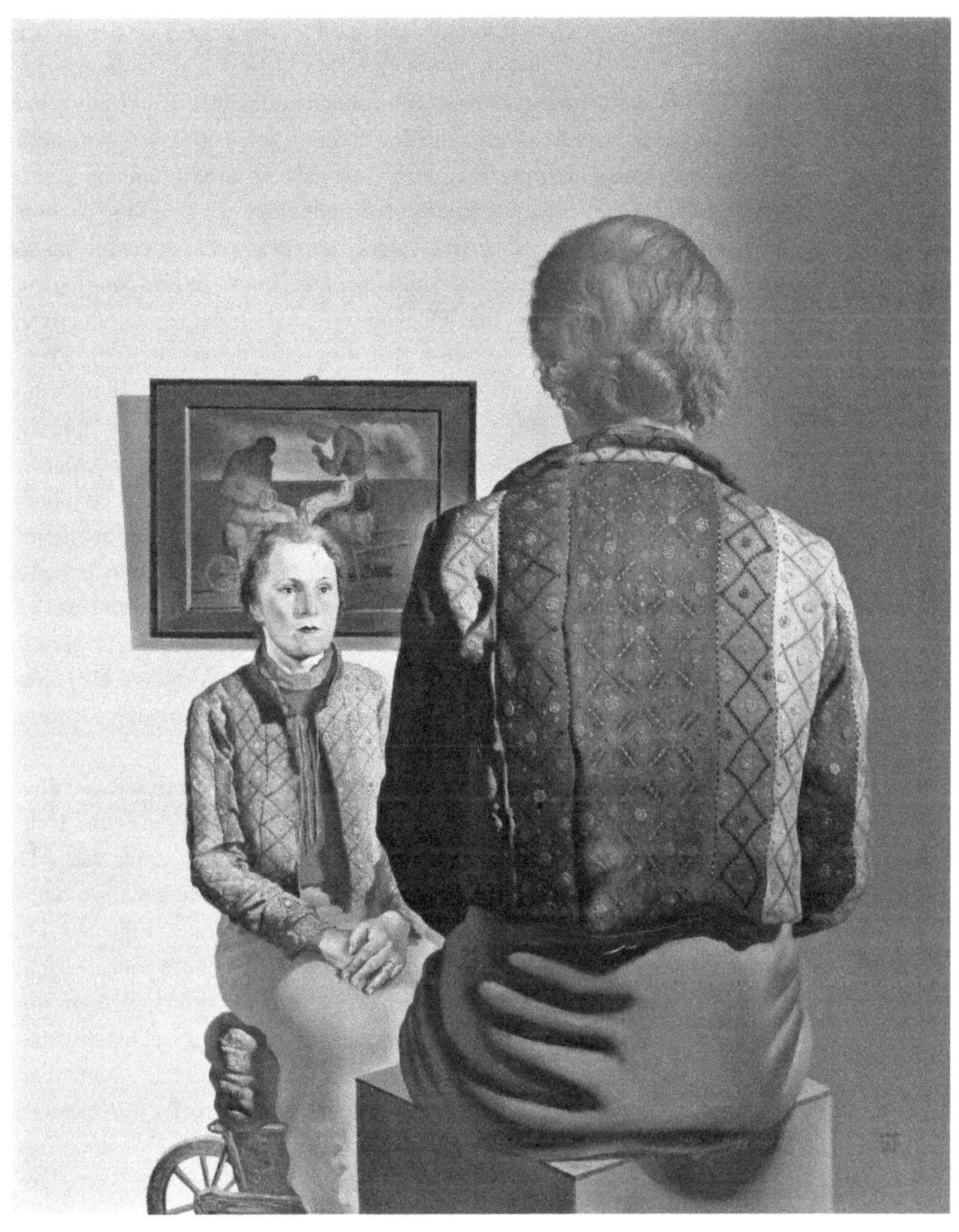

59. Salvador Dalí, *Angelus of Gala (Portrait of Gala)*, 1935. Oil on wood, 32.4 × 26.7 cm (12¾ × 10½ in.). Gift of Abby Aldrich Rockefeller. The Museum of Modern Art, New York NY. Dalí, Salvador (1904–89) © ARS, NY. Digital Image © The Museum of Modern Art/Licensed by SCALA/Art Resource, NY.

Dalí's portraits of Gala distinguish themselves not only from the sadistic aggressivity typical of surrealist depictions but also from the common gestures of avant-gardist transvestitism and comic masquerade. Especially when considered in light of his preference for donning earrings and a pearl necklace (fig. 57), Dalí's identification with Gala calls to mind Duchamp's alter ego, Rrose Sélavy. Although similar in their adoption of a feminine persona, Duchamp's act is structured by ambivalence and performed as camp. Amelia Jones has provided a detailed consideration of Duchamp's gender-bending that provocatively questions whether Duchamp's female masquerade effectively "undo[es] the phallocentric scenarios that structure subjectivity in the West" or whether it "simply operate[s] once again as a masculine strategy to define them as empowered in relation to the a devalued feminine other."[67] By contrast, David Vilaseca has argued that Dalí's "(trans)dressing" involves "taking his own appearance to the very limits of cultural intelligibility, making his own body into a battleground in which patriarchal norms of gender and identity definition are made to clash and ultimately to collapse (as their artificiality emerges on the 'surface,' thereby becoming self-evident)."[68] In addition, Dalí's work is distinguished from Duchamp's by its sobriety and absent eroticism (at least in the case of the women sewing and the portraits of Gala). Although Dalí often makes use of parody and camp performances, in donning women's accoutrements he seems to really mean what he says.[69]

If one were to look for parallels between Duchamp and Dalí, a closer analogy would be found between Duchamp's drag-queen performances and Dalí's comic exaggerations of masculinity. Indeed, Dalí's most recognizable trait — his hypertrophic mustache — makes a mockery not only of the myth of the modern artist as eccentric but also of masculinity and its conventions of display. The mustache — especially in Mediterranean cultures — has long served as a signifier of adult masculinity and its attendant implications of virility, strength, and dominance.[70] Although Dalí's exaggerated mustache is a feature of his post-1940 identity, there are a number of early references to mustaches that situate them as unequivocal signifiers of masculinity. "The Great Masturbator," for example, includes the following description:

The second face of the Great Masturbator
was of a more reduced size than the first
but its expression was proud and softer.
Having been shaved five days before
its barely grown mustache
nibbled on and turned brown

was lightly smeared
with real shit.

In a subsequent passage Dalí contrasts the masculinity of the mustache with the "golden curls" of femininity:

Mythological vases too
adorned with tiny
hermaphrodite faces
with golden
curls
and mustaches
with vomitous
smile
and with very sharp teeth.[71]

References such as these underscore the degree to which Dalí's manipulation of his own facial hair participated in a subversive manipulation of the cultural signifiers of gender.

Dalí's painterly practice, however, owes more to the logic of masochistic identification than it does to parodic mockery. This, it seems to me, is the lesson to be taken from Dalí's 1927 statement that "painting well, consists of *not going beyond the line*" and that painters can be divided into two categories: those who "went beyond the line" and those — like Dalí himself — "who, patiently, and with respectfulness, knew how to just reach their limit." What this statement suggests is that Dalí understood the craft of painting as an unyielding discipline to which the painter is expected to surrender. In that sense Dalí's greatest perversion may well have been his technique, his blind submission to the conventions of the old masters and to their silent but strict insistence that he not go beyond the line.

6

ANACHRONISM

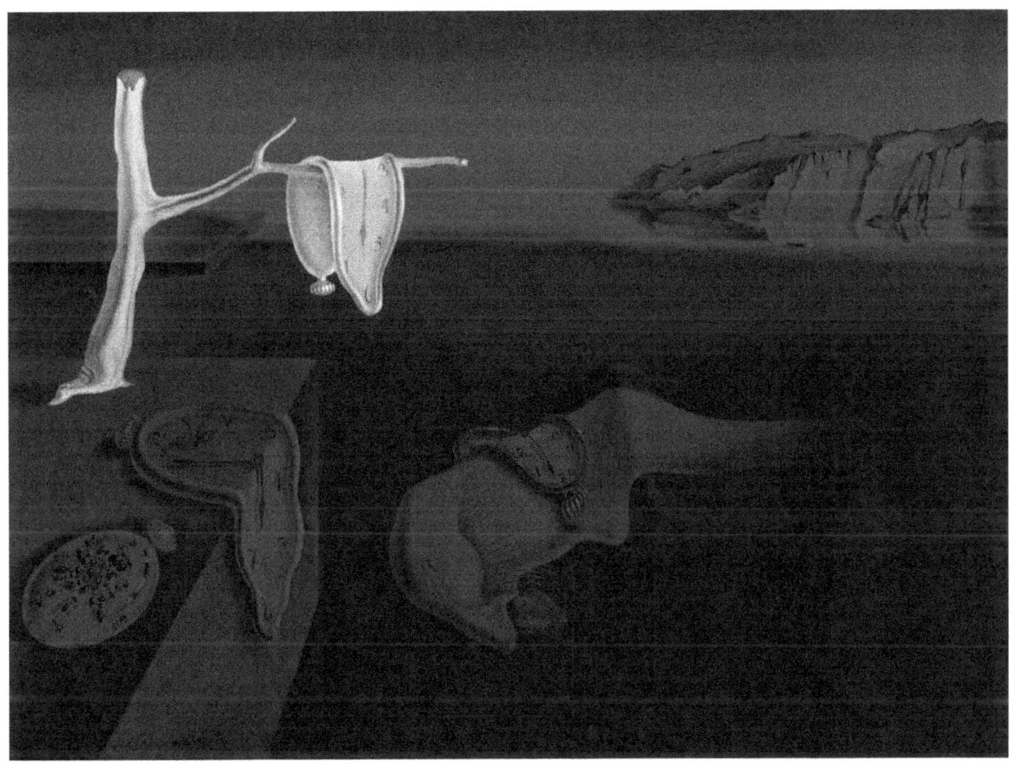

The tree appears to have died years ago, its trunk gray and hollow. The watch that hangs from the one remaining limb adds to the morbidity of the scene, as do the insects searching for nourishment in the rot. Underscoring this panorama of lifelessness is the paint itself: its smooth and glassy surface leaves no trace of the artist's animating touch. Moreover, the technique employed is one that owes little to the imperatives of its time and instead recalls the style of artists long since dead. In this landscape of death the only signs of life belong to the parasites that subsist on its decay.

Each chapter of this book has explored different ways in which Dalí exploited the outmoded and antimodernist techniques of the old masters of the Renaissance and the academicians of the nineteenth century as tools in the service of the small. Chapter 1 examined Dalí's Vermeerian "objectivity" as a tool of "liberation." Chapter 2 explored the paranoiac's camera-like precision as a means of reaggregating these liberated little things into irrational conglomerates. Chapter 3 examined Dalí's conception of Meissonier as a parasite on modernism, while chapter 4 explored the ways in which Dalí reconceived traditional illusionism as an art of superficiality, and chapter 5 followed Dalí as he fashioned the exactitude of the old masters into a device of masochistic self-restraint. This chapter examines one final component of Dalí's surrealism of the tiny: if the history of art could be mined not only for its great achievements but also for its "little things," what would happen if an artist of the present were to bring them back to life? If an artistic style dies a natural death, can it be brought back to life in the present? And if it can, is it reborn in its original form or in an altered state, like that of a ghost or a zombie?

We have been told *ars longa, vita brevis*. But the reality is that most art is as fleeting as human life. Indeed, it is the rare work of art that transcends time. The vast majority of works are discarded soon after they are completed. The works that are more fortunate typically persist just long enough to find themselves renounced by artists of a later generation. Such interest, albeit negative, inevitably fades and disinterest sets in. Eventually they, too, end up abandoned, and no less completely than those that were discarded just moments after they came into being. Such is the life of the "little things" of art history.

One wonders: once lost to history, do such works of art ever reemerge? If so, what happens when we stumble upon them in the present? Dalí's engagement with the techniques of the academicians and old masters raised these very questions about art and its history and in the process suggested that there were certain paintings that occupied a smaller universe. As a consequence of their historical marginality their "liberation" in the present would cause them to be, like the parasite, the simulacrum, and the masochist, a disruptive and potentially subversive force.

Walter Benjamin was the first to recognize the importance that outmoded objects and ideas played in the revolutionary logic of surrealism.[1] He recognized that that yesterday's fashions were, like yesterday's events in the life of an individual, the stuff of the social dreamworld. The surrealists combined their fragments in the same way that individuals combine fragments of their own memories of the previous day into an irrational and seemingly indecipherable yet richly meaningful dream. Building on Benjamin's insight, Hal Foster has pointed out, for example, that Max Ernst's collage novels exploited the parallel between one's individual memory fragments and the various cultural image fragments that can be cut from the pages of old picture postcards, botanical drawings, and nineteenth-century scientific journals. By fusing fragments from these two realms, Foster notes, "Ernst relates the historically outmoded to the psychically repressed at the very level of representation, specifically of representations residual in surrealist childhoods."[2]

Like Ernst, Dalí was interested in the ways in which events and memories are affected by time and even more in the disorienting effect that comes when these events and memories, now distant, are suddenly pressed up against one's face. But Dalí, unlike Ernst and Benjamin, was less interested in the effects of time on fashion and the commodities of capitalism than in the forgotten fragments of art history. The anachronisms that interested Dalí were less the styles of dress that women favored in years past than the styles of painting that artists practiced in decades and centuries past. For Dalí, pictorial "anachronism" was a form of "traumatic renewal" that shaped his conception not only of art history but also of his own art, his own attempt to reach into the past so as to revive it in the present.[3] In other words, whereas Ernst sought to fuse the world of the outmoded with the world of the dream, Dalí set out to *inhabit* the world of the outmoded and to revive it as a "trauma" in the present.

Like Dalí's other guiding concepts (objectivity, paranoia, superficiality, humility, submission), the concept of anachronism was developed over a period of years and was applied in different ways to different objects and actions. In fact, Dalí initially applied the concept not to his own practice but to the strange effect that he perceived in the buildings of Antonio Gaudí and Hector Guimard. As he put it in "The Rotting Donkey": "Here is what we can still like, this imposing mass of frenzied and cold buildings spread all over Europe, despised and neglected by anthologies and scholarly surveys. This is enough to put up against our porcine contemporary aestheticians, defenders of the detestable 'modern art,' and enough even to put up against the whole history of art."[4]

Although the term itself does not appear here, the key elements of "anachronism" are nonetheless visible: within the context of an ever-evolving modernism, the "mass of frenzied and cold buildings" of Gaudí and Guimard is an unsightly residue of a past better left forgotten ("despised and neglected"). Indeed, by 1930 the buildings and decorative objects produced by Gaudí and Guimard no longer enjoyed the enthusiastic reception they had received in the earlier part of the century. Art nouveau was no longer new: the broad appeal of its decorative excess and dramatic asymmetry was anathema to the anti-ornamentalism of the

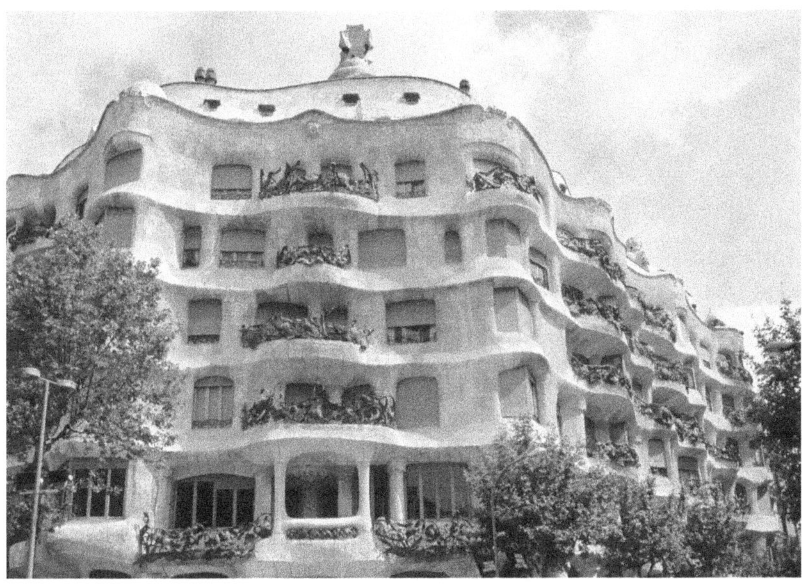

60. Antonio Gaudi, Casa Milà, 1905–10. View of the façade. Casa Mila, Barcelona, Spain. Photo credit: Vanni/Art Resource, NY.

architectural avant-garde of the moment. Gaudí had died in 1926, and by the end of the decade Barcelona's younger generation of architects had oriented themselves around the simplicity and functionalism of Le Corbusier and the Bauhaus.[5] In Paris, Guimard suffered a similar fate. Although he was awarded the Légion d'honneur in 1929, by then the fanciful organicism and elaborate ornamentation that had made him famous had fallen into disrepute. Despite the award, Guimard received no more commissions in Paris. The man, like the movement, was a thing of the past.

Dalí was certainly aware of the modernist discourse within which art nouveau was understood as anathema, for he himself had participated in it just a few years earlier. In his 1928 essay "Poetry of the Mass-Produced Utility," Dalí enthusiastically embraced Le Corbusier's functionalism and emphatically denounced the decorative arts as "horrible," "useless," and "exceedingly pitiful efforts to discover anew procedures and techniques that are dead, devoid of possibilities, uneasily displaced and absurd."[6] But something changed in the years between the publication of "Poetry of the Mass-Produced Utility" and "The Rotting Donkey." Dalí's thought had taken a dialectical turn: it was precisely the outmodedness of the decorative arts that made them so significant to the present. In much the same way as blackheads disrupted the smooth skin of one's face, the "despised and neglected" buildings of Gaudí and Guimard functioned as abrasive intruders upon the homogeneity of the modern city.

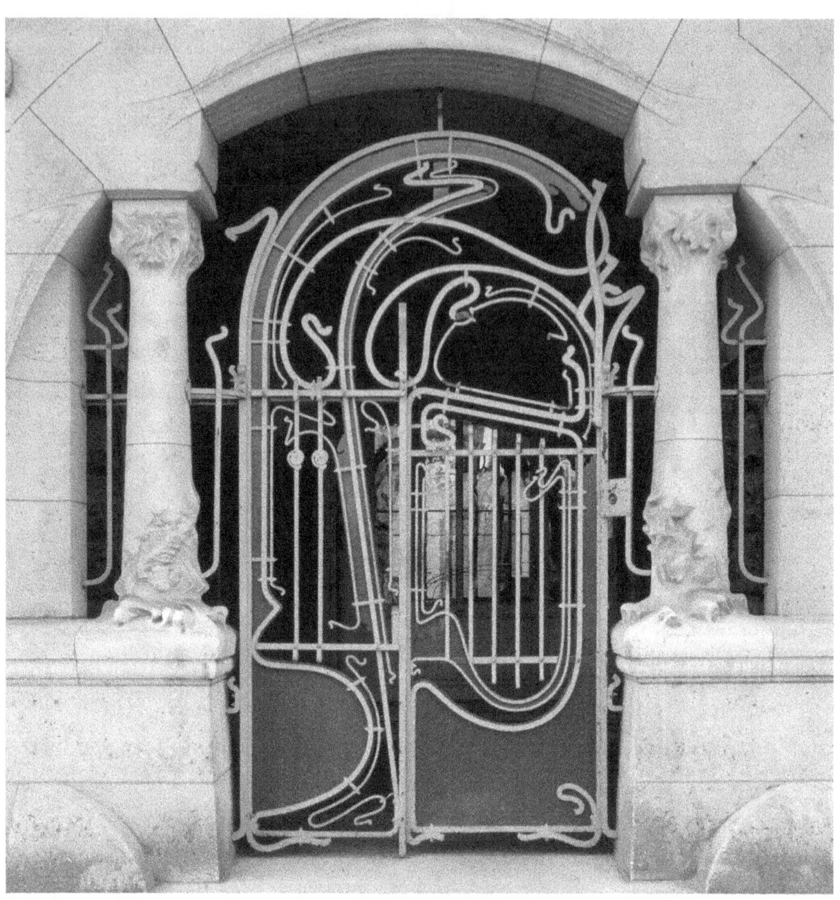

61. Hector Guimard, entrance gate, Castel Béranger, Paris. 1898. Photo credit: Andrea Jemolo/Scala/ Art Resource, NY.

Motifs inspired by Gaudí and Guimard began to appear in Dalí's work in the months leading up to the publication of "The Rotting Donkey" in 1930. *The Enigma of Desire* (fig. 31), for example, includes an enormous rock-like structure in the center of the painting (protruding from Dalí's portrait as the Great Masturbator) that is pocked with a collection of irregular niches in a manner that recalls the façade of Gaudí's Casa Milà in Barcelona (fig. 60). In *The Great Masturbator* (fig. 25) similarly organic elements proliferate; moreover, the large and undulating form on the right side of the painting echoes the organic shapes that grace the façade of Guimard's Castel Béranger (fig. 61). *The Lugubrious Game* (fig. 19) includes not only Gaudian and Guimardian elements similar to those mentioned above but also, in one small section of the painting, a carefully cut and pasted photographic image of a fragment of an elaborately designed architectural embellishment (fig. 62). In *Profanation of the Host* (fig. 63), the

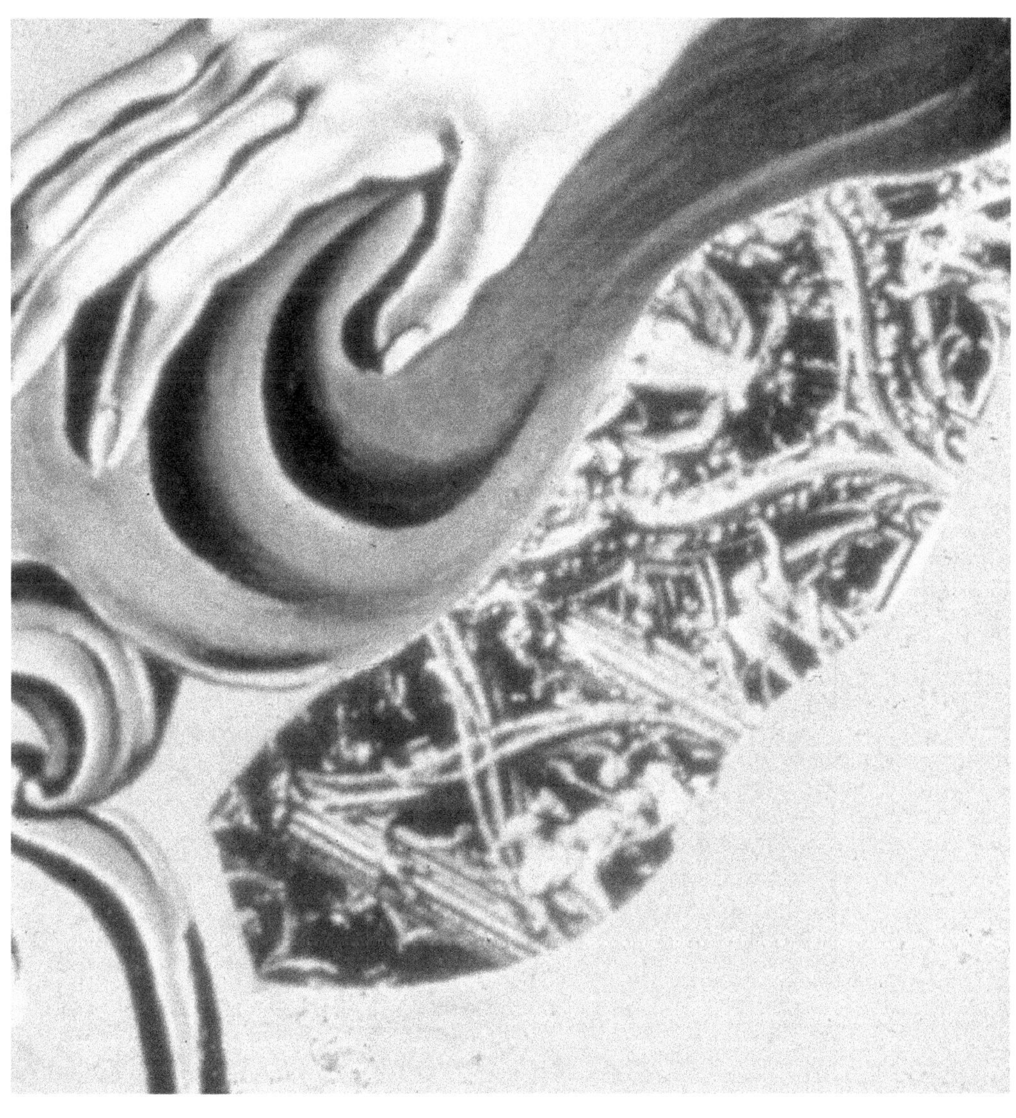

62. Salvador Dalí, detail of *The Lugubrious Game*, 1929. 44.4 × 30.3 cm (17.48 × 11.93 in.). Private collection. Image provided by the Fundació Gala-Salvador Dalí. Dalí, Salvador (1904–89) © ARS, NY.

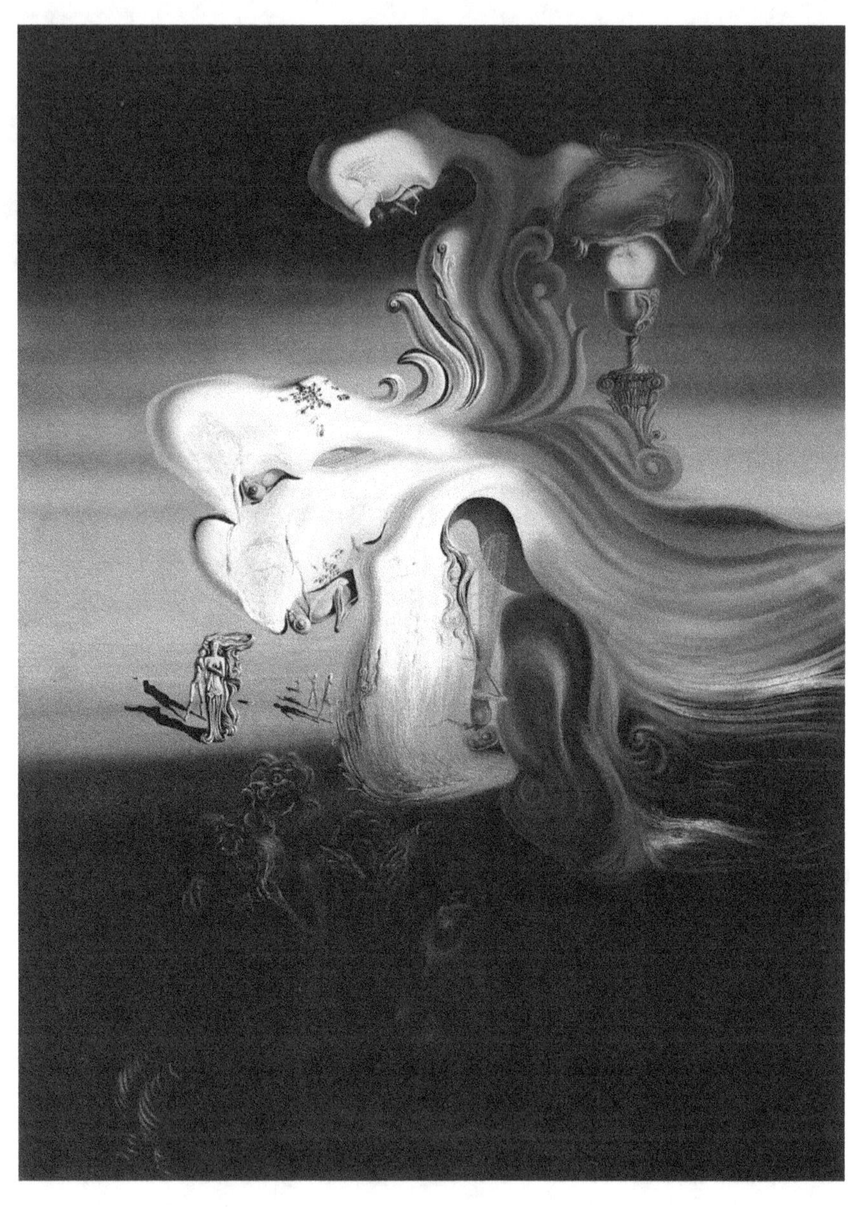

63. Salvador Dalí, *Profanation of the Host*, 1929. Oil on canvas, 100×73 cm (39⅜×28¾ in.). © Salvador Dalí. Fundació Gala-Salvador Dalí (Artists Rights Society), 2011. Collection of the Salvador Dalí Museum, Inc., St. Petersburg FL, 2011.

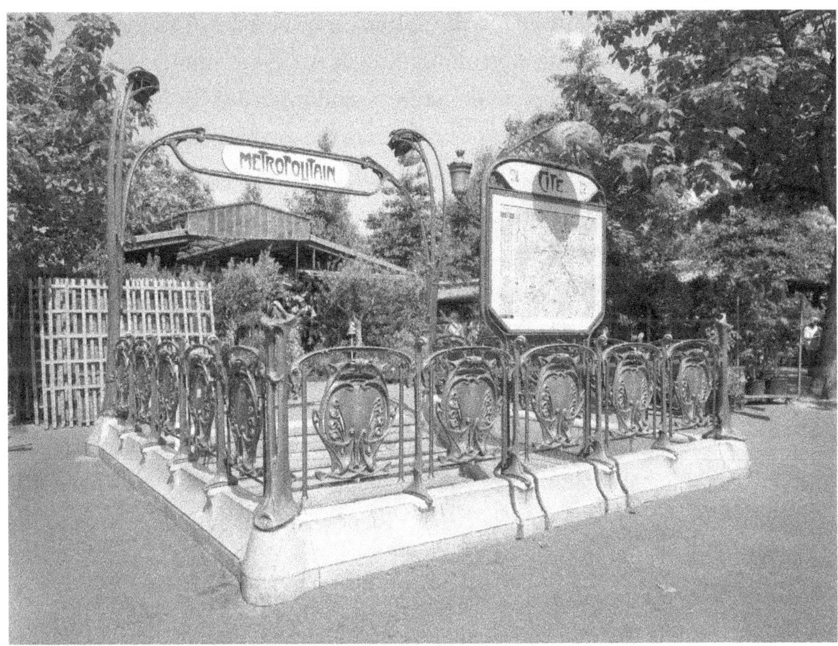

64. Hector Guimard, entrance to the Cité Métro station, Paris. This is one of the eighty-four art nouveau Métro accesses designed by Hector Guimard between 1899 and 1905. Photo credit: Vanni/Art Resource, NY.

proliferating flora common to Guimard's designs for the Paris Métro (fig. 64) have been transformed into Dalí's own, uniquely narcissistic vernacular. As in *The Great Masturbator*, the far right side of the painting is dominated by an enormous wave-like form from which emerge five distinct representations of Dalí's profile. The first (and most abstract) points down and serves as the trunk from which the other four profiles grow. Perched at the top are two profiles that recapitulate, through the differential application of facial hair, the male/female divide that we have already witnessed in *Little Ashes*.

In addition to serving as exemplars of the "despised and neglected," art nouveau played a crucial role in Dalí's psychoanalytic reflections on painting.[7] In "Love," for example, he describes art nouveau as standing alongside the likes of Gustave Moreau, de Chirico, and Joris-Karl Huysmans as a crucial prefiguration of surrealism's amorous depravity: "Everything achieving purity in our eyes bears the unmistakable mark of the vigorous, anti-natural, and depraved aspirations of the amorous imagination. The ancient human sacrifices of the Aztecs have just taken on all the taste and all the light of love. We cherish Sade, the masochism of Thomas Hardy; the metaphysical, artificial, unnatural, and troubling character of de Chirico's mannequins; the backward-looking artifices of Gustave Moreau, of Huysmans; the anti-natural splendor of all the deviations from the Greco-Roman culture culminating in Art Nouveau."[8]

Like the vile corpus of Sadean literature, art nouveau was for Dalí a symbol of both the unconscious and its status as a threat to the established order that sought its eradication. In "The Rotting Donkey" Dalí offered a more precise analogy between art nouveau and the unconscious when he associated the buildings of Gaudí and Guimard with Freud's concept of "infantile neurosis": "Perhaps no simulacrum has created ensembles to which the word *ideal* could apply so well as the great simulacrum constituted by the astounding Art Nouveau ornamental sculpture. No collective effort has managed to create a dream world so pure and so disturbing as the Art Nouveau buildings, which, existing on the fringes of architecture, constitute in themselves a true realization of solidified desires, and where the most violent and cruel automatism terribly betrays a hatred of reality and the need to find refuge in an ideal world, in a manner akin to the way this happens in infantile neurosis."[9]

Although never articulated explicitly, Dalí's conception of art nouveau clearly functions as a parallel and complement to the Dalínian double image. Like the double image, art nouveau is a manifestation of an unconscious process (the former, paranoia; the latter, neurosis). In addition, art nouveau architecture is, like the double image, evidence of a connection between the world of material reality and the world of mental images: the double image is produced by the paranoiac transformation of material reality into a mental image, while the art nouveau building is a neurotic transformation of a mental image into material reality. As Dalí put it, the buildings of Gaudí and Guimard should be recognized as architectural manifestations of "solidified desires."

Initially used as a means of establishing art nouveau's complementary relationship to the double image, the concept of solidified desire was subsequently adopted by Dalí as a general principle of sculptural production. In "Surrealist Objects" (1931), for example, Dalí described four different surrealist sculptures — by Alberto Giacometti, André Breton, Valentine Hugo, and Dalí — as "the embodiment of . . . desires."[10] That is, like the buildings of Gaudí and Guimard, they were the materialization of unconscious processes. Although Dalí himself made only a handful of such objects, his concept of the surrealist object proved to be among his most celebrated.[11] In part this was a consequence of the space that Breton had opened up to his colleagues following the publication of *Surrealism and Painting*. First drafted in 1925 and appearing in installments in *La Révolution Surréaliste*, the full text was published in book form in 1928. Breton's text focused exclusively on works of two dimensions (in addition to painting and drawing, Breton included Ernst's collages and Man

Ray's photograms), which naturally left room for others to provide an analogous study of surrealist sculpture.[12]

In fact, Dalí's subsequent writings on sculpture suggest that he was working to fill the gap that had been left by Breton. In "The Object as Revealed in Surrealist Experiment" (1932) Dalí constructed a typology of surrealist objects, and in "Cher Breton" (1933) he offered an etiological explanation for the emergence of surrealist objects — a parody of the evolutionary logic of modernism whereby one artistic gesture displaces its predecessor only to be displaced by the next.[13] The surrealist object, Dalí insisted, was the natural, evolutionary outgrowth of cubist collage:

> All these objects and ingredients which, at the beginning of the *papier collé*, closely adhered to the picture, were now increasingly hanging from it in an independent, even loose, manner, getting to be less and less stable, less and less stuck. We are already at the point where the shoes and the stones dangle from the picture by a string. One perceives then that the picture has had it, that it is ready to give up the rest of its life, that its life is hanging by a thread, that the object is hanging by a thread; the object physically drops from the picture and begins its prenatal life out of it. The prenatal life of the Surrealist object is our specialty.[14]

In other words, according to Dalí, the true "living continuation of Cubism" was neither Léger nor Mondrian but rather the solidified desires of the sort that first materialized in the art nouveau buildings of Gaudí and Guimard.[15]

SUMMONED TO LIFE AGAIN

Dalí's description of surrealist objects as "the living continuation of Cubism" is all the more significant in that it suggests that they emerged as a consequence of the demise of painting ("one perceives then that the picture has had it, that it is ready to give up the rest of its life, that its life is hanging by a thread"). What, then, might be envisioned for painting now that its life hangs by a thread? Here, too, art nouveau provided a new way of grasping the significance of artistic practices in historical terms — in this instance, the significance of academic and old master painting within the context of modernism.

At stake for Dalí was the issue, first raised in "The Rotting Donkey," of the art historical reception of art nouveau as "despised and neglected." What mattered was not only the fact of art nouveau's "dream world," but also the means by which it was materialized. Dalí addressed this issue in a brief text (roughly two hundred words) written to accompany his 1931 exhibition at the Galerie Pierre Colle (June 3–15). The text, "Ornamental Art above All," was printed on a tri-fold card that also included reproductions of two recently completed paintings, *Profanation of the Host* and *The Persistence of Memory*. The exhibition included twenty-four works by Dalí as well as what was described on the card as "three 'Art Nouveau' objects."[16] By contextualizing the exhibition in this manner — between three art nouveau objects and a two-hundred-word essay on "ornamental art"— Dalí effectively framed his newest paintings as pictorial manifestations of art nouveau architecture.

Brief though it is, the essay attempts to outline a theory of memory (the "persistence" of the past into the present). In particular, it proposes that we understand the construction of architectural history as akin to the construction of dreams — that is, as determined by memories and the unconscious processes enacted on them in sleep. Art nouveau design is thus more than "solidified desire"; it is also the architectural equivalent of the manipulations of memory that take place during sleep. According to Dalí, we should understand the buildings of Gaudí and Guimard as having drawn on the architectural motifs of the past in the same way as a dream draws on motifs from one's past. And just as reason and decorum are violated by one's nocturnal fantasies, so too are reason and decorum violated by the florid and excessive designs of art nouveau. Moreover, in both instances the past is ransacked without regard to the hierarchical order with which history (both personal and architectural) is constructed and sustained. As Dalí put it in the essay's first sentence: ". . . ornamental art above all, the most stereotyped ornamental art, in particular the one that, with the least conviction, repeats and mixes memories of distant and diverse styles [styles lointains et divers], not without a touch of fantasy. It is in such ornamentation that the future will investigate the automatism which is disclosed painfully and with cruelty by each accident, each *cessation*, each *bifurcation*, each *convergence*, that is to say, each symptom of latent content, all unfailingly foul in the most exemplary fashion."[17]

By proposing that art nouveau "repeats and mixes" past styles — regardless of their place or time (styles both "distant and diverse") — and by describing its various processes with terms like "cessation," "bifurcation," and "convergence," Dalí established the designs of Guimard and Gaudí as procedurally analogous to the Freudian dreamwork and its processes of "condensation," "substitution," and "displacement."[18] In other words, art nouveau designs fuse disparate fragments of architectural history in the same way as the dreamwork fuses (distant and diverse) fragments of one's memory.

Dalí's conception of art nouveau as a dreamwork architecture was articulated more elaborately two and a half years later in "Concerning the Terrifying and Edible Beauty of Art Nouveau Architecture" (1933): "With Art Nouveau, architectural elements of the past, in addition to being submitted to a frequent and complete convulsive-formal grinding that will give birth to a new stylization, will be summoned to life again and called to survive under their real original aspect, so that combined with one another, being merged within one another (in spite of their most irreconcilable and implacable intellectual antagonism), they are going to attain the highest degree of aesthetic depreciation, exhibiting in their relations the kind of terrible impurity that knows no equivalent or equal other than the immaculate purity of oneiric intertwinings."[19]

In addition to associating the combinatory process of art nouveau with that of the dream, Dalí's text invokes the trope of the living and the dead: the gaze of the art nouveau architect is necrological and the objects of his consideration are the dead styles of past architecture. The result — as suggested by the notion of a "terrible impurity"— is a kind of monster, a grotesque creature composed of the severed limbs and dry bones of architectural history: "In an Art Nouveau building, Gothic is transformed into Hellenic, into Far-Eastern, and, if ever this comes to mind — through some unintentional fantasy — into Renaissance, which, in its turn, may become pure 'dynamic-asymmetrical' (!) Art Nouveau, all this within the 'imbecilic' time and space of *a single window*, in other words, in the little-known and probably vertiginous time and space that, as we have just insinuated, are none other than those of the dream."[20]

Here, for the first time, Dalí made explicit the fundamental violations of Gaudí and Guimard. The "terrible impurity" of art nouveau derives from the way it combines — without concern for region or history — the motifs of Gothic, Hellenic, far eastern, and Renaissance architecture into a single, "unfailingly foul" structure.

For Dalí, this is the signal achievement of Gaudí and Guimard: to have refused to accept the modernist imperative of contemporaneity, the imperative that the new eclipse the old, the living displace the dead. Art nouveau violates this imperative by reanimating the dead and reinserting it into the present. It was art nouveau's unique condition as the architectural reanimator that led Dalí to conclude that it was "the most original and the most extraordinary phenomenon in the history of art." The refusal of art nouveau to affirm the modernist imperative to contemporaneity distinguished it as "an unprecedented revolution of the 'sentiment of originality.'"[21]

Although the concept of anachronism was, as I have argued above, implicit in Dalí's initial descriptions of art nouveau, the word itself did not appear until the publication of "Concerning the Terrifying and Edible Beauty of Art Nouveau Architecture" in 1933, where it was explicitly associated with the idea of materialized dreams: "*Anachronism*, that is to say, the 'delirious-concrete' (a sole life constant), appears to us in this way (in view of the intellectual aestheticism with which we are credited) as the essence of the 'disoriented-ephemeral' (ridiculous melancholic)."[22] Unfortunately, the text veers off in a different direction and the reader is left wondering what to make of it. However, "The Latest Modes of Intellectual Stimulation for the Summer of 1934" offers a more detailed account of the concept. The essay begins with a definition of anachronism in terms that are consistent with Dalí's earlier account of art nouveau as the reanimation of distant and decrepit styles of architecture: "Anachronism is the single '*imaginative constant*' capable of perpetual '*traumatic renewal*,' thanks to which it becomes possible to snatch raw and living lumps from that hard and extremely thick thing which is the sentimental fog from which are formed the very cheeks of memory." Like the buildings of Gaudí and Guimard, anachronism is the unwelcome interruption of the past into the present, the sudden emergence of that which "goes out of fashion in such a truculent and weighty way that it appears to us right away (a slight hindsight will do) . . . with the shrill characteristics of the 'unprecedented' . . . [and which] haunt[s] us with furor."[23] In this we can see more clearly why Dalí was drawn to art nouveau: not only was it an architecture composed of distant and unrelated motifs, it was itself a style that had recently gone out of fashion. By virtue of their status as outmoded art nouveau buildings "haunt" the cities of Barcelona and Paris like spirits of the deceased.

Dalí is insistent that anachronisms such as art nouveau are by no means benign and inert remnants of bygone eras and should instead be recognized as violent and menacing intruders: "Far from being the unusable, so-called 'stuffed thing,' considered inoffensive by the intellectual pseudo-experience which ironically disposes of it in the 'storehouse of the junk of the ages,' 'anachronism' is, on the contrary, a real and living thing, a thing having flesh and bones."[24] The notion of anachronism as a kind of monster — a grotesque and haunting revenant — is reiterated even more graphically in the following passage: "'Anachronism' is a profoundly sanguinary thing, profoundly biological, and authentically spectral, for which, as you all know from your own life experience, it would be enough to surprise us in a moment of sentimental distraction in order to leave in our flesh and our memories a mark of the real bites of poetry, and in order to rip out from us, with the slashing claw of anxiety, one of the most nutritious pieces of our intellectual anatomy, to the point of exposing out in the open the frightening white of the bare bone of our own death."[25] Like Shelley's Dr. Frankenstein, makers of anachronism produce monsters of the undead: biological yet spectral organisms that parasitize the living.[26]

For Dalí, it was important that his readers understood the degree to which his concept of anachronism was at odds with the common understanding of tradition. Tradition is that which serves as the foundation for the present. It is solid, secure. Tradition is that which "stands the test of time" and serves as the benchmark against which to judge the efforts of the present. Tradition is all that persists in the present as the true and the beautiful: "Outside the grandiose and extra-swift 'anachronisms' there is the thing the aesthetes call beauty; it is always there unchanging, never going out of fashion, always the same, thoroughly identical to itself, thoroughly in good repair, thoroughly abstract, thoroughly turned out; it is eternal; it provokes, as Ozenfant rightly says, an 'uplifting feeling'; it is thoroughly pantheistic, thoroughly and comfortably Catholic, it is there."[27]

Beauty never ages, never decays. It uplifts, comforts, and promises us immortality. Anachronism, on the other hand, is a reminder of the persistence of death. It is beauty's antithesis: traumatic, sanguinary, imbecilic.

BECOMING ANACHRONISTIC

Dalí's understanding of anachronism is thus comprehensible only in relation to the contemporaneous discourse of modernism within which it was developed.[28] Like most avant-garde artists of his generation, Dalí denied that that the past held universal truths to which the present ought to submit; like them, he considered the past a threat to order and advancement. But unlike his contemporaries, he came to believe that it was precisely because of its potential to disrupt the present that the past deserved attention; precisely because it is outmoded and ugly and arbitrary and no longer of universal significance, the past — as anachronism — is able serve a different role in the present. The elements of the past that came to interest Dalí in the thirties were not the time-tested and transcendent monuments we admire as exemplars of universal beauty and wisdom but rather the elements of the past that we wish rather to forget: history's "most shady, discredited, and shameful" acts.[29]

In the years after 1930 Dalí transformed his theory of art nouveau into a pictorial program in which he sought to reanimate history's "most shady, discredited, and shameful" paintings and combine them — in the manner of Gaudí and Guimard — with other "distant and diverse" elements from the history of art. Whereas his reference points in the years before 1930 included Miró, Picasso, Arp, Ernst, Tanguy, and other avant-garde painters of the period, his subsequent reference points were almost exclusively outdated: not only Vermeer and Meissonier but also Arnold Böcklin (1827–1901), Jean-François Millet (1814–75), and Paolo Uccello (1397–1475).

While by no means inconsequential to the history of European art, none of Dalí's reference points can be classified as among the most canonical. As we have seen, in Dalí's day Vermeer was perceived as a figure on the margins. The same is true of both Böcklin and Millet (the latter unquestionably in a class beneath his contemporaries Gustave Courbet and Édouard Manet). Uccello, a painter renowned for his exacting application of geometric perspective, was, like Millet and Böcklin, an artist whose stature was eclipsed by others of his generation (which, in Uccello's case, included Masaccio, Donatello, and Botticelli). And finally, in modeling himself after Meissonier, Dalí was emulating a painter renowned for his obdurate commitment to the techniques of the old masters and dedication to the exacting reconstruction of historical events (down to the tiniest details). Insofar as Meissonier was, for the artists of Dalí's generation, emblematic of all that the avant-garde had laid to rest, he was also emblematic of what made Dalí's anachronisms so grotesque.

The interest that Dalí had in the works of Vermeer, Böcklin, Millet, and Uccello was thus consistent with his abiding identification with all that was small. The artists Dalí collected in his own private pantheon were invariably the *smaller* artists of the Western tradition. This pantheon included neither Leonardo nor Michelangelo, neither Titian nor Rembrandt, neither Monet nor Cézanne (that is, until the 1940s, when Dalí's identifications shifted dramatically). The works of these latter artists are the principal monuments of art history; their value is timeless, their influence universal. On the other hand, the artists to whom Dalí was drawn existed on the margins of art history, their influence on us smaller, our memory of them vaguer. As such, their persistence into the present cannot accord them the same status as the great masters of their respective generations. If Leonardo's *Giaconda* is said to transcend time and place it is precisely because it is perceived to have remained vital to the present. Its historical transcendence is predicated on its distinction from the myriad works of past art that today are of only historical significance, works of art that lived fully in their own time but live no more in ours. The works that Dalí reanimated were those whose time had come and gone, works whose significance was in the past and therefore whose influence on the present — were it to exist at all — would be entirely different than the influence exerted by the timeless works of Leonardo, Raphael, and Rembrandt.

VERMEER, DE CHIRICO, BÖCKLIN

The peculiarity of Dalí's attempted reanimation is especially evident in his treatment of Vermeer. In previous chapters we have seen how Dalí mobilized the image of Vermeer as a model of humility, patience, and machinic objectivity. Vermeer was emblematic not only of an attentiveness to the small but also of superficiality and submission to a rule. It is no surprise, then, that Dalí's advancing identification with the morbid and the decrepit would likewise inflect his reception of his favorite role model. In the text "Daydream" (1930), for example, Dalí proposed that Vermeer's work exhibited "an unconscious funereal feeling."[30] He identified this feeling in de Chirico's work as well and located it, in part, in

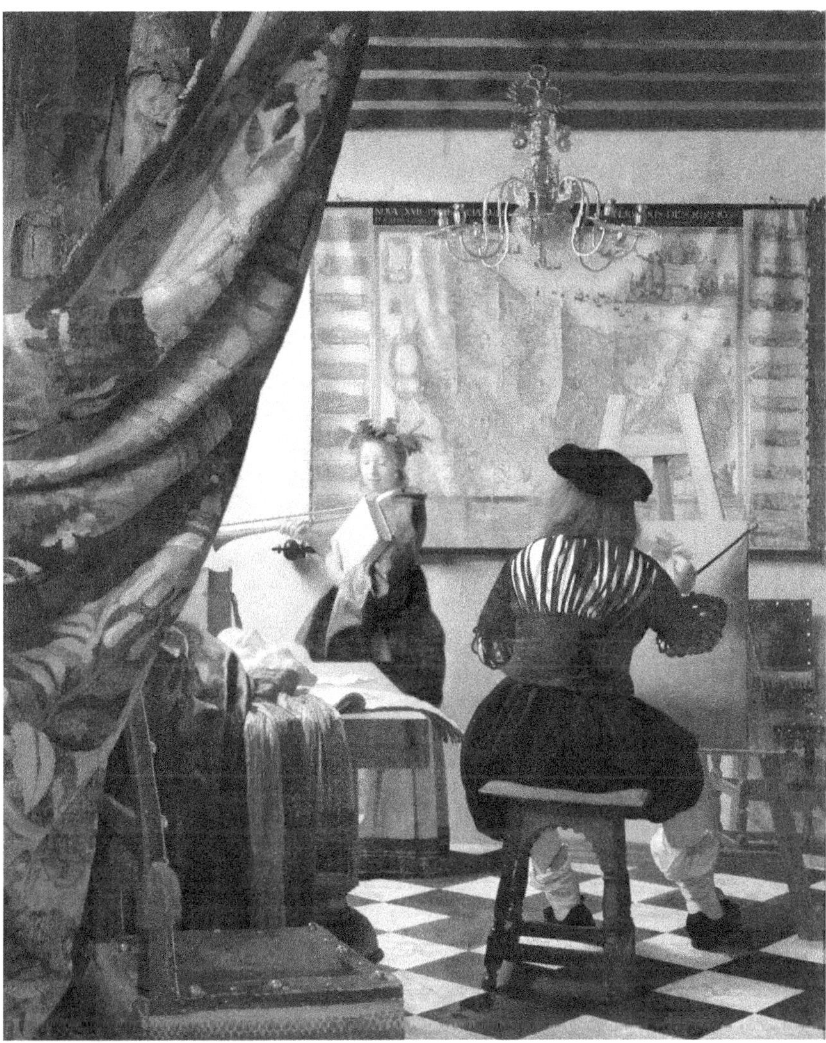

65. Jan Vermeer, *The Painter and His Model as Klio* (*The Allegory of Painting*), 1665–66. Oil on canvas, 120 × 100 cm. Kunsthistorisches Museum, Vienna, Austria. Photo credit: Erich Lessing/Art Resource, NY.

the ways in which the two painters manipulated perspective and lighting. In Dalí's mind, when Vermeer sat before his easel his gaze on the world was not only humble and patient, it was also, if only unconsciously, morbid.

The association between Vermeer and morbidity was articulated pictorially in a small handful of paintings that Dalí completed a few years after the publication of "Daydream." In each instance the "funereal feeling" that Dalí had attributed to Vermeer's work was incorporated directly into the painter's body itself. In all of these works Vermeer is represented from behind, looking out toward the

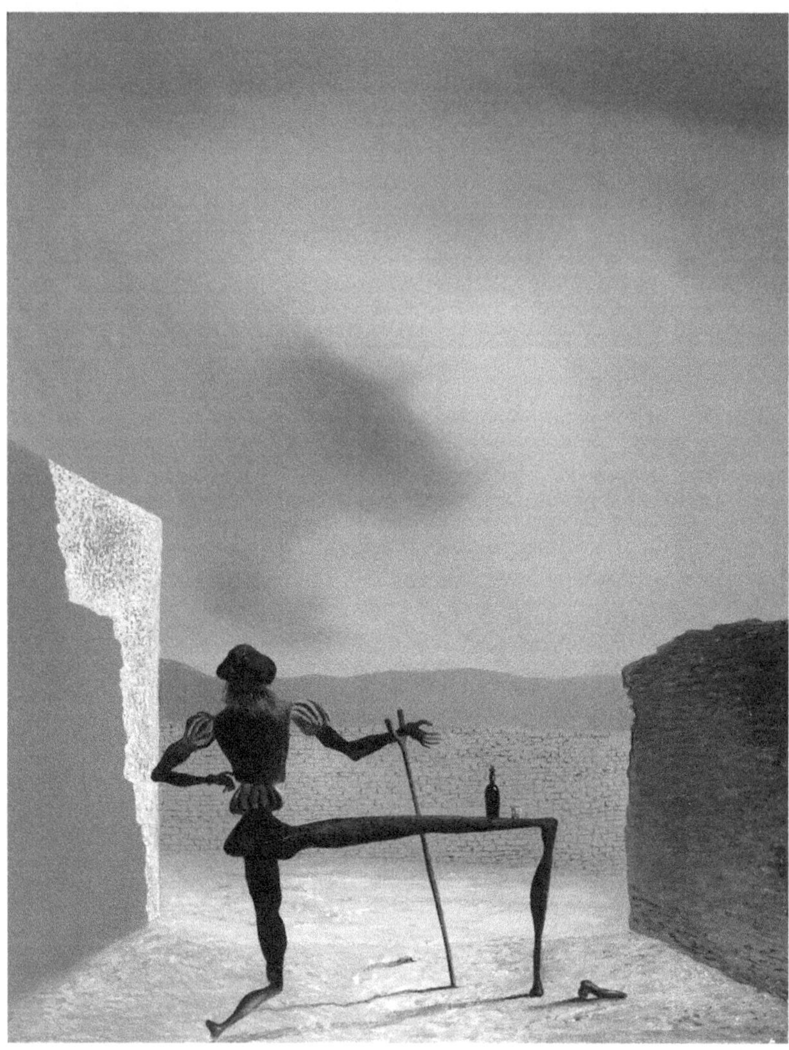

66. Salvador Dalí, *The Ghost of Vermeer of Delft Which Can Be Used as a Table*, 1934. Oil on panel, 18.10 × 13.97 cm (7 1/8 × 5 1/2 in.). © Salvador Dalí. Fundació Gala-Salvador Dalí (Artists Rights Society), 2011. Collection of the Salvador Dalí Museum, Inc., St. Petersburg FL, 2011.

landscape before his (and the viewer's) eyes. The depiction of Vermeer that Dalí used was lifted from the painter's own self-representation in *The Painter and His Model as Klio* (also known as *The Artist's Studio* and *An Allegory of Painting*) (fig. 65). In it Vermeer sits squarely on his wooden bench, his right leg extended at an angle. His left hand holds his mahl stick, which steadies his right hand as he applies a stroke of blue pigment. In paintings such as *Specter of Vermeer* and *The Ghost of Vermeer van Delft Which Can Be Used as a Table* (fig. 66) Dalí has removed the wooden stool so that Vermeer is made to kneel directly on the ground. The mahl stick that had delicately steadied Vermeer's right hand has been replaced by a wooden crutch that supports what now appears to be an entirely limp and lifeless arm. Vermeer's rather plump body has grown frail and emaciated; his right foot, the victim of gangrene or some other rot, is no longer attached to his body. In rendering his most beloved role model as a decrepit and skeletal ghost of his former self, Dalí has reimagined Vermeer as "a real and living thing, a thing having flesh and bones"—that is, as an allegory of anachronism.

De Chirico, the other painter that Dalí associated with the funereal, served an even more significant role in his developing conception of anachronism. In the late twenties Dalí turned to de Chirico's work more than once and described it as marked by "subtle frissons," "concrete hallucinations," and "bloodied perspectives."[31] In the years that followed he introduced de Chirico's frissons, hallucinations, and bloodied perspectives into his own work. Paintings such *The First Days of Spring* (fig. 16), 1929, and *Premature Ossification of a Railway Station*, 1930, for example, emulate and intensify the exaggerated and irregular perspectives as well as the strange juxtapositions and ominously extended shadows that de Chirico had employed in works like *The Red Tower* and *The Enigma of a Day* (fig. 67).[32]

In the years after 1930 Dalí began to acknowledge another aspect of de Chirico's work and, to some extent, to strategically misrepresent it as exemplifying his own anachronistic turn. This new aspect is underscored in the catalog essay that Dalí wrote to accompany his 1933 exhibition at the Galerie Pierre Colle. The essay was written as an open letter to Breton, and Dalí went so far as to include, in mock-epistolary fashion, the precise date (June 11, 1933) and place (Paris) where the letter was supposed to have been written. In it Dalí praised de Chirico's paintings not as exemplars of innovations in space and shadow (there are no references here to "subtle frissons" or "bloodied perspectives") but rather as paragons of stylistic conventionality, that is, as paintings emphatically bereft of technical innovation. The "genius" of de Chirico's work, according to Dalí, was that it "retains all the essential academic conventions: illumination, chiaroscuro, perspective, etc."[33]

In this Dalí was exaggerating, of course. De Chirico can hardly be said to have retained "all the essential academic conventions." That Dalí insisted on this, however, is a sign that it was important for him to establish de Chirico as his precursor. It was important, in other words, for de Chirico to be seen as an artist similarly devoted to the anachronistic exploitation of outmoded techniques and conventions. *The Tower* (fig. 68) is especially emblematic in this regard. Here the barren tower, de Chirico's most iconic architectural element, is exposed to a process of decomposition akin that which was inflicted on Vermeer's body.

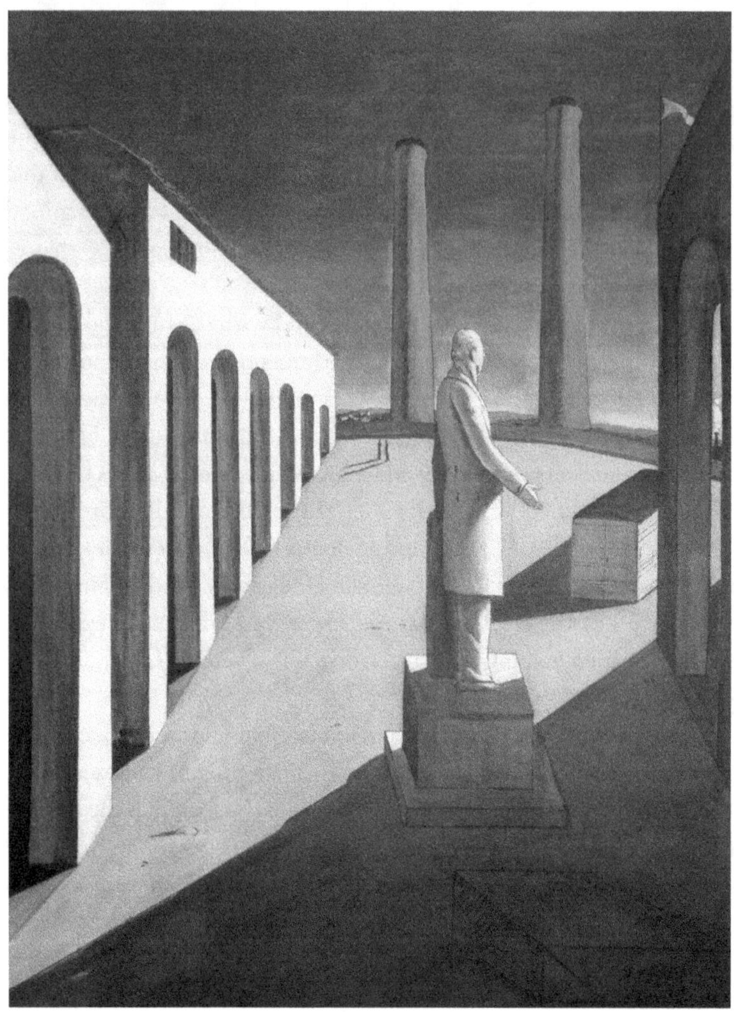

67. Giorgio de Chirico, *The Enigma of a Day*, early 1914. Oil on canvas, 6 ft., 1¼ in. × 55 in. James Thrall Soby Bequest. The Museum of Modern Art, New York NY. Chirico, Giorgio de (1888–1978) © 2011 Artists Rights Society (ARS), New York/SIAE, Rome. Digital Image © The Museum of Modern Art/Licensed by SCALA/Art Resource, NY.

More decrepit than the original on which it was based, Dalí's tower is marred by a jagged crack near the top and two large patches of exposed brick along its side. As had been the case with his anachronistic confrontation with Vermeer's ghost, *The Tower* represents an imaginative encounter with de Chirico that is likewise inflected with morbidity and decay.

De Chirico's tower was inserted into the landscape of a number of Dalí's paintings of the period. In most instances it was used alongside other, similar elements so as to construct the sensation that time and space no longer cohered. In

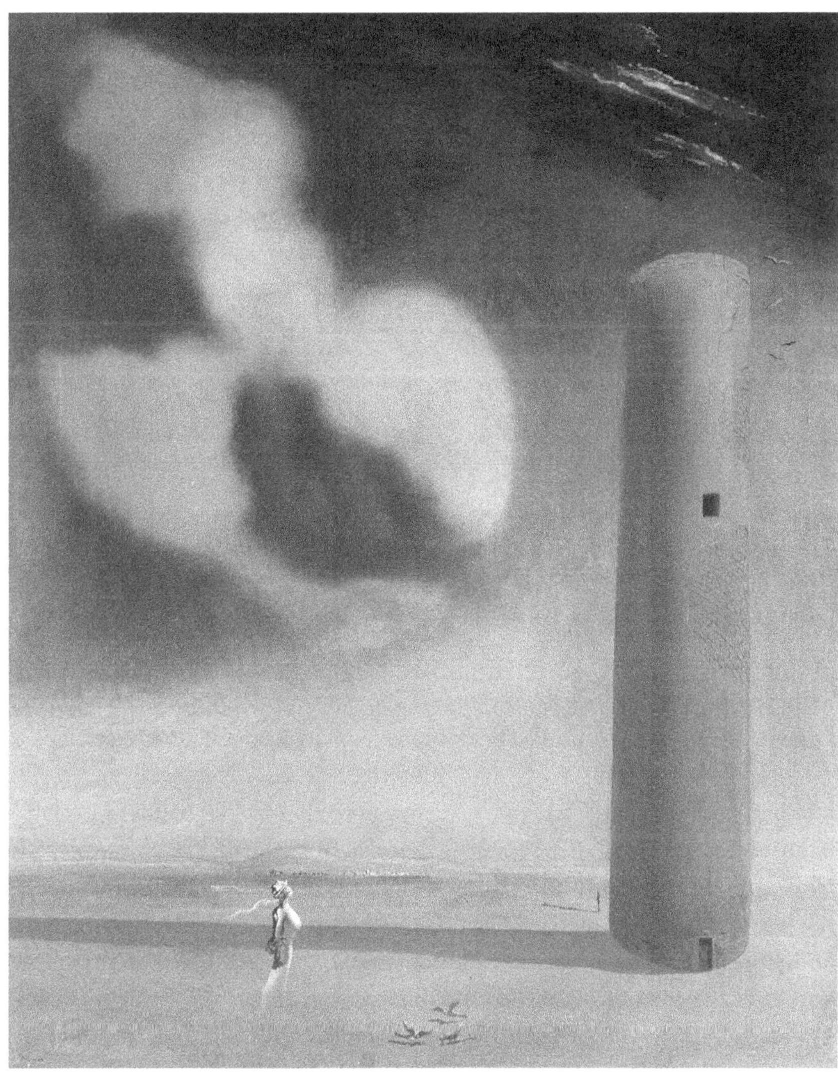

68. Salvador Dalí, *The Tower*, ca. 1935. Oil on canvas, 65.5 × 54.0 cm (25.79 × 21.26 in.). Kunsthaus Zürich, Zurich. Gift of Erna and Curt Burgauer collection. Dalí, Salvador (1904–89) © ARS, NY.

effect, Dalí exploited motifs such as de Chirico's tower and Vermeer's self-portrait in the same way that art nouveau exploited "distant and diverse" architectural motifs. If, as Dalí claimed, one of the defining characteristics of an art nouveau building was that "Gothic is transformed into Hellenic, into Far-Eastern, and, if ever this comes to mind — through some unintentional fantasy — into Renaissance," then the same can be said of Dalí's paintings of the thirties.[34] In them de Chirico is transformed into Vermeer, who is transformed into Böcklin, and so on.

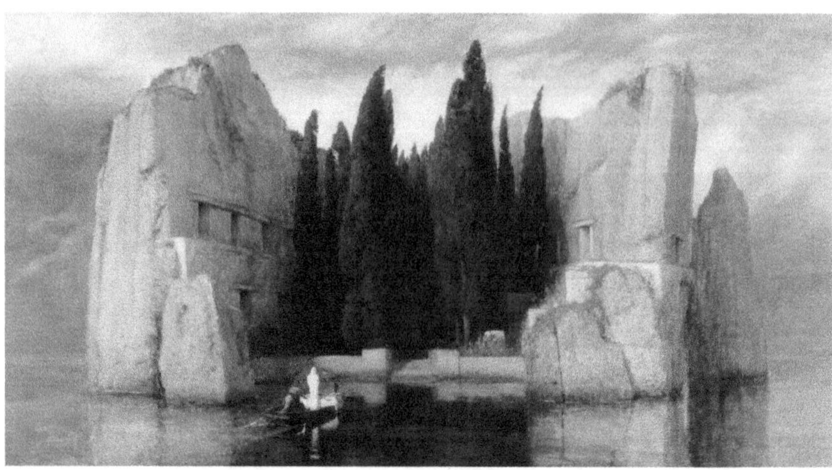

69. Arnold Böcklin, *The Isle of the Dead* (*Die Toteninsel*), 1883. Oil on canvas, 80×150 cm. Inv. 2/80. Nationalgalerie, Staatliche Museen, Berlin, Germany. Photo credit: bpk, Berlin/Nationalgalerie, Staatliche Museen, Berlin, Germany/Andres Kilger/Art Resource, NY.

In fact, the cloud that hovers in the sky of *The Tower* was meant to suggest to the knowing viewer the heavy and ominous storm clouds that one finds in a number of Böcklin's paintings. Böcklin's work — in particular, his depictions of *The Isle of the Dead* (fig. 69) — had influenced de Chirico as well, and by the midthirties Dalí was especially preoccupied not only with the clouds in Böcklin's paintings but also with the cypresses that rise from the rock as a mysteriously vital eruption from within an otherwise moribund island. Dalí first mentioned Böcklin's cypresses in 1930 in "Daydream", the same year in which he included one in *Premature Ossification of a Railway Station*.[35] By 1934 Böcklin's cypresses appeared in over a dozen of Dalí's paintings: sometimes singly, as in *Birth of Liquid Fears*, 1932, and *The Sense of Speed* (fig. 33), 1931, and sometimes in pairs or clusters, as in *Morning Ossification of the Cypress* (fig. 70), ca. 1934, and *Birth of Liquid Desires* (fig. 37), 1931–32.[36] In most instances Böcklin's clouds and cypresses are used as background elements, framing devices akin to the role that art nouveau played in sections of "Daydream," where the architectural elements establish the appropriately dreamlike setting within which surrealist activities take place. In other paintings, however, they function like Vermeer's spindly ghost — that is, as the painting's principal subject, the main actors in the depicted drama.

As was the case with Vermeer, Dalí was particularly fascinated by Böcklin's technique. In "Daydream" he described himself as struck by "the sense of death" evoked by Böcklin's painting, an experience he attributed to the work's near depthlessness.[37] For Dalí, the rigidly planar organization of Böcklin's painting

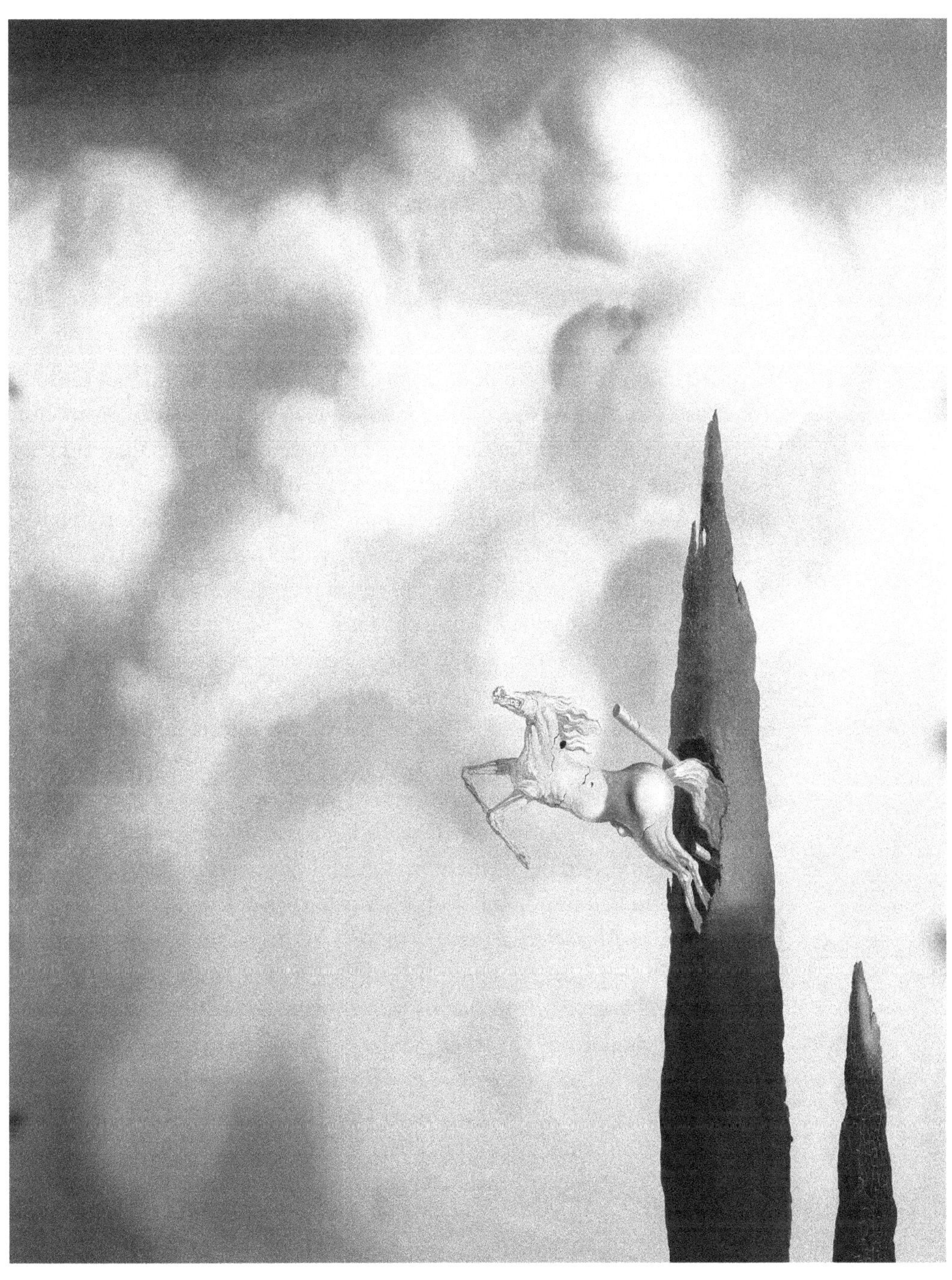

70. Salvador Dalí, *Morning Ossification of the Cypress*, ca. 1934. Oil on canvas, 82 × 66 cm (32.28 × 25.98 in.). Mr. and Mrs. Gilbert Kaplan collection, New York. Dalí, Salvador (1904–89) © ARS, NY. Photo credit: Erich Lessing/Art Resource, NY.

seemed to suggest that the water, island, and sky were somehow stacked on top of each other rather than receding into the distance. The painting's "frontality," as he called it, was no less disorienting than the "perturbations of perspective" he saw in de Chirico's work.[38] And while most of Dalí's paintings of the period deployed de Chirico's vertiginous perspective, a number of works, including *The Old Age of William Tell*, *On the Beach*, and *Birth of Liquid Desires*, adopted Böcklin's alternative manner of spatial construction.[39]

UCCELLO, THE SPECTER

By appropriating iconographic elements and pictorial techniques of artists as diverse as Vermeer, Böcklin, and de Chirico, Dalí was, in effect, constructing for himself a catalog of historical models and outmoded motifs that, although "dead" to the avant-garde of his day, could be reanimated in the manner of art nouveau's own architectural reanimations. Dalí's reanimation involved the fusion of a painter of the Dutch baroque with an Italian neoclassicist and a German symbolist — styles almost as "distant and diverse" as those that he discerned in the buildings of Gaudí and Guimard. In fact, on one occasion all three — Vermeer, de Chirico, and Böcklin — were merged on the plane of a single painting. In *Enigmatic Elements in a Landscape* (fig. 45), 1934, Dalí inserted the bony ghost of Vermeer (this time seated more comfortably on his wooden stool) into a landscape that includes, among other things, Böcklin's cypresses and storm clouds as well as de Chirico's red tower.

Atop the red tower hangs a small, white cloth that is held in place at the end of a long, thin rod. Although barely visible in this particular painting, this motif is readily identified in a number of other paintings of the period. It appears, for example, in *Masochistic Instrument* (fig. 71), 1933–34, where it is shown protruding from the center of one of Böcklin's cypresses. The nail or pin that holds the windswept fabric in place is painted with particular clarity. The motif reappears in similar ways in other paintings as well. In *Eclipse and Vegetable Osmosis*, 1934, the rod pierces the same Böcklinian cypress; in *Morphological Echo*, 1934–36, it emerges from a tiny window; in *Dreams on a Beach*, ca. 1934, it is lodged in some strange object hidden beneath a sheet; and in *Morning Ossification of the Cypress* (fig. 70) the rod has turned white, lost its dangling fabric, and is now accompanied by a striding white horse whose head and forelimbs appear to have, as the title suggests, turned to bone. As far as I can tell, Dalí never identified the source for this peripatetic rod, but its presence alongside a striding horse (in *Morning Ossification of the Cypress*), along with the fact that it is almost always emphatically foreshortened, suggests that the rod is a soldier's lance — in particular, a lance lifted from one of Paolo Uccello's battle

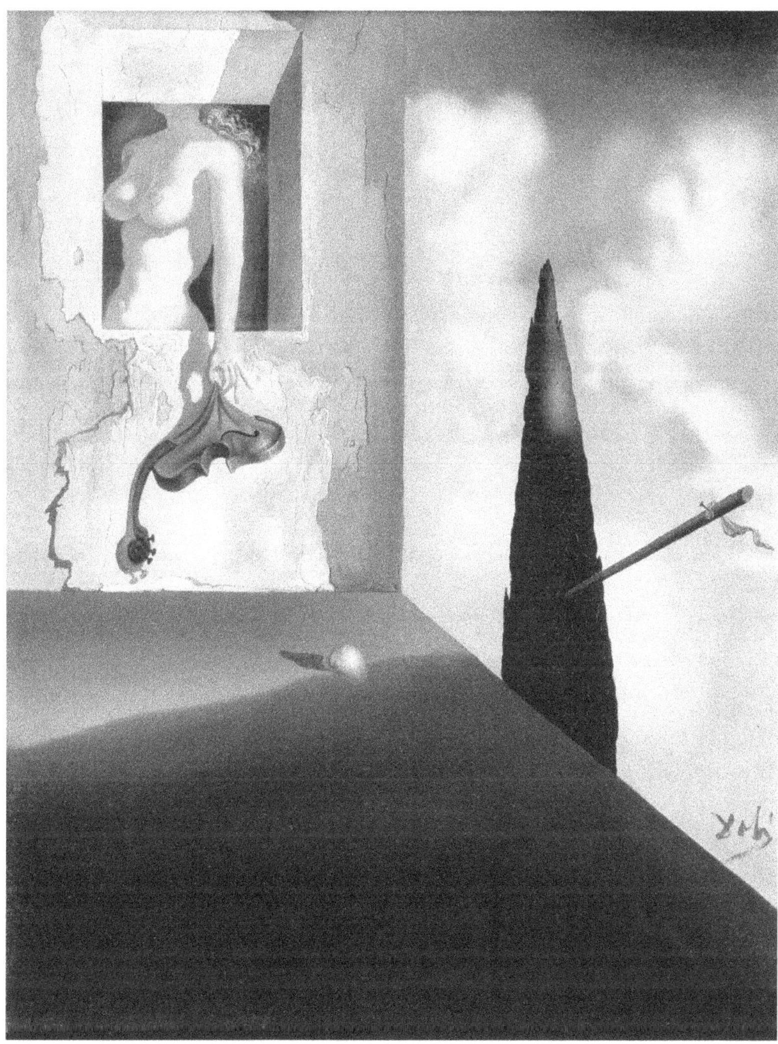

71. Salvador Dalí, *Masochistic Instrument*, 1933–34. Oil on canvas, 62 × 47 cm (24.41 × 18.50 in.). Private collection. Image provided by the Fundació Gala-Salvador Dalí. Salvador Dalí (1904–89) © ARS, NY. Photo credit: Erich Lessing/Art Resource, NY.

scenes. If this is in fact the case, then it would seem that *Enigmatic Elements in a Landscape* includes not only the anachronistic combination of neoclassicism, symbolism, and the Dutch baroque but also a touch of the Italian Renaissance.

References to Uccello appear in two of Dalí's texts from the 1930s. In "The Moral Position of Surrealism" (1930) Uccello is mentioned alongside Trotsky, Freud, Sade, and Heraclitus as one of surrealism's most significant predecessors, and four years later, in "The New Colors of Spectral Sex Appeal," Uccello is described as a "specter" that Dalí associated with "diagonals, staircase banisters,

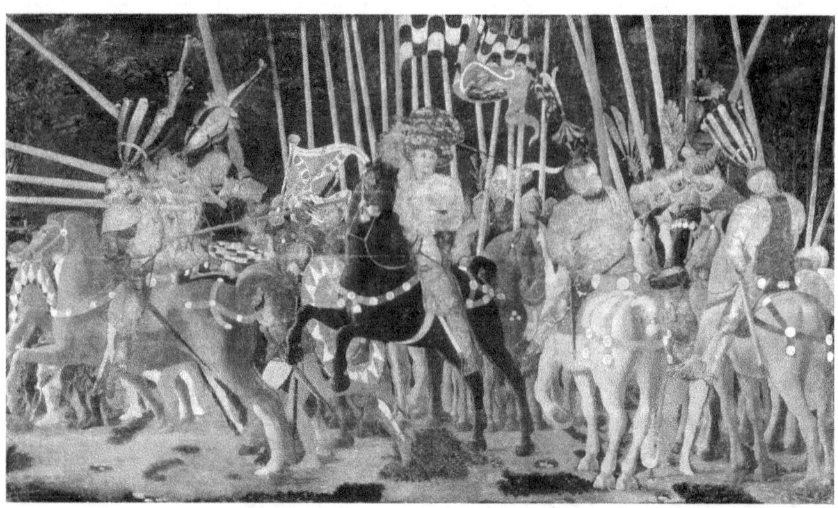

72. Paolo Uccello, *The Battle of San Romano in 1432 (The Counterattack of Micheletto da Cotignola)*, 1450–56. Oil on wood, 180 × 316 cm. Inv.: MI 469. Photo: J. G. Berizzi. Louvre, Paris, France. Photo credit: Réunion des Musées Nationaux/Art Resource, NY.

[and] ridges."[40] It is likely that Uccello was brought to Dalí's attention by Breton, who had mentioned him in his *Manifesto of Surrealism* and again in *Surrealism and Painting*, where Uccello's *The Battle of San Romano in 1432* (fig. 72) was described as a "clash of gold lances under a black sky."[41] In addition, Breton included a reproduction of a section of Uccello's *Profanation of the Host* in the December 1926 issue of *La Révolution Surréaliste* and again, two years later, in *Nadja*.[42] The section Breton reproduced depicts the tense moment when the family that had stolen the Host and attempted to burn it (causing it to bleed) waited nervously as a mob outside struggled to break into the home to rescue it (fig. 73). Uccello's depiction of the interior space as compressed and precipitously diminishing in depth underscored the tension evoked by the mysterious expressions on the figures' faces. To Breton "it seemed . . . full of hidden intentions, and in all respects, quite difficult to interpret."[43] Dalí's 1929 painting *Profanation of the Host* (fig. 63) adopts none of Uccello's spatial coordinates but includes, quite prominently, the bleeding Host of the original. Completed soon after Dalí was introduced to Breton and his group, the painting was likely intended to indicate that the young artist from Spain, although new to the surrealist movement, was already well versed in its principal texts and historical reference points.

Had the experience inspired Dalí to refresh his memory of Uccello's posthumous reputation, he might well have reread Giorgio Vasari's biography of Uccello. And had he done so, he surely would have been struck with the

22 UCCELLO, LE POIL

éprouver. Vivant par l'âme et la matière je n'aurai au jour voulu qu'à lever le doigt pour que ces mirages dérisoires soient balayés avec les premières épaves, au souffle de l'amour réciproque.

Robert Desnos.

UCCELLO, LE POIL

Pour Génica

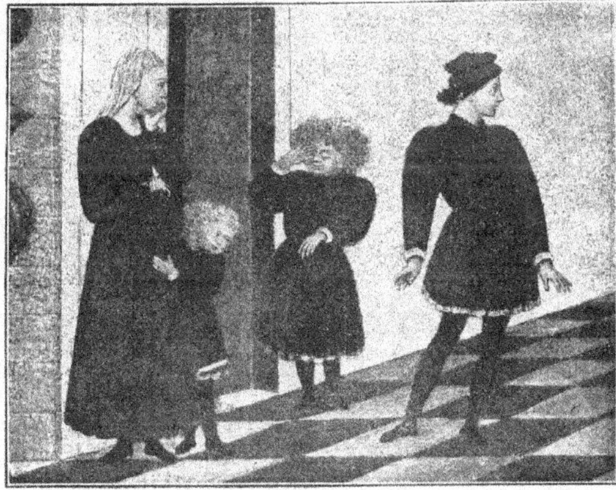

LA PROFANATION DE L'HOSTIE (DÉTAIL). *Paolo Uccello*

Uccello mon ami, ma chimère, tu vécus avec ce mythe de poils. L'ombre de cette grande main lunaire où tu imprimes les chimères de ton cerveau, n'arrivera jamais jusqu'à la végétation de ton oreille, qui tourne et fourmille à gauche avec tous les vents de ton cœur. A gauche les poils, Uccello, à gauche les rêves, à gauche les ongles, à gauche le cœur. C'est à gauche que toutes les ombres s'ouvrent, des nefs, comme d'orifices humains. La tête couchée sur cette table où l'humanité tout entière chavire, que vois-tu autre chose que l'ombre immense d'un poil. D'un poil comme deux forêts, comme trois ongles, comme un herbage de cils, comme d'un râteau dans les herbes du ciel. Etranglé le monde, et suspendu, et éternellement vacillant sur les plaines de cette table plate où tu inclines ta tête lourde. Et auprès de toi quand tu interroges des faces, que vois-tu, qu'une circulation de rameaux, un treillage de veines, la trace minuscule d'une ride, le ramage d'une mer de cheveux. Tout est tournant, tout est vibratile, et que vaut l'œil dépouillé de ses cils. Lave, lave les cils, Uccello, lave les lignes, lave la trace tremblante des poils et des rides sur ces visages pendus de morts qui te regardent comme des œufs, et dans ta paume monstrueuse et pleine de lune comme d'un éclairage de fiel, voici encore les traces augustes de tes poils qui émergent avec leurs lignes fines comme les rêves dans ton cerveau de noyé. D'un poil à un autre, combien de secrets et combien de surfaces. Mais deux poils l'un à côté de l'autre, Uccello. La ligne idéale des poils intraduisiblement fine et deux fois répétée. Il y a des rides qui font le tour des faces et se prolongent jusque dans le cou, mais sous les cheveux aussi il y a des rides, Uccello. Ainsi tu peux faire tout le tour de cet œuf qui pend entre les pierres et les astres, et qui seul possède l'animation double des yeux.

73. *La Révolution surréaliste* (December 1926): 22, with a detail from Paolo Uccello's *Profanation of the Host.*

sense that he had stumbled upon a kindred spirit. Evident throughout Vasari's account is the sense that Uccello was a man obsessed — to the point of near madness — with the intricacies of perspective. According to Vasari, had Uccello been able to temper his singular obsession he might have become the greatest painter of his generation. Instead, he died in near obscurity:

> Paolo Uccello would have been the most delightful and inventive genius in the history of painting from Giotto's day to the present, if he had spent as much time working on human figures and animals as he lost on problems of

> perspective; for although these things are ingenious and beautiful, anyone whose pursuit of them is excessive wastes hour after hour, exhausts his native abilities, and fills his mind with difficulties, quite often turning a fertile and effortless talent into one that is quite often sterile and overworked; and anyone who pays more attention to perspective than to human figures achieves an arid style full of profiles, produced by the desire to examine things in minute detail. Besides this, such a person frequently becomes solitary, eccentric, melancholy, and impoverished like Paolo Uccello who, endowed by Nature with a meticulous and subtle mind, took pleasure only in the investigation of certain problems of perspective which were difficult or impossible, and which, however original and vexing, nevertheless hindered him so much in painting figures that as he grew older, he grew even worse.[44]

Uccello, noted Vasari, was "a timid man" who protected his fragile ego by retreating into solitary study, "as if in the wild, for weeks and months without allowing himself to be seen." One day, after having felt belittled by the sculptor Donatello, "he did not have the courage to leave his house any longer and closed himself inside, devoting himself to perspective, which always kept him in poverty and obscurity until his death."[45]

Vasari's tale of an obsessive whose monomaniacal study of perspective led not only to his personal demise but also to the subsequent glory of Western painting is one that resonates with Dalí's own self-image. As such, the plunging perspectives that one encounters in so many of Dalí's paintings deserve to be understood not only in relation to de Chirico's "bloodied perspectives" but also to Uccello's "spectral" diagonals — above all, the myriad diagonals created by the "clash of gold lances" in *Battle of San Romano*. The singular product of Uccello's obsessive study of perspective, the lances in *Battle of San Romano* point in almost every direction, piercing and slicing not only the soldiers and their horses but also the very space in which the battle is engaged.

In instances where Dalí deployed his own sharply receding lance-like forms (as in *Morning Ossification of the Cypress* and *Masochistic Instrument*), the reference to Uccello's *Battle* is evoked with considerable directness. Like the cypress wrenched from the island in which it originally emerged, Dalí has shorn Uccello's lances from the riders who once held them. Now free to poke and pierce anything they wish (like the "liberated fingers" discussed in chapter 1), these lance-like forms signify the penetration of volume. They are, in this sense, the antithesis of Böcklinian "frontality." By combining the emphatic spatial penetration of Uccello with the equally emphatic flatness of Böcklin, Dalí set out to establish the same "irreconcilable and implacable intellectual antagonism" that distinguished the frenzied anachronisms of art nouveau.

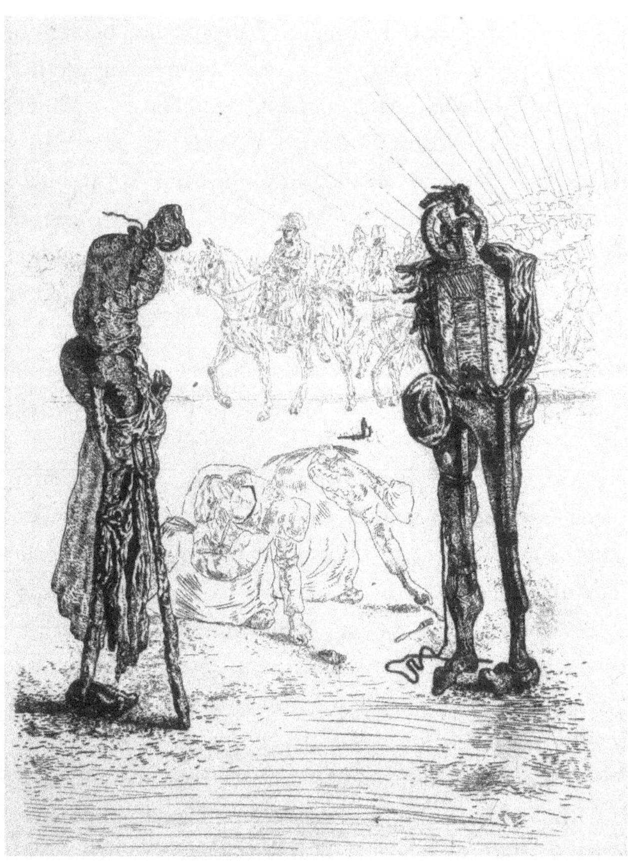

74. Salvador Dalí, illustration for *Les chants de Maldoror*, 1934. Tel Aviv Museum of Art, Tel Aviv, Israel. Salvador Dalí (1904–89) © ARS, NY.

MILLET'S VIOLENT AGITATION

Although Dalí left behind few textual indications of the meaning behind his incorporations of Vermeer, de Chirico, Böcklin, and Uccello, he wrote two detailed studies of Millet's painting *L'Angélus*. The first, a short text, appeared in June 1934 to accompany the exhibition of prints that Dalí had made to illustrate the republication of the proto-surrealist masterpiece *Les chants de Maldoror*, by Isidore Ducasse (Comte de Lautréamont) (fig. 74).[46] The second, much longer study (which appeared in 1963, years after it was written) has proven to be Dalí's most sustained and finely grained application of paranoia-criticism to a single object of analysis.[47] It is, in a sense, an effort akin to Roland Barthes's *S/Z*, in which the structuralist method is applied to every sentence of Balzac's *Sarrasine*.[48]

According to *The Secret Life*, a reproduction of *L'Angélus* had been hung on a wall of Dalí's elementary school in Figueres, where it exerted a mysterious influence on the young boy.[49] As Dalí matured, he came to consider Millet's painting in the same way as had his contemporaries — that is, as a sentimental illustration anathema to the avant-garde. By the thirties he came to the conclusion that, like the "despised and neglected" buildings of Gaudí and Guimard, Millet's *L'Angélus* was an object perfectly suited for anachronistic reanimation: "Due to my intellectual and artistic training, the painting later on merged into the most discredited and ineffective hierarchies of spiritual activity, and, consequently, sank into oblivion, as this was the case of the marvelous Art Nouveau architecture, for whose long and disgraceful repression I similarly try to take revenge."[50]

Dalí claimed that the image of *L'Angélus* appeared to him "all of a sudden, without any recent recollection nor any conscious association that lends itself to an immediate explanation," in June of 1932.[51] Beginning that year and extending into 1935, Dalí included references to *L'Angélus* in more than a dozen paintings and prints. In them Millet's paired figures (and pitchfork and wheelbarrow) are subjected to a variety of distortions and transformations — effects that result in visual analogues to the unconscious mental processes of condensation, substitution, and displacement. In *Archeological Reminiscences of Millet's Angelus* (fig. 75) the two central figures have been transformed into crumbling, de Chirico–like towers, with Böcklinian cypresses emerging from their crevices. In *Atavism at Twilight* (fig. 38) the setting has been shifted from farm to beach, and the tools of the two protagonists grow like tumors from beneath their skin. Other paintings subject Millet's two figures to even more violent mutations. In *Architectonic Angelus of Millet* (fig. 39), for example, a father and child stand together beneath a massive sculptural monument to Millet's protagonists. In this instance the farmers have been transformed into a pair of enormous Gaudian ornamentations, one of which advances toward the other with a gigantic, white, lance-like protrusion. In these and other works of the period Dalí's fusion of Millet, Vermeer, Böcklin, de Chirico, and Uccello functions in much the same way as do art nouveau's transformations of disparate architectural motifs. Folded one into the other, Dalí's "impure" historical quotations are subject to ever more "traumatic" manipulations, the result of which stands as a grotesque reanimation of the dead.

In addition to serving as an exemplary subject of paranoiac-critical analysis and as a source of malleable motifs, Millet's work was also a singular object of emulation. What seems to have astonished Dalí above all was the profoundly deceptive nature of Millet's painting: not only did it depict figures who appeared to have something to hide (the male farmer, Dalí insisted, clasped his hat to his

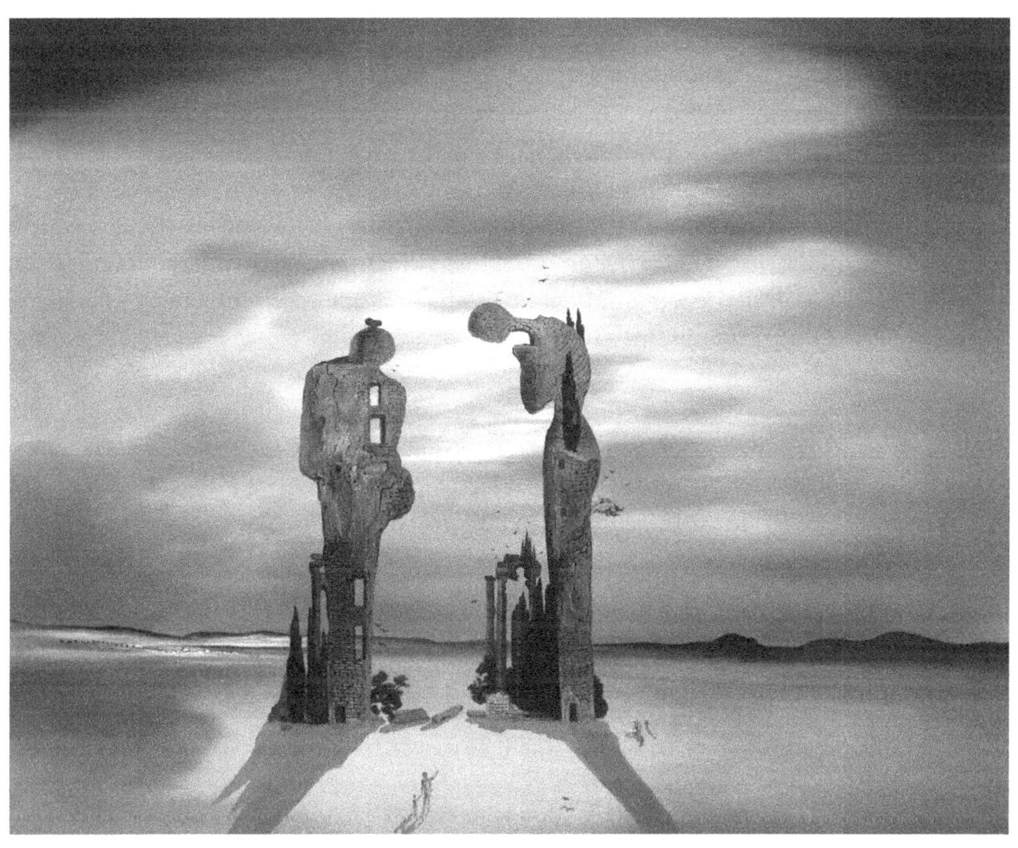

75. Salvador Dalí, *Archeological Reminiscence of Millet's Angelus*, 1933–35. Oil on canvas, 13¾ × 15¼ in. © Salvador Dalí. Fundació Gala-Salvador Dalí (Artists Rights Society), 2011. Collection of the Salvador Dalí Museum, Inc., St. Petersburg FL, 2011.

waist so as "to conceal [his] state of erection"), but the painting itself was, according to Dalí, a deceit. Indeed, the central aim of his paranoiac-critical analysis of *L'Angélus* was to demonstrate that even the most anodyne and sentimental representations sometimes conceal the most repugnant and shameful fantasies. For Dalí, what was most astounding was the contrast between the painting's inarguable sentimentality on the one hand and its traumatizing effect on the other: "The admiration and sudden attraction I felt for this painting contrasted with the paucity, if not almost complete lack of direct means (explanatory or even lyrical) that would have allowed me to objectify, however, poorly, the very serious and very violent agitation on this occasion."[52]

Millet's *L'Angélus* thus served Dalí as evidence that it was possible to construct a painting that was at once incontestably anodyne yet simultaneously, if inexplicably, traumatic. This, I would argue, was the most profound lesson that Dalí drew from Millet's painting. It is a lesson incorporated not only in those paintings that literally appropriate Millet's iconic figures but also, and perhaps more significantly, in those that seek to provoke a similarly inexplicable sensation of distress.

In the midthirties Dalí attempted a number of such paintings, including *Paranoiac-Astral Image* (fig. 48), 1934; *Mediumnistic-Paranoiac Image* (fig. 42), ca. 1934; *Angelus of Gala* (fig. 59), 1935; *The Chemist of Ampurdàn in Search of Absolutely Nothing*, 1936; *The Alert*, 1934; *The Fine, Average, Invisible Harp* (fig. 43), 1932; *Portrait of Gala with Two Lamb Chops Balanced on Her Shoulder* (fig. 30), ca. 1934; *Nostalgia of the Cannibal*, 1932; *Weaning of Furniture-Nutrition*, 1934; and *The Phantom Cart* (fig. 28), 1933. In some, the one or two disruptive elements stand out clearly from otherwise unremarkable features of the landscape (the hole carved from the trunk of the female figure in *Weaning of Furniture-Nutrition*; the bulbous cranial protrusion in *The Fine, Average, Invisible Harp*). In others (*The Phantom Cart*, *Paranoiac-Astral Image*) it is more difficult to pinpoint the cause of one's feeling of discomfort. In all instances, however, the viewer confronts a landscape in which, as in Millet's *L'Angélus*, the exceptional emerges from within the ordinary. Here as well, the method Dalí employed was modeled after the logic of anachronism: the traumatic emergence of the dead within the living.

MEISSONIER'S ACADEMIC FINESSE

Of all the artists that Dalí incorporated into his work in the 1930s, inarguably the most "despised and neglected" was Meissonier. The very attributes that made Meissonier's paintings so popular in their time (their stunning illusionism; their meticulous historical precision) also established them as paradigmatically

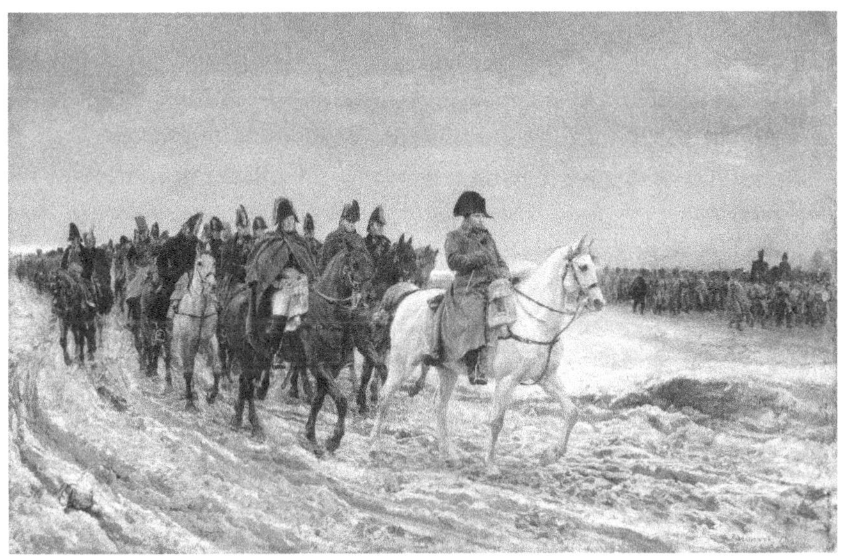

76. Ernest Meissonier, *French Campaign, 1814*, 1864. (Napoleon I followed by Field Marshalls Ney and Berthier and Generals Drouot, Gourgaud, de Flahaut.) Oil on wood, 51.5 cm × 76.5 cm. Inv. RF1862. Photo: Hervé Lewandowski. Musee d'Orsay, Paris, France. Photo credit: Réunion des Musées Nationaux/Art Resource, NY.

reactionary and antimodern. As such, they were for Dalí the perfect vehicle within which to articulate his theoretical practice of anachronism. In fact, for a brief period in the midthirties Dalí seems to have been even more enthralled with Meissonier's work — which he celebrated as models of "academic finesse" and "irrational exactitude"— than he had ever been with Vermeer.[53]

What attracted him to Meissonier was not any one motif or figurative element (as was the case with Millet), although on one occasion (an etching in the series based on Lautréamont's *Les chants de Maldoror*) he did insert the figure of Napoleon from Meissonier's *French Campaign, 1814* (fig. 76) into a landscape dominated by Millet's two farmers (fig. 74).[54] Rather, what drew him to Meissonier was his "ultra-academic" style.[55] Thus, whereas Dalí incorporated Böcklin's cypresses within scenes that included Millet's farmers and Uccello's lances, his appropriation of Meissonier is most evident in the work's meticulous miniaturism. Like the iron Guimard used to construct the entrances to the Paris Métro, Meissonier's "academic finesse" was, in effect, the medium within which Dalí combined Vermeer, Millet, and other outdated practitioners of Western painting.[56] According to Dalí, Meissonier's goal was not simply to represent but to reanimate, to bring back the dead. In his mind *French Campaign, 1814* was painted not to commemorate the event but to bring Napoleon back to life. And not only Napoleon, but also his horse and his soldiers, and all the horses of all his soldiers, and all the flies on all the horses, and all the grass and weeds that had been trampled by all the horses, and all the ants that crawled on all the grass and weeds. His ambition, in other words, was the same as that of the architects of art nouveau: "traumatic renewal."[57]

In 1936 Dalí exhibited *Suburbs of a Paranoiac-Critical Town: Afternoon on the Outskirts of European History* (fig. 77), first in London and then in New York. Its title is especially suggestive, as it suggests that the landscape depicted is, in geographical and historical senses, a site on the margins. The painting's dimensions are small, especially given the multiplicity of figures and architectural details. In fact, it is quite a bit smaller even than Meissonier's *French Campaign, 1814*. Like Meissonier's painting, Dalí's set out to record every inch of the landscape.

Poised at the painting's center, at the spot around which everything circulates, is a depiction of Gala extending her arm to the viewer and grasping in her fingertips an exquisitely rendered bunch of tiny grapes. The grapes recall, of course, Pliny's tale of the painter Zeuxis, whose illusionistic skills were so great that birds mistook his painted grapes for the real thing. As the founding myth of pictorial illusionism, Pliny's tale of trompe l'œil mastery was emblematic of all that modernism opposed, all that was outdated and irrelevant. Surrounding Gala and her grapes are other, more explicitly morbid signs of the passage of time. On the table to the left of Gala sit a skull and a broken amphora; behind her, on the right, a crutch holds up a crumbling structure. The three architectural sites depicted in this painting (one on the left, two on the right) may well have had personal significance to Dalí, but they were by no means buildings of major significance in the history of European architecture (as the painting's title underscores).[58] Moreover, by virtue of their architectural diversity, all three sites suggest radically different geographic and temporal locations. As such, they serve as yet another instance of Dalí's attempt to deploy art nouveau's "imbecilic" amalgamation of the "distant and diverse" architectural motifs as a tool in the service of a "traumatic renewal" of landscape painting.

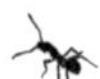

When Dalí first began to exhibit his work in Barcelona, critics accused him of inconsistency, of failing to choose between tradition or modernity. Dalí, they held, was too coy for his own good, offering on the one hand works that preserved the conventions of Renaissance and baroque painting and, on the other hand, paintings that affirmed an allegiance to the avant-garde spirit of rupture. In response to Dalí's 1926 exhibition at Galiere Dalmau, the critic Raphael Benet accused Dalí of playing "the card of tradition" alongside "the card of audacity" in what

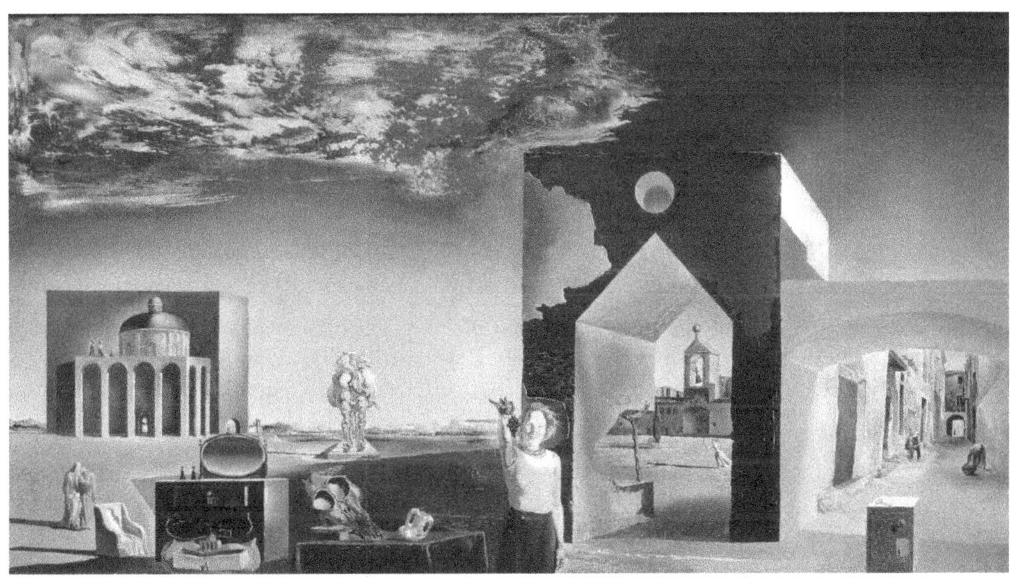

77. Salvador Dalí, *Suburbs of a Paranoiac-Critical Town: Afternoon on the Outskirts of European History*, 1935. Oil on panel, 46 × 66 cm (18.11 × 25.98 in.). Isidore Ducasse Fine Arts. Salvador Dalí (1904–89) © ARS, NY.

Benet believed was an attempt to appeal to both conservative and progressive tastes.[59] Paintings such as *Portrait of My Father* and *Young Girl in Figueres* (figs. 4, 9) seemed to indicate to Benet that Dalí was a sincere adherent of tradition, while paintings such as *Venus and Sailor* (*Homage to Salvat-Papasseit*) and *Still Life by Moonlight* (figs. 3, 5) suggested that Dalí was an authentic member of the avant-garde. The coexistence of these two incompatible styles made Dalí look like a fence-sitter who was too timid to take sides in the debate or as one who was too naïve to recognize the fundamental incongruity of his two styles.

This may well have been the case, but the works that Dalí completed in the thirties suggest a different interpretation. They suggest, that is, that his ambivalent response to the imperative of modernism was the result of neither naïveté nor timidity but was instead an attempt to find a third path — one that would somehow occupy a terrain outside both tradition and modernity. That this might have been his ambition in the twenties is best exemplified in a letter that he wrote to Lorca in 1926. In it Dalí described one of the paintings he had nearly completed as a particularly great achievement because, to him, it "it almost doesn't *look* (because it is) modern (or old)."[60] Like so much of Dalí's subsequent writing, this particular passage is a struggle to unravel, its internal reversals and parenthetical additions demanding that the reader labor to disentangle its meaning. Nevertheless, once unfurled the sentence suggests that Dalí was seeking a pictorial practice in which the old and the new collided in such a way that both would come undone. In retrospect Dalí's paradoxical formulation of an art that "almost doesn't *look* (because it is) modern (or old)" can be seen to have established the foundation for an even more radical conception of the avant-garde — one in which anachronism served as the coordinating concept. Rather than oscillate between "tradition" and "audacity," anachronism transformed tradition *into* audacity. In the process, the history of art was refigured as a collection of corpses awaiting their reanimation.

AFTERWORD

DISINTEGRATION

Throughout the later part of the 1930s, Dalí's relationship with the surrealists grew increasingly conflicted. By the decade's end Breton had become so irritated by what he perceived to be Dalí's opportunism that he expelled him from the group (and took to referring to him anagrammatically as "Avida Dollars"). Following Germany's invasion of France in 1940, Dalí and Gala left Europe and settled in the United States. In 1948 they returned to Spain, now under the dictatorship of Franco.

Having "finished [with] Surrealist malaise and existentialist anxiety," Dalí declared himself a man reborn. As he put it in his autobiography:

> To live! To liquidate half of life in order to live the other half enriched by experience, freed from the chains of the past. For this it was necessary for me to kill my past without pity or scruple, I had to rid myself of my own skin,

that initial skin of my formless and revolutionary life during the Post-War Epoch. . . . I am at this moment, as I write these lines, in the midst of making the last convolutions, which are in reality the end of this chapter, which will allow me to shuffle off and completely detach myself from the prison of my old skin, exactly as snakes do. . . . Instead of stubbornly attempting to use surrealism for purposes of subversion, it is necessary to try to make of surrealism something as solid, complete and classic as the works of the museum. . . . Instead of Reaction or Revolution, RENAISSANCE![1]

In announcing his liberation from his "formless and revolutionary" past, Dalí effectively repositioned himself as a painter at the center of art's history. No longer identifying exclusively with the marginal practices of Vermeer and Meissonier, Dalí now insisted that his work be understood within the context of the most central figures of the Western tradition: Raphael, Velázquez, and above all Leonardo.[2]

This is not to say that his interest in the small disappeared entirely. In fact, in his turn toward particle physics and cell biology Dalí embraced a realm far tinier than any that had interested him before: the universe of the molecular. In his "Anti-Matter Manifesto" (1958–59) he declared that his earlier interest in the little things of the mind was now superseded by his passion for the little things of the material world: "In the surrealist period I wanted to create the iconography of the interior world — the world of the marvelous, of my father Freud. I succeeded in doing it. Today the exterior world — that of physics — has transcended the one of psychology. My father today is Dr. Heisenberg."[3]

As a result, Dalí claimed that his new paintings would no longer be derived from the phobias and fantasies of the unconscious mind and would instead draw from the realm of atomic and subatomic particles: "It is with pi-mesons and the most gelatinous and determinate neutrinos that I want to paint the beauty of the angels and of reality."[4] Likewise was Dalí drawn to the tiny elements that make up the world of living things. In "The Cylindrical Monarchy of Guimard" (1970), for example, he likened the curves and loops of art nouveau design to "the double helix of deoxyribonucleic acid of Crick and Watson."[5] For him, DNA was scientific proof of the transcendent beauty of art nouveau and further evidence that he had been right to have defended it against its modernist detractors. Together, Werner Heisenberg's pi-mesons and James Watson and Francis Crick's deoxyribonucleic acid served Dalí as two of the tiniest and most significant *cosetes* that modern science had ever managed to identify and as the basis of a new direction for painting that would at the same time be a return to the masters of the Renaissance.

An analysis of Dalí's later work and its engagement with the little things of particle physics and human genetics is beyond the scope of this book. Nevertheless, it is worth noting here that both subatomic particles and genetic materials differ in crucial ways from the little things that had so fascinated Dalí in the twenties and thirties. The elements studied by Heisenberg and others are the fundamental components of matter, the most basic stuff of the universe. DNA is likewise a fundamental substance, in this case of organic material. Both of these little things are building blocks, substances from which the larger composites of the world are constructed. By contrast, the hairs on one's arm, boogers in one's nostril, or blackheads in one's pores are little things of an altogether different sort. They are extraneous and parasitical. They build nothing and give life to nothing. Little things like these belong to a fundamentally different class of objects. In abandoning this class in favor of that to which pi-mesons and deoxyribonucleic acid belong, Dalí shifted his attention from the little things on the periphery to the little things at the center. These elements are to the world of nature what the masters of the Renaissance and baroque are to the world of art. As such, it seems appropriate that Dalí's shift from Meissonier to Raphael would be accompanied by a shift from ants to atoms.

Indeed, it is possible to register this shift from ants to atoms by returning one last time to *The Persistence of Memory*. In the two decades since it was painted, *The Persistence of Memory* had become by far his most celebrated painting, and in 1952 Dalí decided to remake it in keeping with his newfound identification with the art of the Renaissance and the science of particle physics. Titled *The Disintegration of the Persistence of Memory* (fig. 78), the painting maintains the same small dimensions as the 1931 original and includes many of its original elements. On the left is the same leafless tree with a single, bifurcated branch, and in the distance are the same jagged rocks and the placid shore of Cadaqués. The three soft watches are still there, as is the flaccid self-portrait. But the red watch and the ants that crawled on them have been removed, as has the fly. The new painting also includes a few additional elements. A forth watch has been added (on the far right), as has a second tree (on the upper left). On the right, in the space that in the original was a wide and empty expanse of sand, Dalí has inserted large fish. Its shape and color echo the self-portrait below it, as if the latter were its wavy reflection in the water. The most significant difference — the difference that gives the painting its name — is that the platform on which the watches and tree once sat has now disintegrated, as has the beach itself. In their place we find an ordered array of golden bricks and conical forms. In addition, everything that in the original rested on the beach now appears to be suspended in liquid. At first one is inclined to imagine that this liquid is the ocean swelling beyond the shoreline. But the second tree in the distance appears to be holding a corner of the sea aloft and as such suggests that what we are witnessing in the foreground is taking place beneath the ocean. Together, the lifted skin of water and the ordered rows of geometrical solids describe a universe that exists inside the visible world: the realm of subatomic particles that fuse and bump and spin about each other as they make, unmake, and remake the world we see and touch.

The ultimate effect of these differences is dramatic. In the original the lines of recession that define the two platforms fail to converge, which invests the scene with a sense that the logical order of the world is itself decaying like the dead tree on the platform. But the units of brick and cone in the later painting are perfectly arranged in the Albertian manner. As a result, this later painting suggests an underlying order and stability that exists despite the presence of so many separate and discrete units. In addition, the shimmering surfaces of the bricks and cones invest the landscape with a vitality entirely absent in the original.

Consider, too, the differing treatment of the self-portrait in the middle of each painting. In the original Dalí depicts himself as stripped of his internal organs, his body flopped over the rocks as if it were a rotting carcass. Disintegration here is the sign and consequence of death. But in the later painting Dalí's self-portrait is rendered quite differently. For one, there are no liquids oozing from his pores. For another, there is no rock on which his body is flopped. Indeed, he does not look dead at all but rather appears to be floating calmly like the fish above him. Suspended within the same invisible substance that maintains the perfect order of the golden bricks and cones, Dalí sleeps peacefully amid a sea of soft watches. In this instance "disintegration" has rendered a world far more at ease, well ordered, and full of life than the original from which it was generated.

Like so many of Dalí's paintings, *The Disintegration of the Persistence of Memory* renders the world of the tiny. But here we find no invasive parasites, no superficial duplicates, no creatures in pain. Here the little things of interest are those that maintain, rather than threaten, the world of the big. In the universe of DNA strands and subatomic particles the small ant and the spot of mucus are rendered, yet again, inconsequential. In this world the little things of consequence are those that live in the center, not on the margin. Here little things still matter, but they no longer prick.

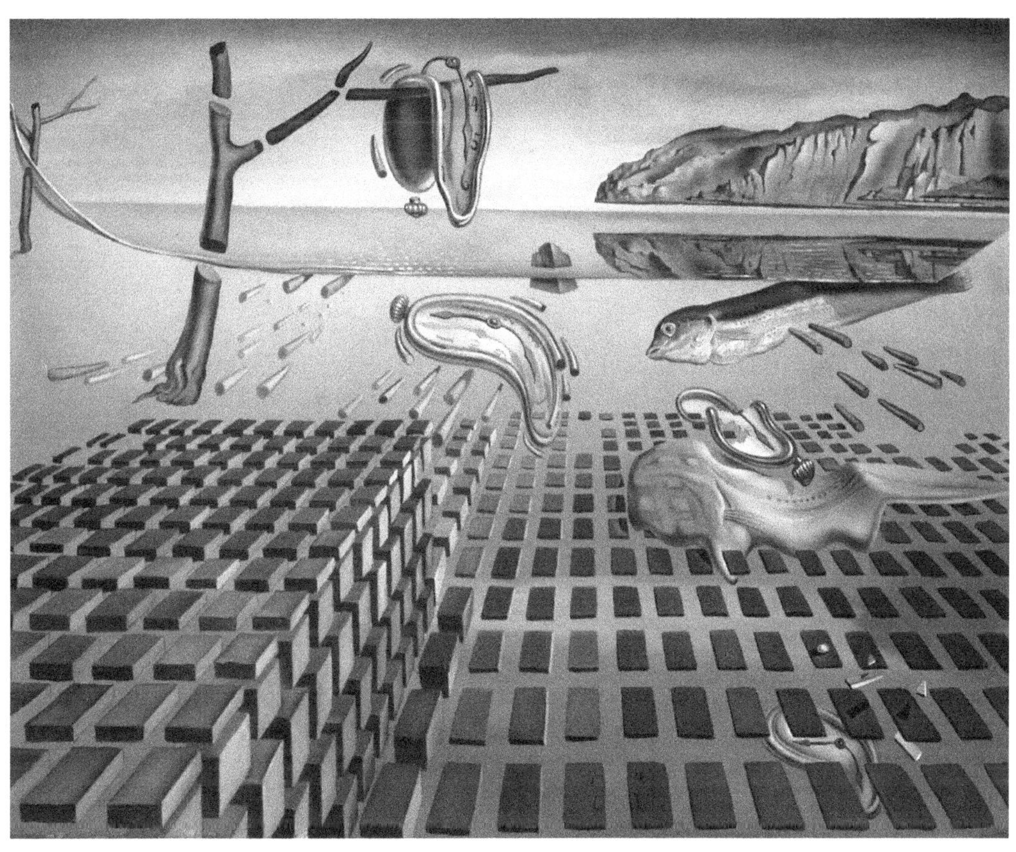

78. Salvador Dalí, *The Disintegration of the Persistence of Memory*, 1952–54. Oil on canvas, 25 × 33 cm (9⅞ × 13 in.). © Salvador Dalí. Fundació Gala-Salvador Dalí (Artists Rights Society), 2011. Collection of the Salvador Dalí Museum, Inc., St. Petersburg FL, 2011.

NOTES

INTRODUCTION

1. Dalí, *Secret Life*, 115, 128–31.

2. Sebastià Gasch, an art critic seven years his senior, encouraged Dalí to publish this poem and other texts in *L'Amic de les Arts*. Gasch had written several columns for the magazine. Dalí dedicated the poem to Gasch, "with all antiartistic delight." Dalí, *Collected Writings*, 27. Dalí had originally written the poem in Spanish and sent it to his friend, the poet Federico García Lorca, in the fall of 1927. See Maurer, *Sebastian's Arrows*, 82–83. The original-language versions of the letters between Dalí and Lorca appear in Santos Torroella, "Dalí escribe," 68–69. The Catalan version that Dalí published in *L'Amic de les Arts* differs slightly from the original Spanish version. For details concerning Dalí's relationship with *L'Amic de les Arts*, see Fanés, *Dalí: Construction of the Image*, 48–50.

3. "Poema de les cosetes"

Hi ha una coseta petita posada alta en un indret.
Estic content, estic content, estic content, estic content.
Les agulles de cosir es claven en els niquelets dolços i tendres.
La meva amiga té la mà de suro i plena de puntes de París.
Una sina de la meva amiga és una calma garota, l'altra un vesper bellugadís.
La meva amiga té un genoll de fum.
Els petits encisos, els petits encisos, els petits encisos, els petits encisos, els petits encisos, els petits encisos, els petits encisos, els petits encisos . . . ELS PETITS ENCISOS, PUNXEN.
L'ull de la perdiu és vermell.
Cosetes, cosetes, cosetes, cosetes, cosetes, cosetes, cosetes, cosetes, cosetes, cosetes, cosetes, cosetes . . .
HI HA COSETES, QUIETES COM UN PA.

My translation differs slightly from translations provided by Willard Bohn and Haim Finkelstein. See Bohn, *Marvelous Encounters*, 113–14; Dalí, *Collected Writings*, 27–28. Finkelstein's annotated collection of nearly all of Dalí's published writings has been an invaluable source to me, and I refer to it throughout this book. On the rare occasions when I have concluded that a particular word or phrase is better translated differently, I have offered my own translation. One recurring difference should be mentioned here.

Throughout his translations, Finkelstein chooses to translate the Catalan *coseta*, the Spanish *cosita*, and the French *petite chose*, as "*small* thing." I have chosen to translate *cosita* as "*little* thing." I have chosen *little* rather than *small* because *little* can be modified with the adverb *tiny* but *small* cannot. In translating *cosita/coseta* as "small thing," Finkelstein is forced to translate phrases such as "pequeña cosita" with the less evocative phrase "*very* small thing." Dalí sometimes modifies the word *cosita* in just this way. For example, in the Spanish version of "Poem of Little Things" (which Dalí sent to Lorca in October 1927), the first line reads, "Hay una pequeña cosita mona, que nos mira sonriendo." In the published, Catalan version of the poem, the line reads, "Hi ha una coseta petita posada alta en un indret." (Bohn translates *coseta* as "little thing" and *cosetes* as "small things." In one instance he translates *petita* as "little," and in another he translates *petits* as "small.")

4. See, for example, Ades, "Morphologies of Desire," 139; Bohn, *Marvelous Encounters*, 114; Finkelstein, *Dalí's Art and Writing*, 39–42.

5. André Breton, "Manifesto of Surrealism" (1924), in *Manifestoes of Surrealism*, 26.

6. Breton, "Première exposition Dalí," 69.

7. Ades, *Dalí*, 119–49.

8. Foster, *Compulsive Beauty*; Lubar, *Dalí: Museum Collection*; Lubar, "Dalí's ParaNONia"; Lomas, *Haunted Self*.

9. Finkelstein, *Dalí's Art and Writing*.

10. Fanés, *Dalí: Construction of the Image*.

11. Vilarasau and Boixadós, *Dalí and Mass Culture*; Mendelson, *Documenting Spain*.

12. Gale, *Dalí and Film*; King, *Dalí, Surrealism and Cinema*; Ruffa, Kaenel, and Chaperon, *Dalí à la croisée*; Parkinson, *Surrealism, Art, and Modern Science*; Maurer Queipo and Rißler Pipka, *Dalís Medienspiele*; M. Taylor, *Dalí Renaissance*; King, *Dalí: Late Work*. A range of perspectives is included in Hine, Jeffett, and Reynolds, *Persistence and Memory*. Two recent biographically oriented studies are Millet, *Dalí and Me*; and Caws, *Salvador Dalí*.

13. For a wide-ranging study of the historical fascination with little things, see Mack, *Art of Small Things*. My consideration of Dalí's work echoes Mack's account of the peculiar power of the microscopic: "Small things are not just experienced passively, they challenge us. We may ignore them because their minute size does not impose itself upon us, but once we are aware of them, they have the capacity to become magnetic. . . . small things resist final possession" (207).

14. The surrealists' "Declaration of January 27, 1925" was issued from the Bureau de recherches surréalistes and included twenty-six signatories. A translation of the document is included in Nadeau, *History of Surrealism*, 240–41.

15. Brown cites Dalí as one of a number of avant-garde figures to have engaged in the "conscious effort to achieve greater intimacy with things, and to exert a different determination for them." Bill Brown, "Thing Theory," in B. Brown, *Things*, 10. The essay was Brown's contribution to a collection he edited for a special issue of *Critical Inquiry* (titled simply "Things" and later published as a book under the same title).

16. B. Brown, *A Sense of Things*; Daston, *Things That Talk*; Blackwell, *Secret Life of Things*; Candlin and Guins, *Object Reader*; Miller, *Stuff*.

17. B. Brown, "Secret Life of Things," 3.

18. B. Brown, "Object Relations," 92–93. Indeed, Brown reminds us that even as Breton was tracking a crisis within subjectivity he was also declaring that the surrealists had uncovered "a fundamental crisis of the object." Breton, "Surrealist Situation of the Object" (1935), in *Manifestoes of Surrealism*, 257; cited in B. Brown, "Objects, Others, and Us," 186.

19. This is Brown's description of Latour's argument. B. Brown, *Things*, 12. See Latour, *We Have Never Been Modern*, 10–11.

20. Baudrillard, *Fatal Strategies*, 111.

21. Baudrillard, *Fatal Strategies*, 113–14.

22. For two recent studies that have taken a close look at surrealist objects, see Malt, *Obscure Objects*; and Mileaf, *Please Touch*

23. Walter Benjamin, "Dream Kitsch" (1927), in *Benjamin: Selected Writings*, 4.

24. Foster, Krauss, Bois, and Buchloh, *Art since 1900*, 191. In this respect it is especially interesting that the book provides a more generous account of Dalí's filmic and photographic projects, despite their infrequency and status as secondary practices in Dalí's career (247–49). I should add that my study would not have been initiated had I not had the good fortune of having been a student of both Rosalind Krauss and Benjamin Buchloh. Their complex reconceptualizations of modernist practice have been crucial formative influences on my attempt to reconsider Dalí's practice and its relation to modernism.

25. Goldring, "Exhibition at Zwemmer's."

26. Alexandrian, *Surrealist Art*, 100.

27. Ades, *Dalí*, 102–3; Finkelstein in Dalí, *Collected Writings*, 125. Finkelstein has argued that Dalí's paintings from the thirties should be seen as a "form of staging . . . in which Freudian concepts . . . are played out." Dalí, *Collected Writings*, 148. Lomas described Dalí's work as "luring the viewer in by means of his technical virtuosity." *Haunted Self*, 159–61. Lomas's reception of Dalí's work is consistent with his larger project concerning surrealism as a whole. Regarding the current state of surrealist scholarship, Lomas writes,

> There has been a flourishing of scholarship on surrealism in the past decade, as witnessed by a plethora of exhibitions and books that have been both popular and intellectually ambitious. One can ascribe this phenomenon to the demise of a formalist hegemony in studies of modern art, leading to a reappraisal of the dada and surrealist avant-gardes which stood outside of, and were in essence unassimilable to, a modernist trajectory. A new agenda, dictated by feminism and poststructuralism, and overtly informed by psychoanalysis in many instances, has taken its place. Questions of identity and sexuality have been paramount in the new art history which, in consequence, has proved to have a fundamental affinity with the concerns that animated the surrealists more than half a century ago. That certainly is how I would choose to situate my project. (*Haunted Self*, 6–7)

In contrast to the studies to which Lomas alludes in this passage, this book is devoted to considering Dalí's work in relation to the "modernist trajectory" to which the painter's work has often seemed, as Lomas put it, "unassimilable."

28. Bosquet, *Conversations with Dalí*, 21. That Dalí generally considered his technique to be less important than his imagery is also suggested by an account he provided in 1958: "In the surrealist period I wanted to create the iconography of the interior world — the world of the marvelous, of my father Freud. I succeeded in doing it." Dalí, *Collected Writings*, 366.

29. It can be argued, in fact, that the very popularity of this painting has served as an impediment to its critical examination. This was provocatively suggested by Michael Taylor in "Conquest of the Irrational."

30. Breton, "Première Exposition Dalí."

31. Bataille, "The Language of Flowers," in *Visions of Excess*, 12.

32. Outraged by this and other essays by Bataille, Breton responded at length in his "Second Manifesto of Surrealism," which he wrote that fall and which appeared in the pages of *La Révolution Surréaliste* in December 1929. "In M. Bataille's case," wrote Breton, "what we are witnessing is an obnoxious return to old anti-dialectical materialism, which this time is trying to force its way gratuitously through Freud." *Manifestoes of Surrealism*, 183.

33. Louis Aragon, "La peinture au défi" (1930), in *Les collages*, 35–71. Translated as "The Challenge to Painting," in Hulten, *Surrealists Look at Art*, 47–74.

34. Aragon associated surreality with "the marvelous," which he defined not as a simple "refusal of reality" but rather as "the emergence of a new rapport, of a new reality which this refusal has liberated." *Les collages*, 36–37; Hulten, *Surrealists Look at Art*, 48.

35. Aragon, *Les collages*, 37; Hulten, *Surrealists Look at Art*, 48.

36. Aragon, *Les collages*, 68, 70; Hulten, *Surrealists Look at Art*, 69–70, 71.

1. LITTLE THINGS

1. Dalí, *Secret Life*, 1.

2. The most complete record of Dalí's life can be found in Gibson, *Shameful Life*.

3. Dalí, *Secret Life*, 81.

4. For accounts of the postwar *rappel à l'ordre*, see Silver, *Esprit de Corps*; Golan, *Modernity and Nostalgia*; Cowling and Mundy, *On Classic Ground*.

5. Fanés, *Dalí: Construction of the Image*, 45–47.

6. In some of these letters Dalí took to describing himself diminutively, as Lorca's "little child" (hijito). In a letter to Lorca that Maurer dates to late February or March of 1926 but Santos Torroella dates to November 1925, Dalí refers to himself as "su hijito." Maurer, *Sebastian's Arrows*, 47; Santos Torroella, "Dalí escribe," 20. In another letter (dated by both Maurer and Santos Torroella to mid-March 1926) Dalí wrote that he was "more your little child than ever" (más hijito que nunca). Maurer, *Sebastian's Arrows*, 54; Santos Torroella, "Dalí escribe," 34.

7. Photographs of Dalí's letter appear in Santos Torroella, "Dalí escribe," 35, 37. In Maurer's translations the written texts have been transferred to typescript, which strips them of their meaningful orientation on the page. *Sebastian's Arrows*, 53–55.

8. Gasch recalls Dalí's strange penmanship, full of orthographic errors and written so small as to sometimes require a magnifying glass. *L'expansió de l'art català*, 144.

9. Deleuze and Guattari, *Kafka*, 20–21.

10. B. Brown, "Secret Life of Things," 2.

11. B. Brown, "Secret Life of Things," 2–3.

12. B. Brown, "Secret Life of Things," 3 (ellipses in original).

13. Bill Brown, "Thing Theory," in B. Brown, *Things*, 4.

14. Bill Brown, "Thing Theory," in B. Brown, *Things*, 4.

15. Dalí, letter to Lorca, early December 1927, in Maurer, *Sebastian's Arrows*, 91; and in Santos Torroella, "Dalí escribe," 80. Torroella suggests that Dalí is referring to *Little Ashes* (142).

16. Dalí, "The New Limits of Painting, Part Two" (April 30, 1928), in *Collected Writings*, 87.

17. Dalí, letter to Lorca, September 1928, in Maurer, *Sebastian's Arrows*, 102; and in Santos Torroella, "Dalí escribe," 91.

18. Dalí, letter to Lorca, September 1928, in Maurer, *Sebastian's Arrows*, 103; and in Santos Torroella, "Dalí escribe," 91. Lorca's understanding of Dalí's opposition to established poetic conventions was clearly expressed in "Corazón bleu y coeur azul," a poem Lorca began in 1927 or 1928 but never completed. The poem pits two figures against each other in dialogical format: a poet (referred to as "YO") and a painter (referred to as "MI AMIGO"). The poet defines his task as that of finding the "fragile thread that joins all things to each particular thing, and each thing to all." His interlocutor, however, insists that he has it all wrong: "You shouldn't be concerned about the relation [between things]," says the painter, "but about the things themselves, in isolation. . . . One must break the bonds that relate things visibly and invisibly; one must permit objects and concepts to wander freely wherever they want to, and to fight and fly." Lorca, "Corazón bleu y coeur azul," in *Poemas en orosa*, 91. A translation of this poem appears in Maurer, *Sebastian's Arrows*, 12–13.

19. The image of the liberated minute hand appeared again in a later iteration. Writing in 1929, now within the context of surrealism, Dalí wrote, "The idea of minute hands made of millet (PRODUCED, ONE SHOULD ASSUME, BY SPECIALISTS IN THIS MATTER) had not ceased from coming back to my thoughts with great intensity while following quite different paths." ". . . A Young Man," in *Collected Writings*, 32.

20. Dalí, letter to Lorca, Fall 1927, in Maurer, *Sebastian's Arrows*, 81; and in Santos Torroella, "Dalí escribe," 67.

21. Dalí, letter to Lorca, November 1927, in Maurer, *Sebastian's Arrows*, 84; and in Santos Torroella, "Dalí escribe," 71.

22. Ramón and his ilk "adore the weight of the water jug on the head, that makes girls' teeth fall off." Dalí, "For the Sitges 'Meeting,'" (May 1928), in *Collected Writings*, 65.

23. Dalí, letter to Lorca, November 1927, in Maurer, *Sebastian's Arrows*, 85; and in Santos Torroella, "Dalí escribe," 71. For Dalí's attitude toward Ramón, see Ades, "Morphologies of Desire," 139; Fanés, *Dalí: Construction of the Image*, 68–70. In one letter to Lorca Dalí went so far as to describe himself as "the anti-Juan Ramón." Maurer, *Sebastian's Arrows*, 84; Santos Torroella, "Dalí escribe," 71. In the same letter Dalí described Ramón's imagery as "anecdotal." By this he meant that it was based not on observation but on comprehension. Real observation — objective observation — reveals imagery that

escapes understanding. Dalí's objection was, as he put it to Lorca, that "even the purest, most uncontrollable of images can be explained like a riddle." If a poetic image can be explained like a riddle then it must be that this image has been made to be explicable, made to be hospitable to subjective comprehension; and if this is the case, the image does not deserve to be called objective.

24. Here, too, Dalí's practice resonates with Deleuze and Guattari's understanding of Kafka's writing: "Kafka deliberately kills all metaphor, all symbolism, all signification, no less than all designation. Metamorphosis is the contrary to metaphor. There is no longer any proper sense or figurative sense, but only a distribution of states that is part of the range of the word. The thing or other things are no longer anything but intensities overrun by deterritorialized sound or words that are following their line of escape." Deleuze and Guattari, *Kafka*, 22.

25. "Platero es pequeño, peludo, suave; tan blando por fuera, que se diría todo de algodón, que no lleva huesos. Sólo los espejos de azabache de sus ojos son duros cual dos escarabajos de cristal negro." Ramón Jiménez, *Platero y yo*, 17.

26. Dalí, "My Pictures at the Autumn Salon" (October 31, 1927), in *Collected Writings*, 52.

27. Dalí, "The Liberation of the Fingers," in *Collected Writings*, 99. Dalí elaborated on his concept of anti-metaphorical poetry by addressing the image that inspired the essay's title. He described a series of exchanges he had with a man named Eugenio Sánchez, whom he had met during his year of military duty in 1927. "I am indebted to this extraordinary man," Dalí wrote, "of whom unfortunately I have lost all trace, for some of the most intense hours of my entire life, and, furthermore, for a few texts of exceptional interest." Dalí recalled that Sánchez was particularly obsessed with the image of what he described as a "liberated" finger: "Probably due to a hypnagogic image appearing just before falling asleep, in which he confessed to having seen a detached finger floating about, the image of an isolated finger appeared frequently in the texts which he assiduously handed over to me to examine." Dalí was fascinated by Sánchez's "liberated finger" and began to see it even while he was awake. He saw it when he looked at a mother and child whose hands were clasped together such that, from a certain angle, "only the fingers of one of these stuck out." He claimed to have seen it frequently when he painted, at the moment when he would momentarily catch a glimpse of his thumb protruding through the hole in his wooden palette: "Often my own thumb gave me a sudden turn, despite my being used to seeing it isolated, sticking out of the hole in my palette like something disturbing and unusual." For a psychoanalytic interpretation of Dalí's "liberated fingers," see Ades, "Morphologies of Desire," 144–45; and Finkelstein, *Dalí's Art and Writing*, 90–91. For an interesting account of the role of hands in surrealist work (one that unfortunately does not discuss Dalí's notion of the liberation of fingers), see Powell, "Hands-On Surrealism."

28. Dalí, "Pez perseguido por una uva," letter to Lorca, November 1927, in Maurer, *Sebastian's Arrows*, 87; and in Santos Torroella, "Dalí escribe," 76. The original Catalan versions of Dalí's early publications have been collected in Dalí, *L'alliberament*. "Peix perseguit per un raïm" was first published in *L'Amic de les Arts* 3:28 (September 31, 1928): 217–18, and is reprinted in Dalí, *L'alliberament*, 121–23.

29. Dalí, "Fish Pursued by a Grape," in *Collected Writings*, 28; and in *L'alliberament*, 121. Here and below, my translation includes slight modifications of Finkelstein's.

30. "L'oliva quieta porta una petita faldilla. Jo tinc una bonica foto de Nova York." Dalí, "Fish Pursued by a Grape," in *Collected Writings*, 30; and in *L'alliberament*, 123.

31. Dalí, letter to Lorca, June 1927, in Maurer, *Sebastian's Arrows*, 72–73; and in Santos Torroella, "Dalí escribe," 58–59. Dalí praised Le Corbusier in a 1926 letter to Lorca (Maurer, *Sebastian's Arrows*, 58; Santos Torroella, "Dalí escribe," 42) as well as in a number of published texts: "Saint Sebastian" (1927), in *Collected Writings*, 23; "Poetry of the Mass-Produced Utility" (March 1928), in *Collected Writings*, 57. Le Corbusier is also mentioned in the "Yellow Manifesto" of March 1928 that Dalí wrote with Lluís Montanyà and Sebastià Gasch. Dalí, *Collected Writings*, 63.

32. Le Corbusier, "The Lesson of the Machine," in *Decorative Art of Today*, 110, 112, 114.

33. Dalí, "Poetry of the Mass-Produced Utility" (March 31, 1928), in *Collected Writings*, 57; Dalí, "Two Pieces in Prose" (November 30, 1927), in *Collected Writings*, 25; Dalí, "For the Sitges 'Meeting,'" (May 31, 1928), in *Collected Writings*, 65–66.

34. Dalí, "Poetry of the Mass-Produced Utility," in *Collected Writings*, 58.

35. Dalí, ". . . Always, Above Music, Harry Langdon" (March 31, 1929), in *Collected Writings*, 70. On Dalí's interest in Chaplin and Keaton, see Finkelstein, *Dalí's Art and Writings*, 66, 83; Gibson, *Shameful Life*.

36. Dalí, "Photography, Pure Creation of the Spirit," in *Collected Writings*, 46; and in *L'alliberament*, 34.

37. Dalí, "Photography: Pure Creation of the Spirit" (September 30, 1927), in *Collected Writings*, 45–46. The "Yellow Manifesto" includes an affirmation of the phonograph, "which is a little machine," and the camera, "which is another little machine." (HI HA el gramòfon, que és una petita màquina. HI HA l'aparell de fotografiar, que és una altra petita màquina.) Dalí, *Collected Writings*, 62; Dalí, *L'alliberament*, 103.

38. Dalí, "Photography: Pure Creation of the Spirit," in *Collected Writings*, 46–47.

39. See, for example, Latour, "Where Are the Missing Masses? The Sociology of a Few Mundane Artifacts," in Candlin and Guins, *Object Reader*, 229–54, which focuses in particular on the seat belt in contemporary automobiles.

40. Latour, *Aramis*, 61.

41. Latour, "On Technical Mediation," 46.

42. Latour, "Technology Is Society Made Durable," 117.

43. "Créame, señorito, el pintor más grande que ha habido es Vermeer de Delft, no sé si ya te lo había dicho en otra carta." Dalí, letter to Lorca, March 1926, in Maurer, *Sebastian's Arrows*, 54; and in Santos Torroella, "Dalí escribe," 34. Although one of Dalí's earliest references to Vermeer, it was not his first. Dalí mentioned Vermeer in late 1925 in a letter to another friend, the poet José Moreno Villa. Fanés, *Dalí: Construction of the Image*, 31–32.

44. "Estoy pintando una 'niña en Figueras,' hace 5 días que pinto paciente y devotamente su pescuezo acabado de afeitar, me sale muy bien, *tanto* que casi no *parece* (porque lo es) moderno (ni antiguo)." Dalí, letter to Lorca, March 1926, in Maurer, *Sebastian's Arrows*, 54; and in Santos Torroella, "Dalí escribe," 34.

45. Most scholars believe that Dalí is referring to *Young Girl in Figueres*, which was included in Dalí's second Dalmau exhibition in December 1926. See Finkelstein, *Dalí's Art and Writing*, 20; Santos Torroella, "Dalí escribe," 127.

46. Ades, *Dalí*, 32.

47. The influence of de Chirico and Morandi on Dalí's work is detailed in Ades, *Dalí*; Fanés, *Dalí: Construction of the Image*; and especially Finkelstein, *Dalí's Art and Writing*.

48. For information about the reception of Vermeer, see Broos, "Vermeer."

49. "Vous êtes de ceux qu'attirent l'Inconnu et le Méconnu. Vous êtes à la fois curieux du mystère et de la réalité, de l'ombre et de la lumière, — les deux extrémités de l'art et de la vie." Bürger, "Van der Meer de Delft," 297.

50. Bürger, "Van der Meer de Delft," 459.

51. "Quand un musée possède un seul Vermeer de Delft, souvent ce tableau modeste devient son plus précieux joyau." Vanzype, *Vermeer de Delft*, 11–12.

52. "By means of this humble and subdued reality," Vaudoyer wrote in *L'Opinion* in 1921, Vermeer's "modest painting becomes its most precious jewel," quoting Vanzype's very line. Vaudoyer's text appears in the appendix to Arasse, *Vermeer*, 87.

53. Vaudoyer, in Arasse, *Vermeer*, 88.

54. Vaudoyer mentions "monotony" before saying, "We are dealing with a magician." Arasse, *Vermeer*, 94, 95.

55. Dalí owned a copy of the tiny booklet *The Masterpieces of De Hooch and Vermeer*. See Fanés, *Dalí: Construction of the Image*, 32.

56. Dalí, letter to Lorca, September 1926, in Maurer, *Sebastian's Arrows*, 63; and in Santos Torroella, "Dalí escribe," 44. Unfortunately, Lorca's letters to Dalí no longer exist, so we have no record of how he responded to Dalí's enthusiasm. But Dalí's subsequent letter to Lorca suggests that the poet was bewildered. In the face of his bewilderment, Dalí responded with this: "How could you ever think I don't really like the Dutch painters? When you see what I'm doing now, you'll realize you're wrong." Dalí, letter to Lorca, March 1927, in Maurer, *Sebastian's Arrows*, 66; and in Santos Torroella, "Dalí escribe," 48.

57. Dalí, "Saint Sebastian," in *Collected Writings*, 19.

58. Dalí, "Photography, Pure Creation of the Spirit," in *Collected Writings*, 46; and in *L'alliberament*, 34. I have modified this translation based on my translation of the Catalan.

59. Dalí, "Photography, Pure Creation of the Spirit," in *Collected Writings*, 46; and in *L'alliberament*, 34.

60. Dalí, "Art Film, Antiartistic Film" (December 1927), in *Collected Writings*, 55; and in *L'alliberament*, 56–57.

61. Dalí, "New Limits of Painting," in *Collected Writings*, 81; and in *L'alliberament*, 64.

2. PARANOIA

1. Pierre Loeb to Dalí, December 7, 1927, cited in Aguer and Fanés, "Illustrated Biography," 33.

2. For a concise account of Dalí's aesthetic borrowing in this period, see Ades, *Dalí*, 55–63. For a detailed account, see Fanés, *Dalí: Construction of the Image*.

3. The distance Dalí had traveled in just twelve months is clearly evident in his essay "Reality and Surreality" (October 1928). As late as June 1927 Dalí wrote to Lorca that he was most interested in the works of "Léger, Picasso and Miró." Maurer, *Sebastian's Arrows*, 73. In "Reality and Surreality," however, Dalí recognized that Léger's work stood as surrealism's antithesis and as such insisted that, along with Miró, "the artists most alive today are Picasso, Arp, Ernst, and Tanguy." *Collected Writings*, 94. It is worth noting that although Dalí abandoned a number of the artists that interested him in 1926 and 1927 — not only Léger but also Le Corbusier and Cocteau — he still insisted on the importance of Vermeer. And this despite the fact that, at the time, his work had almost nothing in common with Vermeer's miniaturist realism. It is also the case that although Dalí abandoned the celebratory modernism of the journal *L'Esprit Nouveau*, he still held fast to his earlier belief that photography remained the most crucial invention of the moment.

4. Breton, *Surrealism and Painting*, 36.

5. "Miró pinta pollitos con *pelos* y sexos." Dalí, letter to Lorca, Fall 1927, in Maurer, *Sebastian's Arrows*, 81–82; and in Santos Torroella, "Dalí escribe," 67. For a compelling reinterpretation of Miró's work and its complex relationship to Bretonian Surrealism, see Palermo, *Fixed Ecstasy*.

6. See Gibson, *Shameful Life*, 241.

7. Dalí, "The Photographic Data," in *Collected Writings*, 68–69.

8. Dalí, "The Photographic Data," in *Collected Writings*, 68, 69.

9. Dalí, "The Photographic Data," in *Collected Writings*, 68.

10. Dalí, "The New Limits of Painting, Part Two" (April 30, 1928), in *Collected Writings*, 87.

11. Dalí, "The Photographic Data," in *Collected Writings*, 69.

12. "Sotmetre . . . a llur pròpia llibertat." Dalí, "At the Moment," in *Collected Writings*, 102; and in *L'alliberament*, 164.

13. For a richly detailed account of Dalí's interest in documentary theory and practice and its relation to both modernist and popular practices in Spain at the time, see Mendelson, *Documenting Spain*.

14. Dalí, "Review of Antiartistic Tendencies," in *Collected Writings*, 104.

15. Dalí, "Review of Antiartistic Tendencies," in *Collected Writings*, 105.

16. Dalí, "The Liberation of the Fingers," in *Collected Writings*, 99.

17. Dalí, "A Young Man," in *Collected Writings*, 32–33.

18. Dalí, "Documentary — Paris — 1929," pt. 1 (April 26, 1929), in *Collected Writings*, 108.

19. Dalí, "Documentary — Paris — 1929," pt. 1, in *Collected Writings*, 105–6.

20. Dalí, "Documentary — Paris — 1929," pt. 1, in *Collected Writings*, 106.

21. Dalí, "Documentary — Paris — 1929," pt. 2 (April 28, 1929), in *Collected Writings*, 108–9.

22. "I apologize to my readers," Dalí began, "for breaking today the promise I made in my first article not to add one more line of theory." "Documentary — Paris — 1929," pt. 5 (June 7, 1929), in *Collected Writings*, 114.

23. Letter to Lorca, November 1927, in Maurer, *Sebastian's Arrows*, 84; and in Santos Torroella, "Dalí escribe," 71.

24. Dalí described the riddle as "a very strange gathering of pieces of information that are objective, very precise, and often meticulous" but are structured in such a way that it is "difficult (at times impossible) to recognize the object of which they are a part and of which they come to constitute a sort of documentary." "Documentary — Paris — 1929," pt. 5, in *Collected Writings*, 114.

25. Dalí, "Documentary — Paris — 1929," pt. 5, in *Collected Writings*, 115.

26. Dalí, "Documentary — Paris — 1929," pt. 6 (June 28, 1929), in *Collected Writings*, 117.

27. In *Secret Life*, Dalí recalls that while in Paris "I always carried a painting under my arm as a sample." One day he carried *The First Days of Spring* with him to a meeting with the surrealist poet Robert Desnos. Desnos wanted to buy it straight away but did not have any money (213).

28. "Podem sotmetre ENCARA les coses a la seva pròpia llibertat." Dalí, "The Liberation of the Fingers," in *Collected Writings*, 101; and in *L'alliberament*, 162.

29. Dalí, "The Photographic Data," in *Collected Writings*, 68.

30. Dalí, "The Rotting Donkey," in *Collected Writings*, 223. For an extensive treatment of Dalí's response to Breton's concept of automatism, see Harris, *Surrealist Art and Thought*, 178–94.

31. Dalí, "The Rotting Donkey," in *Collected Writings*, 224.

32. See Garrabé, "Clérambault, Dalí, Lacan."

33. Freud, *Introductory Lectures*, 308, cited in Gibson, *Shameful Life*, 310. Gibson, who considers Dalí's latent homosexuality a crucial clue to the painter's work, suggests that Dalí's interest in developing the concept of paranoia into a method was perhaps a "defense against a sexual temptation that racked him with anxiety" (310). Gibson also notes that Dalí's grandfather suffered from a kind of persecution mania akin to that which Freud described and that this was perhaps another source of the painter's interest in the illness (309–10).

34. Freud, "Psychoanalytic Notes," 59.

35. See Dowbiggin, "Delusional Diagnosis?" Ades provides a thumbnail history of the diagnosis in *Dalí*, 122.

36. Sérieux and Capgras, *Les folies raisonnantes*, cited in Lomas, *Haunted Self*, 150. Ades claims that delusions of persecution were not essential to the definition of paranoia and that it was broadly understood as a "reasoning madness": "a delirium of interpretation in which suites of images, ideas or events are perceived as having causal connections, or are all related to one central idea, and are internally coherent for the subject of the delusion though meaningless to an outside observer." Ades, *Dalí*, 122.

37. Dalí's debt to the literature is clear from his statement in "The Moral Position of Surrealism" (1930): "The paranoiac who thinks he is being poisoned discovers in all the things that surround him, down to their most imperceptible and subtle details, preparations for his death." *Collected Writings*, 221.

38. "Défient presque toujours l'analyse psychologique." Dalí, "The Rotting Donkey," in *Collected Writings*, 224; and in Dalí, *Oui*, 154.

39. For an alternative argument, see Lomas, *Haunted Self*. "Though the paranoiac-critical method was a confection of various things, the conception of paranoia upon which it relied, and especially the fundamental concept of an interpretive delirium derives in large measure from sources in French psychiatry" (150). "The terminology of Sérieux and Capgras and each one of the clinical features they ascribe to the condition is faithfully reproduced when Dalí puts into practice his paranoiac-critical method" (151).

40. Freud, "Psychoanalytic Notes," 81–82.

41. For an account of Schreber's machinic self-understanding, see Roberts, "Wired."

42. For Freud, the symptoms of a patient with *dementia paranoides* are windows into the workings of the unconscious. The willing articulation of inner thoughts and feelings characteristic of the paranoiac offers the psychoanalyst an exceptional opportunity in that it is often unnecessary to witness the patient directly. Their loquaciousness with regard to their symptoms enables diagnosis from a distance: "The psychoanalytic investigation of paranoia would be altogether impossible if the patients themselves did not possess the peculiarity of betraying (in distorted form, it is true) precisely those things which other neurotics keep hidden as a secret. Since paranoiacs cannot be compelled to overcome their internal resistances, and since in any case they only say what they choose to say, it follows that this is precisely a disorder in which a written report or a printed case history can take the place of personal acquaintance with the patient." Freud, "Psychoanalytic Notes," 9.

43. Dalí's awareness of this distinction is evident in a statement he made in October 1929. After discussing the behavior and biology of anteaters, Dalí notes, "Psychoanalysis may analyze the most subtle psychic mechanisms and study anew the *human* facts. But, for all this, neither these facts nor the tongue of the anteater will turn less enigmatic and irrational." Dalí, "Un chien andalou" (October 1929), in *Collected Writings*, 135. Evidence of Dalí's awareness of the distinction between his own notion of paranoia and that of Freud appears in *The Conquest of the Irrational* (1935). In it Dalí contrasts the images produced by the paranoiac process and those produced by what he considered to be *passive* processes, such as hallucinations, dreams, and automatism:

> The images obtained in these processes offer two serious inconveniences: 1. they cease being unknown images, because, in falling into the domain of psychoanalysis, they are readily reduced to ordinary and logical language, although they continue to offer an uninterpretable residue and also an authentic and very vast margin of enigma, especially for the public at large; 2. their essentially virtual and chimerical character no longer satisfies our desires and our "principle of verification," announced for the first time by Breton in the *Discourse on the Paucity of Reality*. From that time, the delirious images of Surrealism have been desperately tending toward their tangible possibility, toward their objective and physical existence in reality. . . . The new delirious images of concrete irrationality tend toward their physical and real "possibility"; they go beyond the realm of psychoanalyzable phantasms and "virtual" representations. (Dalí, *Conquest of the Irrational*, in *Collected Writings*, 266)

Indeed, Dalí insisted that his own paranoiac images were uninterpretable even to himself: "I myself, the one to have 'made' them, do not understand them either" (265). This is not to say, however, that the images have no meaning: "The fact that I myself, at the moment of painting, do not understand the meaning of my paintings does not indicate that these paintings have no meaning: on the contrary, their meaning is so deep, complex, coherent, involuntary, that it escapes the simple analysis of logical intuition" (265).

44. As early as 1928 Dalí had argued that the photographic instrument produces the very sort of confusion that he would later describe as the "systematized confusion" of the paranoiac. For example, in "Reality and Surreality" (October 1928), Dalí described photography's precise and objective documentation as irrefutable evidence that the world is neither rational nor meaningful and that one's confidence in the mind's ability to organize coherently the objects and events one perceives (what Dalí typically referred to as "facts") is thus entirely misplaced: "The photographic datum sets up—as much photogenically as through the infinite figurative associations to which it may submit our mind—a constant revision of the external world, which becomes increasingly an object of doubt, and, at the same time, displays more unusual possibilities of a lack of cohesion." *Collected Writings*, 95; *L'alliberament*, 126.

45. "The paranoiac who thinks he is being poisoned discovers in all the things that surround him, down to their most imperceptible and subtle details, preparations for his death." Dalí, "The Moral Position of Surrealism" (1930), in *Collected Writings*, 221; and in *L'alliberament*, 224. Dalí, "The Rotting Donkey," in *Collected Writings*, 223.

46. Dalí, "The Rotting Donkey," in *Collected Writings*, 224.

47. Dalí, "The Photographic Data," in *Collected Writings*, 69. Earlier in the chapter this phrase is quoted in full.

48. Hence Rabaté's proposal that with paranoia "the main issue is not reality and surreality but rationality and surrationality." Rabaté, "Loving Freud Madly," 70.

49. Eburne put it similarly in "That Obscure Object of Revolt": "Dalí's paranoia rethinks Surrealism's epistemological problems in terms of a formal device that is neither merely an attempt at simulating 'madness,' nor a materialist analysis of 'reality' effected as if imagination and representation didn't exist at all. Rather, like the 'photographic donnée' of Dalí's photography, it represents a hyper-development of interpretive faculties, an empiricism whose scrutiny 'liberates' material facts from their logical positions, yet in a way which reproduces this liberation for others to encounter as well: not through the rhetorical or propagandistic methods of ideological praxis, but through an 'objective crystal,' a 'glass of real poetry'" (202).

50. Dalí, "The Rotting Donkey," in *Collected Writings*, 224. Dalí reiterated this claim in a number of places. For example, in "Love" (1930) he attributed the ability to transform reality to the power of the paranoiac's desire: "Thanks to love, the images of the external world will increasingly come to illustrate my own thought, things will finally be obediently commensurate with my tastes and will become the clever vocabulary of my own paranoiac will." *Collected Writings*, 191. The identification of the paranoiac's process with that of photography remained a common feature of Dalí's thought throughout the thirties. In *The Conquest of the Irrational* (1935), Dalí described paranoia (which he now referred to as "paranoia-criticism") as "l'appareil précis de l'activité paranoïaque-critique à la main"—that is, quite literally, a camera. *Collected Writings*, 263; *Oui*, 256.

51. For recent studies of Dalí's work with cinema, see King, *Dalí, Surrealism and Cinema*; and Gale, *Dalí and Film*.

52. Dalí, "Un chien andalou," in *Collected Writings*, 134.

53. Dalí, "Un chien andalou," in *Collected Writings*, 134. To which Dalí added, "Only the imbecility and cretinism that are consubstantial with the majority of the men of letters and the people in particularly utilitarian ages could make us believe that real facts are endowed with clear meaning, with a normal sense that is both coherent and *suitable*. From this derives the official suppression of mystery, the admission of logic into human acts, etcetera, etc." (134–35).

54. Dalí, "Un chien andalou," in *Collected Writings*, 135.

55. That Dalí continued to associate the objectivity of photography with the paintings of Vermeer is evidenced by the appearance of a reproduction of *The Lacemaker* in an early scene from *Un chien andalou*.

56. Dalí, "Un chien andalou," in *Collected Writings*, 135.

57. Ades explains:

> At first glance it looks as though Dalí has revived the old tradition of adding significant attributes to the portrait to say something about the occupation, taste and so on of the sitter. However, the objects Dalí has added belong to him rather than to Éluard, and many are familiar from other paintings: the grasshopper, whose likeness to the "slobberer" fish is neatly underlined by making its head the fish's eye, and the woman-jug, for example. The hand on the poet's forehead refers to Dalí's own experience while painting [*The Lugubrious Game*]: "I would feel the protective fingers of my imagination scratch me reassuringly between my two eyebrows . . . ," and sometimes he would feel a pecking just behind his brow which here he translates into butterflies. (Ades, *Dalí*, 78)

3. PARASITISM

1. Although Dalí never explicitly described himself as a parasite, in later years he joked that modern art was a cuckold and he was the one who had been sleeping with its lover behind its back. Dalí, *Dalí on Modern Art*.

2. Serres, *Parasite*, 244.

3. Serres, *Parasite*, 35. Serres offers the following, abstract definition: "The parasite is a differential operator of change. It excites the state of the system" (196).

4. Serres, *Parasite*, 38.

5. Serres, *Parasite*, 190. For studies of Serres's notion of the parasite, see: Abbas, *Mapping Michel Serres*; Assad, *Reading with Michel Serres*; Assad, "Language, Nonlinearity, and the Problem of Evil"; S. Brown, "Michel Serres."

6. Serres, *Parasite*, x.

7. Serres, *Parasite*, 190. There are, however, a few moments in Serres's text when the reader may detect something akin to identification. The final page of the book is perhaps the most compelling in this regard: "The parasite doesn't stop. It doesn't stop eating or drinking or yelling or burping or making thousands of noises or filling space with its swarming and din. The parasite is an expansion; it runs and grows. It invades and occupies. It overflows, all of a sudden, from these pages. Inundation, swelling waters." The passage continues in this way until the very end, when a reversal of perspective is introduced and the identificatory relationship is severed: "It finally is separated from me.

Thus the horrible insect slowly left my room, through the creaking door, one May morning, in Venice. Something had begun. Quiet, serene, no anxiety. The high seas" (253).

8. For an account of Dalí's reception by the surrealists in Paris, see Polizzotti, *Revolution of the Mind*, 329–34.

9. Dalí, "The Great Masturbator" (1930), in *Collected Writings*, 179–80; and in *Oui*, 159–60. In "The Liberation of the Fingers" Dalí described his "real dread of grasshoppers" as the consequence of a childhood experience in Cadaqués. *Collected Writings*, 100. See Lubar, *Dalí: Museum Collection*, 85. For an account of the literature on the figure of the Great Masturbator, see Fèlix Fanés's entry on *The Great Masturbator*, 1929, in Taylor and Ades, *Dalí*, 116–18. For the appearance of this self-portrait in *The First Days of Spring*, 1929, see Lubar, *Dalí: Museum Collection*, 55.

10. Burke, *Philosophical Enquiry*, pt. 1, sec. 7, p. 72.

11. Burke, *Philosophical Enquiry*, pt. 2, sec. 7, p. 66.

12. In 1935 Dalí evoked the miniature sublime in yet another fashion when he wrote of the pleasure he received while playing with pebbles on the beach, piling them on each other and rearranging them. Often the pebbles seemed to Dalí to transform themselves into living beings. Dalí described it as a game of "making a mass of small 'monumental' objects," that is, objects imagined to be "enlarged to enormous proportions":

> For this game I make use of various sites, couplings and "situations" of pebbles and stones from the beach. These stones are extremely variegated and complex; they by themselves are rich in an endless number of striking small plastic and "evocative"conflicts. Most of them have extraordinarily smooth and rounded forms, polished over the centuries by the mechanical action of the waves; these stones, although far more irregular than pebbles, manage to give the illusion of having almost flesh-like consistency; others, on the contrary, worn down by erosion, show fleshless forms riddled with holes; they present tortured and dynamic surfaces and are reminiscent of strange animal skeletons in savage attitudes. ("The Tragic Myth of Millet's *L'Angélus*: Paranoiac-Critical Interpretation" [1963], in *Collected Writings*, 284)

13. For example: "A FEATHER, that is no FEATHER, but an exceedingly small herb, representing a sea horse, my gums upon the hill, and at the same time a lovely spring landscape." Dalí, "A Feather," in *Collected Writings*, 35–36; Dalí, *L'alliberament*, 190.

14. "Río abajo vive un moco en una cabaña." Dalí, "UNA PLUMA . . . ," in *L'alliberament*, 190. Finkelstein translates *un moco* as "a mucus." While literally correct, this is especially awkward as, in English, *mucus* is an uncountable noun. *Boogers*, on the other hand, are countable, and thus, to my mind, that term is the more appropriate translation.

15. Dalí, "The Great Masturbator," in *Collected Writings*, 188; and in *Oui*, 169.

16. See, for example, Georges Bataille, "The Use Value of D.A.F. de Sade," in *Visions of Excess*, 91–102.

17. See Derrida, "Forcener le subjectile," 86. The surrealist interest in feces, urine, and spit was also influential in shaping Julia Kristeva's concept of the abject, a concept in which all sorts human waste serve as figures of the collapsed distinction between inside and outside, subject and object, living organism and inert thing. For an account of Kristeva's concept of abjection as it relates to Dalí, see Lomas, *Haunted Self*, 159–68.

18. Dalí's interest in mucus did not preclude an interest in feces, an interest for which Dalí was roundly criticized by Breton. Dalí's coprophilia is addressed in chapter 5.

19. Its mutability makes it especially amenable to incorporation within what Ades and Finkelstein have shown to be Dalí's expansive interest in metamorphosis and illusions of transformation. Ades, "Morphologies of Desire," 129–60; Finkelstein, *Dalí's Art and Writing*, 147–50.

20. Dalí, "With the Sun," in *Collected Writings*, 34; and in *L'alliberament*, 158. I have modified Finkelstein's translation (see chapter 3, note 14, concerning the translation of *un moco*.)

21. One might also be inclined to consider this strange little thing in relation to Jacques Lacan's notion of the *object petit a*. For a Lacanian reading of other aspects of Dalí's work, see Lubar, "Dalí's ParaNONia"; and Lubar, "Salvador Dalí: Portrait." Finkelstein examines similar territory in various sections of *Dalí's Art and Writing*. For a study of Dalí's influence on Lacan, see José Ferreria, *Dalí-Lacan*. I have resisted applying Lacan's concept to Dalí's engagement with the small because it seems to me to be a problematic match. As Lacan makes clear, the *objet petit a* is not strictly speaking an actual object, but an imaginary object, a hallucination. See Nasio, *Five Lessons*, 73–95. Over time Lacan's understanding of the concept grew more abstract. Indeed, he famously insisted to his English translator, Alan Sheridan, that the term remain untranslated so as to underscore its ontological status as akin to that of "an algebraic sign." Lacan, *Écrits*, xi). Lacan's mathematical conception of the *objet petit a* is especially evident in the seminars of 1968–69: Lacan, "Le un et le petit *a*" (January 22, 1969), in *Le séminaire*, 121–36. See also Kirshner, "Rethinking Desire."

22. Dalí, "Aerodynamic Apparitions of 'Beings-Objects,'" in *Collected Writings*, 207, 208.

23. Dalí, "Aerodynamic Apparitions of 'Beings-Objects,'" in *Collected Writings*, 210.

24. Gavin Parkinson proposes that the inspiration for Dalí's account of the pleasures of manipulating one's blackheads is likely the passage in Freud's 1915 essay "The Unconscious" in which Freud describes a patient who is depressed by the condition of his skin but who nevertheless derives pleasure from squeezing his blackheads. Freud concludes that the patient's act is "clearly to him a substitute for masturbation." Freud, "The Unconscious," 205. Parkinson associates Dalí's account of "aerodynamic apparitions" not only in light of Freud's writing but also in light of Dalí's interest in Einstein's theory of relativity. Parkinson, *Surrealism, Art, and Modern Science*, 185.

25. Dalí, "The Rotting Donkey" in *Collected Writings*, 223, 224.

26. Dalí claimed to have definitively proven that Millet's painting was in fact a "literal illustration" of *Les chants de Maldoror*'s most famous line, "as beautiful as the encounter of an umbrella and a sewing machine on a dissecting table." Much has been written about Dalí's application of his paranoiac-critical method to Millet's work. See, for example, Finkelstein, *Dalí's Art and Writing*, 211–26; Bradley, "Dalí as Myth-Maker."

27. Dalí, "Non-Euclidean Psychology of a Photograph" (June 1935), in *Collected Writings*, 302. Unfortunately for readers of Finkelstein's translation, the reproduction that accompanies the translation was cropped a bit too aggressively, and as a result the spool does not appear in the photograph (303).

28. "The 'threadless' spool [la bobine 'sans fil'], begging provisionally for the same filiation, can have no other maternity than that of pure intuition, who is, all things considered, Kant's legitimate daughter [la fille légitime de Kant]." Dalí, *Collected Writings*, 304; *Oui*, 251.

29. Dalí, "Non-Euclidean Psychology of a Photograph," in *Collected Writings*, 303–4.

30. Ian Walker has argued that Dalí's concept of the "bobine sans fil" is usefully understood in relation to Roland Barthes's concept of the photographic "punctum." See Walker, *City Gorged with Dreams*, chapter 1. Suggestively, Barthes describes the punctum as "that accident which *pricks me* (but also bruises me, is poignant to me)." (Le *punctum* d'une photo, c'est ce hasard qui, en elle, *me point* [mais aussi me meurtrit, me poigne].) Barthes, *La chambre claire*, 49. Barthes's argument, however, turns on the question of the ontology of the photograph and thus the visual signifier, whereas Dalí's concern is not the photograph itself but the reality of that which the photograph represents.

31. Dalí, "Non-Euclidean Psychology of a Photograph in *Collected Writings*, 306; *Oui*, 254. Finkelstein translates *minime et débile* as "negligible and feeble."

32. Spools did, however, appear in a number of Dalí's forty-two etchings that illustrated the republication of Lautréamont's *Maldoror*, *Le chants de Maldoror* (Paris: Albert Skira, 1934). Lautréamont most famous line ("as beautiful as a sewing machine and an umbrella on a dissecting table") practically demands their inclusion.

33. Dalí's fascination with anachronism, as evidenced in the amphora, is addressed at length in chapter 6. For an analysis of Dalí's interest in the amphora as evocative of the ancient artifacts left behind by the Phoenician and Greco-Roman civilizations that had once occupied his native Catalonia, see Ades, *Dalí*, 132; and Michael Taylor's entry for *Paranoiac-Astral Image*, in Taylor and Ades, *Dalí*, 230.

34. Other works in which the amphora appears include: *Apparition of My Cousin Carolinetta on the Beach at Rosas*, 1934; *Sun Table*, 1936; *Suburbs of a Paranoiac-Critical Town: Afternoon on the Outskirts of European History*, 1936 (fig. 77); and *The Invention of Monsters*, 1937.

35. *White Calm* is the largest of the three at about sixteen by thirteen inches, but the figures are all placed beneath an enormous expanse of empty sky and occupy only the bottom quarter of the painting, a thin horizontal band measuring less than 16 cm (6 in.) high.

36. Dalí, "First Morphological Law Concerning the Hairs on Soft Structures" (October 1936), in *Collected Writings*, 315.

37. Dalí, "I Defy Aragon" (March 1937), in *Collected Writings*, 329–31.

38. Dalí, "Cher Breton" (June 1933), in *Collected Writings*, 249, 250.

39. Dalí's conception of Meissonier as modernism's antithesis is also underscored by the letter's presentation of his academicism as the inverse of Picasso's stylistic radicalism: "Picasso, as everyone knows, revolutionizes the 'means of expression' in an amazing and sensational manner." *Collected Writings*, 250.

4. SUPERFICIALITY

1. Georges Braque, "Thoughts and Reflections on Art" (December, 1917), in Chipp, *Theories of Modern Art*, 260.

2. Raynal, "What Is Cubism?," 129.

3. "Ninguna época había conocido la perfección como la nuestra; hasta el invento de las Máquinas no había habido cosas perfectas, y el hombre no había visto nunca nada tan *bello* ni *poético* como un motor *niquelado*. La máquina ha cambiado *todo*. . . . Estamos, pues, rodeados de una belleza perfecta inédita, motivadora de estados nuevos de poesía." Dalí, letter to Lorca, June 1927, in Maurer, *Sebastian's Arrows*, 72; and in Santos Torroella, "Dalí escribe," 58.

4. "Soy superficial y lo externo me encanta." Dalí, letter to Lorca, June 1927, in Maurer, *Sebastian's Arrows*, 73; and in Santos Torroella, "Dalí escribe," 59. Dalí made a similar pronouncement to Gasch: "The inside of things is still a superficial reality; the most profound is still an epidermis." (Puc ben dirte amic Gasch que per a mi l'interior de les coses, es encara una realitat superficial; lo més profont es encara una epidermis.) Gasch, *L'expansió de l'art català*, 146; cited in Monegal, "Las palabras y las cosas," 152. Although the connection between superficiality and objectivity is not immediately obvious, it was a connection that Dalí clearly believed in: "Things have no significance beyond that of their complete objectivity; in this, for me, is their source of miraculous poetry." (Les coses no tenen cap significat fora de la seva abstracta objectivitat; en això, per a mi, resideix la seva miraculosa poesia.) Gasch, *L'expansió de l'art català*, 146. Dalí expressed the same connection to Lorca: "The outside of things is what delights me, because in the end it is the outside of things that is objective. At the moment, the poetry of the outside of things is for me the most pleasing of all, and only in the outside of things do I see the trembling of the ethereal." (Lo externo me encanta, porque lo externo al fin y al cabo es lo objetivo. Hoy lo objetivo poéticamente es para mí lo que me gusta más, y sólo en lo objetivo veo el estremecimiento de lo Etéreo.) Dalí, letter to Lorca, June 1927, in Maurer, *Sebastian's Arrows*, 73; and in Santos Torroella, "Dalí escribe," 59. Although Dalí's private correspondence establishes a clear connection between superficiality and objectivity, his public statements make this association less explicitly. In "Saint Sebastian," for example, a text that he described as an articulation and defense of his "aesthetic of objectivity," Dalí included a reference to an experience he once had at the beach when, moved by the clear, cool ocean breeze, he closed his eyes for a moment. So as to forestall the reader's inclination to interpret this scene within the established convention of romanticism wherein the artist stands frozen in nature and closed in on himself, Dalí insisted that in shutting his lids he was not seeking some kind of interior vision or dialectical incorporation of the world within the self but rather was attending to a small and purely superficial sensory experience: "I shut my eyes," he wrote, "not out of mysticism, nor to better see my inner self — as might be said platonically — but simply for the sensuality of the physiology of my eyelids." *Collected Writings*, 21.

5. "Petit fonògraf." Dalí, "Poetry of the Mass-Produced Utility" (March 1928), in *Collected Writings*, 57; and in *L'alliberament*, 95.

6. Dalí, "Poetry of the Mass-Produced Utility" in *Collected Writings*, 58; and in *L'alliberament*, 96–97. My translation differs slightly from Finkelstein's.

7. In this regard Dalí was responding, at least in part, to Freud's concept of the fetish. What distinguishes Dalí's engagement in this instance is that it fixes not on the material object itself but rather on its surface effect (an echo, perhaps, of Freud's own consideration of the "shine on the nose"). Freud, "On Fetishism," 152. Accounts of the

role of fetishism in surrealism in general and for Dalí in particular include Ades, "Surrealism"; Kropf, *Dalí Objects / Dalí Fetishes*; Malt, *Obscure Objects*.

8. Ades, *Dalí*, 58–60.

9. Bergson, *Comedy*, 157, 158, 162. A similar notion appeared in Konrad Fiedler's 1881 statement "Modern Naturalism and Artistic Truth": "The decisive turning point in our striving for knowledge takes place when, on deeper reflection, we realize that external reality, which appears to be the absolutely real, is in fact a deceptive illusion." Fiedler, "Modern Naturalism," 701. On the "passion for the real," see Badiou, *Le siècle*. Shortly before Badiou's book appeared in print, Slavoj Žižek began using the notion of "the passion of the real" as a centerpiece of his thought. See, for example, Žižek *Welcome to the Desert*. Although Badiou does not include Bergson in his account, his argument clearly echoes Bergson's. As Badiou put it, "The question of the face-to-face is the heroic question of the [twentieth] century." *Le siècle*, 30. Badiou's line of thought echoes Henri Peyre's proposal that we understand the Bergsonian ambition to "bring us face to face with reality itself" as modernism's "all pervading obsession." Peyre, *Literature and Sincerity*, 237.

10. Rivière, "Present Tendencies," 76 (italics in original).

11. "Les premières peintures furent seulement une ligne qui entourait l'ombre d'un homme faite par le soleil sur la terre. Mais combien sommes-nous loin, avec nos moyens contemporains, de ce simulacre, nous qui possédons la lumière." Delaunay, cited in in Apollinaire, *Chroniques*, 348.

12. Hartman, *Unmediated Vision*, 156. For his more recent formulation of this historical understanding, see Hartman, *Scars of the Spirit*.

13. Breton, "Second Manifesto of Surrealism" (1930), in *Manifestoes of Surrealism*, 137.

14. Nadeau, *History of Surrealism*, 21.

15. Deleuze, *Logic of Sense*, 87.

16. Deleuze, *Logic of Sense*, 93.

17. "És igual. Però millor en el quadro, perquè en ell les ones es poden comptar." Dalí, "Sant Sebastià," in *L'alliberament*, 15. My translation differs slightly from Finkelstein's ("Saint Sebastian," in Dalí, *Collected Writings*, 19).

18. "Yo he pintado toda la tarde, 7 olas duras y frías como son las del mar . . . , mañana pintaré 7 más; estoy tranquilo porque las he pintado *bien*, además cada vez el mar se parece más al que yo pinto." Dalí, letter to Lorca, September 1926, in Maurer, *Sebastian's Arrows*, 62; and in Santos Torroella, "Dalí escribe," 44. My translation differs slightly from Maurer's. As late as 1969 — some forty years after his tale of Enriquet and his letter to Lorca about the seven waves he had painted one afternoon — Dalí expressed a similar notion in his interview with Alain Bosquet: "That's one of my permanent mottos: I always encourage people to reproduce my paintings because I find the reproductions much better than the originals." Bosquet, *Conversations with Dalí*, 22. Dalí's provocative claim was offered in the middle of a discussion about the relationship between Dalí's early work and Bosch's (Dalí said that he had known of Bosch's painting largely through reproduction). Perhaps because it was a digression of sorts, Bosquet did not follow up on it and instead returned to Dalí's claim that his paintings had very little in common with Bosch's. That Bosquet did not pursue it is unfortunate, as it might well have illuminated

an aspect of Dalí's work that has for too long remained obscured by the very elements that the two of them were in the middle of discussing. Instead, the conversation continued to address what has always been the focus of Dalí's work — its imagery. The prospect that what mattered most may not have been the things that Dalí painted but the manner in which he painted them was likely as inconceivable to Bosquet as it has been to so many of Dalí's admirers.

19. "Wax-museum figures on view at side-shows are as real as a puff of smoke or a nose." (Els esguerros de cera exhibits a les barraques són la realitat igual que un fum, que un nas.) Dalí, "New Limits of Painting, Part II," in *Collected Writings*, 87; and in *L'alliberament*, 76.

20. Hildebrand, *Problem of Form*, 113.

21. Flaubert, *Correspondance*, 427.

22. Ortega y Gasset, *Dehumanization of Art*, 14, 29.

23. "Servia de falses tovalles." Dalí, "Have I Disowned Perhaps?" (December 31, 1928), in *Collected Writings*, 30; and in *L'alliberament*, 147.

24."Fausses briques; les cruel ornements d'or faux; médailles en faux bronze; l'apparemment fausse sauterelle composée d'une infinité de minuscules et pourtant très nettes photos de requins." Dalí, "The Great Masturbator," in *Collected Writings*, 179, 180, 183, 188; and in *Oui*, 159, 161, 164, 170.

25. Dalí, letter to Breton, March 1937, cited in Ades, "Dalí and Duchamp," 11. In the forties, in response to Hitchcock's invitation to supply a dream sequence for *Spellbound*, Dalí prepared a scene in which fifteen grand pianos would be hung from the ceiling above the heads of the ballroom guests. When he went to witness the filming in Selznick's studio, he was "stupefied at seeing neither the pianos nor the cutout silhouettes which must represent the dancers. But right then someone pointed out to me some tiny pianos in miniature hanging from the ceiling and about 40 live dwarfs who, according to the experts, would give perfectly the effect of perspective that I desired. I thought I was dreaming. Even so, they maneuvered with the false pianos and the real dwarfs (which should be false miniatures). . . . Neither Hitchcock nor I liked the result, and we decided to eliminate the scene. In truth, the imagination of the Hollywood experts will be the only thing that will ever have surpassed mine." Dalí, in Taylor and Ades, *Dalí*, 503; originally in the *Dalí News*, November 20, 1945.

26. Dalí, *Secret Life* 38. In the midthirties Dalí made a number of paintings that included a young boy looking onto a perplexing figure or landscape. For example, in *Atavistic Vestiges after the Rain* (1934) and *Architectonic Angelus of Millet* (1933) he included a depiction of a boy and his father; in *Spectre of Sex Appeal* (1934), *Paranoiac-Astral Image* (1934), and *Enigmatic Elements in the Landscape* (1934) he included a painted copy of a photograph of himself wearing a wide-brimmed hat and holding a large hoop.

27. "Anècdotes completament falses." Dalí, "The Liberation of the Fingers," in *Collected Writings*, 100; and in *L'alliberament*, 160. My translation differs slightly from Finkelstein's.

28. Dalí, *Secret Life*, 230, 231.

29. Dalí, *Secret Life*, 231.

30. Dalí, *Secret Life*, 219.

31. A similar scene, in which the man's act of coprophagia is more readily discernible than it is in the frontispiece, is present in a drawing from 1931, *Projet pour le menu de la Société du roman philosophique*. The relation between coprophagia, masochism, and submission is addressed in chapter 5.

32. Hollier, *Against Architecture*, 107. See also Rabaté, "Loving Freud Madly," 65. For analyses of various Bataillean aspects of Dalí's work, see Raymond Spiteri, "Beyond the Lugubrious Game."

33. Dalí, "The Great Masturbator," in *Collected Writings*, 181–82; and in Oui, 162. My translation differs slightly from Finkelstein's.

34. See, for example, Finkelstein, *Dalí's Art and Writing*, 185.

35. In "The Great Masturbator," for example, Dalí described a sculpture depicting William Tell as "a simulacrum." *Collected Writings*, 183; *Oui* 163. This is also the sense in which Dalí uses the term in *Secret Life* when he describes the image of the man with the soiled pants as "merely a simulacrum" (219).

36. "These new and menacing simulacra will act skillfully and corrosively." Dalí, "The Rotting Donkey," in *Collected Writings*, 223; and in *Oui*, 153. In "Love" Dalí described simulacra in more explicitly parasitistic terms as destructive intruders, "liable to injure us." *Collected Writings*, 190.

37. Dalí, "The Rotting Donkey," in *Collected Writings*, 223.

38. Lomas, "Simulacra," 204.

39. Finkelstein, on the other hand, has proposed that Dalí conceived of simulacra as the set of universal forms in which reality is represented by the mind: "[Dalí] seems to imply that what we normally perceive of external reality persistently assumes certain forms — the simulacra — that attain a measure of universality." Finkelstein, *Dalí's Art and Writing*, 140.

40. Gilles Deleuze, "Plato and the Simulacrum," in *Logic of Sense*, 262, 263. The paintings of René Magritte, which Dalí knew, also exploited this opposition between surface and depth; good copy from faulty simulacrum. The classic account is Michel Foucault, *This Is Not a Pipe*. See also Rothman, "Against Sincerity"; Rothman, "Mysterious Modernism"; and Rothman, "René Magritte."

41. Dalí, "The Rotting Donkey," in *Collected Writings*, 223–24.

42. Dalí, "The Rotting Donkey," in *Collected Writings*, 224.

43. Dalí, "The Moral Position of Surrealism," in *Collected Writings*, 221.

44. Dalí, "The Rotting Donkey," in *Collected Writings*, 225.

45. Lomas, *Haunted Self*, 159–68.

46. Kristeva, *Powers of Horror*.

47. Dalí, "The Rotting Donkey," in *Collected Writings*, 225.

48. Dalí, "The Rotting Donkey," in *Collected Writings*, 225.

49. Dalí, "The Rotting Donkey," in *Collected Writings*, 225.

50. Dalí, "Concerning the Terrifying and Edible Beauty of Art Nouveau Architecture" (December 1933), in *Collected Writings*, 193–200.

51. Dalí, "The Rotting Donkey," in *Collected Writings*, 225.

52. Dalí, "The Sanitary Goat" (1930), in *Collected Writings*, 226.

53. Dalí first articulated the distinction between appearance and reality with reference to Heraclitus's famous dictum "nature likes to hide itself." He had come across the statement in a text by Alberto Savinio. Following Savinio, Dalí referred to the distinction as "irony." For Savinio, irony was a metaphysical concept, which he defined at one point as "the essence of appearance." "To reproduce this essence in its complete genuineness," wrote Savinio, "is the highest aim of art." Savinio, "Anadyomenon." Dalí's first mention of Heraclitus appears in the opening passage in "Saint Sebastian"— a passage subtitled "Irony": "Heraclitus tells us, in a fragment collected by Themistius, that it pleases Nature to hide itself. Alberto Savinio believes that this same self-hiding is a phenomenon of modesty. It has to do — so he tells us — with an ethical reason, for this modesty is born of the relationship between Nature and man. And he finds this to be the primary cause for the engendering of irony." *Collected Writings*, 19. For Surrealism's multifaceted reception of Heraclitus, see Eburne, "That Obscure Object of Revolt."

54. Given his fascination with the deceptiveness of appearances, it is unsurprising to find that Dalí was especially drawn to the writings of Raymond Roussel (Roussel's *Impressions of Africa* was one of the two books found on Dalí's bedside table when he died in 1989). Gibson, *Shameful Life*, 678. Roussel had been of interest to many of Dalí's contemporaries, including Duchamp, Picabia, and Apollinaire, as well as many of the surrealists. André Breton reflects on Roussel's influence in *Conversations*, 83. For Roussel's reception by the surrealists (including Dalí), see Ford, *Raymond Roussel*. One wonders if Dalí was as drawn to Roussel's "detachment from the real" as Michel Leiris was when he met Roussel in 1922. Leiris, "Conception et réalité," 18. For a range of responses to Roussel's life and work, see Brotchie, Green, and Melville, *Raymond Roussel*. Although the works of artists who have adopted this contrary position have not been systematically studied en masse, the issues that these works introduce have not been entirely overlooked by scholars. See, for example, Weiss, *Popular Culture of Modern Art*. For a compelling account of Duchamp's exploitation of the complexities of inauthenticity, see Singer, "In the Manner of Duchamp."

55. Dalí, "The Sanitary Goat," in *Collected Writings*, 229.

56. Dalí attributed his awareness of the peculiar eeriness of "frontality" to the paintings of Arnold Böcklin. "Daydream," in *Collected Writings*, 151–52.

57. Dalí, "The New Colors of Spectral Sex-Appeal," in *Collected Writings*, 203.

58. Dalí, "The Spectral Surrealism of the Pre-Raphaelite Eternal Feminine," in *Collected Writings*, 312.

59. Dalí, "The Spectral Surrealism of the Pre-Raphaelite Eternal Feminine," in *Collected Writings*, 312.

60. In "The Spectral Surrealism of the Pre-Raphaelite Eternal Feminine" Dalí quoted a passage from *Principe de morphologie generale* in which Monod-Herzen refers to catenaries as "found . . . more or less distinctly, in the folds of curtains or draperies." *Collected Writings*, 313.

61. Descharnes, *World of Salvador Dalí*, 142.

5. SUBMISSION

1. Dalí, "Photography: Pure Creation of the Spirit" (September 1927), in *Collected Writings*, 46; and in *L'alliberament*, 34. My translation differs slightly from Finkelstein's.

2. Dalí described Vermeer as "humble" in both "Photography: Pure Creation of the Spirit" (*Collected Writings*, 46) and "The New Limits of Painting," pt. 1 (*Collected Writings*, 81).

3. Dalí, letter to Lorca, September or October 1927, in Maurer, *Sebastian's Arrows*, 80; and in Santos Torroella, "Dalí escribe," 64.

4. Dalí, "Saint Sebastian," in *Collected Writings*, 24.

5. Gibson, *Shameful Life*, 187; Finkelstein, *Dalí's Art and Writing*, 25–26; Santos Torroella, "Madrid Years," 87.

6. Dalí, "Saint Sebastian," in *Collected Writings*, 19–20; and in *L'alliberament*, 15–16.

7. Dalí, "Reflections" (August 1927), in *Collected Writings*, 45.

8. Baudelaire, "Salon of 1859," in *Art in Paris*, 162–63.

9. "Courbet . . . inaugurated a realistic impulse which runs through all modern efforts. Yet he remained the slave of the worst visual conventions. Unaware of the fact that in order to display a true relation we must be ready to sacrifice a thousand apparent truths, he accepted, without the slightest intellectual control, all that his retina presented to him." Gleizes and Metzinger, "Du Cubisme."

10. Miró, in a letter to Leiris in 1924, wrote, "I am freeing myself of all pictorial convention (that poison)." Miró, *Écrits*, 97–98; cited by Lubar in "Miró in 1924," 55.

11. "Le seul mot de liberté est tout ce qui m'exalte encore." André Breton, "Premier Manifeste," in *Les manifestes du surréalisme*, translation in *Manifestoes of Surrealism*, 4. "La révolte absolue, . . . l'insoumission totale." Breton, *Les manifestes du surréalisme*, 94, translation in *Manifestos of Surrealism*, 125.

12. Georges Bataille, "The 'Lugubrious Game,'" in *Visions of Excess*, 27.

13. Bataille, *Accursed Share*, 124, 198.

14. Delaunay's perspective is underscored by the following: "The first paintings were simply a line encircling the shadow of a man made by the sun on the surface of the earth. But how far removed we are, with our contemporary means, from these effigies [simulacre] — we who possess light." Delaunay and Delaunay, *New Art of Color*, 93.

15. Malevich, "Non-Objective Art."

16. Paul Klee, "On Modern Art" (1924), in *On Modern Art*, 47; reprinted in Herbert, *Modern Artists*, 88.

17. As Jenny Anger has richly demonstrated, the gendered discourse surrounding the contemporary reception of Klee's work was fraught with conflict and defensiveness. See Anger, *Paul Klee and the Decorative*.

18. Apollinaire, *L'œuvre*, 17. For Breton's reference to Apollinaire see Breton, *What Is Surrealism?*, 242.

19. Bataille, *Oeuvres complètes*, 253. Bataille's statement is cited in translation in Rosalind Krauss, "No More Play," in *Originality of the Avant-Garde*, 54.

20. Nadeau, *History of Surrealism*, 70.

21. Nadeau, *History of Surrealism*, 50–51.

22. Maurice Blanchot, "Sade's Reason" (1949) in *Lautréamont and Sade*, 7–41. To a considerable extent, Bataille's *Accursed Share* was an effort to extend Blanchot's analysis more broadly. For Bataille's references to Blanchot and Sade, see Bataille, *Accursed Share*, esp. 174–75.

23. Solomon-Godeau, "Dark Night," 35, 37, 39.

24. Foster, *Compulsive Beauty*, 109.

25. S. Taylor, *Hans Bellmer*; Lichtenstein, *Behind Closed Doors*.

26. Solomon-Godeau, "Dark Night," 37.

27. Foster, *Compulsive Beauty*, 122.

28. S. Taylor, *Hans Bellmer*, 94, 96.

29. Lyford, *Surrealist Masculinities*. Lyford examines a number of artists, including Dalí. Whereas she proposes that we understand Dalí's "investigation of bodily dismemberment and sexual ambiguity" as consistent with the mainstream of surrealism (25), I believe that Dalí's work is different in crucial respects from the surrealist mainstream. Nevertheless, I consider our accounts of surrealism and masculinity to be, in general, complementary rather than contradictory: the anxiety for which sadism is celebrated as compensation by the surrealists is complemented by the willfully masochistic submission exemplified by Dalí's pictorial practice.

30. The literature on the surrealist representation of women is immense and contentious. One of the earliest and most influential is Xavière Gauthier's critical assessment in *Surréalisme et sexualité*. Following Gauthier's work, American feminists in the seventies and eighties struggled over the degree to which surrealist depictions of violence toward women could be interpreted as affirmations of misogyny or as critiques. (Interpretations of Bellmer's work, mentioned in the notes above, are characteristic.) Perhaps the clearest indication of the current debate over how to interpret surrealism's relation to women can be gleaned by comparing Susan Rubin Suleiman's negative assessment in *Subversive Intent* with Rosalind Krauss's argument in *Bachelors*. See also Caws, "Ladies Shot and Painted"; and Rudolf E. Kuenzli, "Surrealism and Misogyny," in Caws, Kuenzli, and Raaberg, *Surrealism and Women*, 17–26.

31. For an extended discussion of Sade's influence, see Eburne, *Surrealism and the Art of Crime*.

32. The surrealists' "Declaration of January 27, 1925" was issued from the Bureau de recherches surréalistes and included twenty-six signatories. A translation of the document is included in Nadeau, *History of Surrealism*, 240–41.

33. Dalí "The Moral Position of Surrealism" (1930), in *Collected Writings*, 220.

34. Dalí, "Love" (1930), in *Collected Writings*, 192; Dalí, "The Moral Position of Surrealism, " in *Collected Writings*, 220.

35. Dalí, "Les pantoufles de Picasso" (1935), in *Collected Writings*, 297–301. For an account of the writing of this essay, see Finkelstein, *Dalí's Art and Writing*, 224–26.

36. Bataille, *Accursed Share*, esp. 14–16, 198.

37. Bataille, *Accursed Share*, 437n2.

38. Georges Bataille, "The 'Lugubrious Game,'" in *Visions of Excess*, 29. Fanés suggests that this figure is derived from a depiction of Venus as she appears in a painting

by Titian that Dalí would have been able to see in the Museo del Prado. Fanés, *Dalí: Construction of the Image*, 144.

39. Dalí, "Love," in *Collected Writings*, 191.

40. Cited in Descharnes, *World of Salvador Dalí*, 61.

41. Freud, *Civilization and Its Discontents*, 58. My thanks to Genevieve Brassard for directing me to this passage.

42. Freud, "Economic Problem of Masochism," 162.

43. Freud, "Economic Problem of Masochism," 162.

44. Silverman, *Male Subjectivity at the Margins*, 209, 212–13.

45. Deleuze, *Masochism*, 86, 87.

46. Deleuze, *Masochism*, 88, 89.

47. For further considerations of Silverman's conception of the relation between Sade, Sacher-Masoch, and the avant-garde, see Stewart, *Sublime Surrender*; and Bersani, *Freudian Body*. For an illuminating discussion with Bersani that includes Silverman, among others, see Bersani, Dean, Foster, and Silverman, "Conversation with Leo Bersani."

48. For an analysis of masochism as articulated in Dalí's autobiographical writings, see Vilaseca, *Apocryphal Subject*. Vilaseca's analysis draws on a wide range of psychoanalytic texts, including not only those of Freud and Lacan but also those of Julia Kristeva, Leo Bersani, Shoshana Felman, Jane Gallop, Jean Laplanche, Eve Kosofsky Sedgwick, and others. Vilaseca does not, however, address Silverman's account of masochism and the gendered subject.

49. Although Steven Harris has argued that the passivity of Bretonian automatism invokes a feminine position and the activity of Dalínian paranoia invokes a masculine position, the analyses of Silverman and Deleuze enable a different perspective on the question of gender and reveal Dalí's femininity to be compatible with the active position of paranoia. See Harris, *Surrealist Art and Thought*, 182, 196.

50. It is unclear who was responsible for having invented this scene. Soon after the film was shot, Buñuel was reported to have said that Dalí came up with the idea; later in life he said that the idea had been his. Gibson, *Shameful Life*, 244–45.

51. As this scene is among the most famous in the history of avant-garde cinema, it has been subjected to a wide range of interpretations — rhetorical, biographical, semiotic, and of course and above all, psychoanalytic. For the range of interpretations of this scene and the film as a whole, see François Piazza, "Considérations psychanalytiques"; Matthews, *Surrealism and Film*, 84–90; Oswald, "Figure/Discourse"; Williams, *Figures of Desire*, 53–104; Murcia, *Un chien andalou*, 75ff; Short, *Age of Gold*, 68–76.

52. Allen Thiher aptly described this scene as "a visual rape." *Cinematic Muse*, 27.

53. Gibson, *Shameful Life*, 245.

54. For an account of how such seemingly radical gender transgressions are in fact quite typical in contemporary horror films, see Clover, "Her Body, Himself"; and Clover, *Men, Women, and Chain Saws*.

55. Mulvey, "Visual Pleasure."

56. Silverman, *Male Subjectivity at the Margins*, 204–5.

57. The needle is an obvious phallic symbol, yet the earliest of Dalí's references to it that I have found dates to 1934. In analyzing Lautréamont's famous phrase, Dalí writes,

Facing it [the umbrella, which Dalí elsewhere in the essay refers to as a "flagrant and well-known symbol of erection"], the sewing machine, an extremely characteristic feminine symbol that everyone knows, goes as far as to avail itself of the deadly and cannibalistic virtue of its stitching needle, whose action becomes identified with the superfine perforation made by the praying mantis "emptying" its male; that is to say, emptying its umbrella, transforming it into that martyrized, flaccid and depressive victim that every closed umbrella becomes following the grandeur of its tense and paroxysmal amorous functioning of a little while back. (Dalí, "Millet's *L'Angélus*" [1934], in *Collected Writings*, 281–82).

58. Santos Torroella, "Madrid Years," 82.

59. Dalí, letter to Lorca, September 1926, in Maurer, *Sebastian's Arrows*, 62.

60. It would be illuminating to consider the relationship between Dalí's distinctive mode of identifying beholder and subject and modes of identification characteristic of eighteenth- and nineteenth-century painting that Michael Fried has discussed at length. See Fried, *Absorption and Theatricality*; Fried, *Manet's Modernism*.

61. The women engaged in needlework also figure prominently in Lorca's poetry and in Buñuel's films. Delgado, "Dalí and the Surreal Story."

62. Alpers, "Art History," 187.

63. Alpers, "Art History," 198.

64. Dalí, *Secret Life*, 226–27.

65. The two photographs on which this painting was based (one of Gala's face, one of the well at Port Lligat) are reproduced in Descharnes and Néret, *Dalí: The Paintings*, 1:200.

66. Silverman, *Male Subjectivity at the Margins*, 206.

67. Jones, *Postmodernism*, 152. Historical accounts of the cultural politics of cross-dressing can be found in Gilbert and Grabar, *No Man's Land*; and Garber, *Vested Interests*.

68. Vilaseca, *Apocryphal Subject*, 160.

69. For a discussion of the figure of the hermaphrodite in Dalí's painting, see Finkelstein, *Dalí's Art and Writing*, 193, 238–39.

70. See Davis, *People of the Mediterranean*, 22. For an extensive consideration of masculine norms in Mediterranean cultures, see David D. Gilmore, "Performative Excellence: Circum-Mediterranean," in *Manhood in the Making*, 30–55.

71. Dalí, "The Great Masturbator," in *Collected Writings*, 181, 187–88.

6. ANACHRONISM

1. Walter Benjamin, "Surrealism: The Last Snapshot of the European Intelligentsia" (1929), in *Reflections*, 177–92.

2. Foster, *Compulsive Beauty*, 176.

3. Dalí, "The Latest Modes of Intellectual Stimulation for the Summer of 1934," in *Collected Writings*, 253.

4. Dalí, "The Rotting Donkey," in *Collected Writings*, 225–26.

5. For accounts of the Catalan discourses around art nouveau (*modernisme*), see Robinson, Falgàs, and Lord, *Barcelona and Modernity*.

6. Dalí, "Poetry of the Mass-Produced Utility," in *Collected Writings*, 59.

7. Of the four texts published together in *La femme visible* (1930), all but "The Sanitary Goat" include at least one explicit reference to art nouveau. In "The Great Masturbator" art nouveau is deployed in two ways. First, as an object of desire: "the faces of women / with rubbed out mouths / in Art Nouveau reliefs." *Collected Writings*, 187. Second, as a site within which desire flourishes: "The successive contemplation of all these medallions conjured up in detail the scene of the female praying mantis devouring the male and also the decoratively colored stained-glass windows exhibiting metamorphosis motifs that exist only in these infamous Art Nouveau interiors in which there is seated at the piano a very beautiful woman with wavy hair with terrifying look hallucinating smile magnificent throat ready to howl out a song that is imminent, menacing, imperial, sweet, proud, priggish, battered, drooping, stoned to death, smiling, special, theatrical, retarded, springlike, perfumed, altered, commemorative, historical, artistic." *Collected Writings*, 186. Although art nouveau does not appear by name in "The Sanitary Goat," its significance is implicitly invoked in Dalí's description of various curved lines and their relation to what he called the "curve of thought": thought that refuses to follow the straight line of reason and propriety. *Collected Writings*, 227.

8. Dalí, "Love," in *Collected Writings*, 192.

9. Dalí, "The Rotting Donkey," in *Collected Writings*, 225.

10. Dalí, "Surrealist Objects," in *Collected Writings*, 232.

11. In addition to *Surrealist Object Functioning Symbolically*, Dalí made five other objects in the thirties: *Retrospective Bust of a Woman* (1933), *Aphrodisiac Jacket* (1936), *Venus de Milo with Drawers* (1936), and *Lobster Telephone* (1936).

12. Recently surrealist objects have been the subject of more systematic and wide-ranging study. See, for example, Malt, *Obscure Objects*; Harris, *Surrealist Art and Thought*; and Mileaf, *Please Touch*.

13. In his typology Dalí divided the production of surrealist objects into four phases: "1. The object exists outside us, without our taking part in it (anthropomorphic articles); 2. The object assumes the immovable shape of desire and acts upon our contemplation (dream-state articles); 3. The object is movable and such that it can be acted upon (articles operating symbolically); 4. The object tends to bring about our fusion with it and makes us pursue the formation of a unity with it (hunger for an article and edible articles)." *Collected Writings*, 243–44. The essay was published initially in English, translated by David Gascoyne, in *This Quarter* (September 1932). In "Psychoatmospheric-Anamorphic Objects" (May 1932) Dalí entertained a logic similar to his etiological explanation in "Cher Breton" when he applied an evolutionary formula to the internal development of surrealist objects: "Here, in effect, the stage of cannibalism of objects becomes outmoded [dépassé], and so does, I suspect, any symbolical stage in general as well, and this thanks to the plan for the scrupulous confection of the forthcoming Psychoatmospheric-Anamorphic Objects." *Collected Writings*, 245.

14. Dalí, "Cher Breton," in *Collected Writings*, 251.

15. According to Dalí's account, the historical justification for the emergence of the surrealist object was obscured by "the mean and smug bureaucrats of aesthetics and pseudo-good-taste, who have reduced Cubism to its current level of decay known to all,

with its official and reassuring label of 'modern art,' its plastic — and succulent — austere — sickening orchestration, the apogee of comfort, frank French premeditation. Is Léger a Cubist? To go on, the living continuation of Cubism should then be sought, not among the Cubists, but, on the contrary, it could be seen in Picasso himself and among artists such as Duchamp, Miró, Tanguy, Giacometti, Arp." "Cher Breton," in *Collected Writings*, 251.

16. To my knowledge, none of these three objects has been identified.

17. Dalí, "Ornamental Art above All," in *Collected Writings*, 192 (ellipsis in the original).

18. Dalí made reference to these unconscious processes in a number of texts, including "Concerning the Terrifying and Edible Beauty of Art Nouveau Architecture," in *Collected Writings*, 198, and "The Tragic Myth of Millet's *L'Angélus*: Paranoiac-Critical Interpretation," in *Collected Writings*, 294.

19. Dalí, "Concerning the Terrifying and Edible Beauty of Art Nouveau Architecture," in *Collected Writings*, 194–95.

20. Dalí, "Concerning the Terrifying and Edible Beauty of Art Nouveau Architecture," in *Collected Writings*, 195.

21. Dalí, "Concerning the Terrifying and Edible Beauty of Art Nouveau Architecture," in *Collected Writings*, 194.

22. Dalí, "Concerning the Terrifying and Edible Beauty of Art Nouveau Architecture," in *Collected Writings*, 193.

23. Dalí, "The Latest Modes of Intellectual Stimulation for the Summer of 1934," in *Collected Writings*, 253.

24. Dalí, "The Latest Modes of Intellectual Stimulation for the Summer of 1934," in *Collected Writings*, 253. The full quotation includes other suggestive associations:

> Anachronism is the single "*imaginative constant*" capable of perpetual "*traumatic renewal*," thanks to which it becomes possible to snatch raw and living lumps from that hard and extremely thick thing which is the sentimental fog from which are formed the very cheeks of memory. — "Anachronism" is always a "sentimental cataclysm" sparkling with the ulterior motives of a "new skin." Far from being the unusable, so-called "stuffed thing," considered inoffensive by the intellectual pseudo-experience which ironically disposes of it in the "storehouse of the junk of the ages," "anachronism" is, on the contrary, a real and living thing, a thing having flesh and bones. (*Collected Writings*, 253)

25. Dalí, "The Latest Modes of Intellectual Stimulation for the Summer of 1934," in *Collected Writings*, 253. Dalí developed the concept of "specters" (and their complement, "phantoms") at far greater length in "The New Colors of Spectral Sex-Appeal," *Minotaure* (February 1934). In that essay Dalí defined phantoms as beings that create the illusion of volume and specters as beings that disintegrate and destroy the illusions of volume. According to Dalí, examples of phantoms include plaster, cotton, curves, Spinoza, La Gioconda, and Greta Garbo. Examples of specters include asbestos, silk, Uccello, and Harpo Marx. *Collected Writings*, 204–6.

26. Shelley's description of the doctor's labors: "I collected bones from charnel houses; and disturbed, with profane fingers, the tremendous secrets of the human frame. In a solitary chamber, or rather cell, at the top of the house, and separated from all the other apartments by a gallery and staircase, I kept my workshop of filthy creation: my eye-balls were starting from their sockets in attending to the details of my employment. The dissecting room and the slaughterhouse furnished many of my materials." Shelley, *Frankenstein*, 54–55.

27. Dalí, "The Latest Modes of Intellectual Stimulation for the Summer of 1934," in *Collected Writings*, 254.

28. Foster makes a related point when he notes that Dalí "sets up anachronism as a process of 'uprooted ephemera' in implicit opposition to modernism as a process of continuous innovation." Foster views Dalí's engagement with anachronism with ambivalence. On the one hand he suspects it of complicity with capitalist cycles of fashion ("the retro recovered as risqué"), and on the other he sees in it the potential to critique fascism's attempt to revive classicism under the banner of a transcendent order. Foster, *Compulsive Beauty*, 186–87.

29. Dalí, "Concerning the Terrifying and Edible Beauty of Art Nouveau Architecture," in *Collected Writings*, 195.

30. "Le sentiment funèbre inconscient." Dalí, "Daydream," in *Collected Writings*, 152.

31. Dalí, "Federico García Lorca: Exhibition of Color Drawings" (1927), and "The New Limits of Painting" (1928), in *Collected Writings*, 48, 84.

32. For an account of the de Chirico–like elements in *Premature Ossification of a Railway Station*, see Michael Taylor's entry in Taylor and Ades, *Dalí*, 140.

33. Dalí, "Cher Breton," in *Collected Writings*, 250, 252.

34. Dalí, "Concerning the Terrifying and Edible Beauty of Art Nouveau Architecture," in *Collected Writings*, 195.

35. Dalí, "Daydream," in *Collected Writings*, 153, 154. Dalí also referred to Böcklin's clouds and cypresses in "The New Colors of Spectral Sex-Appeal" (1934), in *Collected Writings*, 204.

36. Other paintings in which Dalí inserted either Böcklin's clouds or his cypresses include *Central Courtyard from the Isle of the Dead (Reconstructive Obsession after Böcklin)*, 1934; *Atavistic Vestiges after the Rain*, ca. 1934; *Dreams on a Beach*, ca. 1934; *The Signal of Anguish*, ca. 1932–36; *Surrealist Architecture*, ca. 1932; *The Fine, Average, Invisible Harp*, ca. 1932; and *Archeological Reminiscence of Millet's Angelus*, ca. 1934.

37. Dalí, "Daydream," in *Collected Writings*, 153. In "Daydream" Dalí mentions that his study of Böcklin was to form a significant part of a book he was writing on historical precursors to surrealism, *La peinture surréaliste à travers les âges* (Surrealist painting throughout the ages). He mentioned the book, which was never completed, again in 1933 in "Cher Breton," in *Collected Writings*, 249.

38. Dalí, "Daydream," in *Collected Writings*, 151, 152.

39. Ades addresses Dalí's interest in Böcklin's "frontality" in Taylor and Ades, *Dalí*, 170.

40. Dalí, "The Moral Position of Surrealism" and "New Colors of Spectral Sex Appeal," in *Collected Writings*, 222, 204.

41. Breton, *Manifestos of Surrealism*, 27, and *Surrealism and Painting*, 8. Breton's fascination with Uccello persisted over many years: as late as 1952 the poet continued to maintain that Uccello was, in his own way, a precursor to surrealism. "Goya was *already* a Surrealist, as was Dante, Uccello, or Lautréamont, or Gaudí. Centuries from now, any art that takes new paths toward a greater emancipation of the mind will be Surrealist." Breton, *Conversations*, 238.

42. *La Révolution Surréaliste* 8 (December 1926): 22; Breton, *Nadja*, 95.

43. Breton, *Nadja*, 94.

44. Vasari, *Lives of the Artists*, 74.

45. Vasari, *Lives of the Artists*, 75, 83.

46. Dalí, L'Angélus *de Millet*, in *Collected Writings*, 279–82.

47. Dalí, *Le mythe tragique*. For an extensive analysis of this text, see Finkelstein, *Dalí's Art and Writing*, chapter 15.

48. Barthes, *S/Z*.

49. Dalí, *Secret Life*, 64.

50. Dalí, "The Tragic Myth of Millet's *L'Angélus*: Paranoiac-Critical Interpretation," in *Collected Writings*, 289.

51. Dalí, "The Tragic Myth of Millet's *L'Angélus*: Paranoiac-Critical Interpretation," in *Collected Writings*, 282.

52. Dalí, "The Tragic Myth of Millet's *L'Angélus*: Paranoiac-Critical Interpretation," in *Collected Writings*, 283.

53. Dalí, "Cher Breton," in *Collected Writings*, 250.

54. Dalí, "The New Colors of Spectral Sex-Appeal," in *Collected Writings*, 205; "The Tragic Myth of Millet's *L'Angélus*: Paranoiac-Critical Interpretation," in *Collected Writings*, 282; "Cher Breton," in *Collected Writings*, 250.

55. Dalí, "The Conquest of the Irrational," in *Collected Writings*, 269.

56. Dalí's various historical references extend beyond the artists I have examined in this chapter. As Michael Taylor has noted, in works such as *Cardinal, Cardinal!* (originally *Cardenera, Cardenera* [Goldfinch, goldfinch]), 1934, "the streakily painted male protagonists look back to the work of Jacopo Tintoretto and other 16th-century Venetian painters, who often created similarly dematerialized figures whose forms are picked out of the darkness by carefully delineated highlights." Taylor and Ades, *Dalí*, 234.

57. Dalí, "The Latest Modes of Intellectual Stimulation for the Summer of 1934," in *Collected Writings*, 253.

58. Taylor has pointed out that the architectural elements were drawn from Catalan towns in which Dalí had lived. The building on the far left was from Palamós, near the town where Dalí painted this picture. The center section depicts buildings from Vilabertràn, a town near his home in Figueres. The street depicted on the far right is the Calle de Cal, in Cadaqués. Taylor and Ades, *Dalí*, 248.

59. "Dalí juega dos cartas aparentemente opuestas: 'Muchacha cosiendo' que representa aquí la carta tradicional; 'Figura en unas rocas,' que representa la carta de la audacia." Raphel Benet, "El Saló de Tardor" I, *La Veu de Catalunya*, October 20, 1926, cited in Fèlix Fanés, *Salvador Dalí: La construcción de la imagen 1925–1930* (Madrid: S.

E. Electa, 1999), 49; translation in Fanés, *Dalí: Construction of the Image*, 33. As Fanés has shown, Benet's interpretation of Dalí's work was shared by other critics at the time.

60. "Estoy pintando una 'niña en Figueras,' hace 5 días que pinto paciente y devotamente su pescuezo acabado de afeitar, me sale muy bien, *tanto* que casi no *parece* (porque lo es) moderno (ni antiguo)." Maurer, *Sebastian's Arrows*, 54; Santos Torroella, "Dalí escribe," 34.

AFTERWORD

1. Dalí, *Manifeste mystique* (Paris: Robert J. Godet, 1951), translated as "Mystical Manifesto" in *Collected Writings*, 365; Dalí, *Secret Life*, 393, 397, 398. Ades has described Dalí's later work as a "single-handed attempt to revive epic painting and rival the achievements of the old masters." (Ades, "Dalí and Duchamp," 13). In recent years more attention has been paid to Dalí's work, and new issues have emerged to enrich our picture of this later period. See, in particular, the essays collected in M. Taylor, *Dalí Renaissance*.

2. For Dalí's engagement with Leonardo, see Lomas, "Painting Is Dead."

3. Dalí, "Anti-Matter Manifesto" (1958–59), in *Collected Writings*, 366. For a detailed account of Dalí's postwar engagement with scientific discourse, see Parkinson, *Surrealism, Art, and Modern Science*.

4. Dalí, "Anti-Matter Manifesto" (1958–59), in *Collected Writings*, 366–67.

5. Dalí, "The Cylindrical Monarchy of Guimard" (1970), in *Collected Writings*, 374.

BIBLIOGRAPHY

Abbas, Niran, ed. *Mapping Michel Serres*. Ann Arbor: University of Michigan Press, 2005.

Ades, Dawn. *Dalí*. London: Thames and Hudson, 1995. Originally published as *Dalí and Surrealism* (New York: Harper and Row, 1982). Page numbers in the notes refer to the 1995 edition.

———. "Dalí and Duchamp." In Hine, Jeffett, and Reynolds, *Persistence and Memory*, 11–16.

———. "Dalí and the Myth of William Tell." In *Salvador Dalí: A Mythology*, ed. Dawn Ades and Fiona Bradley, 32–50. London: Tate Gallery, 1998.

———. "Morphologies of Desire." In Raeburn, *Dalí: The Early Years*, 129–60.

———. "Surrealism: Fetishism's Job." In *Fetishism: Visualizing Power and Desire*, ed. Anthony Shelton, 73–78. London: South Bank Centre, 1995.

Aguer, Montserrat, and Fèlix Fanés. "Illustrated Biography." In Raeburn, *Dalí: The Early Years*, 17–48.

Alexandrian, Sarane. *Surrealist Art*. Translated by Gordon Clough. London: Thames and Hudson, 1970.

Alpers, Svetlana. "Art History and It Exclusions: The Example of Dutch Art." In *Feminism and Art History: Questioning the Litany*, ed. Norma Broude and Marty D. Garrard, 183–99. Boulder CO: Westview Press, 1982.

Anderson, Thomas C. *Sartre's Two Ethics: From Authenticity to Integral Humanism*. Peru IL: Open Court Publishing, 1993.

Anger, Jenny. *Paul Klee and the Decorative in Modern Art*. Cambridge: Cambridge University Press, 2004.

Apollinaire, Guillaume. *The Cubist Painters*. Translated by Lionel Abel. New York: Wittenborn, 1949.

———. *Chroniques d'art: 1902–1918*. Edited by L. C. Breunig. Paris: Éditions Gallimard, 1960.

———. *L'œuvre du Marquis de Sade*. Introduction by Apollinaire. Paris: Bibliothèque des curieux, 1909.

———. *Selected Writings*. Translated by Robert Shattuck. New York: New Directions, 1950.

Aragon, Louis. *Les aventures de Télémaque*. Paris: Nouvelle Revue Française, 1923.

———. *Les collages*. Paris: Hermann, 1965.

Arasse, Daniel. *Vermeer: Faith in Painting*. Translated by Terry Grabar. Princeton NJ: Princeton University Press, 1994.

Assad, Maria. "Language, Nonlinearity, and the Problem of Evil." *Configurations* 8:2 (2000): 271–83.

———. *Reading with Michel Serres: An Encounter with Time*. Albany: State University of New York Press, 1999.

Badiou, Alain. *Le siècle*. Paris: Éditions du Seuil, 2005.

Bakhtin, Mikhail. *Rabelais and His World*. Translated by Helene Isswolsky. Bloomington: Indiana University Press, 1984.

Barthes, Roland. *La chambre claire: Note sur la photographie*. Paris: Éditions de l'Étoile, Gallimard, 1980.

———. *S/Z*. Translated by Richard Miller. New York: Hill and Wang, 1974.

Bataille, Georges. *The Accursed Share: An Essay on General Economy*. Vols. 2 and 3 (two vols. in one). Translated by Robert Hurley. New York: Zone Books, 1993.

———. *Oeuvres complètes*. Vol. 1. Paris: Gallimard, 1970.

———. *Visions of Excess: Selected Writings, 1927–1937*. Edited and translated by Allan Stoekl. Minneapolis: University of Minnesota Press, 1985.

Baudelaire, Charles. *Art in Paris: Salons and Other Exhibitions*. Edited and translated by Jonathan Mayne. London: Phaidon Press 1965.

Baudrillard, Jean. *Fatal Strategies*. Translated by Phillip Beitchman and W. G. J. Niesluchowski. New York: Semiotext[e], 1990.

———. *Jean Baudrillard: Selected Writings*. 2nd ed. Edited by Mark Poster. Stanford CA: Stanford University Press, 2001.

Bell, Linda A. *Sartre's Ethics of Authenticity*. Tuscaloosa: University of Alabama Press, 1989.

Bellori, G. P. *Le vite de' pittori, scultori, ed architetti moderni*. Rome, 1674.

Benjamin, Walter. *Reflections: Essays, Aphorisms, Autobiographical Writings*. Edited by Peter Demetz. Translated by Edmund Jephcott. New York: Shocken, 1978.

———. *Walter Benjamin: Selected Writings*. Vol. 2: *1927–1934*. Translated by Rodney Livingston et al. Edited by Michael Jennings, Howard Eiland, and Gary Smith. Cambridge MA: Harvard University Press, 1999.

Bergson, Henri. *Comedy*. Translated by Wyle Sypher. New York: Doubleday, 1956.

Bersani, Leo. *The Freudian Body*. New York: Columbia University Press, 1986.

Bersani, Leo, Tim Dean, Hal Foster, and Kaja Silverman. "A Conversation with Leo Bersani." *October* 82 (Fall 1997): 3–16.

Blackwell, Mark, ed. *The Secret Life of Things: Animals, Objects, and It-Narratives in Eighteenth-Century England*. Lewisburg PA: Bucknell University Press, 2007.

Blanchot, Maurice. *Lautréamont and Sade*. Translated by Stuart Kendall and Michelle Kendall. Stanford CA: Stanford University Press, 2004.

Bohn, Willard. *Marvelous Encounters: Surrealist Responses to Film, Art, Poetry, and Architecture*. Lewisburg PA: Bucknell University Press, 2005.

Bosquet, Alain. *Conversations with Dalí*. Translated by Joachim Neugroschel. New York: E. P. Dutton, 1969.

Bradley, Fiona. "Dalí as Myth-Maker: The Tragic Myth of Millet's *Angelus*." In *Salvador Dalí: A Mythology*, ed. Dawn Ades and Fiona Bradley, 12–28. London: Tate Gallery, 1998.
Breton, André. *Conversations: The Autobiography of Surrealism*. Translated by Mark Polizzotti. New York: Random House, 1993.
———. *Manifestoes of Surrealism*. Translated by Richard Seaver and Helen R. Lane. Ann Arbor: University of Michigan Press, 1972. Originally published as *Les manifestes du surréalisme* (Paris: Éditions du Sagittaire, 1946).
———. *Nadja*. Translated by Richard Howard. New York: Grove Press, 1968.
———. "Premiére exposition Dalí" [November 1929]. In *Point du jour*, 67–70. Paris: Gallimard, 1970. Translated by Mark Polizzotti and Mary Ann Caws as *Break of Day* (Lincoln: University of Nebraska Press, 1999), 51–53.
———. *Surrealism and Painting*. Translated by Simon Watson Taylor. Boston: MFA Publications, 2002.
———. *What Is Surrealism? Selected Writings*. Edited by Franklin Rosemont. New York: Pathfinder, 1978.
Broos, Ben. "Vermeer: Malice and Misconception." In *Vermeer Studies*, edited by Ivan Gaskell and Michiel Jonker, 19–33. New Haven CT: Yale University Press, 1998.
Brotchie, Alastair, Malcolm Green, and Antony Melville, eds. *Raymond Roussel: Life, Death, and Works*. London: Atlas Press, 1987.
Brown, Bill. "Object Relations in an Expanded Field." *Differences: A Journal of Feminist Cultural Studies* 17:3 (2006): 88–106.
———. "Objects, Others, and Us (The Refabrication of Things)." *Critical Inquiry* 36:2 (Winter 2010): 183–217.
———. "The Secret Life of Things (Virginia Woolf and the Matter of Modernism)." *Modernism/Modernity* 6:2 (1999): 1–28.
———. *A Sense of Things: The Object Matter of American Literature*. Chicago: University of Chicago Press, 2003.
———, ed. *Things*. Chicago: University of Chicago Press, 2004.
Brown, Steve. "Michel Serres: Science, Translation and the Logic of the Parasite." *Theory, Culture and Critique* 19:1 (2002): 1–27.
Bürger, William [Theophile Thoré]. "Van der Meer de Delft." *Gazette des Beaux-Arts* 21 (1866): 297–33, 458–70.
Burke, Edmund. *A Philosophical Enquiry into the Origin of Our Ideas of the Sublime and Beautiful*. Edited by Adam Phillips. Oxford: Oxford University Press, 1990.
Caillois, Roger. "La mante religieuse." *Minotaure* 5 (December 1934): 23–26.
———. "Mimétisme et psychasthénie légendaire." *Minotaure* 7 (Fall 1935): 4–10.
Candlin, Fiona, and Raiford Guins, eds. *The Object Reader*. London: Routledge, 2009.
Caws, Mary Ann. "Ladies Shot and Painted: Female Embodiment in Surrealist Art." In *The Female Body in Western Culture*, ed. Susan R. Suleiman, 262–87. Cambridge MA: Harvard University Press, 1986.
———. *Salvador Dalí*. London: Reaktion, 2008.
Caws, Mary Ann, Rudolf E. Kuenzli, and Gwen Raaberg, eds. *Surrealism and Women*. Cambridge MA: MIT Press, 1991.

Cézanne, Paul. *Conversations with Cézanne*. Edited by Michael Doran. Translated by Julie Lawrence Cochran. Berkeley: University of California Press, 2001.

Chave, Anna. "Minimalism and the Rhetoric of Power." *Arts Magazine* 64:5 (January 1990): 44–63.

Cheetham, Mark. *The Rhetoric of Purity: Essentialist Theory and the Advent of Abstract Painting*. Cambridge: Cambridge University Press, 1991.

Chipp, Herschel B., ed. *Theories of Modern Art: A Source Book by Artists and Critics*. Berkeley: University of California Press, 1968.

Clover, Carol J. "Her Body, Himself: Gender in the Slasher Film." *Representations* 20 (1987): 187–228.

———. *Men, Women, and Chain Saws: Gender in the Modern Horror Film*. Princeton NJ: Princeton University Press, 1992.

Courshon, W. L. "Salvador Dalí's Exclusion from the Surrealist Group." *Dada/Surrealism* 5 (1975): 80–89.

Cowling, Elizabeth, and Jennifer Mundy, eds. *On Classic Ground: Picasso, Léger, de Chirico and the New Classicism, 1910–1930*. London: Tate Gallery, 1990.

Cumming, Robert, ed. *The Philosophy of Jean-Paul Sartre*. New York: Vintage, 1965.

Dalí, Salvador. *L'alliberament dels dits: Obra Catalana completa*. Edited by Fèlix Fanés. Barcelona: Quaderns Crema, 1995.

———. *L'amour et la mémoire*. Paris: Éditions Surréalistes, 1931.

———. L'Angélus *de Millet*. Paris: Galerie des Quatre Chemins, 1934.

———. *Comment on devient Dalí. Les aveux inavouables de Salvador Dalí, récit présenté par André Parinaud*. Paris: Robert Laffont, 1973.

———. *Dalí on Modern Art: The Cuckolds of Antiquated Modern Art* [French and English text]. Translated by Haakon M. Chevalier. New York: Dial Press, 1957.

———. *Un diari: 1919–1920. Les meves impressions i records íntims*. Edited by Fèlix Fanés. Barcelona: Fundació Gala-Salvador Dalí, 1994.

———. *Diary of a Genius*. Translated by Richard Howard. New York: Doubleday, 1965.

———. *La femme visible*. Paris: Éditions Surréalistes, 1930.

———. *Le mythe tragique de* L'Angélus *de Millet: Interprétation "paranoïaque-critique"*. Paris: Jean-Jacques Pauvert, 1963.

———. *Oui*. Edited by Robert Descharnes. Paris: Éditions Denoël, 2004.

———. "Les pantoufles de Picasso." *Cahiers d'art* (Paris) 10:7–10 (1935): 208–12.

———. *The Collected Writings of Salvador Dalí*. Edited and translated by Haim Finkelstein. Cambridge: Cambridge University Press, 1998.

———. *The Secret Life of Salvador Dalí*. Translated by Haakon M. Chevalier. New York: Dial Press, 1942.

———. *The Unspeakable Confessions of Salvador Dalí*. As told to André Parinaud. Translated by Harold J. Salemson. New York: William Morrow, 1976.

Daston, Lorraine, ed. *Things That Talk: Object Lessons from Art and Science*. New York: Zone Press, 2004.

Davis, John. *People of the Mediterranean*. London: Routledge, 1977.

Delacroix, Eugène. "On Romanticism" [journal entry, August 3, 1855]. Translated by Walter Pach. In *Art and Theory, 1815–1900: An Anthology of Changing Ideas*, ed. Charles Harrison, Paul Wood, and Jason Gaiger, 26–30. London: Blackwell, 1998.
Delaunay, Robert, and Sonia Delaunay. *The New Art of Color: The Writings of Robert and Sonia Delaunay*. Edited by Arthur A. Cohen. Translated by David Shapiro and Arthur A. Cohen. New York: Viking Press, 1978.
Deleuze, Gilles. *The Logic of Sense*. Translated by Mark Lester. New York: Columbia University Press, 1990.
———. *Masochism: Coldness and Cruelty*. New York: Zone Books, 1991.
Deleuze, Gilles, and Félix Guattari. *Kafka: Toward a Minor Literature*. Translated by Dana Polan. Minneapolis: University of Minnesota Press, 1986.
Delgado, Manuel. "Dalí and the Surreal Story of the Needle and the Lacemaker." Paper presented at Bucknell University, Lancaster PA, September 14, 2005.
Derrida, Jacques. "Forcener le subjectile." In *Antonin Artaud: Dessins et portraits*, ed. Paule Thévenin and Jacques Derrida, 55–105. Paris: Gallimard, 1986.
Descharnes, Robert. *Salvador Dalí*. New York: Viking Press, 1976.
———. *The World of Salvador Dalí*. Translated by Haakon Chevalier. New York: Harper and Row, 1962.
Descharnes, Robert, and Gilles Néret. *Salvador Dalí: The Paintings*. Translated by Michael Hulse. Cologne: Benedikt Taschen, 1994.
Dowbiggin, Ian. "Delusional Diagnosis? The History of Paranoia as a Disease Concept in the Modern Era." *History of Psychiatry* 11 (2000): 37–69.
Eburne, Jonathan P. *Surrealism and the Art of Crime*. Ithaca NY: Cornell University Press, 2008.
———. "That Obscure Object of Revolt: Heraclitus, Surrealism's Lightning-Conductor." *symplokē* 8:1–2 (2000): 180–204.
Evans, Dylan. *An Introductory Dictionary of Lacanian Psychoanalysis*. London: Routledge, 1996.
Fanés, Fèlix. "The First Image — Dalí and His Critics: 1919 to 1929." In Raeburn, *Dalí: The Early Years*, 90–96.
———. *Salvador Dalí: The Construction of the Image 1925–1930*. New Haven CT: Yale University Press, 2007.
Ferreria, José. *Dalí-Lacan, la rencontre: Ce que le psychanalyste doit au peintre*. Paris: Editions L'Harmattan, 2003.
Fiedler, Konrad. "Modern Naturalism and Artistic Truth" [1881]. Translated by Jason Gaiger. In *Art in Theory, 1815–1900: An Anthology of Changing Ideas*, ed. Charles Harrison, Paul Wood, and Jason Gaiger, 691–702. London: Blackwell, 1998.
Finkelstein, Haim. *Salvador Dalí's Art and Writing, 1927–1942: The Metamorphosis of Narcissus*. Cambridge: Cambridge University Press, 1996.
Flaubert, Gustave. *Correspondance*. Paris: Louis Conard, 1910.
Ford, Mark. *Raymond Roussel and the Republic of Dreams*. Ithaca NY: Cornell University Press, 2000.
Foster, Hal. *Compulsive Beauty*. Cambridge MA: MIT Press, 1993.
———. "Prosthetic Gods." *Modernism/Modernity* 4:2 (1997): 5–38.

Foster, Hal, Rosalind Krauss, Yve-Alain Bois, and Benjamin H. D. Buchloh. *Art since 1900: Modernism, Antimodernism, Postmodernism*. Vol. 1. London: Thames and Hudson, 2004.

Foucault, Michel. *This Is Not a Pipe*. Translated and edited by James Harkness. 1973; reprint, Berkeley: University of California Press, 1983.

Freud, Sigmund. *Civilization and Its Discontents*. Translated and edited by James Strachey. New York: W. W. Norton, 1961.

———. "The Economic Problem of Masochism" [1924]. In *The Standard Edition of the Complete Psychological Works*, ed. and trans. James Strachey, 19:157–70. London: Hogarth Press, 1961.

———. *Introductory Lectures on Psychoanalysis*. Part 3, *General Theory of Neurosis* [1916–17]. Vol. 16 of *The Standard Edition of the Complete Psychological Works*, ed. and trans. James Strachey. London: Hogarth Press, 1963.

———. "New Introductory Lectures on Psycho-Analysis" [1933]. In *The Standard Edition of the Complete Psychological Works*, ed. and trans. James Strachey, 22:3–182. London: Hogarth Press, 1964.

———. "On Fetishism" [1927]. In *The Standard Edition of the Complete Works of Sigmund Freud*, ed. and trans. James Strachey, 21:152–59. London: Hogarth Press, 1961.

———. "Psychoanalytic Notes on an Autobiographical Account of a Case of Paranoia (Dementia Paranoides)" [1911]. In *The Standard Edition of the Complete Psychological Works*, ed. and trans. James Strachey, 12:3–82. London: Hogarth Press, 1958.

———. "The Unconscious." In *On Metapsychology*, 159–222. Penguin Freud Library, vol. 11. Harmondsworth UK: Penguin, 1991.

Fried, Michael. *Absorption and Theatricality: Painting and Beholder in the Age of Diderot*. Berkeley: University of California Press, 1980.

———. *Manet's Modernism, or The Face of Painting in the 1860s*. Chicago: University of Chicago Press, 1996.

Fry, Edward R., ed. *Cubism*. Translated by Jonathan Griffin. London: Thames and Hudson, 1978.

Gale, Matthew, ed. *Dalí and Film*. London: Tate, 2007.

Garber, Marjorie. *Vested Interests: Cross-Dressing and Cultural Anxiety*. New York: Routledge, 1992.

Garrabé, Jean. "Clérambault, Dalí, Lacan et l'interprétation paranoïaque." *Annales Médico Psychologiques* 163 (2005): 360–63.

Gasch, Sebastià. *L'expansió de l'art català al món*. Barcelona: Clarasó, 1953.

Gaskell, Ivan, and Michiel Jonker. *Vermeer Studies*. New Haven CT: Yale University Press, 1998.

Gauthier, Xavière. *Surréalisme et sexualité*. Paris: Gallimard, 1971.

Gibson, Ian. *The Shameful Life of Salvador Dalí*. New York: W. W. Norton, 1997.

Gilbert, Sandra, and Susan Grabar. *No Man's Land: The Place of the Woman Writer in the Twentieth Century*. Vol. 2: *Sexchanges*. New Haven CT: Yale University Press, 1989.

Gilmore, David D. *Manhood in the Making: Cultural Concepts of Masculinity*. New Haven CT: Yale University Press, 1990.

Gleizes, Albert, and Jean Metzinger. "Du Cubisme" [1912]. In Chipp, *Theories of Modern Art*, 207–8.

Golan, Romy. *Modernity and Nostalgia: Art and Politics in France between the Wars*. New Haven CT: Yale University Press, 1995.

Goldring, Douglas. "Exhibition at Zwemmer's." *The London Studio* (January 1935): 36.

Gray, Frances. *Women and Laughter*. Charlottesville: University of Virginia Press, 1994.

Greeley, Robin Adèle. *Surrealism and the Spanish Civil War*. New Haven CT: Yale University Press, 2006.

Harris, Steven. *Surrealist Art and Thought in the 1930s: Art, Politics, and the Psyche*. Cambridge: Cambridge University Press, 2004.

Harrison, Charles, and Paul Wood, eds. *Art in Theory, 1900–2000: An Anthology of Changing Ideas*. London: Blackwell, 2003.

Harrison, Charles, Paul Wood, and Jason Gaiger, eds. *Art in Theory, 1815–1900: An Anthology of Changing Ideas*. London: Blackwell, 1998.

Hartman, Geoffrey. *Scars of the Spirit: The Struggle against Inauthenticity*. New York: Palgrave Macmillan, 2002.

———. *The Unmediated Vision: An Interpretation of Wordsworth, Hopkins, Rilke, and Valéry*. New Haven CT: Yale University Press, 1954.

Herbert, Robert L., ed. *Modern Artists on Art*. Englewood Cliffs NJ: Prentice-Hall, 1964.

Hildebrand, Adolf. *The Problem of Form in Painting and Sculpture* [1893]. Translated by Max Meyer and Robert M. Ogden. New York: G. E. Stechert, 1907.

Hine, Hank, William Jeffett, and Kelly Reynolds, eds. *Persistence and Memory: New Critical Perspectives on Dalí at the Centennial*. St. Petersburg FL: Salvador Dalí Museum, 2004.

Hokenson, Jan Walsh. *The Idea of Comedy: History, Theory, Critique*. Madison NJ: Fairleigh Dickenson University Press, 2006.

Hollier, Denis. *Against Architecture: The Writings of Georges Bataille*. Translated by Betsy Wing. Cambridge MA: MIT Press, 1989.

Hulten, Pontus. *The Surrealists Look at Art*. Venice CA: Lapis Press, 1990.

Jewell, Edward Alden. "Dalí, an Enigma? Only His Exegesis." *New York Times*, November 21, 1945.

Jones, Amelia. *Postmodernism and the En-Gendering of Marcel Duchamp*. Cambridge: Cambridge University Press, 1994.

Kahnweiler, Daniel-Henri. "The Rise of Cubism" [1915]. Translated by Henry Aronson. In Chipp, *Theories of Modern Art*, 248–59.

King, Elliot H. *Dalí, Surrealism and Cinema*. London: Kamera Books, 2007.

———, ed. *Salvador Dalí: The Late Work*. New Haven CT: Yale University Press, 2010.

Kirshner, Lewis A. "Rethinking Desire: The Objet Petit A in Lacanian Theory." *Journal of the American Psychoanalytic Association* 53:1 (2005): 83–102.

Klee, Paul. *On Modern Art*. Translated by Paul Findlay. London: Faber and Faber, 1948.

Krauss, Rosalind. *Bachelors*. Cambridge MA: MIT Press, 1999.

———. "Corpus Delicti." In *L'Amour Fou*, ed. Rosalind Krauss and Jane Livingston, 57–100. New York: Abbeville Press, 1985.

———. *The Originality of the Avant-Garde and Other Modernist Myths*. Cambridge MA: MIT Press, 1985.

Kristeva, Julia. *Powers of Horror: An Essay on Abjection*. Translated by Leon S. Roudiez. New York: Columbia University Press, 1982.

Kropf, Joan R. *Dalí Objects / Dalí Fetishes*. St. Petersburg FL: Salvador Dalí Museum, 2002.

Lacan, Jacques. *Écrits: A Selection*. Translated by Alan Sheridan. New York: W. W. Norton, 1977.

———. *Le séminaire de Jacques Lacan*. Book 16, *D'un autre à l'autre, 1968–1969*. Edited by Jacques-Alain Miller. Paris: Éditions du Seuil, 2006.

LaFountain, Marc J. *Dalí and Postmodernism: This Is Not an Essence*. Albany NY: SUNY Press, 1997.

Latour, Bruno. *Aramis, or The Love of Technology*. Translated by Catherine Porter. Cambridge MA: Harvard University Press, 1996.

———. "On Technical Mediation — Philosophy, Sociology, Genealogy." *Common Knowledge* 3 (Fall 1994): 29–64.

———. *We Have Never Been Modern*. Translated by Catherine Porter. Cambridge MA: Harvard University Press, 1993.

———. "Technology Is Society Made Durable." Translated by Gabrielle Hecht. In *A Sociology of Monsters: Essays on Power, Technology, and Domination*, edited by John Law, 103–31. London: Routledge, 1991.

Le Corbusier. *The Decorative Art of Today* [1925]. Translated by James I. Dunnett. Cambridge MA: MIT Press, 1987.

Lee, Pamela M. *Chronophobia: On Time in the Art of the 1960s*. Cambridge MA: MIT Press, 2006.

Leiris, Michel. "Conception et réalité chez Raymond Roussel" [1954]. In *Épaves précédé de* Conception et réalité chez Raymond Roussel *par Michel Leiris*, by Raymond Roussel, 9–34. Paris: Jean-Jacques Pauvert, 1972.

Lichtenstein, Therese. *Behind Closed Doors: The Art of Hans Bellmer*. Berkeley: University of California Press, 2001.

Lomas, David. *The Haunted Self: Surrealism, Psychoanalysis, Subjectivity*. New Haven CT: Yale University Press, 2001.

———. "Painting Is Dead — Long Live Painting! Notes on Dalí and Leonardo." In *The Dalí Renaissance: New Perspectives on His Life and Art after 1940*, ed. Michael R. Taylor, 153–189. Philadelphia: Philadelphia Museum, 2008.

———. "Simulacra and the Order of Mimesis in Salvador Dalí and Glenn Brown." In Hine, Jeffett, and Reynolds, *Persistence and Memory*, 201–10.

Lorca, Federico García. *Poemas en prosa*. Edited by Andrew A. Anderson. Granada, Spain: La Valeta, 2000.

Lubar, Robert S. "Dalí's ParaNONia." In Hine, Jeffett, and Reynolds, *Persistence and Memory*, 123–29.

———. "Miró in 1924: Cubism and the Subject of Vision." In *Joan Miró: 1917–1934*, ed. Angès de la Beaumelle, 52–59. Paris: Centre Georges Pompidou, 2004.

———. "Salvador Dalí: Modernism's Counter-Muse." *Romance Quarterly* 46:4 (Fall 1999): 230–38.
———. "Salvador Dalí: Portrait of the Artist as (An)Other." In *Salvador Dalí: A Mythology*, ed. Dawn Ades and Fiona Bradley, 106–116. London: Tate Gallery, 1998.
———. *Dalí: The Salvador Dalí Museum Collection*. Boston: Bulfinch Press, 2000.
Lyford, Amy. *Surrealist Masculinities: Gender Anxiety and the Aesthetics of Post–World War I Reconstruction in France*. Berkeley: University of California Press, 2007.
Mack, John. *The Art of Small Things*. Cambridge MA: Harvard University Press, 2007.
Malevich, Kasimir. "Non-Objective Art and Suprematism." In *Malevich: Suprematism and Revolution in Russian Art 1910–1930*, ed. Larissa Zhadova, 282–83. New York: Thames and Hudson, 1982.
Malt, Johanna. *Obscure Objects of Desire: Surrealism, Fetishism, and Politics*. Oxford: Oxford University Press, 2004.
Marinetti, Filippo Tommaso. "The Foundation and Manifesto of Futurism" [1909]. In *Marinetti: Selected Writings*, trans. R. W. Flint, 39–44. New York: Farrar, Straus and Giroux, 1972.
Markus, Ruth. "Surrealism's Praying Mantis and the Castrating Woman." *Woman's Art Journal* 21:1 (Spring–Summer 2000): 33–39.
Massumi, Brian. "Realer than Real: The Simulacrum According to Deleuze and Guattari." *Copyright* 1 (1987): 90–97.
The Masterpieces of De Hooch and Vermeer. London: Gowans and Gray, 1911.
Matthews, J. H. *Surrealism and Film*. Ann Arbor: University of Michigan Press, 1971.
Maurer, Christopher, ed. and trans. *Sebastian's Arrows: Letters and Mementos of Salvador Dalí and Federico García Lorca*. Chicago: Swan Isle Press, 2004.
Maurer Queipo, Isabel, and Nanette Rißler Pipka, eds. *Dalís Medienspiele: Falsche Färten und paranoische Selbstinszenierungen in den Künsten*. Bielefeld, Germany: Transcript Verlag, 2007.
Mendelson, Jordana. *Documenting Spain: Artists, Exhibition Culture, and the Modern Nation, 1929–1939*. University Park: Pennsylvania State University Press, 2005.
———. "Joan Miró's *Drawing-Collage*, August 8, 1933: The 'Intellectual Obscenities' of Postcards." *Art Journal* 63:1 (Spring 2004): 24–37.
Mileaf, Janine. *Please Touch: Dada and Surrealist Objects after the Readymade*. Hanover NH: University Press of New England, 2010.
———. "Smoking Jacket and Pumps." In Hine, Jeffett, and Reynolds, *Persistence and Memory*, 89–92.
Miller, Daniel. *Stuff*. Cambridge MA: Polity Press, 2010.
Millet, Catherine. *Dalí and Me*. Chicago: University of Chicago Press, 2008.
Miró, Joan. *Écrits et entretiens*. Edited by Margit Rowell. Paris: D. Lelong, 1995.
Mondrian, Piet. "Natural Reality and Abstract Reality" [1919]. Translated by Michael Seuphor. In Chipp, *Theories of Modern Art*, 321–23.
Monegal, Antonio. "Las palabras y las cosas, según Salvador Dalí." In *El aeroplano y la estrella: El movimiento de vanguardi en los países catalanes (1904–1936)*, ed. Joan Ramon Resina, 151–76. Amsterdam: Rodopi, 1997.

Monod-Herzen, Édouard. *Principes de morphologie générale.* Vol. 1. Paris: Gauthier-Villars et Cie., 1927.

Mulvey, Laura. "Visual Pleasure and Narrative Cinema." *Screen* 16:3 (Fall 1975): 6–18.

Murcia, Claude. *Un chien andalou, l'age d'or, Luis Buñuel: Étude critique.* Paris: Nathan, 1994.

Nadeau, Maurice. *The History of Surrealism.* Translated by Richard Howard. New York: Macmillan Press, 1965.

Nasio, Juan-David. *Five Lessons on* The Psychoanalytic Theory of Jacques Lacan. Translated by David Pettigrew and François Raffoul. Albany: SUNY Press, 1998.

Ortega y Gasset, José. *The Dehumanization of Art and Other Essays on Art, Culture, and Literature.* Translated by Helene Weyl. Princeton NJ: Princeton University Press, 1968.

Oswald, Laura. "Figure/Discourse: Configurations of Desire in *Un chien andalou.*" *Semiotica* 33:1–2 (1981): 105–22.

Palermo, Charles. *Fixed Ecstasy: Joan Miró in the 1920s.* University Park: Pennsylvania State University Press, 2008.

Parkinson, Gavin. *Surrealism, Art, and Modern Science: Relativity, Quantum Mechanics, Epistemology.* New Haven CT: Yale University Press, 2008.

Peyre, Henri. *Literature and Sincerity.* New Haven CT: Yale University Press, 1963.

Piazza, François. "Considérations psychanalytiques sur *Un chien andalou.*" *Psyché* 27–28 (January–February, 1949): 147–56.

Poggi, Christine. "Dreams of Metallized Flesh: Futurism and the Masculine Body." *Modernism/Modernity* 4:3 (1997): 19–43.

Polizzotti, Mark. *Revolution of the Mind: The Life of André Breton.* New York: Farrar, Straus and Giroux, 1995.

Poussin, Nicolas. "Observations on Painting." In *Artists on Art,* 3rd ed., ed. Robert Goldwater, 154–57. New York: Pantheon, 1958.

Powell, Kirsten H. "Hands-On Surrealism." *Art History* 20:4 (December 1997): 516–33.

Purdie, Susan. *Comedy: The Mastery of Discourse.* Toronto: University of Toronto Press, 1993.

Rabaté, Jean-Michel. "Loving Freud Madly: Surrealism between Hysterical and Paranoid Modernism." *Journal of Modern Literature* 25:3/4 (Summer 2002): 58–74.

Raeburn, Michael, ed. *Salvador Dalí: The Early Years.* London: South Bank Centre, 1994.

Ramón Jiménez, Juan. *Platero y yo.* Madrid: Aguilar, 1957.

Raynal, Maurice. "What Is Cubism?" [1913]. In Fry, *Cubism,* 128–30.

Rivière, Jacques. "Present Tendencies in Painting" [1912]. In Fry, *Cubism,* 75–81.

Roberts, Mark S. "Wired: Schreber as Machine, Technophobe, and Virtualist." In "Experimental Sound and Radio," special issue, *TDR* 40:3 (Autumn 1996): 31–46.

Robinson, William H., Jordi Falgàs, and Carmen Belen Lord. *Barcelona and Modernity: Picasso, Gaudí, Miró, Dalí.* New Haven CT: Yale University Press, 2007.

Rothman, Roger. "Against Sincerity: René Magritte, Paul Nougé and the Lesson of Paul Valéry." *Word and Image* 23:3 (July–September 2007): 290–99.

———. "A Mysterious Modernism: René Magritte and Abstraction." *Konsthistorisk Tidskrift—Journal of Art History* 76:4 (2007): 224–39.

———. "René Magritte and 'The Shop-Window Quality of Things.'" *The Space Between: Literature and Culture 1914–1945* 3:1 (2007): 11–28.

———. "Two Sublimes of Surrealism." In *Modernism and Theory: A Critical Debate*, ed. Stephen Ross, 49–59. London: Routledge, 2008.

Roussel, Raymond. *Épaves précédé de* Conception et réalité chez Raymond Roussel *par Michel Leiris*. Paris: Jean-Jacques Pauvert, 1972.

Ruffa, Astrid, Philippe Kaenel, and Danielle Chaperon, eds. *Salvador Dalí à la croisée des saviors*. Paris: Éditions Desjonquères, 2007.

Santos Torroella, Rafael. "The Madrid Years." In Raeburn, *Dalí: The Early Years*, 81–89.

———. *La miel es más dulce que la sangre: Las épocas lorquiana y freudiana de Salvador Dalí*. Barcelona: Seix Barral, 1984.

———. ed. "Salvador Dalí escribe a Federico García Lorca." Special edition, *Poesía: Revista Ilustrada de Información Poética* (Ministerio de Cultura, Madrid) 27–28 (April 1987).

Sartre, Jean-Paul. *Being and Nothingness: An Essay on Phenomenological Ontology*. Translated by Hazel E. Barnes. New York: Philosophical Library, 1956.

Savinio, Alberto. "Anadyomenon: Principles in the Evaluation of Contemporary Art" [1919]. In *Metaphysical Art*, ed. Massimo Carrà, trans. Caroline Tisdall, 155–62. New York: Praeger, 1971.

Schlipp, Paul Arthur, ed. *The Philosophy of Jean-Paul Sartre*. Peru IL: Open Court Publishing, 1981.

Sérieux, Paul, and Joseph Capgras. *Les folies raisonnantes: La délire d'interpretation*. Paris: Alcan, 1909.

Serres, Michel. *The Parasite*. Translated by Lawrence R. Schehr. Baltimore: Johns Hopkins University Press, 1982.

Shelley, Mary. *Frankenstein*. 1818; reprint, London: Oxford University Press, 1969.

Short, Robert. *The Age of Gold: Surrealist Cinema*. London: Creation Books, 2003.

Silver, Kenneth. *Esprit de Corps: The Art of the Parisian Avant-Garde and the First World War, 1914–1925*. Princeton: Princeton University Press, 1989.

Silverman, Kaja. *Male Subjectivity at the Margins*. New York: Routledge, 1992.

Singer, Thomas. "In the Manner of Duchamp, 1942–47: The Years of the 'Mirrorical Return.'" *Art Bulletin* 86:2 (June 2004): 346–69.

Solomon-Godeau, Abigail. "Dark Night of the Doll" (book review). *Art in America* 90:9 (September 2002): 35–39.

Spiteri, Raymond. "Beyond the Lugubrious Game: Dalí, Bataille and the Culture of Surrealism." In Hine, Jeffett, and Reynolds, *Persistence and Memory*, 55–58.

Stewart, Suzanne R. *Sublime Surrender: Male Masochism at the Fin-de-Siecle*. Ithaca NY: Cornell University Press, 1998.

Stone, Robert. "Sartre on Bad Faith and Authenticity." In *The Philosophy of Jean-Paul Sartre*, ed. Paul Arthur Schlipp, 246–56. Peru IL: Open Court Publishing, 1981.

Suleiman, Susan Robin. ed. *The Female Body in Western Culture*. Cambridge MA: Harvard University Press, 1986.

———. *Subversive Intent: Gender, Politics, and the Avant-Garde*. Cambridge MA: Harvard University Press, 1990.

Taylor, Michael R. "The Conquest of the Irrational: Salvador Dalí and the Limits of Surrealism." Lecture, Bucknell University, Lewisburg PA, October 12, 2004.

———. ed. *The Dalí Renaissance: New Perspectives on His Life and Art after 1940.* Philadelphia: Philadelphia Museum of Art, 2008.

Taylor, Michael R., and Dawn Ades. *Dalí.* Philadelphia: Philadelphia Museum of Art, 2005.

Taylor, Sue. *Hans Bellmer: The Anatomy of Anxiety.* Cambridge MA: MIT Press, 2000.

Thiher, Allen. *The Cinematic Muse: Critical Studies in the History of the French Cinema.* Columbia: University of Missouri Press, 1979.

Vanzype, Gustave. *Vermeer de Delft.* Brussels: G. van Oest, 1908.

Vasari, Giorgio. *The Lives of the Artists.* Translated by Julia Conaway Bondanella and Peter Bondanella. Oxford: Oxford University Press, 1991.

Vilarasau, José, and Ramon Boixadós. *Dalí and Mass Culture.* Barcelona: Fundació Gala-Salvador Dalí, 2004.

Vilaseca, David. *The Apocryphal Subject: Masochism, Identification, and Paranoia in Salvador Dalí's Autobiographical Writing.* New York: Peter Lang, 1995.

Walker, Ian. *City Gorged with Dreams: Surrealism and Documentary Photography in Interwar Paris.* Manchester, UK: Manchester University Press, 2002.

Weiss, Jeffery. *The Popular Culture of Modern Art: Picasso, Duchamp, and Avant-Gardism.* New Haven CT: Yale University Press, 1994.

Werth, Léon. "Picasso." In Fry, *Cubism*, 57–58.

Williams, Linda. *Figures of Desire: A Theory and Analysis of Surrealist Film.* Urbana: University of Illinois Press, 1982.

Žižek, Slavoj. *Welcome to the Desert of the Real! Five Essays on September 11 and Related Essays.* London: Verso, 2002.

INDEX

Page numbers in italic indicate illustrations

www.ingramcontent.com/pod-product-compliance
Lightning Source LLC
LaVergne TN
LVHW081258100826
845148LV00005B/907